Our demands most moderate are:
we only want the EARTH.

The Lost & Early Writings of
JAMES CONNOLLY
1889–1898

This first edition published by *Iskra Books* © 2024

10 9 8 7 6 5 4 3 2 1

Iskra Books
WWW.ISKRABOOKS.ORG
US | England | Ireland

Iskra Books is an independent, nonprofit, scholarly publisher—publishing original works
of revolutionary theory, history, education, and art, as well as edited collections, new
translations, and critical republications of older works.

ISBN-13: 979-8-3304-3531-9 (Softcover)
ISBN-13: 979-8-3304-3521-0 (Jacketed Hardcover)

British Library Cataloguing in Publication Data
A catalogue record for this book is available from the British Library

Library of Congress Cataloging-in-Publication Data
A catalog record for this book is available from the Library of Congress

Cover Art, Typesetting, and Design by Ben Stahnke
Editing, Proofing, and Development by Róisín Dubh

The Lost & Early Writings
of
JAMES CONNOLLY
1889–1898

EDITED BY
CONOR MCCABE

ISKRA BOOKS
US | ENGLAND | IRELAND

I will not yield
I will not fall
I will eat dynamite
And one day I will explode
Like a volcano

—PATRICK GALVIN. *Song for a Raggy Boy* (1991)

CONTENTS

Part II: Lost Fiction

PUBLISHER'S NOTE

Iskra Books would like to acknowledge the fantastic Polish translation work by our impeccable colleague, Paweł Wargan. We would also like to acknowledge the brilliant Dr. Kerron Ó Luain for his time on behalf of Iskra Books in supporting McCabe's critical analysis of Desmond Greaves' problematic and incorrect claim of James Connolly joining the British Army.

Go raibh míle maith agaibh!

INTRODUCTION

KILMAINHAM JAIL is about two miles from Dublin Castle. It would take a horse-drawn wagon around fifteen minutes to cover the distance at a fast pace under normal conditions. On the morning of 12 May 1916, with the city under military curfew, it might have taken only ten. Twilight began around 3:30am. Such an early dawn was due to Dublin time, which ran twenty-five minutes behind London. Daylight saving had yet to be introduced.

The route taken by the wagon, the one carrying James Connolly to his execution, is not entirely known.[1] The most direct way is up past Christchurch, with a left turn onto Thomas Street, giving you an almost clear run via James' Street and the Old Kilmainham Road to the large wooden gates that open onto the stonebreakers' yard. It would have taken Connolly past the area where he once lived as well as the Obelisk where he often held public talks and meetings. General service wagons were open topped, with no roof or sides.[2] He was seated between soldiers for

---

1   Michael T. Soughley was a constable in the Dublin Metropolitan Police (DMP), attached to Kilmainham police station in 1916. He said that a "four-wheeled general service wagon drawn by two horses came along the Old Kilmainham Road at a very fast pace, swung to the right and went into the prison." He saw "a man sitting in the wagon surrounded by a number of soldiers who were sitting around him... A short time after the wagon entered the jail a volley rang out and we later learned that the victim was James Connolly." Witness Michael T. Soughley, WS 189, 4-5, Bureau of Military History, Dublin.

2   Two eyewitnesses stated that the method of transportation was a horse-drawn general service wagon, and so not the ambulance truck usually depicted: Major Harold Heathcote, who was in charge of the firing squad and saw the wagon when it arrived at Kilmainham Jail; and constable Michael T. Soughley. These accounts are contained in the Bureau of Military History archive collection, the files of which were sealed until 2003. Both eyewitness accounts, hidden from public view for decades, cast doubt on the 'Christian martyr' narrative peddled by Capuchin cleric (and virulent anti-communist) Fr. Aloysius Travers in the years following the execution. Neither Soughley nor Heathcote made any mention of a priest with Connolly.

the journey, giving him a clear view, in theory at least, of his surroundings. He may not have been too aware of them though. Major Harold Heathcote, the officer in charge of the firing squad, said that Connolly appeared to have been heavily drugged. He was also unconscious the whole time, at least that was the impression the Major gave Robert Barton, an officer in the Royal Dublin Fusiliers, who talked with him shortly afterwards.[3] Connolly was still in his medical ward pyjamas when the wagon arrived and he was wearing a blindfold when the Major first saw him. The soldiers carried him to a kitchen chair in the yard 'where he sat in an extended position with his head falling backwards.'[4] Once the order to fire was given, the bullets hit Connolly in the head, chest and abdomen.[5] He died without any sign of movement, 'the back of the chair on which he sat was shattered by the volley, a piece being completely blown out of the top of it.'[6] His remains were then taken across the Liffey and laid to rest in Arbour Hill.[7]

Connolly did not leave a plan for his personal archive. During his incarceration in Dublin Castle he expressed the hope that his friend and comrade, Francis Sheehy-Skeffington, would publish a collection of songs and give the proceeds to his wife, Lillie.[8] This seems to have been

---

3   Witness Robert C. Barton, WS 979, 5. Bureau of Military History, Dublin.

4   Brian Barton, *The Secret Court Martial Records of the Easter Rising.* (Cheltenham: The History Press, 2010), 343. Robert Barton later went on to join the Republican movement and was a member of the negotiating team that signed the Anglo-Irish Treaty in 1921. He later repudiated its terms and joined the anti-treaty side during the Irish Civil War.

5   Heathcote told Barton he instructed two of the firing squad to aim for the head. Both bullets struck.

6   Barton, *Secret Court*, 343.

7   Connolly was shot in a different location to the others in the stonebreaker's yard. The spot is immediately beside the large wooden gates; the other executions occurred at the far end of the yard. This would suggest that Connolly was brought in via the gates, put in a chair, and shot in a rather rushed affair. The time of Connolly's execution is not recorded. Seán MacDiarmada, who preceded him, was executed at 3:45am. Constable Soughley said that about half an hour after what he presumed was the final execution he observed the carriage carrying Connolly enter the Gaol. This would suggest that Connolly's execution occurred sometime between 4am and 4:30am, which is between 5:25am and 5:55am today.

8   Nora Connolly, *The Unbroken Tradition* (New York: Boni and Liveright, 1918), 180.

the extent of the request.[9] However, Sheehy-Skeffington was himself executed during the Rising by a British officer later court-martialled for the
offence. Some of the manuscripts and papers were shared among Connolly's children. Eventually, though, the bulk of the archive fell under the
control of William O'Brien, a former colleague of Connolly's and future
general secretary of the Irish Transport and General Workers' Union (IT-
GWU). It included many of his articles, as well as personal letters and
drafts of speeches and lectures. Added to this was O'Brien's personal copy
of an almost complete run of *Workers' Republic* (1896-1903), all of which
he kept under lock and key for over fifty years, publishing only what he
saw fit in censored editions.[10]

Five of Connolly's pamphlets and two of his books were the focus
of publication in the years that followed.[11] A small number of articles
were reprinted in the ITGWU's *Voice of Labour* and in the Communist
Party of Ireland's *Workers' Republic* (1921-23). In 1925 the *Socialist Review* published five letters from Connolly to Kier Hardie and in 1931 *An
Phoblacht* republished a short series of articles, edited by Roddy Connolly, which were taken from *The Harp*, Connolly's American newspaper.
However, the bulk of his work—over seven hundred articles and speeches—remained un-republished.

It was not until March 1941 that a new collection was produced
in book form. It was entitled *A Socialist and War* and was edited by PJ
Musgrove, Connolly Club activist and member of the editorial board of

---

9   This has not stopped later biographers from claiming that Sheehy-Skeffington had been entrusted by Connolly as his literary executor, in charge of the
management of the papers and unpublished works, despite the lack of evidence that
this is what Connolly meant by his request for a once-off book of songs as an income
for his family.

10   Connolly referenced O'Brien's personal copy of *Workers' Republic* in a
letter to O'Brien in 1914. See "Letter from James Connolly to William O'Brien 5 October 1914," MS 13,908/1/84, William O'Brien Collection, National Library of Ireland, Dublin. O'Brien also added to the archive over the years, sourcing Connolly's
letters from former comrades in Ireland and Scotland, most notably John Carstairs
Matheson.

11   These were (with original publication dates): *Erin's Hope: The End and the
Means* (1897); *The New Evangel* (1901); *Songs of Freedom* (1907); *Socialism Made Easy*
(1909); *Labour, Nationality and Religion* (1910); *Labour in Irish History* (1910); and *The
Re-Conquest of Ireland* (1915).

Irish Freedom.[12] "With the exception of a few published works" wrote Musgrove, "the writings of James Connolly lie buried in museum files of obscure periodicals. This virtual suppression of the mass of Connolly's writings is but part of the campaign to 'omit, obliterate and distort the revolutionary side of its doctrine, its revolutionary soul.'"[13] Musgrove reprinted nineteen articles, either in full or in part, all from 1914-1916: two from *Forward*; five from *Irish Worker*; and twelve from *Workers' Republic* (1915-1916). The purpose of the book was to drum up anti-war sentiment, a tactic quietly shelved when the Soviet Union was attacked under Operation Barbarossa in June 1941. It had the effect, though, of raising Connolly's Marxism once again, after years of conservative shoehorning of Connolly into the paradigm of *Rerum Novarum* and 'social justice.'[14]

Meanwhile, the release of his complete works seemed as far away as ever. The first major attempt was made in 1923 by his son, Roddy Connolly. He established the James Connolly Publishing Company and ten titles were drawn up, covering articles, pamphlets, letters, speeches, songs, poems, and a play.[15] Only one was ever completed though: *The Irish Revolution*, a reprint of *Erin's Hope*. The idea was then revived in April 1937 by William O'Brien who said that he was preparing 'the first complete edition' of Connolly's writings and that the 'first edition will be issued at a cheap price in the autumn.'[16]

O'Brien was very clear as to the purpose of the publication. 'It is to

---

12   PJ Musgrove (ed), *A Socialist and War 1914-1916* (London. Lawrence & Wishart, 1941).

13   Musgrove, *A Socialist*, 11. The quote is from chapter one of *The State and Revolution* by Lenin.

14   First published in May 1891, *Rerum Novarum* was the Catholic Church's attempt to counter the rise of working-class socialism and trade unionism. It played a significant role in the Irish Free State post-partition, acting as an intellectual and moral justification for class appeasement within the industrial and political labour movement.

15   The proposed volumes were: *The Irish Revolution*; *Jim Larkin—the Man and his Fight*; *'98—Tone and Emmet'*; *The Workers' Republic: Selected Editorials*; *The New Evangel*; *Revolutionary Songs, Poems, and a Play*; *Two Glorious Triumphs—1913-1916*; *National Independence or Social Emancipation*; *Selected Speeches and Short Stories—Part I*; *Life, Works, and Letters—Part I*. See *Workers' Dreadnought*, 4 August 1923, 8.

16   "What Connolly Wrote," *Irish Press*, 7 April 1937, 6.

help the public to understand Connolly's policy that Mr. O'Brien has undertaken the editing of these writings' said the *Irish Press*.[17] He told the newspaper that 'Connolly gave him all his cuttings from American, Scottish and Irish newspapers at O'Brien's request' and that Connolly 'asked O'Brien to do several things, including the furthering of the Union, of which Mr. O'Brien is now secretary, the extensive organisation of unskilled workers, the advancement of a policy of industrial unions and the formation of 'OBU', 'one big union.' All of this was almost certainly a fabrication on O'Brien's part, who was not even a member of the ITGWU at the time of the Rising; in fact, he did not join the union until January 1917.[18] We also know that Connolly left no plans for his personal archive. It was only after his death that it eventually ended up in the hands of O'Brien.[19] The purpose of the proposed collection was to *justify*, as much as it could, the direction the ITGWU and the Irish Labour Party had taken since 1922, using Connolly as cover.[20]

However, the task of corralling Connolly into the truncated dreams and ambitions of 1930s Free State trade unionism proved to be more difficult than O'Brien expected. In August 1937 he said that the work would 'not be completed in the autumn, as expected'[21] owing to the recent general election in which O'Brien was a candidate. Four years later the historian Desmond Ryan said that he was 'now editing the writings

---

17   "What Connolly Wrote."

18   "Diary of William O'Brien, 1917," 6 January 1917, MS 15,705/10, William O'Brien Collection, National Library of Ireland, Dublin.

19   Ina Connolly-Heron, daughter of James, once told Desmond Greaves that "Cathal O'Shannon took a whole sackful of letters from the house in Belfast and gave them to O'Brien." See "8 December 1956," Desmond Greaves Journal, Vol.12, 1956-7, accessed 5 May 2024, https://desmondgreavesarchive.com/journal/desmond-greaves-journal-vol-12-1956-7/.

20   "The Church rarely mobilised against Labour, but only because Labour was assiduous in ensuring that it was never given cause to do so. The degree of self-censorship was enormous in both policy and language; Labour's amendment of the Workers' Republic constitution; its silence over the Spanish civil war; and its failure to support social reforms such as non-means-tested social welfare benefits or health reforms which would have, in the eyes of the Church in Ireland, been contrary to Catholic social teaching... Offering little and delivering less, Labour received the support it deserved." Niamh Puirséil, *The Irish Labour Party 1922-73* (Dublin: UCD Press, 2007), 310-311.

21   "James Connolly's Works," *Irish Press*. 13 August 1937, 4.

of James Connolly, in whose work from 1897 to 1916... he found much interesting material.'[22] Ryan told the *Irish Press* that he began editing in June 1940 and that it was almost completed. Five years later William O'Brien said that he was now 'engaged in the preparation of an edition of the works of James Connolly.'[23] Finally, in March 1948, eleven years after the original announcement, *Socialism and Nationalism* was published by Sign of the Three Candles Press with a significant subsidy from the IT-GWU. It was the first of three volumes. The second, *Labour and Easter Week*, was published in 1949. The third volume, *The Workers' Republic*, was published in 1951, along with a reprint of *Labour in Ireland*. All four volumes made a set with matching covers and layout, giving the appearance of a collected works.

Alas, all was not what it seemed. Most of the articles were clipped, with sentences and entire paragraphs deleted. Very few were presented as originally intended. Some were given titles they never had while others were composites with extracts taken from different articles but presented together as if original. O'Brien and his main assistant, Desmond Ryan, also surgically removed any complimentary remarks Connolly made towards Larkin, as well as his warnings on the 'dangers of trade union officialdom and the need for a rank-and-file fight' which, as the historian Aindrias Ó Cathasaigh noted, 'were mysteriously absent.'[24] It was a direct continuation of a strategy O'Brien initiated in 1924 when the ITGWU published two books, *The Attempt to Smash the Irish Transport and General Workers' Union*, and *Some Pages From Union History*. They contained highly edited extracts from Connolly's personal letters which O'Brien manipulated in order to attack James Larkin and PT Daly in a vicious and highly personalised struggle over control of the ITGWU—one from which O'Brien emerged victorious.[25]

O'Brien's personal papers also show that the original plan was a lot

---

22   "People and Places," *Irish Press*, 13 October 1941, 2.

23   "Mr. O'Brien to Resign ITGWU Position," *Irish Press*, 21 January 1946, 1.

24   Aindrias Ó Cathasaigh, *The Lost Writings: James Connolly* (London. Pluto Press, 1997), 9.

25   For more on this see, Francis Devine, *Organising History: A Centenary of SIPTU* (Dublin: Gill & Macmillan, 2007), 148-175.

more substantive than the final 121 articles eventually published.[26] The three volumes represented only twenty-one percent of the 577 articles identified by O'Brien.[27] The errors, composites, and ideological bias which saturate the O'Brien/Ryan editions were compounded in the 2000s when the Marxist Internet Archive began transposing Connolly's writings online. The versions used, in many cases, were taken from O'Brien/Ryan and not from the originals. This had the unfortunate effect of reproducing the political and ideological bias of William O'Brien and Desmond Ryan. One of the articles they republished was 'Nationalism and Socialism,' first published in *Shan Van Vocht* in January 1897. The omissions made by them in that article, corrected in the version presented here, give an insight into the kind of editorialism that O'Brien/Ryan inflicted on Connolly's writings.

From 1966 to 1976, there was a renewed interest in his life and work, in part due to the anniversaries of the 1916 Rising and Connolly's birth in 1868, but also because of the Troubles and the heightened radicalism of the period. It saw a somewhat languid descent into the archives and a rediscovery of sorts. Firstly, the O'Brien/Ryan editions were reissued as part of the 50th anniversary commemorations of the Easter Rising. This was quickly followed by *The Best of Connolly*, a fairly nondescript publication of quotes and extracts mainly sourced from O'Brien/Ryan.[28] However, in 1968 New Books, printing press of the Irish Workers Party (IWP), added to the canon with the release of *Revolutionary Warfare*, a collection of articles on street-fighting and urban warfare originally written for the Irish Citizen Army and published in *Workers' Republic* (1915-1916).[29] 'This first-ever reprint of Connolly's military articles is not merely a historical event on the occasion of the centenary of his birth' wrote Michael O'Riordan in the introduction, 'they also reveal him still clearer in his role of a revolutionary soldier who approached revolution-

---

26   The original plan was for 184 articles—sixty-three less than the final volumes. See "List of titles of published writings of James Connolly, 1897-1916," MS 13,920/2, William O'Brien Collection, National Library of Ireland, Dublin.

27   "Lists of titles of published writings of James Connolly in Ireland and the United States, 1895-1916," MS 13,920/1, William O'Brien Collection, National Library of Ireland, Dublin.

28   Proinsias MacAonghusa and Liam Ó Régáin (eds), *The Best of Connolly* (Cork. Mercier Press, 1967).

29   James Connolly, *Revolutionary Warfare* (Dublin. New Books, 1968).

ary war not as a romantic... [but] as a serious business, subscribing to Engel's dictum that 'fighting is to war what cash payment is to trade.'[30] O'Riordan directly linked Connolly with anti-colonial, anti-fascist and anti-imperialist struggle 'in the Russian October Revolution, the liberation of China, the Spanish Peoples Anti-Fascist war, the Anti-Nazi resistance, in Cuba, and in countless battles in other parts of the world' including 'the revolutionary people of Vietnam in their epic struggle against the powerful, and, in this case, impotent imperialism of America.'[31] It was a version of Connolly that was a million miles away from the Christian socialist and bureaucratic trade unionist of O'Brien/Ryan's truncated editions.

In 1969, the Irish Communist Organisation (ICO) republished six articles on trade unionism by Connolly which it said were 'suppressed by the bourgeoisie and the opportunists' and which expose 'those "followers of Connolly" in the leadership of the trade union movement who have been one of the main props of capitalism in the Free State for almost fifty years.'[32] The articles were originally published in *Forward* during 1913-14. It followed these with two other small selections, *The Connolly-Walker Controversy,* (a series of articles in *Forward* in 1911), and *Socialism and the Orange Worker* (a reprint of 'A Forgotten Chapter of Irish History' first published in Forward in 1913).[33] The same year *Under Which Flag,* Connolly's long-lost play, was rediscovered among the recently-deposited O'Brien papers in the National Library of Ireland and performed as a reading in Liberty Hall on 13 May 1969. In terms of Connolly's writings, it proved to be a bit of a false dawn. The focus on the night was not Connolly per se but Francis Sheehy-Skeffington, with all proceeds going towards the erection of a plaque to Skeffington in Cathal Brugha Barracks. Tributes on the night were paid to John Dillon, leader of the Home Rule Party, and to a British officer who apparently said some kind words to

---

30   Connolly. *Revolutionary Warfare*, vi.

31   Connolly. *Revolutionary Warfare*, vi.

32   James Connolly, *Yellow Unions in Ireland and other Articles* (London. Connolly Books, 1968), 1. James Connolly, *Press Poisoners in Ireland and other Articles* (London. Connolly Books, 1968).

33   James Connolly, *Socialism and the Orange Worker* (London. Connolly Books, 1969); James Connolly, *The Connolly-Walker Controversy* (London. Connolly Books, 1969).

Skeffington. The text of the play was not republished until 2007, reflecting the shrugged indifference to the O'Brien collection and the wealth of new writings it contained. [34] For the next thirty years the archive was mainly used by researchers looking at the life of Connolly but not his writings.

This period of semi-heightened interest in Connolly's work was bookended in 1973 with the release of two collections: Dudley-Edwards/Ransom's *Selected Political Writings*, and Beresford Ellis' *Selected Writings*.[35] The Dudley-Edwards/Ransom selection was a scholarly affair, containing a number of new articles including one from *Labour Chronicle* (1894-1895). Beresford Ellis chose to source his article selection from O'Brien/Ryan, the pamphlets produced by the IWP and ICO, as well as Dudley-Edwards/Ransom, despite availability of the original documents. As such it contains the same errors/omissions as the others. Both collections marked a return to the "Christian socialist/trade unionist" thesis, a reaction to the anti-imperialist, anti-colonial Connolly which had come to the fore as a result of the Troubles.

As a coda of sorts, the Cork Workers Club produced two pamphlets which contained new material—*Ireland upon the Dissecting Table: James Connolly on Ulster & Partition* (1975), and *The Connolly-DeLeon Controversy on Wages, Marriage and the Church* (1976). These essentially marked the end of any rediscovered articles in book/pamphlet form for the next twenty years. The Communist Party of Ireland (CPI) did produce a two-volume *Collected Works* in 1987 and 1988, but unfortunately it wasn't a collection of all the known writings, merely a scanned reissue of the four O'Brien/Ryan volumes along with *Revolutionary Warfare* from 1968.[36] It had the side-effect, though, of consolidating the general view that, notwithstanding the odd article or two, the publication of Connolly's writings was more or less complete. Nothing could have been

---

34   James Moran, ed., *Four Irish Rebel Plays* (Dublin. Irish Academic Press, 2007).

35   P. Beresford Ellis, ed, *James Connolly: Selected Writings* (London. Penguin Books, 1973); Owen Dudley Edwards and Bernard Ransom, eds., *James Connolly: Selected Political Writings* (London. Jonathan Cape, 1973).

36   James Connolly, *Collected Works Vol I* (Dublin. New Books, 1987); James Connolly, *Collected Works Vol II* (Dublin. New Books, 1988). The articles from *Revolutionary Warfare* were given the title, "Insurrectionary Warfare."

further from the truth.

By the late 1990s, there was at least some acceptance that the on-going situation with Connolly's writings needed to be challenged. The first movement in this direction was in 1997 when Pluto Press published *The Lost Writings: James Connolly*, edited by Aindrias Ó Cathasaigh. It reproduced sixty-five new articles from 1896 to 1916 and at a stroke increased the Connolly canon by almost a third. 'This collection means that the gaping hole in the publication of Connolly's writings won't gape so much' wrote Ó Cathasaigh, 'but it remains a huge one all the same.'[37] He pointed out that hundreds of articles and letters remained buried in the O'Brien Papers, as well as in libraries and archives across Scotland, England, and the United States. 'The ambitious project of Connolly's heirs has to be resurrected' he said, 'a start has to be made on the complete works of James Connolly.'[38] Ó Cathasaigh did not slouch from his own call. He continued his work in *Red Banner*, a socialist magazine produced in Dublin from 1997 to 2016. It ran for sixty-three issues, during which Ó Cathasaigh transcribed an additional 164 articles, all republished for the first time. When coupled with *Lost Writings*, this meant that Ó Cathasaigh, working alone and with no resources, more than *doubled* the entire amount of republished Connolly articles, adding a total of 229 to the canon. *Red Banner* moved to an online-only publication in 2016 and at time of writing is in the process of moving the Hidden Connolly articles to its website.[39]

The other major development was in April 2001 and the announcement by Manus O'Riordan, head of research at SIPTU, that the union had agreed to sponsor a multi-volume publication of all of Connolly's articles and letters. This would, he said, 'at last enable us to appreciate Connolly's own originality and greatness to the full.'[40] Donal Nevin, veteran trade unionist and author, was placed in charge of the project. The first volume was published in 2005 and to some surprise it was not

37   Ó Cathasaigh, *Lost Writings*, 12.

38   Ó Cathasaigh, *Lost Writings*, 13.

39   *Red Banner*, accessed 7 April 2024, https://redbannermagazine.wordpress.com/tag/hidden-connolly.

40   Aindrias Ó Cathasaigh. 'Where, oh where, is our James Connolly?' 12 September 2017, https://theirishrevolution.wordpress.com/2017/09/12/where-oh-where-is-our-james-connolly/.

a collection of writings but a rather eccentric and somewhat rambling biography of Connolly, written by Nevin. He said it was built upon three pillars: Connolly's letters, his writings, and C. Desmond Greaves' 1961 biography of James Connolly.[41] The final pillar was a strange choice for any biographer as Greaves famously declined to reveal the sources or evidence for his claims about Connolly's life. He even refused to update his book after the O'Brien Collection was made available to the general public, restating with some arrogance that the information available in 1961 was sufficient to tell Connolly's story and that the hundreds of unseen letters contained in the O'Brien Collection were 'unlikely [to] materially alter the conclusions drawn.'[42] It is unusual, to say the least, for a biographer to *reject* an archive containing hundreds of letters and articles written by the subject. Greaves not only did so, but then bragged about it afterwards. Any new biography that placed such scholarship as its bedrock was doomed from the start. Nevin, it seems, did not mind at all. Unfortunately, he carried the same attitude towards Connolly's writings.

The second volume in SIPTU's project, and the first to contain his words, was *Between Comrades: James Connolly Letters and Correspondence 1889-1916.*[43] It was published in 2007 to decidedly mixed reviews. On the one hand a significant selection of Connolly's letters was now at least publicly available; on the other the reproduction of those letters, along with the supporting research, was amateurish, clumsy and dull.[44] Nevin did not give sources for the individual letters, he merely listed the various repositories. There were errors in transcription, including wrong dates, addresses and text; whole paragraphs were omitted from some, with Nevin stating that pages were missing when this was not the case; other letters were left out of the collection with no explanation; the footnotes were unreliable, and in some cases simply wrong. It contained 652

---

41   Donal Nevin, (*James Connolly: A Full Life* (Dublin. Gill & Macmillan, 2005), xix.

42   C. Desmond Greaves, *The Life and Times of James Connolly* (London: Lawrence & Wishart [1961], 1986), 9.

43   Donal Nevin, ed., *Between Comrades: James Connolly Letters and Correspondence 1889-1916* (Dublin. Gill & Macmillan, 2007).

44   It starts with the very first letter, dated 7 April 188[9]. Nevin has 'for me in my position' in the opening paragraph, whereas Connolly wrote 'for one in my position' [my emphasis]. It may seem minor, but Connolly was expressing his firm grasp of the English language—only to be let down by Nevin's lack of same.

letters of which only 278 (43%) were written by Connolly. This meant that more effort was put into reproducing letters *not* by Connolly than into letters actually written by him, which made the conscious omission of known letters all the more frustrating. Ó Cathasaigh, in his review of the book, said that it 'joins a line of Connolly's collections that have raised hopes only to dash them' adding that 'The editor's failure is fundamental: he has not provided a fully accurate and reliable version of the text themselves.'[45] An acknowledgment of sorts was made by Nevin in 2009 in *Saothar*, journal of the Irish Labour History Society. Two letters written by Connolly in 1912, as well as missing paragraphs from three others, were reproduced.[46] However, the majority of errors and omissions were not addressed and the volume itself was not updated, nor republished.

Two years later, Nevin produced *Political Writings 1893-1916* and *Collected Works*.[47] The two-volume collection, the last in the promised series, was published by SIPTU whereas *A Full Life* and *Between Comrades* had both been published by Gill & Macmillan. Nevin said that 580 editorials and articles by Connolly were identified by a Japanese academic in 1980, to which about 'a score' had been added since.[48] This tallied somewhat with the William O'Brien list of 577 articles, manifestos, and election leaflets written by Connolly.[49] The O'Brien list gave names, dates, and publication information for every article—and almost all of them available in the National Library of Ireland, around a twenty-minute stroll from Liberty Hall. Despite this, the collection contains only 268

---

45   Aindrias Ó Cathasaigh, "Donal Nevin (ed), *Between Comrades*," *Saothar* 32 (2007): 110.

46   Donal Nevin, "Between Comrades," *Saothar* 34 (2009): 135-138.

47   Donal Nevin, ed., *James Connolly Political Writings 1893-1916* (Dublin: SIPTU, 2011); *Writings of James Connolly Collected Works* (Dublin: SIPTU, 2011).

48   Nevin, *Political Writings*, xxi. I have been unable to source a copy of the original Horikoshi paper but a review of it appeared in *Saothar* no. 7 (1981). It was somewhat critical of Horikoshi's methodology as well as the glaring omissions in his research. The review does not cite how many articles Horikoshi sourced and given Nevin's somewhat potted history with accuracy and facts I am unable to confirm that what Nevin stated is actually what Horikoshi wrote. See Fintan Cronin, "Notes on Sources," *Saothar* 7 (1981): 112-113.

49   "Lists of titles of published writings of James Connolly in Ireland and the United States,1895-1916," MS 13,920/1, William O'Brien Collection, National Library of Ireland, Dublin.

pieces—around 46% of the material at hand. Nevin said he published 234 pieces, but this is actually thirty-four *less* than the actual contents of the book.[50] Nevin apparently did not even know what was in the book he edited.

Nevin also decided to remove whole sections from articles, just as William O'Brien and Desmond Ryan had done before him. There are nineteen articles in *Political Writings 1893-1916* that are also in this present collection. However, of those, only twelve were reproduced in full by Nevin; the other seven he cut with no explanation. Indeed, of the earliest 101 articles published by Nevin (covering the period 1893 to 1903), only fifty-six were published in full; the rest are incomplete, peppered with inaccurate footnotes, references, and assumptions. Nevin was clearly the wrong person for the job yet was given state and trade union funds over a ten-year period to produce such Sunday League results.[51] Today, the two-volume set is almost impossible to track down. There are no copies in the National Library of Ireland, the British Library, nor in any university library in Ireland or Britain.[52] It is not for sale and it has not been republished. Most of the copies left in existence are in the hands of private collectors.[53]

Since the Nevin editions, three publications have made available new material by Connolly—two in book form and one online. These are: *James Connolly & The Re-Conquest of Ireland* by John Callow (2013); *Old Wine in New Bottles: Some Lessons of the Dublin Lockout* by D.R. O'Connor Lysaght (2013); and 'New early letters: creating James Connolly', *Treason Felony Blog* (2020). Haymarket Books published *A James Connolly Reader* in 2018, edited by Shaun Harkin, but it did not contain any new material. It also sourced many of the articles from the flawed O'Brien/Ryan editions rather than the original publications.

All of which leads us to today and the present collection, the ratio-

---

50   Nevin, *Political Writings*, xxii.

51   Aindrias Ó Cathasaigh said that at least €105,000 was made available for the project. See "Where, oh Where, is our James Connolly?"

52   I've been able to track down three copies worldwide: the storeroom in Bray Public Library; the Des Brannigan collection in Dún Laoghaire Library (appointment only); and the Connolly Centre, Falls Road, Belfast.

53   I am indebted to Joe Mooney for allowing me to borrow his copy for the purposes of this research.

nale for which I hope at this stage is clear. There is no complete edition of Connolly's entire writings, and of the published work the most neglected period is that prior to the first issue of *Workers' Republic* in August 1898. This collection will address this gap, providing for the first time ever all the known works, as well a significant number of previously unknown works which I discovered in the course of my investigations.

LOST & EARLY WRITINGS 1889–1898

The early writings, lectures, and speeches offer up a radically different view of Connolly from that presented by many of his biographers. His first recorded work is a letter on the nature of wealth and labour under capitalism, published in August 1891 when he was only twenty-three years of age. His activism began before this, informing Lillie around 1890 that he may have to cancel a promised trip to Dundee due to an industrial dispute in his workplace. 'As my brother and I are ringleaders in the matter' he wrote, 'it is necessary we should be on the ground.'[54] Yet despite the popular image of Connolly as a trade unionist, this offhand reference in a private letter to a strike is one of only a tiny handful he made to trade union activity, normally consisting of simple and general support for strikes, apart from an article for *Justice* in 1893 where he criticised trade union support for cooperation businesses that paid less than trade union rates of wages.[55]

Connolly was, first and foremost, a political agitator. He remained one his entire life. It was his one guiding principle: the raising of class-consciousness through journalism, books, pamphlets, lectures, political campaigns, street agitation, and industrial organisation. His great innovation, from a Marxist perspective, was the application of class consciousness-raising to Ireland, the Empire, and the colonial dynamic—an application often routinely misunderstood or cynically misrepresented since his death by political and trade union actors with an altogether different agenda.

The James Connolly that emerges from these early writings was a so-

---

54   "Letter from James Connolly to Lillie Connolly about arrangements for their wedding," MS 13,911/6, William O'Brien Collection, National Library of Ireland, Dublin.

55   "Scottish Notes," *Justice*, 26 August 1893, 3.

cialist internationalist and an anti-imperialist Irish republican. If there was a contradiction in this—as others have suggested—then it was one that was shared by Marxist anti-imperialist nationalists across what is now known as the Global South. The anti-colonial struggles that followed in the wake of the First and Second World Wars were nationalist by design—the imperial and colonial projects of the US and European states ensured that this was so. Connolly's Marxist republicanism fits perfectly into this dynamic. He did not see it as some kind of tactic to win over the Irish working classes to socialism. He saw it as a *scientific necessity*, arrived at through the application of Marxism to the colonial capitalist relations of production and exchange in Ireland, and the very particular colonial class dynamics that arose out of those relations. He could see that Britain's presence in Ireland was part and parcel of a wider imperial capitalist project. He could also see a type of middleman class in Ireland that benefitted from those relations, and that unless those relations (and that class) were shattered the exploitation of the Irish working class would continue as before.

Connolly's republicanism has been explained away by mainstream historiography in ways that refuse to acknowledge the path that took him—as with others across the globe—to an anti-imperialist, anti-colonial, republican Marxism. Thus we read that it was a Fenian uncle, or John Leslie, or the fallout from the 1913 Lockout, that somehow "corrupted" his socialism and led him to nationalism. However, when he is placed alongside other Marxists who were also engaged in anti-colonial and anti-imperialist liberation, we see not only where he belonged, but where he wanted to take us. For example, the Peruvian Marxist José Carlos Mariátegui wrote in 1925 that 'the function of the socialist idea changes in politically or economically colonial peoples [where] socialism acquires, by force of circumstance, without denying entirely any of its principles, a nationalist attitude.'[56] Similarly, the Guinea-Bissau independence leader and Marxist Amilcar Cabral said that "Independence is not just a simple matter of expelling the Portuguese, of having a flag and a national anthem. The people must be secure in the knowledge that no one is going to steal their labour, that the wealth of the country is

---

56   José Carlos Mariátegui, *Selected Works*, trans. Christian Noakes (Madison: Iskra Books, 2021), 103. I am indebted to Seán Byers for highlighting Mariátegui's work to me.

not going into somebody else's pocket."[57] It immediately brings to mind Connolly's article for *Shan Van Vocht* in 1897: "If you could remove the English army tomorrow and hoist the green flag over Dublin Castle, unless you set about the organisation of the Socialist Republic, your efforts would be in vain." In 1968 the Lebanese Marxist Mahdi Amel argued that the "insertion of new relations of production in colonised countries processed through... a radical change in the historical logic of these countries' development"[58]—a firm echo of Connolly's own analysis in *Labour in Irish History*.[59] Maybe Irish historiography is right, though, to ignore the dynamics of national struggle and anti-colonial, anti-imperialist Marxism across the globe. Maybe Mariátegui, Cabral and Amel simply had Fenian uncles.

Once Ireland's historiographical diviners, however, are left to their bone-throwing causality, other voices enter the fray. "From the postcolonial perspective, it was Connolly—whose very name sounds like a wilful resisting reversal of the word 'colony'—who was among the very first to combine the politics of socialism with the demand for national self-determination in the colonial arena,' wrote Robert J.C. Young in 2001. 'His revolutionary anti-colonial violence always remained embedded within the larger political perspective of socialist objectives.'[60] "Connolly is remarkably ahead of his time because of the historical determined temporal differentials of British colonialism," said Spurgeon Thompson in 2008, who saw in Connolly's play, *Under Which Flag*, "a unique mode of indigenous theory production directly involved in the context of in-

---

57   Quoted in Walter Rodney, *Decolonial Marxism: Essays from the Pan-African Revolution* (London: Verso, 2022), 4.

58   Mahdi Amel, *Arab Marxism and National Liberation: Selected Writings of Mahdi Amel*, ed.Hicham Safieddine, trans. Angela Giordani (Chicago: Haymarket Books, 202), 57.

59   "Communal ownership of land would, undoubtedly, have given way to the privately owned system of capitalist-landlordism, even if Ireland had remained an independent country, but coming as it did in obedience to the pressure of armed force from without, instead of by the operation of economic forces within, the change has been bitterly and justly resented by the vast mass of the Irish people, many of whom still mix with their dreams of liberty longings for a return to the ancient system of land tenure-now organically impossible." James Connolly, *Labour in Irish History* (Dublin: Maunsel & Co.), 4.

60   Robert J.C. Young, *Postcolonialism: An Historical Introduction* (Oxford: Blackwell Publishing, 2001), 305.

surrectionary anticolonial politics."[61] Catherine Morris and Thompson point out that Connolly's ideological framework was "anti-imperialist, feminist, multilingualist, pro-immigration, anti-racist, and it was forged in the context of theory meeting practice, directly, daily, where often Connolly's own personal and political survival was at stake."[62] The importance of Connolly's theoretical creativity was summed up by Gregory Dobbins in 2000. "If one is to construct a genealogy of Irish critical responses to colonization that might [be] seen in relation to what eventually would come to be known as postcolonial theory," he said, "a critical recovery of Connolly's works is a crucial site from which to begin that process."[63] The articles, letters and stories reproduced in this volume—many for the first time—present an opportunity to carry on that critical work of rediscovery.[64]

In terms of the writings themselves, the starting point is the list of 577 articles compiled by O'Brien. He recorded twenty pieces of writing that were published before the first issue of *Workers' Republic* (13 August 1898), which is the cut-off point for this book. Connolly's articles for *Labour Chronicle*, along with his Scottish reports for *Justice*, were not included by O'Brien, but were known about and referenced by Desmond Greaves and Samuel Levenson in their respective biographies. In 1998 the historian Paul Dillon rediscovered two more articles: 'Famine in Ireland' first published in *Weekly People* (New York) in 1898; and 'Socyalizm w Irlandyi', which was published in the London-based Polish journal Świątła the same year.[65] Finally in 2020 three letters written by Connolly

---

61   Spurgeon Thompson, "Indigenous Theory: James Connolly and the Theatre of Decolonization," *Interventions* 10, no.1 (2008): 23.

62   Catherine Morris & Spurgeon Thompson, "Postcolonial Connolly," *Interventions* 10, no.1 (2008): 5.

63   Gregory Dobbins, "Whenever Green is Red: James Connolly and Postcolonial Theory." *Nepantla: Views from the South* 1, no.3 (2000): 607.

64   For all of his brilliance, it is hard not to see the outsized influence of Edward Said on Irish postcolonial studies, in particular his rejection of Marxism as an analytical tool, as having had a somewhat detrimental effect in terms of a deeper understanding of Connolly—notwithstanding the work of Dobbins, Young, Morris and Thompson, among others.

65   Paul Dillon, "James Connolly and the Kerry Famine of 1898," *Saothar* 25 (2000): 29-42. Carl Reeve and Ann Barton Reeve had previously mentioned that Connolly supplied articles on Kerry for the *Weekly People* but did not give any further details. See Carl Reeve and Ann Barton Reeve, *James Connolly and the United States* (New

and first published in *Dundee Weekly News* in 1891 were rediscovered by the historian John Ó Néill and republished online at *Treason Felony Blog*.[66]

Also included are fifteen of the sixteen letters contained in *Between Comrades* that were written by Connolly during 188[8/9]-1898. Unfortunately, I have been unable to locate the original source for one of the letters published in *Between Comrades* and given Nevin's track record I feel uncomfortable with its reproduction. I have no doubt the letter exists—it is one that Connolly wrote to Lillie in 1890—I simply failed to locate the original in time for this volume. I took the decision therefore to exclude it from the list of confirmed writings and place it instead in the appendices as reference. That leaves fifty previously known articles and letters written by Connolly between April 1889 and July 1898, of which only thirty-one to date have been republished in full. The remaining nineteen items are republished here, complete and unedited, for the first time ever.

The present collection also contains eighteen previously unknown and lost items authored by Connolly. These consist of eleven newspaper pieces, four works of fiction, and three personal letters.[67] I have also included nineteen secondary accounts of speeches and lectures given by Connolly, of which only a handful were previously known. Finally, I have included seven appendices. These cover Connolly's local election campaigns; the various lectures and talks he gave in Scotland, England, and Ireland; a short collection of the known writings of his brother, John; some items either of uncertain authorship or where the originals are not available; and a reflection on the myths and rumours regarding his early life, with a special focus on the highly influential and frustratingly unprovable tales of C. Desmond Greaves.

Jersey. Humanities Press. 1978): 19. They erroneously say that this was at the request of Daniel De Leon. It was in fact an initiative undertaken by Connolly and Maud Gonne alone, who knew each other when Connolly was still living in Edinburgh.

66   "New early letters: Creating James Connolly," *Treason Felony Blog*, 4 June 2020, https://treasonfelony.wordpress.com/2020/06/04/new-early-letters-creating-james-connolly/.

67   The bulk of these items were found in digitised newspaper archive collections. It is almost certain that there are more pieces out there in collections yet to be digitised. The three letters were found in the Independent Labour Party papers, London School of Economics.

Taken together, these writings and speeches reflect an original and piercing intellect coupled with an energetic activism. Similarly, they show his closeness to his brother, John, six years older than him and a clear influence on Connolly in terms of his politics and activism. Indeed, it would be highly unusual, given such closeness, that Connolly made this journey to an anti-colonial Irish republicanism Marxism all on his own. So much has been lost over the years, especially in regard to John, but even with that it is still possible to move him, however gently, back into the picture. Many of Connolly's biographers have argued that Connolly was hugely influenced by John Leslie, as reflected in the short series of articles on Ireland written by Leslie for *Justice* in 1895. I would argue that the opposite is the case: it was Leslie that was more than likely influenced by the Connolly brothers, not the other way round. There is so much more to discover about Connolly, and this volume is presented simply as the opening step of a greater journey into this half-remembered world.

PART I
LOST WRITINGS

INTRODUCTION

THIS SECTION contains eleven previously unknown pieces written by Connolly, consisting of seven letters to the editor of *Edinburgh Evening News*, published between October 1893 and August 1894; two pieces for *Labour Leader* published in summer 1895; and two articles on food distress in Kerry in 1898, published in *Cork Daily Herald* and *Irish World* (New York) respectively.

The letters and articles in the *Evening News* and *Labour Leader* display an intelligent and confident young Marxist, already seasoned through years of street agitation and intense research and reflection. Indeed, Connolly's first known published work was a letter on the nature of wealth and labour power under capitalism, published in *Dundee Weekly News* in August 1891.[1] This was followed by two other letters on socialism and the world's wealth.[2] This was no singular bookish journey. He undertook his political education alongside his brother, John, and fellow socialists, Marxists, and radicals in Edinburgh. The letters rediscovered and republished here show a deepening of his understanding of the general economic and political theories of Marx, as well as his first moves (in print at least) towards the application of that understanding to the realities of Ireland, the UK and the British Empire.

They also show that the theoretical and conceptual apparatuses used by Connolly throughout his lifetime were there from the beginning. He built upon them as his research and analysis developed and deepened but there is no break to speak of, no 'mature' and 'immature' Connolly to any major degree. What we see instead from 1895 onwards is an increasing focus on the Irish question—in print, public talks, and finally with the

---

1   James Connolly, "What is Wealth?" *Dundee Weekly News*, 8 August 1891.

2   James Connolly, "What do Socialists Want?" *Dundee Weekly News*, 24 October 1891; "The World's Wealth," *Dundee Weekly News*, 31 October 1891.

establishment of the ISRP itself. This is not done at the expense of his Marxism but rather was an expansion of it, one that incorporated the nuanced reality of colonialism within the so-called 'imperial core' of the United Kingdom—as indeed Marx and Engels had done before him.[3]

The letters to the *Evening News* and *Labour Leader* are peppered with lines that would resonate throughout his life: 'the political equality of the ballot-box must be supplemented by the economic equality of the workshop'; 'our experience in the past has shown us the utter folly of trusting to middle class gentlemen for working-class reform'; 'Freedom as a gift from above is valueless, but when won by the active rebellion of the oppressed against the oppressor it becomes a boon more precious than life itself'; 'socialism... insists upon the working class recognising the duty of rebellion against the classes whose manipulation of the productive forces of society have caused the empty stomachs in the midst of plenty'; 'Home Rule would be of little use to the Irish worker while he was at the mercy of the Irish landlord, who could throw him out on the roadside, or the Irish employer, who could turn him upon the street.'

These sentiments were built upon the ideological apparatus which underpinned them: 'labour creates capital, maintains the capitalist, and dies in the process'; 'The wealth of the upper class is simply that portion of the earnings of labour which they have stolen from the workers in the name of rent, interest, and profit'; 'even under political freedom the owners of land and capital are virtually the masters of the people's lives.' When Connolly wrote of the need for economic equality in the workshop, he was clear as to what it meant: 'This, socialism teaches, can only be realised by substituting the public ownership and control of industry for the individual enterprise of the capitalist, and transforming the capitalist himself from an irresponsible hunter after profit into a public servant, fulfilling a public function.' Not for Connolly the Christian socialist dream of a partnership between the classes of labour and capital, all working together for the glory of a benevolent deity in the sky. This was class struggle, a scientific necessity under Marxism for the realisation of a socialist society.

The two *Labour Leader* pieces were published under the pseudonym

---

3   Karl Marx and Frederick Engels, *Ireland and the Irish Question* (Moscow: Progress Publishers, 1971).

'Brehon.' The main evidence for Connolly as Brehon is laid out in the Lost Fiction section of this book. However, there are two phrases in 'To the Electors' that point to Connolly as author. These are: 'last and meanest form of human slavery'; and 'from the dark Egypt of our capitalistic anarchy to the promised land of industrial freedom.'

In September 1897 Connolly wrote an article for *The People* (New York) entitled "Ireland's Address to the Working Class Irish of America." It was republished later that year in the American edition of *Erin's Hope: The Ends and the Means* and contains the following line:

> ...no stronger blow could be struck for the liberties of "the old land" than will be given on the day when a majority of the electorate of the United States vote for the installation of a socialist administration, pledged to uproot that **last and meanest form of human slavery**, the wage system of capitalism. [My emphasis.]

It is a unique formula of words. Indeed, a Google search produces a single hit to the aforementioned article. The Hathi Trust collections also reveals only one (that of *Erin's Hope*), while a search of the British Newspaper Archive produces a single result: 'To the Electors':

> The heart and intellect of mankind are in revolt against it; it is already tottering to its fall, and with its disappearance **the last and meanest form of human slavery** will disappear from off the face of this old earth of ours. [My emphasis.]

The second phrase, 'from the dark Egypt of our capitalistic anarchy to the promised land of industrial freedom,' was first used by Connolly in an article for *Labour Chronicle* in December 1894 which he wrote under the pseudonym 'R.Ascal.' It said, with a slight variation:

> ..., to create such a public feeling in our favour as shall enable us to bridge the gulf between the old order and the new, and lead the people **from the dark Egypt of our industrial anarchy, into the Promised Land of industrial freedom**. [My emphasis.]

It is a phrase unique to Connolly. Its next appearance was in a manifesto issued one month later in January 1895 by the Socialist Election Committee of Edinburgh Central Division, extracts from which were republished in a number of Scottish newspapers.[4] Here the word 'indus-

---

4   "A Socialist Manifesto," *Edinburgh Evening News*, 29 January 1895, 2; "Edinburgh Socialists and the Central Division," *Scotsman*, 30 January 1895, 6; "Mr H Paul MP in Edinburgh," *Dundee Advertiser*, 31 January 1895, 3.

trial' was changed to 'capitalistic' but otherwise it is exactly the same. The manifesto was later republished in full in *Labour Leader* as 'To the Electors.' It said:

> ...to make the people in a democratic state the sole masters of the land and instruments of labour by which they live, to organise and lead the workers in their onward and upward pilgrimage **from the dark Egypt of our capitalistic anarchy to the promised land of industrial freedom**. [My emphasis.]

Brehon also wrote a letter to the editor of the *Labour Leader*, Kier Hardie, in which he offered advice on how the newspaper could increase its circulation. 'I was in Rochdale the other week' he wrote, 'and although the ILP branch there boasts a membership of over 600, I found it impossible to procure the paper at a single newsagents in the town, and had eventually to go to the rooms in order to purchase it. In Bury the same state of matters was existent.' The letter was written some time in August 1895 and at the time Connolly was on a lecture tour of the Greater Manchester and Liverpool area. He addressed two meetings in Bury on 21 July.[5]

The final two articles in this section are from 1898 and relate to the food distress in Kerry that year. The historian Paul Dillon did much to highlight the work that Connolly and Maud Gonne did regarding Kerry in an article first published in 2000.[6] The articles uncovered here serve to supplement his analysis, which remains the best written account of the campaign. The *Irish World* article was signed by Connolly, while the *Cork Daily Herald* article was uncovered using textual and contextual analysis which identifies Connolly as the journalist in question.

5   "Provincial Notes—Bury," *Justice*, 27 July 1895, 236.

6   Dillon, "James Connolly."

*****

LETTERS TO THE EDITOR
EDINBURGH EVENING NEWS,
24 OCTOBER 1893, P.2

JAMES CONNOLLY, secretary, Labour Election Committee, writes: Your correspondent, "Working Man," seems to be somewhat astray in his logic. [1] After informing us that it is the duty of all true liberals to secure the return of labour members to the Town Council, he next proceeds to demand the withdrawal of the labour candidate; but how we are to return labour members by withdrawing them he nowhere condescends to explain. Now, to bring the question to a direct issue. Why should we wish for the return of labour members at all? Simply because our experience in the past has shown us the utter folly of trusting to middle class gentlemen for working-class reform; because it is not safe to trust landlords to carry out city improvements, involving the purchase of slum property; because we believe that if workmen have sufficient discernment to elect and instruct representatives, they have surely the ability to act as representatives. Now, as we recognise no difference between Tory landlords and Liberal landlords, betwixt Liberal employers and Tory employers, as we believe the difference is simply the difference betwixt Tweedledum and Tweedledee, why we should withdraw our man to make room for one any more than another passes my comprehension. If our friend believes

---

1   See *Edinburgh Evening News*, 23 October 1893, 2: ""Working Man" writes: We are to have a three- cornered fight in George Square Ward, and every true Liberal will deplore this state of matters. As working men we must all do our best to return Labour members to the Council, wherever possible; but a Labour candidate with a Tory and a man like Bailie Steel in the field has not the remotest chance. If Mr Hamilton has the cause of labour at heart he will be prudent and retire, as otherwise it will be a win for the retrogressive party. We may not all be pleased with Bailie Steel, but he is surely a good deal better than a Tory misrepresenting the opinion of the Ward in our Town Council." Bailie is an elected position in Scottish local government.

in working-class representation let him vote for his fellow workman, and not for a man who has been the bitterest enemy of all real social reform,[2] and who can only begin to see the existence of grievances requiring remedy, when his eyes are opened by the approach of the day of reckoning.

2   James Steel (1830-1904), builder, property developer, and Liberal Party councillor. Steel held the position of Bailie at the time.

*****

MR. LABOUCHÈRE ON SOCIALISM
EDINBURGH EVENING NEWS
10 FEBRUARY 1894, P.4

JAMES CONNOLLY writes: Your statement that "Mr Labouchère[1] is to be congratulated on meeting one of the ablest exponents of socialism face to face" will be readily endorsed by every socialist who has read even the fragmentary reports of his speech, as it appears in today's newspapers. We could not in justice withhold our admiration from an opponent who so light-heartedly entered upon a contest for which he was so poorly equipped. For the ignorance of economics displayed by Mr Labouchère is only equalled by his audacity in displaying it. To take an example of his arguments: 'Capital,' he said, 'creates labour by consuming it.' Now, labour-power, which is really what capital consumes, is simply the powers or energies inherent in our minds or bodies; is, in fact, inseparable from the labourer—lives with him and dies with him. And capital only consumes labour in order that in the process of consumption labour may not only preserve and perpetuate capital, its master, but may also make a free gift to the capitalist of an added value to the raw material, which added

---

1 Henry Du Pré Labouchère (1831-1912), English politician and at the time Liberal MP for Northampton. He took part in a debate on socialism which was held in Northampton on 8 February 1894. His opponent was Henry Hyndman (1842-1921), founder of the Social Democratic Federation. During the debate Labouchère said that Hyndman "exaggerated the evils of the present system. However wealthy men might waste their money and spend it upon luxuries, these luxuries had to be produced ... There was no more incontrovertible fact than this, that the more capital there was in the country the better it was for the country and the better for labour. It created labour by consuming it," See "Mr. Labouchère and Socialism," *Edinburgh Evening News,* 9 February 1894, 4. Labouchère was also responsible for the 1885 Labouchère Amendment, which criminalised all male homosexual activity in the United Kingdom. It was under this law that Oscar Wilde was prosecuted in 1895.

value appears in his ledgers as profit. Thus labour creates capital, maintains the capitalist, and dies in the process. And Mr Labouchère might be challenged to search the world over for a single instance in which inanimate capital has created labour, the vital energy of a human being. In fact, capital is to labour what a tool is to the individual workman, i.e. an instrument which in his hands increases his efficiency, but becomes useless when he lays it down. Destroy the tool and the workman may replace it by his labour, but destroy the labourer and the tool (or capital) is useless lumber. Yet Mr Labouchère gravely informs us that capital creates labour. Again, he revives an old economic fallacy that the expenditure of the idle rich upon luxuries for personal gratification confers a benefit upon the workers by giving employment. However ingenious this may be as an excuse for the heartless luxury of the rich amid the misery of the poor, as a statement of economics it is simply ridiculous. The wealth of the upper class is simply that portion of the earnings of labour which they have stolen from the workers in the name of rent, interest, and profit. By expending this wealth upon luxuries they simply command the services of a number of workers who would otherwise be employed in the production of necessaries. As the same amount of necessaries is still required, the workers engaged in their production are compelled to work harder and longer to make good the deficit caused by the withdrawal of their quondam fellow-workers, who are now making luxuries for the idle rich. But if the workers had in the first instance been left in possession of the wealth they had created, the existence of an idle class would be impossible, and our capitalist and landlord friends would find themselves lending a hand in the useful work of the community, and not merely devouring its substance. If any man imagines that an idler confers a benefit upon society by his presence in it, or produces wealth by destroying, let him try the experiment in his own family. His faith in Mr Labouchère would quickly vanish. But it would take more space than is allotted to a letter to the newspaper to even allude to all the economic fallacies to which Mr Labouchère gave utterance in the course of his speech.

*****

SOCIALIST ECONOMICS
EDINBURGH EVENING NEWS
12 FEBRUARY 1894, P.2

JAMES CONNOLLY writes: It would, perhaps, save much confusion of thought on the part of non-socialists if we define what we mean by socialism before proceeding with a discussion on the subject. Socialism teaches that the industrial system of a free people, like their political system, ought to be administered on the lines of the broadest democracy, by the people, for the people, and in the interests of the people. That the political equality of the ballot-box must be supplemented by the economic equality of the workshop. This, socialism teaches, can only be realised by substituting the public ownership and control of industry for the individual enterprise of the capitalist, and transforming the capitalist himself from an irresponsible hunter after profit into a public servant, fulfilling a public function. This is the bare idea upon which socialism rests, and the point in dispute between individualism and socialism is the respective merits and justice of public and private ownership. All other ideas are subservient to this central doctrine, which does not stand or fall with any one definition of what constitutes labour, Mr Mallock notwithstanding.[1] Socialists in speaking of labour do not exclude intellectual labour—indeed in the letter you were courteous enough to publish I expressly defined labour as "the powers or energies inherent in our *mind* and bodies." Surely that is explicit enough. And if you will allow me to

---

1 Connolly is referencing an *Edinburgh Evening News* editorial, 19 January 1894, which quoted from William Hurrell Mallock's book, *Labour and the Popular Welfare* (1893). The editorial said "That great inequalities exist no one denies, but a dip into Mr Mallock's book on "Labour and the Popular Welfare," reveals the fact that the period of the greatest wealth production has also been the period of the greatest wealth distribution."

say so, the whole argument based upon this erroneous conception of socialism is a mere beating of the wind. Further, while we do not forget that the labour of the manual worker is as necessary to the full fruition of the work of genius as the aid of capital can be, we nevertheless do not wish to disparage the enormous benefits conferred upon society by a Watt, a Stephenson, an Arkwright, or a Fulton.[2] But we do think that unless you are prepared to argue, and this we will scarcely credit, that the capitalist class of today are a race of intellectual giants upon whose brain power society rests for its support, unless you are prepared to maintain such an absurd position, your whole argument is beside the question. One swallow does not make a summer, nor yet do a whole flock of swallows. The appearance of a few inventive geniuses in a generation, does not justify the action of the whole host of sordid human leeches who take advantage of the fruits of other men's genius to enrich their own coffers, while the man whose brain creations they are exploiting, very often dies, as did Elias Howe, in a garret.[3] The man of ability today must sell his ability and his inventiveness and his genius to the class without whose capital his ideas would never be realised. Moreover, to point the moral of the absolute uselessness of the present-day capitalist, it is well known that in every country in which capitalism has found a footing, the conduct and management of all industries are now entrusted to salaried managers and officials; while the functions of the real capitalist are reduced to the arduous task of drawing and signing for his quarterly dividends. Thus the stern logic of facts works out before your eyes the problem your brain refuses to grasp, befogged by the mists of class prejudice.

---

2   James Watt (1736-1819); George Stephenson (1781-1848); Richard Arkwright (1732-1792); Robert Fulton (1765-1815), designers of a steam engine, steam locomotive, spinning frame, and steamboat respectively.

3   Elias Howe (1819-1867) American inventor and designer of a sewing machine. His patent was stolen by Isaac Singer among others who ended up paying royalties to Howe after a successful lawsuit. Despite Connolly's image of Howe dying in a lonely attic room ("in a garret"), Howe earned nearly $2 million from his patent from 1854 to its expiration in 1867, the year of his death.

*****

THE SCHOOL BOARD ELECTION
EDINBURGH EVENING NEWS
23 MARCH 1894, P.2

JAMES CONNOLLY writes: As we are now fairly entered upon a contested election for the School Board[1], it may interest your readers to know why the Independent Labour Party interfered with the arrangement arrived at by the various parties interested in preventing a contest. The middle class are already, in our opinion, vastly over-represented on every legislative and administrative body in the country, and it was surely a small measure of justice to expect that in such a matter as the administration of the education of their children the claims of the workers should not be overlooked. But in the list of candidates drawn up by the retiring Board and their committees not one working man or woman was included. And even when under pressure of a requisition signed by over 700 electors Mr Alex Dickinson[2] consented to stand as an Independent Labour candidate, the compromise suggested came in the form of a deliberate insult to the workers. The overwhelming majority, in fact nearly 90 per cent, of the children attending our board schools are drawn from the ranks of the working class, yet it was gravely suggested that the three candidates who should retire to avoid a contest should be as follows: the Independent Labour candidate (of course), another working class, and

---

1   Connolly was a candidate in the election for the St Giles ward. See appendix B.

2   Alec ("Alex") Dickinson was a printer from Fountainbridge, Edinburgh. In January 1894 he was secretary of the southern division of the Edinburgh Independent Labour Party. In 1895 he was the publisher of the Labour Chronicle. He died in December of that year. See Bernard Campbell Ransom, "James Connolly and the Scottish Left 1890-1916" (PhD diss., University of Edinburgh, 1975), 39-66, and "Alec Dickinson," *Justice*, 14 December 1895.

one middle class candidate. In other words, two working men out of four and one middle class member out of fourteen. The cool insolence of the proposal fairly takes our breath away. Yet all those estimable ladies and gentlemen will tell you they are in favour of working-class members. How adroitly they have disguised their sentiments. But we cannot be a party to any attempt to play fast and loose with the right of the people to control the education of their children. An education is today the only heritage the most of us can leave our offspring. This is the ideal that inspires the Independent Labour Party in entering upon this contest, and from any task we shall never turn back until our ideal is realised.

***** *****

THE LABOUR WAR IN THE STATES
EDINBURGH EVENING NEWS
11 JULY 1894, P.2

J AMES CONNOLLY, 21 South College Street, writes: Would you kindly allow me the use of your columns to point out to your readers the real significance of, and lesson to be drawn from, the labour riots at Chicago[1]. To judge from the reports appearing in the newspapers at present, one would imagine the strikers to be fiends in human shape, animated by no other motive than love of destruction. But a closer study reveals the employers themselves in a light scarcely less credible. In a recent issue appears a report stating that the strike leaders have repeatedly offered to submit to arbitration, but have had their offer declined by the Pullman Company[2], who are apparently indifferent to the sufferings inflicted upon the outside world, and can afford to view with equanimity the destruction of property, conscious that, as you pointed out in a recent issue, for all the damage to property occasioned the inhabitants of the state will be compelled to pay full and ample compensation. Is this the tyranny of trade unionism, or is it not rather a signal proof of the helplessness of the public in the grip of organised capital? The anarchy at present rampant in the United States is the direct outcome of our capitalist system, and a striking proof of the truth of the socialist contention that even under political freedom the owners of land and capital are virtually the masters of the people's lives. The lesson to be learned from Chicago is the necessity of using our political power to accomplish our industrial emancipation, instead of allowing the life and wellbeing of the entire nation to be at the

---

1   The riots were linked to the Pullman railway strike (Chicago) May–July 1894.

2   The Pullman Palace Car Company manufactured railroad cars.

mercy of contending groups of masters and slaves.

*****

SOCIAL DEMOCRACY VERSUS STATE SOCIALISM
EDINBURGH EVENING NEWS
21 JULY 1894, P.2

JAMES CONNOLLY writes: "In your editorial of Friday *in re* the social-ist movement in Germany you apparently commit the too common error of confounding social democracy, the socialism of the people, with its spurious aristocratic namesake.[1] The success of socialism cannot be judged by the failures of the imitation article fathered by Prince Bismarck. Collectivists look to the adoption of their principles to abolish discontent by abolishing its causes, but they do not hope to attain that end by learning the people to lean upon the protecting arms of middle-class state officials.[2] Indeed, so far is this from being the case, that in countries

1   "Collectivists in this country, who look to the adoption of their principles to abolish discontent, would do well to study the Socialistic movement in Germany. There can be no doubt that in paternalism Germany is far ahead of us. Bismarck was the first to introduce state socialism into Germany.... What has been the result? Are what are called the "weaker members" of the State more contented? This does not appear to be the case, for several instances lately have proved that aggressive socialists exist even among the Government employees... It may be taken as an axiom that the more the government of any country insist on their ability to rectify evils the greater will be the popular discontent when government interference fails to remove all grievances." *Edinburgh Evening News*, 20 July 1894, 2.

2   Connolly used the verb 'to learn' for 'to teach' on at least two other occasions: 'have long ere now learned the intelligent worker' in 'Labour Representation,' *Workers' Republic*, 27 August 1898, 4; and 'you cannot learn starving men Gaelic' in 'Home Thrusts,' *Workers' Republic*, 1 October 1898, 1. Nevin changed the latter to 'teach' in *Political Writings*, believing the use of 'learn' to be an error. However, it was a popular enough colloquialism for Kenneth Grahame to discuss its usage in *The Wind in the Willows* (1908): "I'm very sorry," said the Rat humbly. "Only I think it ought to be 'teach 'em,' not 'learn 'em.'" "But we don't want to teach 'em," replied the Badger. "We want to learn 'em—learn 'em, learn 'em! And what's more, we're going to do it,

like Germany where, the government being appointed by the Emperor, irrespective of the strength of parties in the Reichstag, the possibility of the people attaining immediate administrative power does not exist, the Socialist party does not even encourage such projects as the gradual absorption by the state of all industries, nor the extension of state interference in any direction. In Britain, on the other hand, where the vote of the people does elect the government, the Socialist party makes such proposals as the above chief planks in their programme. The reason for such seemingly divergent policies is, of course, obvious. In Germany, state paternalism or the nationalisation of separate industries would simply increase the power of the horde of officials who compose the middle-class state, and be of no permanent benefit to the workers, who might as well be exploited by the individual capitalist as by the capitalist state official. But in Britain, where the people absolutely control the government, to place the control of our industry in the hands of the state is to make it the property of the people. If under such auspices public control of our industrial affairs is still marked by tyranny and despotic officialism, it will only be because the people are not thoroughly alive to the vital importance of the powers the franchise has endowed them with. When they are and insist upon our public officials applying to our industrial affairs the same principles of democracy to which we adhere in our political affairs, government interference will not mean state paternalism arousing nothing but discontent, but will mean the gradual assumption by the people of the ownership and control of the means by which the people exist.

---

too!" Grahame was born at 32 Castle St Edinburgh in 1859, around a twenty-minute walk from where Connolly grew up. The colloquialism was also used by Shakespeare, of whom Connolly was an avid and dedicated reader. Caliban says 'learning' for 'teaching' in The Tempest, act I, scene II, line 368: 'you taught me language, and my profit on't / Is I know to curse. The red plague rid you / For learning me your language!' I am indebted to Paul Anderson for the reference to *Wind in the Willows*. See also Ó Cathasaigh, "Where, oh where, is our James Connolly?"

*****

SOCIALISM V. INDIVIDUALISM
EDINBURGH EVENING NEWS
8 AUGUST 1894, P.2

JAMES CONNOLLY writes: Will you allow me the use of your columns to point out a few of the inaccuracies contained in your article of Tuesday on the above subject.[1] To deal with them all would, I am afraid, require too much space. When Mr JH Levy[2] seeks to discredit socialism by the remark that it has its paternal origin in the empty stomachs of its disciples, he is not reasoning with us, he is only throwing mud.[3] If the fact that the people are suffering under political or social oppression is to be taken as a reason why their arguments should be scorned or their revolt discountenanced, then farewell to all hopes of political or social progress. Freedom as a gift from above is valueless, but when won by the active rebellion of the oppressed against the oppressor it becomes a boon more precious than life itself. And the strength and dignity of socialism lies just in this fact—that it insists upon the working class recognising the duty of rebellion against the classes whose manipulation of the productive forces of society have caused the empty stomachs in the midst of

---

1   See *Edinburgh Evening News*, 7 August 1894, 2. Editorial in question begins with the line: "Naturally Mr Hyndman is jubilant about the success of socialism."

2   Joseph Hiam Levy (1838-1913). English author, economist, and anti-vaccinationist.

3   "Mr. JH Levy, in his carefully reasoned pamphlet, 'The Outcome of Individualism,' sums up the situation by the remark that the father of socialism is an empty stomach, and its mother a fertile and somewhat distorted brain.' ibid. 'The Outcome of Individualism' was first delivered as a lecture by Levy at the National Liberal Club on 10 January 1890. It was subsequently revised and published as a pamphlet. The *News* slightly misquotes Levy. The actual line is: 'The father of socialism is an empty stomach and its mother a fertile, though perhaps somewhat distorted, brain.' See Levy, *The Outcome of Individualism* (London, 1890): 4.

plenty. The more political power the workers possess the more peaceful will that rebellion be. But it is when Mr Levy speaks of the mother of socialism being a "disordered brain" that he becomes most truly humorous. The brightest names in contemporary science, art, and literature are those of socialists. Count Leo Tolstoi, philosopher and novelist;[4] Elisee Reclus, foremost geographer of our day;[5] Alfred Russel Wallace, scientist, sharing with Darwin the honour of the greatest scientific discovery of the age;[6] Grant Allen, scientist and novelist;[7] Walter Crane, artist;[8] William Morris, poet and artist;[9] Edward Carpenter, poet and scientist;[10] Walt Whitman, poet[11]—those are a few whose names rise to the lips of every educated man or woman like a litany when thinking on the bright galaxy of genius whose rays shed a lustre on European literature today, and every one of them is a confirmed and avowed socialist. Disordered brain, forsooth. "Individualism," Mr Levy informs us, "would purify marriage by ridding it of masculine domination... It would bring their duties home to parents, and hold them responsible for their fulfilment." But he neglects to inform us that it is individualism which has corrupted marriage, as it has also corrupted every institution in our midst. It has founded society on the basis of a universal scramble for existence—a scramble in which the weakest are trampled underfoot without remorse and without scruple. Woman, the mother of the human race, by reason of her sexual functions, is unable to take part in this scramble during long periods of her life, and as a direct result of this physical and honourable weakness finds herself totally dependent on the exertions of the man, her husband. He may be an angel or he may be a brute, but whatever he may be he is

---

4   Leo Tolstoy (1828-1910) Russian novelist and Christian anarchist/socialist.

5   Jacques Élisée Reclus (1830-1905) French geographer, writer and anarchist.

6   Alfred Russel Wallace (1823-1913) scientist and socialist.

7   Grant Allen (1848-1899) Canadian scientist and writer, atheist and a socialist.

8   Walter Crane (1845-1915) English artist, writer and socialist.

9   William Morris (1834-1896) English artist, writer and socialist.

10   Edward Carpenter (1844-1929) English writer, utopian socialist.

11   Walt Whitman (1819-1892) American poet, essayist, and journalist. Whitman was adopted by the British socialist movement, although he was more an advocate of universal democracy than outright socialism.

the bread-winner, and she is to all intents and purposes his slave, bound to obey his will for her own sake and for the sake of her children. How many of us know of women married to men whose character is a disgrace to our age, whose influence is destroying the life prospects of their children, but yet are compelled to remain in their power, for the sake of the maintenance they ought to be guaranteed by the state in recognition of their services as the mothers of its future citizens. Socialism would deprive fathers of no status of recognition, except that of lord and master of the woman they had promised to love and cherish. In so far as they fulfilled the true duties of husbands and fathers they would receive their due honour, but when they attempted to transgress that point and enforce obedience on those whom they should delight to serve, their wives and children, then the State would be within its right in intervening to secure for its citizens and citizenesses that full individual freedom to which our system of private property is opposed.

*****

TO THE ELECTORS[1]
LABOUR LEADER
6 JULY 1895, P.4

FELLOW ELECTORS—In the General Election of 1892 three political parties—Conservative, Liberal, and Labour—sought your suffrages. We who, believing in the policy of independent opposition as the one best calculated to advance the interests of the workers, were mainly responsible for the appearance upon the field at that time of the third party in defiance of the wishes and in disregard of the plans of the official Liberal and Tory wirepullers, who generally "boss" the political show, desire now to recall to your memory the charges of treachery so freely hurled at us by those reformers who resented our independent action.

They accused us of being in the pay of the Tories, of opposing only the Liberals, who were the true friends of progress, of a desire to split the liberal vote, and so let in the Tories, who were opposed to the reform of our Land Laws, which the Liberals were in favour of, as they were in favour of every measure for the benefit of the people, for whom alone they made and administered the laws.

We ask you also to remember our answers to those charges, that we recognised neither Liberal nor Tory as having an exclusive right to interfere in politics, that all political parties drew their strength from the people and existed only for the people, who had therefore a perfect right to destroy them when they ceased to serve their purpose, that the Liberals and Tories were not two parties but only two sections of one party—the party of property—that their political antagonism had no deeper foun-

---

1   The article was signed by "Brehon" and based on a manifesto issued by the Socialist Election Committee of Edinburgh Central Division in January 1895.

dation than a difference of opinion as to the best method of keeping the poor contented in their misery and excluded from their inheritance, that we also were Home Rulers, but believed that a fundamental social change was urgently needed in the interests of the working classes of England, Scotland, and Ireland alike, since even Home Rule would be of little use to the Irish worker while he was at the mercy of the Irish landlord, who could throw him out on the roadside, or the Irish employer, who could turn him upon the street.

But even as the apostles of Christianity itself were first received with contumely and derision by the people whose salvation they were seeking, so we were laughed at and our advice scorned, while in almost every instance the candidate who represented our views was relegated to the bottom of the poll.

But now, on the eve of another general election—now, as we once more appeal for your suffrages—we invite you first to look upon the political history of the last three years, upon the record of the liberal government from whom you expected so much, and then tell us have events not amply justified our action.

Who declared that Home Rule blocked the way of social reform, that it must be immediately passed in the interests of the people, and then while one million men were out of work and the evicted tenants were starving on the hillsides of Ireland signalised their advent into office by voting themselves a six months' holiday? *The Liberal Government.*

Who sent the military into Hull to assist the Shipping Federation in their endeavour to terrify Hull dockers into unconditional submission to their tyrannical behests?[2] *The Liberal Government.*

Who sent the military into Wales against the wishes of the county authorities, to assist the Welsh mine owners in reducing the wages of Welsh miners? *The Liberal Government.*

Whose anxiety to take sides with the rich against the poor enabled the Yorkshire coal owners to command English soldiers to butcher English miners at Featherstone? *The Liberal Government.*

Who, when out of office, are forever denouncing the system of pen-

---

2   The Hull Dock Strike, April-May 1893. The government sent police and soldiers to protect strike-breakers.

sioning royal and aristocratic paupers, and when in office demanded the continuance of the pension to the Duke of Edinburgh, a foreign sovereign? *The Liberal Government.*

Who by this vote declared their belief in the right of princes "made in Germany" to quarter their useless lives on the backs of the British people? *The Liberal Government.*

When Mr. Sam Woods, MP,[3] proposed to restore to the people the mining rights and royalties of which the landlord class have robbed them, who opposed and defeated the measure? *The Liberal Government.*

Who thus voted side by side with the Tories to protect the interests of the landlords against the rightful claims of the people? *The Liberal Government.*

When 25,000 children in the east-end of London go to school every morning without a morsel of food for breakfast, who has no time to consider a remedy for this disgrace to our civilisation? *The Liberal Government.*

Who has plenty time to pass votes of congratulation on the birth of one "royal" baby? *The Liberal Government.*

Who, while themselves drawing from the nation salaries ranging from £955 to £8000 per annum, yet declared nineteen shillings per week to be a sufficient wage for working men to live and rear a family upon? *The Liberal Government,* when they refused to advance the standard wage of Woolwich Dockyard labourers beyond that point.

Who refused to appeal to the country when Ireland was deprived of the benefits of Home Rule, but did appeal to the country when one of their number was deprived of his salary? The Liberal Government.

Who during their term of office have been always ready to lick the dust at the feet of royalty, to cringe and toady to the rich, to insult, betray, and trample upon the poor? *The Liberal Government.*

Who have aided, abetted, and encouraged the Liberal Government in their every act against the reforming tendencies of the times? *The Tory opposition.*

---

3   Sam Woods (1846-1915). British trade unionist. Elected Liberal-Labour MP for Ince in 1982.

Fellow electors, the political farce is at last played out.

The system of partyism which has so long dominated our political life has long survived whatever usefulness it may have ever possessed. Today every candidate returned under the auspices of a Liberal or Tory organisation is pledged to support the Liberal or Tory party in all its actions, even when those actions are in direct conflict with the teachings of his own conscience. Should he fail to do so he is denounced as a traitor to his party, and all the powers of the party press and caucus are put in motion to ruin him.

In Parliament, whatever useful measure may be introduced by one party is certain of the opposition of the other, who feel bound to prevent the enemy obtaining credit for a desire to serve the people.

As a result of this criminal squabbling no great measure of reform has ever passed the Houses of Parliament unless backed up by an outside agitation, popular enough and strong enough to threaten the existence of both political parties.

So well do they recognise this fact that the leading men of both parties have carefully avoided identifying themselves with any useful and therefore contentious legislation, but have been satisfied to limit their activities to theatrical displays of eloquence over matters of too trivial and unimportant a character to excite serious opposition. Thus the old parties have resolved politics from being the science of government into a conscienceless scramble for the spoils of office.

Fellow-workers, what, then, is your duty in face of the political impotence of those who in the past have ruled and governed us? The Liberal and Tory parties can no longer aid you—nay, they exist only to betray you. They represent only landlordism and capitalism, the two sides of the evil social system under which we groan and suffer to-day—a system founded upon that robbery of the poor so eloquently denounced by the prophet of old.[4] The heart and intellect of mankind are in revolt against it; it is already tottering to its fall, and with its disappearance the last and meanest form of human slavery will disappear from off the face of this old earth of ours.

---

4   Ezekiel 22:29. "The people of the land have used oppression, and exercised robbery, and have vexed the poor and needy: yea, they have oppressed the stranger wrongfully."

We ask you, then, to refuse to vote for either Liberal or Tory—instead of your vote to give them that contempt they so richly deserve, to reserve your vote for an Independent Labour or Social-Democratic candidate, or for none at all, and thus to signify your adhesion to a party pledged to uproot every form of political or social bondage, to make the people in a democratic state the sole masters of the land and instruments of labour by which they live, to organise and lead the workers in their onward and upward pilgrimage from the dark Egypt of our capitalistic anarchy to the promised land of industrial freedom.[5]

---

5   See "Plain Talk," *Labour Chronicle*, 1 December 1894. "...to create such a public feeling in our favour as shall enable us to bridge the gulf between the old order and the new, and lead the people from the dark Egypt of our industrial anarchy, into the Promised Land of industrial freedom."

*****

FURTHER OPINIONS AND COMMENTS
LABOUR LEADER
24 AUGUST 1895, P.2

I[1] HAVE PLEASURE in submitting the following thoughtful letter from one of our most esteemed contributors:

> "Would you allow me to make a few suggestions to your readers, and to ILP branches generally, relative to the sale of the *Labour Leader*?
>
> I am convinced, from what I have seen in the course of my wanderings since the late dissolution of Parliament,[2] that if the *Leader* has not a large sale among the general public who attend our meetings it is entirely the fault of the branches themselves.
>
> I was in Rochdale the other week[3], and although the ILP branch there boasts a membership of over 600, I found it impossible to procure the paper at a single newsagents in the town, and had eventually to go to the rooms in order to purchase it. In Bury the same state of matters was existent. Indeed, in the latter place, even at the ILP club they had not the current week's issue until the Wednesday or Thursday following the Friday on which it ought to have been procurable. I am mentioning those two branches because they are in large towns, but they are only a sample of a state of matters pretty general here.
>
> Now, I would like to ask our comrades do they think it good policy or business tactics to restrict the sale of their paper to the clubs? What, for instance would be the circulation of a Liberal or Tory journal which could only be procured at a Liberal or Tory committee-room? *I think that if branches are really desirous of maintaining the paper they should be prepared to forego the few pennies of profit on its sale, and put it*

---

1   **Ed. Note:** original ellipsis omitted for the sake of typesetting.

2   Parliament was dissolved on 5 July 1895.

3   Connolly was in the greater Manchester/Liverpool area on a lecture tour for most of August and September 1895. He spoke in Little Hulton 11 August; Salford 18-21 August; Stockport 25 August; Wigan 1-7 September; Liverpool 8-14 September.

instead in the hands of the newsagents.

Let each branch make out a list of members who are prepared to regularly purchase the *Labour Leader*, then select some newsagent in a populous and busy locality and ask him or her to take in each week a number of copies proportionate to the number of names you have obtained.

Stipulate that the *Leader* bill shall be exhibited each week, and that if they suffer any loss on the transaction, by the members neglecting to purchase their paper, the branch will recoup the newsagent for the loss. In almost every case the offer will be accepted.

If a sufficiently large number of names are obtainable they may be spread over a number of agents in various districts. This would ensure (1) *that the weekly placard of the Leader would be exhibited in prominent positions, and would be seen by thousands for the scores who see it today; (2) that copies of this paper would lie on the newsagent's counter, and would thus attract the eye of the chance customers who would never dream of going to a political club to buy it.*

I would also like to advise our friends who act as chairmen at ILP propagandist meetings to devote a little time to introducing the paper to the audience at the beginning and end of each lecture. Fasten upon some event of political or social importance which may have been noticed in your local capitalist papers, and advise the audience to buy your paper in order to learn the socialist side of the question. This will stimulate their interest, and cause them to purchase the *Leader*, if only for the same reason as that which induces them to attend your meetings, viz, curiosity. In conclusion, I hope our comrades will take my advice in good part. I know that in many cases it is superfluous, but I also know that in a great many more it is much needed."

—Yours fraternally, Brehon

I am glad Brehon has drawn attention to the necessity of securing the best possible service from newsagents, for I am convinced that with them lies the power to make or mar the success of a newspaper. Peg at the newsagents, interest them in the sale of the *Leader*, urge the displaying of contents bill, and do it often.[4]

---

4   Not everyone was pleased with Brehon's advice. The contributor Busy Bee wrote: "I see by the *Labour Leader*, 24th August, that Brehon has been delivering himself of some pretty statements, which would be very bad against Bury ILP if they were true. I must inform you that there are two newsagents who both sell and show the *Labour Leader* bill every week—Mr. Slater and Mr. Hill of Bolton Street. The LIP sells dozens per week through Mr Slater, and some of our members get them through Mr. Hill. I myself have done all I can along with other comrades to push the paper both at meetings and by chalk on hoardings, and making arrangements from the chair at two Sunday meetings." See "Bury," *Labour Leader*, 7 September 1895, 10.

*****

DISTRESS IN CAHIRCIVEEN, COUNTY KERRY
CORK DAILY HERALD
20 APRIL 1898, P.6

A PRESS REPRESENTATIVE[1] having called upon the Rev Mr O'Halloran[2], rector of the Church of Ireland in the parish of Cahirciveen, Co. Kerry, in reference to the reported distress in his district, elicited in answer to inquiries the following important and alarming facts:—

There were, he estimated, 650 families in the rural districts surrounding Cahirciveen, of these there could not be less than one-half in very great distress, amounting in many cases to an actual want of food.[3]

The entire number were this year in exceptionally bad circumstances owing to the failure both of the expected return from fishing and of the potato crop, but perhaps, one-half, although suffering greatly through this visitation, would manage to tide over the summer without help, but the other and poorer half were, without doubt, in great danger of actual famine. He was fully convinced that if the shopkeepers of the town were to refuse credit there would be absolute famine in the district. He had personally discovered a case in which the produce of shellfish mixed with meal[4] and boiled for food, was eagerly devoured by the children of the

---

1 Although unsigned, the journalist in question is undoubtedly Connolly, based on the quotes in the article and police reports of Connolly's activities in Cahirciveen, Co. Kerry in April 1898. See, "The Famine in Kerry," *Irish World* (New York), 4 June 1898, 5; Paul Dillon, 'James Connolly.'

2 Rev Thomas Halloran in other reports.

3 See "The Famine in Kerry," *Irish World* (New York), 4 June 1898.

4 Indian meal.

family in lieu of a more nourishing diet.

In another part of the parish a case had recently occurred of a family in such dire distress that the partly decomposed remains of a cow which had died of disease had been used as food.

The Relief Committee in the district had received twenty tons of seed potatoes from the Mansion House Committee. This they had distributed in the most careful manner. In order to avert all danger of unscrupulous persons simulating poverty, exhaustive private inquiries into the circumstances of every farmer in the district had been made before the donation of seed was made known. As a result the committee came to the conclusion that three hundred and fifty families were in such straitened circumstances that they could not possibly purchase seed without the aid of the committee or of the charitably disposed persons whom the committee represented. The committee had, therefore, distributed the seed to the persons approved of, but he (Rev O'Halloran) was of opinion that the quantity of seed set this year was at least one-third less than the usual for the district. This, of course, made the prospects of the poor people in and around Cahirciveen very gloomy indeed for the coming year.

The moneys received from the Mansion House had been expended partly in relief works on the roads and partly in donations for food where the distress was known.

*****

THE FAMINE IN KERRY
IRISH WORLD (NEW YORK)
4 JUNE 1898, P.5

T HE FOLLOWING LETTER, which was addressed to Miss Maud
Gonne, is forwarded by that lady for publication in the *Irish World*:

* * *

CAHIRCIVEEN, County Kerry.

Dear MISS GONNE:

In the course of last week I had an opportunity of seeing your letter to the
Irish World, upon the state of the famine-stricken districts in the County Mayo. I can assure you that in the horrible rivalry for the position of
the most unfortunate, County Kerry bids fair at the present moment to
outbid even Mayo.

I have lately made a tour of the county round the southwestern coast,
and in the course of my travels have called upon men in almost all sorts
of representative positions, have visited the houses of and conversed with
the people, have attended and taken notes of the meetings of the various
relief committees, and have everywhere met the same condition of matters; poverty in its acutest form, hunger the rule and not the exception,
misery long-drawn out and accepted with heart-breaking resignation, as
too inevitable to awaken resentment of demand investigation.

The district round from Sneem to Cahirdaniel and Waterville is for
the most part a wild, picturesque, rocky country, affording but little re-

muneration, at the best of times, to those who spend their lives in an attempt to work its stubborn soil into productivity. It is such a countryside as a peculiarly vindictive, revolutionary government might, in the event of success, choose as a place of punishment for recalcitrant conservative or ditch-lining Orangemen, but would never expect faithful, unoffending citizens to occupy while more fertile territory remained in possession of the beasts of the field.

In my journey hither from Dublin, the train passes through miles upon miles of splendid cultivatable land, on which no vestige of a house or human habitation can be seen; the whole thing given up to cattle or desolation; and it is only when you pass from the area of what might be good fertile soil, and enter upon a territory of alternate bog and mountain, into which the people have been driven, that you begin to feel once more that Ireland is not quite depopulated, and that what naturalists call "that rare specimen of the genus homo, an Irish peasant," still exists. In other words, our lords and masters have cleared the Irish off the land upon which they might live in comfort, and have placed it in the possession of cattle: and upon the land where the cattle would die they have left the Irish peasant to live.

I found that [in] Cahirdaniel, Barrymore and Waterville, although it was generally agreed that the present season is the worst the district has passed through since '47, yet the people have, with a most commendable pride, striven to stifle their craving for food and refrained from making their destitution public. In their desire to prevent themselves and their country from appearing once more before the world as paupers depending upon public charity there are few who will not sympathize with them; but there is another aspect of the case to which it is well to direct public attention. This grim endurance of poverty is not a public necessity. If our beneficent government were to expend upon developing the resources of this district one-hundredth part of the sum it spends, with a light heart on expeditions against sundry tribes of aborigines in central Africa, if it were to make it possible for these poor people to obtain loans of money, when needed, for their little enterprises, without plunging into debt to banks or gombeen men, as if in all its dealings with these people the government were to think more of advancing the interests of those who are unfortunately its subjects, and less of securing a percentage of interest upon all money advanced, the chronic poverty of these people might be gradually eliminated from their midst.

Therefore, to keep silence on this terrible condition of affairs, while perhaps commendable enough in the people most affected, is by no means the duty of those who do not share their lot. It should rather be made known throughout the world, that the world might know and understand to the full the blessings of civilization on the British imperial pattern.

I have been assured by shopkeepers in the district before named, and have heard the statement corroborated privately by the tenants themselves, that three-fourths of the population are only preserved from actual famine by the credit generously advanced by the shopkeepers. One hears on many sides of debts of £220, £230 and even £240 pounds contracted by poor tenants, whose whole stock of worldly goods consists of a few acres of poor land, a pig or two, perhaps a cow, and a brood of hens. When you venture to suggest to the shopkeeper that he or she has advanced a great deal upon mighty poor security, you get for answer a look of resignation, and "sure, what could we do, sir? We couldn't let the craythure[1] starve." But this generosity has, of course, its limits; a time must come when the shopkeeper must pay his debts to the wholesale merchant, and then, unable to collect from his own customers what they owe him and would pay if they could, but cannot, it is hard to see in what manner general bankruptcy can be avoided.

But after bankruptcy comes inevitable famine. One most depressing feature of the whole matter is that owing to the potato failure of last year, and the inability of the people to purchase seed in sufficient quantity to repair the loss, at least one-third less than the usual amount of seed was planted this year. This is an average taken for the entire district, and is rather an understatement than otherwise. Thus there is an absolute certainty that next year will be a year, if not of absolute famine, at least of most terrible suffering. The foregoing, be it remembered, refers mainly to the districts where, according to the public press, the distress has not yet reached its acute form. They are facts verified by my own observation. But of the distress in Cahirciveen I do not dare to trust myself to speak. I know that in your position, you must be careful to avoid anything ap-

---

1   Although "craythur" is now the accepted form, "craythure" was also used at the time.

proaching the nature of mere declamation; and, as I have been so moved by what I have seen around here, I am afraid I could not prevent my pen from recording my feelings as well as my observations. So, not being able to school myself into acting as an automaton, I have preferred to give you the evidence of one whom those acquainted with Irish politics will readily admit as an unbiased authority. The gentleman in question is Mr O'Halloran,[2] Protestant rector of Cahirciveen, and a strong Unionist in politics. I transcribe from my notes, taken in the course of an interview with this gentleman the following statement of the position in Cahirciveen:

"There were," he estimated, "650 families in the rural district around Cahirciveen. Of those there could not be less than one-half in very great distress, amounting in many cases to an absolute want of food. The entire farming population was this year in exceptionally bad circumstances, owing to the failure of both fishing and potato harvest, but perhaps one-half, although suffering greatly through this visitation, would manage to tide over the summer without assistance, but the other and poorer half were, without doubt, in very great danger of actual famine."[3] He was convinced that "if the shopkeepers in the town were to refuse credit there would be absolute famine in the district." He did "not understand how the shopkeepers were to be repaid." The people were honest and would undoubtedly pay if they could, but he did not think they could. "The people were, as a whole, striving manfully to hide their distress." He had personally discovered a case in which the produce of shellfish mixed with Indian meal, and boiled as food, was eagerly devoured by the children of a family in lieu of better nourishment. In another part of the parish a cow had recently died of disease, and the family to which it belonged were in such dire distress that the semi-decomposed remains of the animal were being used as food, when the unexpected arrival upon the scene of the priest

---

2   Reverend Thomas Halloran.

3   Quotes from this interview with Rev. Thomas Halloran appeared word for word in the *Cork Daily Herald*, 20 April 1898. The article said that a "press representative" had called upon "Rev Mr O'Halloran, Rector of the Church of Ireland in the parish of Cahirciveen...' The press representative could indeed have been Connolly—police reports at the time say that he introduced himself as a journalist in Kerry in April 1898 while researching a piece on the famine, telling locals in Cahirciveen that he was a journalist for 'the American press and that he was visiting Ireland for the purpose of looking after the poor and evicted." See Paul Dillon, "James Connolly," 35.

prevented the consummation of an act which might have brought epidemic upon the whole district. The relief committee in the district had received twenty tons of seed potatoes from the Mansion House fund, which they distributed in the most careful manner. They had made private inquiries into the case of every recipient of such relief, and had found that it would be impossible for them to buy seed. He was convinced that there was a deficit of one-third in the amount of potatoes planted this year, a fact which made the outlook for the future very gloomy indeed.

They had received no help whatever from the government. The relief works in the district were not operated by government, but were simply tests they, the committee, had instituted in order to prevent any indiscriminate appeals for help from the funds at their disposal.

The people, he had found, were very willing to give labor in return for any relief afforded. He had been thirty-one years in the parish and knew it well.

When a gentleman in the position, and with the political leanings of Mr O'Halloran, speaks in such a manner there is little reason for doubt upon the awful gravity of the situation of these poor people. I do not like to speak of it, but I have stood by and watched these victims of poverty, with the wild longing look of hunger in their faces, actually fighting for precedence when some members of the committee were distributing tickets for food, and as I looked and noted the bright natural intelligence in their faces fading away, almost before my eyes, and giving place to a fierce, wolfish expression, I began to realize the manner in which the Celt, hunted and famine-stricken, had so often been driven to swell the ranks of the parishes of the large cities of Britain and the New World; but as I realized it I added another item to the long standing debt which we will yet pay to the uttermost.

PART II
LOST FICTION

INTRODUCTION

CONNOLLY WAS no stranger to creative writing. His preferred medium was poetry and song, with selections published in *Songs of Freedom* in 1907. There were also limited forays into prose and theatre. He wrote a short story entitled 'The Mendicity and its Guests' that he originally offered to Alice Milligan and *Shan Van Vocht*.[1] It was eventually published in *Workers' Republic* and is a sombre tale of a homeless man from Monaghan who is staying at the Mendicity Institute on Usher's Quay in Dublin.[2] Desmond Ryan, co-editor of Connolly's writings with William O'Brien, decided that the story 'had to be suppressed' and it was left out of their collections.[3] It was not republished until 2009.[4] Connolly also wrote *Under Which Flag*, a play performed in 1916 in the weeks before the Rising. His daughter, Nora, in her memoir of her father, mentioned another play, 'The Agitator's Wife', which is considered lost.

For decades this was believed to be the sum of his creative output. However, from June 1895 to June 1896 Connolly wrote four short stories which were published in the *Labour Leader* under the pseudonym Brehon. We can identify Connolly as Brehon through the use of four distinct and unique phrases. Two of these phrases are contained in the 1895 election manifesto discussed in the previous section; the other two—'Malahide codfish waiting for the tide to come in,' and 'dung to manure the pasture lands of the rich expropriator'—are contained in the

---

1   Alice Milligan to James Connolly, [July] 1897. See Nevin, *Between Comrades*, 91.

2   'The Mendicity and its Guests.' *Workers' Republic*, 27 August 1898, 3. Connolly used the pseudonym 'Senanta' for the piece.

3   "27 December 1956," Desmond Greaves Journal, Vol.12, 1956-7, accessed 5 May 2024, https://desmondgreavesarchive.com/journal/desmond-greaves-journal-vol-12-1956-7/.

4   *Red Banner*, March 2009.

short stories.

Having a mouth like a Malahide cod was a Dublin expression, often used as a synonym for surprise.[5] Connolly used a variation of it in *Workers' Republic* in his Home Thrust column, 27 August 1898:

> Nothing impresses the reader so much as what he does not understand. That is why we have so long admired the Home Rule leaders. They but needed to open their mouths and talk, and talk, and talk, and still to talk, and the more they talked the less we understood, and consequently the more we admired them. We just stood around them **with our mouths open like a Malahide codfish waiting for the tide to come in**—And gazed and gazed, and still the wonder grew / Where such mere men could learn all they knew.[6] [My emphasis.]

There are very few instances of the phrase in print, although it has remained part of the oral tradition in Dublin.[7] The exact phrasing here, though, in particular the use of 'codfish' instead of 'cod,' is unique to Connolly, his very own literary fingerprint. The only other example of its use anywhere is by Brehon in 1895:

> Give me that plate of fancy bread out of the window, an' for God's sake don't stand there staring **with your mouth open like a Malahide codfish waiting for the tide to come in**. [My emphasis.]

The second phrase shared by Connolly and Brehon is a slight variation on a quotation from the Russian anarchist writer, Peter Kropotkin. The first English translation of his pamphlet, *An Appeal to the Young*, was serialised in *Justice* in 1884:

> Do you want your husband, your lads to be ever at the mercy of the first comer who has inherited from his father a capital to exploit them with?' he wrote. 'Are you anxious that they should remain slaves for a master, food for powder, mere **dung; wherewith to manure the pasture lands of rich expropriators?**[8] [My emphasis.]

Connolly used a version of this line in an article he wrote for *Irish Worker* in December 1914:

---

5   George A. Little, "About Malahide," *Dublin Historical Record*, Vol.10, no.1 (Mar-May 1948): 14.

6   "Home Thrusts," *Workers' Republic*, 27 August 1898, 1. The couplet is taken from The Deserted Village, by Oliver Goldsmith (1728-1774). Connolly changed the last line. The original: "And still they gazed, and still the wonder grew / That one small head could carry all he knew."

7   Orla Timmins, "Drama of the City's Poor," *Herald* (Dublin), 6 July 2013, 29.

8   Peter Kropotkin, "An Appeal to the Young," *Justice*, 11 October 1884, 3.

The children were only children of the poor, and the poor, whether Protestant or Catholic were only esteemed, perhaps are only esteemed today, by the rich, as, in Krapotkin's [sic] words "mere **dung to manure the pasture lands of the rich expropriator.**"[9] [My emphasis.]

Brehon uses the same version in the short story 'The Transfusion of Blood':

I do not wish to create fresh armies of surplus labourers to enrich the dividend-hunting capitalist, or to become what Krapotkine [sic] calls "more **dung to manure the pasture lands of the rich expropriator.**" No, I wish to destroy, not to help, the robber crew. [My emphasis.]

The use of 'more' instead of 'mere' may be a typo; nonetheless, the part of the phrase highlighted is unique to Connolly even though it is a quotation from Kropotkin. The dropping of 'wherewith' and the change of 'rich expropriators' to 'the rich expropriator' are the key markers.

There is also circumstantial evidence which links Brehon to Connolly. The character and setting of 'A Free Breakfast Table', for example, are similar to that of 'The Mendicity and its Guests.' The links are more pronounced, though, with 'An Agitator's Wife', a short story with a play-like setting, consisting entirely of dialogue, which matches the description given by Nora Connolly of her father's 'lost play.'[10] In 2019 Maria-Daniella Dick, Kirsty Lusk, and Willy Maley wrote an article for *Irish Studies Review* which reproduced a short story first published in *Labour Prophet* in 1894 which they said could be an early iteration of the play.[11] The piece itself, though, lacks textual or contextual evidence to link it to Connolly outside of its title. In 2024 *Liberty*, the newspaper of SIPTU (Services Industrial Professional and Technical Union), republished the *Labour Prophet* short story, declaring Connolly to be the author with a

9   James Connolly, "German and Irish Schools," *Irish Worker*, 5 December 1914, 1. See also *The Reconquest of Ireland* (1915), 43. In the *Irish Worker*, 'exproprietor' is used. This was almost certainly a typo as Connolly corrected it to 'expropriator' in *Reconquest* a year later.

10   "That play you wrote, 'The Agitator's Wife,' is just our life, isn't it?" "Yes," said daddy, laughing. "But I made the wife say things you never said, Lillie, though I'm sure you often felt them.'" Nora Connolly, *James Connolly: Portrait of a Rebel Father* (Dublin: Talbot Press, 1935; Dublin: Four Masters Press, 1975), 97. Citation refers to the Four Masters edition.

11   Maria-Daniella Dick, Kirsty Lusk and Willy Maley, "The Agitator's Wife" (1894): the story behind James Connolly's lost play?" *Irish Studies Review*, vol. 27, no.1 (2019): 1-21.

confidence that is lacking in the original study by Dick et al., who merely suggested it as a possible Connolly piece which deserved more scrutiny.[12] SIPTU gave the author a pseudonym, 'R.Ebel,' even though the original piece is unsigned.[13] It then declared that this was used by James Connolly. However, Connolly never used 'R.Ebel' as a pseudonym; he used 'R.Ascal.' The piece also said that Connolly worked as a union activist in Dundee—a point that is simply wrong.[14] It is disappointing that this type of mythical material about Connolly, in the tradition of William O'Brien, is still being published by an Irish trade union, 108 years after his execution.

What, then, of the stories themselves? Three of them are humorous with a self-deprecating tone. 'A Free Breakfast Table' is about a tramp who finds a gold sovereign on the street. It is set in Dublin, even though Connolly was living in Edinburgh at the time, and contains an almost Joycean stroll through the city, from Drumcondra Bridge to Thomas Street in the Liberties. 'The Transfusion of Blood' describes the overworked life and strains of a political agitator with a delightfully surreal twist. 'An Agitator's Wife' is essentially a monologue on the sexual politics of political activism and marriage. The other story, more serious in tone, is 'What May Happen.' It is about a private in the army who is called out with his unit to protect a factory during a strike. As already stated, it will most certainly add to the speculation as to whether Connolly was in the army or not, although my own conclusion is that it was written with his brother, John, in mind. Taken together, the stories show that Connolly was as much a writer as agitator, one that brought both skills together with considerable skill and talent.

---

12   Frank Connolly, "The Agitator's Wife," *Liberty*, February 2024, 15.

13   Anon, "The Agitator's Wife," *Labour Prophet*, Vol.3, No.26 (Feb 1894): 26-28

14   Connolly's sole reference to trade union activity in Scotland is in a letter to Lillie he wrote while in Edinburgh sometime in 1890. "By the way if we get married next week I shall be unable to go to Dundee as I promised' he wrote, 'as my fellow-workmen in the job are preparing for a strike on the end of this month, for a reduction in the hours of labour. As my brother and I are ringleaders in the matter it is necessary we should be on the ground." Far from working as a trade union activist in Dundee, Connolly said that he was unable *to go to Dundee* because he was involved in possible strike action in Edinburgh. Connolly was working as a carter at the time. He did not work as a trade union activist until 1907, when he lived in the United States.

*****

AN AGITATOR'S WIFE
LABOUR LEADER
1 JUNE 1895, P.4

SCENE: A working-man's home. A small room serving as a kitchen by day and a bedroom by night.

TIME: The present. Hour: 12pm

CHARACTERS: A Socialist agitator, his wife, and babies.

WIFE (IN A LOUD VOICE): "Ay, a nice time of night this to come home at, indeed. Twelve o'clock, and me and the children might be dead, or the house burned down, or anything awful happened for all you know or cared. Socialist meeting, you say. Oh, yes, the same old story, working for freedom and keeping your own wife a prisoner inside the four walls of the house.

"Other men's wives have their husband beside them sometime. There was Mrs. Gillespie that's married on Mr. Thomson's wife's brother, her man goes in for politics too, but he can stay beside her every night in the week, and she gets four bags of coal every quarter from the ladies who come to see him.

"That's the kind of politics and the kind of man I would like to have, but I'd no such luck. My husband, my intelligent husband, 'our gifted and energetic comrade,' spends his days at work, and his nights at committee or other meetings, and his Sundays on top of a four-legged stool ranting like a Hallelujah lassie,[1] and I am left stuck up here to look after

---

1   "My own recollections of Connolly go back to the days immediately preceding the formation of the ILP as a national organisation at Bradford in 1893... On his invitation I addressed frequent meetings on the Leith Links and Edinburgh Meadows—he and I often, especially on the Sunday mornings, bearing the "stool"

his squalling children, and cook his meals, and wash his clothes, and then he will mount the platform and tell the crowd that the Socialist party are the only party who, in seeking the emancipation of women, are actuated by principle, and not by expediency.

"Oh, for a right hypocrite, give me a socialist. Cant, pure unblushing cant and humbug, my dear husband. Coming home at twelve o'clock at night when all decent people ought to be in bed. Why, there was Mr. Gillespie—What d'ye say, don't bother you about Mr. Gillespie. I hadn't so much to say about him when he was carried home drunk on Saturday night singing Rule Britannia,' after spending all his wages in boose.

"Don't bother you, indeed. And who are you that I shouldn't speak to you; who are you, I would like to know? That's not the way you spoke to that brazen-faced jade who came to lecture for you last month. You didn't tell her not to bother you. Oh, no; it was, 'Would you like a glass of lemonade before you speak, or in the middle of your address,' or 'I will hold your wraps for you, if you please,' and then, when Comrade what d'ye-call him got up and said how pleased you all were to have the company of a true woman in this fight, you could be heard all over the field shouting Hear, hear."

"But you are not over-fond of the company of your own wife, it seems, or you would stay with her oftener, you hard-hearted wretch (tears) I'm not a true woman, I suppose (sobs and tears).

"What d'ye say, 'We must all try to leave the world a little better than we found it?' Rubbish; leave the world a little better than we found it. Ha! ha! and you're a nice-looking character to leave anything better than you found it. You've left me, anyway, a great deal worse than you found me."

"There, now, you have wakened the baby with your scolding."

"Wakened the baby, indeed! *Me* wakened the baby! Oh, no; but it was the sound of your voice that wakened the baby, for it is very seldom, indeed, the poor darling hears the voice of its respected parent; very seldom, indeed. He has to save it all up for the propaganda. Hush-a-bye, baby, there's a darling. Don't be frightened; it's only the man who comes

and the literature between us." J. Bruce Glazier, "James Connolly: In Memoriam," *Labour Leader*, 17 May 1917, 7.

here to take his meals and change his clothes. He won't hurt you, oh, no; he would not intrude for the world. He is so bashful that he never comes here if he can avoid it. Hush-sh-sh, hush-a-bye. That, baby, is only your father, your respected parent, your affectionate sire; that, baby, is the socialist agitator, the apostle of the new righteousness, who tells people that 'society in the future must be founded upon a right perception of love and duty,' and then neglects his own wife and children, and stays out till twelve at night attending meetings, and discussing problems on the way home. Yes, baby, your father.

"'Hush-a-bye, baby, don't you cry,

Daddy is coming by-and-by.'

"I wonder if the person who wrote that verse was the wife of an agitator? If not, she must have been inspired. Hush-a-bye, baby, look at him, your beloved, respected, darling father, your male parent of my cherub, the revolutionist, the man who talks of planting the flag of the future upon the barricades,' but turns white with fear if I ask him to hold the baby whilst I run a message.

"'The flag of the future upon the barricades'[2] is only a metaphorical expression, you say? Oh, yes, and explained it away, of course. What is there a Socialist can't explain away? It's no wonder you hated old Gladstone; he was the only rival you had at the explaining-away business, But, of course, I am only an ignorant woman, fit for nothing but washing dishes and looking after children (SOBS). I know nothing about economics (TEARS), nothing about the theory of value (SOBS AND TEARS), nor the law of wages (MORE SOBS); but I'm the woman you married and promised to love and cherish, and I love my babies and my home, and won't have them neglected for no meetings, my poor darling little pets." (KISSES THE CHILDREN AND, SOBBING, FALLS ASLEEP.)

AGITATOR (DRAWING A LONG BREATH): "Phew! That was a storm. That knocks the sentimental nonsense out of a fellow's head. One cannot

---

2   "Will you claim that these weavers should be thrown into prison who in a moment of desperation have set fire to a mill? That this man who shot at a crowned murderer should be imprisoned for life? That these insurgents should be shot down who plant the flag of the future on the barricades?—no, a thousand times no!" Peter Kropotkin, "An Appeal to the Young," *Justice*, 6 September 1884, 3. Translated by H.M. Hyndman from ""Aux Jeunes Gens," *Le Révolté* (June-August 1880) and serialised in *Justice* Feb.-Oct. 1884. Republished as a pamphlet in 1885.

live very long in rapt inward contemplation of the joys of life and living under socialism when he has to face the music provided for him by the partner of his joys and sorrows, especially when she does not care a brass farthing for socialism, and is more concerned about a rise in the price of coals than about the future of civilisation. But this sort of thing is really getting monotonous. (BEGINS SLOWLY TO UNDRESS.) The worst of it is there is so much truth in all she says.

"I think I remember reading of Socrates telling an inquirer that he who aspired to rule the State must first learn to rule his own family; and as the person in question was troubled with a shrewish wife it appears this initial step in the art of governing was too difficult, for he was never more heard of. Now, should I take Socrates' advice? I think not. In the first place, I don't want to rule the State, and in the second I would rather have my wife as a comrade than as a subject. And, by hokey (LAUGHING), she would make an excellent propagandist. Why, she could talk for an hour at a stretch without drawing her breath! And such eloquent invective, such fine sarcasm, such cutting irony! They would make the fortune of a paid agitator. Oh, there is no doubt about it, our working women, the women of the people, possess a fund of eloquence and a stock of debating power that, if properly cultivated, would far outshine the middle-class collegians we think so much of today. That's a good idea; I must move a resolution on the subject." (DROPS OFF ASLEEP.)

*****

A FREE BREAKFAST TABLE
LABOUR LEADER
15 JUNE 1895, P.10

THIS IS NOT a political fulmination, exhortation, or oration.

It is a brief examination of the situation in which the hero found himself after two months' semi-starvation.

It is not written in blank verse, nor in flowing Whitmanesque.[1]

It has a hero—a noble-minded, generous, whole-souled, ragged, and hungry hero.

He was in Dublin, the capital of Ireland, bounded on the west by the emigrant ship, on the east by the House of Commons, and on the south by Cork, known to the initiated as God's own town and the devil's own people, and on the north by Derry, the Maiden City, whose inhabitants to a man would die in the last ditch in defence of Protestant ascendency, provided always the ditch was a clean one and that the rebellion could be arranged for evening, after work was over.

Dublin is a great city. There the very air is redolent of patriotism and rebellion and Dublin Bay herring. There the Nationalist alderman suns himself on the steps of the Mansion House and the Nationalist worker out of work sleeps off his hunger on the steps of Nelson's Pillar. There the aristocratic Irish beauty, half naked and wholly unashamed, throngs to the Viceregal ball, "where low-born bareness wafts perfume to pride,"[2]

---

1   In a letter to the *Edinburgh Evening Post* in 1894, Connolly cites Whitman as one of "a few whose names rise to the lips of every educated man or woman like a litany when thinking on the bright galaxy of genius whose rays shed a lustre on European literature today, and every one of them is a confirmed and avowed socialist." See "Socialism v Individualism," *Edinburgh Evening Post*, 8 August 1894.

2   From "An Ode in Imitation of Alcaeus," by Sir William Jones (1746-

while Irish matrons in the service of Irish employers crouch with advertising boards in their grasp beneath the lamp-posts in their leading thoroughfares. There the form of Tom Moore, the sweetest singer of Irish music, stands before the world in the ugliest statue the hand of man has ever formed.[3] There the unskilled labourer, enthusiastic in the cause of freedom, enrolls himself a member of the same political association as his employers, who are paying him his sixteen-shilling wage. There you have streets named after the oppressors of the people—Marlborough Street, the site of Beresford's riding school, in which the 98 rebels were flogged and tortured, and where on each succeeding Sunday the clink of the collection-plate at the pro-cathedral can be heard arising like silvery music upon the summer air. There you have Dan O'Connell's statue, with his coat buttoned upon the wrong side, and that of Lord Gough's horse without shoes on its feet. There you have Christ Church and St. Patrick's Cathedral restored by the rival efforts of two dealers in strong drink. There you have the stately Liffey, the silvery Dodder, and the commerce-laden canal, the mention of which recalls my wandering pen. Our hero arose from his couch upon the banks of the canal, and removing the hay from his hair, dodged the watch-dog, shut his ears to the seductive wailings of the rent provider and landlords' friend, yclept the pig, scrambled out upon Drumcondra Bridge and looked around him.[4]

It was a lovely morning, nature smiled upon him—and the policeman moved him on. Such is the way of fate and the instructions of the inspector.

The turf-laden barges sailed placidly along the bosom of the canal; the waters reflected the blue dome of the heavens above.

1794), also known by its first line, "What Constitutes a State?" Connolly slightly misquotes the original line which reads: "Where low-browed baseness wafts perfume to pride.' The misquotation may be intentional, with 'low-born bareness' Connolly's own description of the attendees at the Viceregal ball.

3   Thomas Moore's statue is at the junction of College St and Westmoreland St. Erected in 1857 it was poorly received with the *Irish Builder* describing it as a 'hideous caricature of our national bard.' See *Freeman's Journal*, 9 September 1863, 4.

4   'Yclept' is an archaic adjective meaning 'by the name of'; the word represents Old English gecleopod, past participle of cleopian 'call.' Its meaning here is uncertain, but could signify being called or shouted at.

"All nature seemed smiling by moorland and lea."[5]

And he was hungry—desperately hungry. So he wandered forth toward the great city, and there arose within him thoughts of sweet and succulent food. Thoughts of the capabilities of human enjoyment and the powers of the human stomach. Thoughts of the time when in his home in the Black North he had feasted right royally upon potatoes and salt, washed down with a "naggin of buttermilk," and had scorned the wealth of kings. Thoughts of the feasts he had seen and heard of, of what he would do if his guardian angel were then and there to endow him with a fortune, how he would sample the contents of the baker's window he had just passed, how he would revel in clearing of its contents that steaming tray of delicacies just being carried into that refreshment saloon. Thoughts of rebellion, on-rushing and triumphant, of hungry mobs sacking the palaces of the rich and casting out the robbers; thoughts of tables spread with good cheer and the outcasts and down-trodden of the city installed in the place of the oppressors of the people; thoughts of the coal porters from the quay and the denizens of Montgomery Street rioting in the mansions of Merrion Square, and holding levees at the castle; thoughts of the ponds of Stephen's Green drained of water and filled with wine, of the rookeries transformed into luscious edibles and given away to the people. Thoughts, in fact, of every kind an empty stomach could force upon a weakened brain.

And on he walked, and unconsciously his feet kept pace with his imagination, and in the midst of his reveries he heeded not the stares of the passers-by, who occasionally turned to look after the swiftly moving, hungry, ragged outcast.

On he rushed, past the Rotunda, along O'Connell Street, past the offices of the National League, under the shadow of the British flag flying from the topmost point of Nelson's monument, past the Post Office, Abbey Street, Bachelors' Walk, across Carlisle Bridge,[6] on towards the Bank.

---

5   I have been unable to source this quote.

6   Carlisle Bridge was built in 1794 and rebuilt by the Dublin Ports and Docks Board in 1880, when it was renamed O'Connell Bridge by the City council. The use of "Carlisle Bridge" seems an anachronism, although a search of newspapers for the period shows that the old name was still in use in the 1880s and 1890s.

Beauty, wealth, fashion, pomp, pageantry, loyalty, cant, flunkeyism, pride, piety—what are they all to a man who is hungry? And he was hungry.

For three months he had looked in vain for employment. For three months he had beseeched a situation from those sterling Nationalist employers who denounce landlord tyranny in the country and in the towns use the misery of its victims to drive down wages to starvation point. For two months he had lived on the charity of the Mendicity institution.[7]

He was hungry, desperately hungry. Even the thought of work had left him in the overpowering desire for food. He reached the Bank, be essayed to cross the street; as he did so there rounded the corner of Grafton Street a company of red-coated soldiers on their way to relieve their comrades on duty in some of the garrison guards. For a moment the bright, flashing bayonets of the soldiers riveted the attention of our hero, as with shouldered arms they marched past the sentry who guards her Britannic Majesty's treasures at the Bank. Then he stepped forward again and stopped. For, lo! there on the ground before him lay a coin—yellow, glittering, shining, stamped with the counterfeit presentment of the old lady[8] who does us the honour to rule over us. A coin to all appearance the equivalent of a workman's weekly wage.[9]

Have you seen a ragged street arab[10] clutch at a crust and thrust it into the recesses of his clothing lest his bigger playmates should claim a share of the spoil? Then you have an idea of the manner in which our hero seized that coin, hiding it at once in his pocket from the prying eyes of the policeman; into his pocket, while his fingers carefully felt it over to ascertain whether it had indeed that jagged, notched edge accompanying a golden coin. It had. Eureka! Here was a fortune. Feasting galore, a warm bed to lie in, a fire to sit beside, breakfast, dinner, and supper for a week to come.

Straightway he turns upon his heel, along Dame Street, up Cork Hill,

7   Connolly published a short story, "The Mendicity and its Guests," in *Workers' Republic*, 27 August 1898.

8   Queen Victoria.

9   The hero believes he has found a gold sovereign, value one old pound, or 240 pence.

10   A homeless child; a street urchin.

past the castle, along Thomas Street, and dives headlong into a third-rate eating-house he had known in his palmy days.

"It's a fine mornin', sir."

"Two slices of bread and butter, two cups of tea, and half a pound of cooked rashers (bacon)."

"Yes, sir; yes, sir."

"An' have you any taters ready. No? Then get me a plate of taters an' a bowl of broth, quick; I'm starving. An', holy Heaven, what kind of rashers is that to put before a hungry man; an' bread, sure I could read Tim Healy's speeches through it. Give me that plate of fancy bread out of the window, an' for God's sake don't stand there staring with your mouth open like a Malahid codfish waiting for the tide to come in.[11] Get your taters done, or I'll be finished with this mouthful before you are ready. Eaten half-a-crown's worth already, you say. I don't care if I had eaten five shillings' worth, ma'am. I can afford it this blessed morning, thanks be to God. Look here, ma'am, and let me dazzle your eyes and comfort your ould heart; for although I've eaten your mouldy bread and drunk your watery tea before paying for it, it's meself[12] can so drive away your cares with a sight of the face of the widow woman we neither love nor honour[13]—at least, except on the back or front, which ever you like to call it, of a yellow sovereign like this one."

So saying, our hero suited the action to the word, and drawing his hand from his pocket slapped down upon the table the coin—a brand new, shining, polished *halfpenny*[14].

Dublin is a great city.

---

11   Malahide codfish. Connolly re-used this line in "Home Thrusts," *Workers' Republic*, 27 August 1898, 1. "We just stood around them with our mouths open like a Malahide codfish waiting for the tide to come in."

12   Meself.

13   Queen Victoria's image on the coin.

14   The punchline of the story. The halfpenny was the second-lowest coin in value, the lowest being a farthing. It was made of copper which had, when new, a shiny appearance. The hero, in his famished state, mistook its shine for that of a gold sovereign. He has already eaten half-a-crown's worth of food, or 30 old pence.

*****

WHAT MIGHT HAPPEN
LABOUR LEADER
11 APRIL 1896, P.122

IF THIS WERE a narration of facts, what effect would their frequent recurrence have upon the solution of the social question,

"Party, attention, slope arms, fours, right, quick march, right wheel, by the left"; and as the last section of fours passed the gate the bugler on the regimental guard raised his bugle to his lips and sounded the reveille, arousing the sleeping battalion. A curious circumstance, truly.

Peace between the nations. No one had trod upon the tail of the British Lion. That dignified old monster was still lying, in calm and undisturbed repose, watching the antics of the Russian bear as it cavorted around our Indian frontier; or else with self satisfied complacency, listening to the excited crowing of the Gallic cock, as it scratched fresh scandals from its financial dunghills.

Peace between the nations, and yet a detachment of seventy men, non-commissioned officers and privates, under the command of the oldest officer in the regiment, marched out of barracks that grey winter's morning with fifty rounds of ball-cartridge in their pouches. It was not a mere shooting party, although Lieutenant Evesham had facetiously described it as such. Shooting parties do not usually seek the least frequented thoroughfares, or have their approach to the railway station guarded by bodies of police, or anxiously awaited by the civil magistracy; shooting parties are not composed of men carefully selected from every company in the regiment, paraded before reveille in the barrack square, and then, after a few words from the commanding officer, marched off with white faces and discontented looks.

Colonel Walker was one of those men who, in the terse language of Tommy Atkins,[1] are known to be "as regimental as a buff-stick."[2] He had earned for his regiment the reputation of being a smart corps, a reputation generally earned at the expense of a rank and file driven to death by excess of discipline; but he had also set the example of making no regulation for his men to which he did not conform himself. So, when he appeared upon the parade ground, dressed in full regimentals, between tattoo and reveille, the detachment drawn up there awaiting his inspection felt no little uneasiness as to the nature of the expedition which had prompted such unheard of conduct, an uneasiness increased by the secrecy attending their muster.

"All present, Major Eldridge?"

"Present and correct, sir."

"Very good, you will please order their arms, and let them know I wish to speak to them before their departure."

"Party, order arms, eyes right, dress, steady, now that will do, eyes front. Now, men, the commanding officer wishes to speak to you before you are marched off. I need hardly remind you to keep silence in the ranks and await his instructions."

"Men," Colonel Walker spoke in an unusually low tone of voice, but, nevertheless, so clearly and distinctly, that No.2 sentry upon the hospital post, catching his first accent wafted across the parade ground on the still morning air, ordered his arms, and listening intently, heard every word he uttered. "Men, you are today being sent out upon a duty as disagreeable and at the same time as honourable as any that has fallen to your lot since first you enlisted beneath the flag of your country. Many of you have served with me, I am proud to say, upon the field of battle against the enemies of our country, in Egypt, in India, in South Africa, and wherever we have been we were never, I think, sparing of our energies, or over careful of our lives, in the strife against the foes of England. It would be well for us if it were always against such foes, speaking a different tongue or of a different colour, that we had to bear arms; but I am sorry to say, that now, loyal men are fain to recognise that England has other foes than

---

1   Generic name for a common soldier.

2   A small piece of wood covered with leather used to polish brass uniform buttons.

those who speak a different tongue or claim another country. England, men, has fallen upon troublous times. There are now, as you are perhaps aware, strikes, lock-outs, and industrial disputes in almost every corner of it. The poorer classes, stirred up by the seditious teaching and glib words of the socialist agitators, are formulating the most ridiculous demands for higher wages and shorter hours, irrespective of the condition of trade or the stress of competition. The authorities are openly defied, and in the town to which you are being sent today, an attempt has actually been made to blow up the offices of a factory in order, it is presumed, to punish the owner for having formed an employers combination to resist the demands of the agitators. Now, men, I hope there will be no need for your intervention, but I also hope that if there is you will remember your duty as soldiers, and your oath of allegiance, and act promptly to the word of command, whatever that may be. You have with you Major Eldridge, your oldest and most trusted officer, and he I am sure will act with all care and moderation in these trying circumstances."

As the old colonel proceeded with his speech his voice, which had faltered a little at first, gradually grew harsher and his tone more vitriolic and to the close observer it was plain that long before the end of his remarks, the spirit of the aristocrat had triumphed over that of the patriot, completely obliterating in his mind the distinction between foreign foes and native agitators, to both of whom he would without hesitation have measured out the same short shrift,

"Major Eldridge."

"Yes, sir."

"March off your party."

* * * * *

Private Thomas Molyneux, numbering off left of the right half company, had, with the remainder of the party, listened to the words of the colonel, at first with a feeling of intense curiosity, but finally with an overmastering sensation of horror. Private Molyneux, unlike most of his room-mates had closely watched the progress of the strike in the town and factory referred to. To him the daily narrative of its progress had possessed a fascination stronger than any allurement within the power of military life to offer. Years before, when the hot blood of youth was still pulsating through his veins, he had served in that factory as one of its most promising hands. Respected by his mates and trusted by his superiors, he was in a fair way of developing into a model British working man. But just as the boy had developed into the man, and at that period of life when in times of peace we sway between the contending currents of smug respectability and free and easy vagabondage, er in times of social change between conservatism and revolution, there entered into his life two influences, deeply rooted in their mutual antagonism, and yet irresistibly cooperating to mould the destiny of their victim into one shape and form.

On the 1st of May he had been induced to listen to a lecture delivered under the auspices of a local socialist society in the town in which he lived. From that day he had constantly attended their meetings, and by the end of August, becoming thoroughly imbued with their doctrines, had joined their ranks as an enrolled member. And on the 1st of September, on entering the factory he found installed in the office, and listened to the few sharp words addressed to the assembled workpeople by the new managing partner, Mr. Roland. Between the old manager, Mr. Bow, and himself there had ever existed a kindly feeling born of the fact that he was in an especial sense Mr. Bow's own apprentice, having received his technical education under that gentleman's personal supervision. But Mr. Roland was not only a manager, he was also a partner. He was determined, as he carefully informed his workpeople on the morning of his installation, to conduct his business on strictly commercial principles, and commercial principles, he was gracious enough to instruct them, meant the greatest possible return to the firm for the smallest possible outlay.

From that day forward hard times set in for the employees of Roland & Co.'s factory, and from that day a storm raged in the heart of Tom Molyneux. Reduction of wages followed reduction, fines accumulated upon fines, the lives of the workers were rendered miserable by the petty tyrannies and vexatious interferences of their overseers. Each little underling and petty "gaffer" took his cue from the head of the firm, and vied with each other in harassing the work-people. The braver spirits among the latter at last made an effort to organize them to resist this tyranny; and finally, after a well-attended meeting of the employees, at which many eloquent speeches were made and courageous resolutions passed, Tom Molyneux was appointed a spokesman to interview the manager.

Tom knew and appreciated the risk he ran, but his life for some time past had become almost unendurable. Insults which to an ordinary man might have passed unheeded, fell upon his soul, saturated with Socialist doctrines, like steel upon flint, and he resolved to run the risk and interview the tyrant. He did, was immediately discharged, black-listed through the town, and deserted by his fellow-workers, who at the first intimation of the fate which had befallen him, disowned his action, and slunk like sheep to their places. Finally, hungry, workless, and sick at heart of the cowardice of his fellows, he had ended by enlisting and smothering his conscience in order to fill his stomach. And now after many years of absence he was about to return to his native town, but in what a guise and on what an errand.

Mechanically he obeyed the orders of his officer as the party passed out through the gates and along the almost deserted thoroughfares to the railway station. Almost unconsciously his mind recorded the fact that they passed a mill worker who was apparently tramping in at that early hour, from her home in the suburbs, to be in time for her work in the town, drunken swell being gently pioneered homewards in the affectionate grasp of a policeman, shivering outcast whose looks betrayed the fact that he had spent the night in fitful slumber inside some friendly archway, a milk-cart, a ball-party, a servant girl with towsy hair and grinning countenance, and finally, that they arrived at the railway station and were rapidly entrained and sent whirling upon their journey.

Then shutting his eyes he leant back in the carriage, and, unheeding the somewhat forced badinage of his comrades, his mind wandered back to bygone times, to old familiar scenes and faces. He recalled the aspect of the lanes and streets in which he had spent his boyhood days, the friends he had known, the happy hours he had spent, the escapades and pranks in which he had taken part and of which he had been so proud. Then he remembered—and the remembrance stirred him to the very heart—the bright smiling face, the winsome looks, the cheery laughter, the supple sinuous form of a certain factory 'hand,' in whose presence he at one time thought he had anticipated the joys of heaven.

"A shooting party," said Lieutenant Evesham, the words came back to his memory with stunning force, "My God, if it should prove a prophecy. If we should have to fire upon the people, and I, Tom Molyneux, the socialist, the rebel, should have to fire upon a crowd in which might be my schoolmates, my best chums· aye, my own relations—flesh of my flesh, and blood of my blood. God almighty, perhaps the bullet that leaves my rifle would find its billet in the heart of the girl for whose happiness I would willingly give my life itself. No! I'm damned if it will. Before I'd fire upon the people, I'll smash the rifle upon the stones at my feet even if I were to get penal servitude."

His teeth closed together with a crunch, his nails sank into his flesh, and he sprung involuntarily to his feet as he mentally registered this vow; and at that moment the engine drew its carriages alongside the platform at their destination.

* * * * *

The streets were crowded with people. From early morning the town had been astir. Bands of strikers paraded the streets cheering their leaders, booing their late employers, vowing vengeance upon the blacklegs, and generally giving vent to the pent-up hatred aroused by years of oppression. Around the buildings constituting the factory of Roland and Company the chief interest seemed to centre, and thither accordingly the majority of the populace had bent their footsteps, until the adjacent streets became one moving mass of humanity. Late the previous evening the strike leaders had received intimation that a body of blacklegs in the employment of the Free Labour Agency were on their way to the town, and that, as if in order to provoke a conflict, it had been arranged to delay their entrance until midday, when they were to be marched through the streets by the soldiery and lodged in Roland & Co.'s factory. On protesting against this senseless parade of force, the strike committee were curtly told that it was intended to demonstrate the determination of the authorities to uphold the freedom of the citizens and to safeguard the rights of property.

In times of great public excitement there seems to be a peculiar kind of magnetism in the air which somehow influences the minds of men, and almost without the necessity of a spoken word inspires great mobs at the same moment with the same idea. Thus, when the strike committee, after a short and earnest deliberation, resolved to recommend their followers and sympathisers to surround Roland & Co.'s factory and oppose a passive resistance to the passage of the blacklegs and their escort, leaving only the necessary pickets and a line of communication to give warning of any strategic move upon another base, they found upon their descent into the street, from the room in which their meeting was hell, that the people had already anticipated their wishes and were rapidly moving off in the direction they desired.

As the day wore on the excitement increased; the mob surged backwards and forwards, the police in vain endeavouring to keep clear a passage to the factory gate, charging and clearing a lane through the people, only to find the human flood closing in behind them as they passed.

Ever and anon the mood of the people seemed to change. At one time fierce curses were hurled at the heads of the police, the magistrates, the blacklegs, the crown, the constitution, the political parties, the established order generally; at another gibes and laughter would be heard on all sides; everybody and everything seemed to come in for the ready wit and ridicule of the people. Again cheers for their leaders would rend the air, immediately followed by deep-toned choruses of revolutionary songs, interspersed with snatches of some music hall ballad.

In the midst of one of these bursts of feeling a sudden murmur passed through the crowd, succeeded by a silence so intense as to be almost oppressive.

"The soldiers are coming! The soldiers are coming!"

The whisper passed from lip to lip, and eyes were strained and necks were stretched to get a glimpse of the red coats, as with measured tread they moved forward upon what was to most of them a highly disagreeable duty. In front of their array marched the arch-enemy of the workers, Mr Roland himself, proudly arrogant in what he deemed his hour of triumph, whilst the blacklegs (one hundred strong) were placed in the position of safety between the two half-companies of soldiery. The silence which had fallen upon the people upon the appearance of the soldiery lasted only until they had penetrated into the centre of the crowd, when the most deafening chorus of noises again broke forth. The crowd surged backwards and forwards, cursing and yelling, alternately threatening the blacklegs with all sorts of pains and penalties, or promising them monetary rewards if they would only come out and refuse to work. At one time the swaying mob swung right across the pathway, and so completely blocked the passage to the gate that the military were obliged to charge with fixed bayonets in order to clear the way. This proceeding for a moment terrified the people, and before they could recover from their temporary stupor, the escort, advancing rapidly, swept the gateway clear of the opposing crowd, then wheeling outwards in half-companies, allowed the blacklegs to pass in safety through the factory gate; then wheeling into line again, fronted towards the threatening multitude.

Tom Molyneux, who with averted face and downcast looks had kept his place in the ranks that day with all the precision but with scarcely more than the consciousness of an automaton, now for the first time raised his eyes towards the people, and in doing so met a sight that in a moment froze his blood in mingled shame and horror. In any excited crowd the persons who occupy the most prominent position are not always those who deserve that position. In the tumultuous tossing of a human wave, the most shrinking and the least assertive are as likely to find themselves in the front ranks as are the bold or aggressive.

Thus when Tom looked out towards the mass of people he saw right in front of him, at a distance of about fifty yards, the form of a young woman struggling to keep her feet in the crowd, and as she turned her face towards him he recognised in an instant the visage of his one-time sweetheart. A dry groan, coupled with a prayer to God that the earth might open and swallow him before he was recognised, had just burst from his lips, when his attention was arrested by the first of that fatal chain of accidents which have made this strike so memorable in the industrial history of England.

As the soldiery had wheeled into line before the factory gate, Mr. Roland, Tom's arch enemy, and the man who, above all others, was responsible for the strife and tumult incidental to the strike, was left standing amid a knot of police and magistrates, a little to the right of the soldiers, but between them and the crowd. Throughout the day his insolent and arrogant demeanour had aroused the people to an ungovernable fury. In him they saw incarnated the spirit of capitalistic oppression, in him they saw the cause of all the suffering and misery they were undergoing, and they accordingly hated him with all the force of their nature, a hatred he freely returned and made no pretence to hide. As the last of the Free Labour men were safely ensconced inside the factory gate, Mr. Roland raised his hat, and swinging it round his head, shouted at the pitch of his voice,

"Three cheers for freedom of contract, and to hell with the strike."

Before the words had well left his lips the crowd made a sudden rush forward as if to seize him, and then as suddenly swayed back again, as a stone flung by an unknown hand came whizzing through the air, and missing Mr. Roland for whom it was no doubt intended, struck Major Eldridge on the right arm, almost fracturing the bone, while his sword fell clattering to the ground. Major Eldridge, a choleric, hot-tempered aristocrat, thoroughly despising the rabble, at once lost control of his temper, and as the surging crowd again moved forward with threatening looks and gestures, Tom Molyneux heard the command:

"With ball cartridges ready!"

In a mechanical manner he obeyed the order while he looked out towards the crowd and saw his sweetheart, with outstretched arms and appealing eyes, gazing, as he thought, towards him, and standing right in his line of fire.

"God Almighty! Must I fire, must I fire, must I fire? Shall I fire in the air and thus absolve myself at least of the murder, although the moral guilt of complicity would still be on my soul? Or, shall I hurl my rifle at that accursed scoundrel, Roland, and so create a diversion which may save the people?"

As with lightning-like rapidity these thoughts passed through his brain, he looked towards his enemy and observed him gazing with approving glances towards the military.

"Present!" The order rang out clear and threatening. Tom Molyneux raised his rifle to his shoulder and sank his cheek upon the stock, while his lips repeated the drill book formula, "Bottom notch up the backsight, tip up the foresight, and centre of the object: to be aimed at." As he did so he noticed, with a strange lack of interest, that his aim was taken true and correct upon the watch pocket of Mr. Roland's vest, that that gentleman wore a hair chain curiously plaited around a silver ornament in the shape of a hand, that even then his left hand was toying with a jewelled pendant in the old well-remembered manner in which it had toyed with it on the evening he, Tom, had received his dismissal.

"It's no use talking, Mr. Thompson." Mr. Roland's voice reached him across the intervening space without seemingly arousing his interest. "It's no use talking, this socialist agitation requires strong measures; these people must be taught a lesson."

"In the air; fire!"

Crash! The bullets passed harmlessly over the heads of the people as Mr Roland sprang into the air, spun round three times and fell with a thud upon the ground, the blood spurting from his mouth, his hands convulsively clutching at the pavement.

A bullet had drilled a hole through his heart.

*****

THE TRANSFUSION OF BLOOD
LABOUR LEADER
6 JUNE 1896, P.190

"YES, MEN AND WOMEN, the forces of mammon have too long dominated the lives of our people, narrowing our mental vision, stultifying our unblest efforts, and mocking at our highest aspirations. We must cast off all thoughts of self, and prove our faith by our willingness to give all our energy, all our ability, aye, even our life itself to the grand work of human emancipation, and think ourselves well repaid if we can go down to the grave with the consciousness that we have opened out a way to freedom for the toiling peoples of the world."

As I stepped off the stool which served as a platform, after concluding an hour's speech with the foregoing peroration, I was exceedingly gratified by the vehement clapping of hands with which the audience testified their approval of the sentiments to which I had given voice.

It was in a big city, one of those blots on the face of the earth of which commercialism is so fruitful, and the meeting was the last of a series of seven I had addressed under the auspices of the local socialists. Alike from the standpoints of numbers, collections, and new members, the meetings had been uniformly successful, and I was just in the mood when the true agitator feels the real revolutionary enthusiasm stirring in his blood, and longs to throw aside the narrow trammels and sordid details of political warfare, and stake his whole hopes upon the reckless hazard of a revolutionary uprising. With such thoughts surging in my brain, I stood looking at the departing crowd until a hand touched my elbow, aroused me from my reverie and caused me to turn sharply to face the individual to whom the hand belonged.

"Good evening, sir, I believe you are the speaker."

It was an old man apparently on the wrong side of sixty, but with a firmness of voice and decision of manner that gave evidence of an abiding vitality not common to his age.

"Yes, I believe I am the speaker."

"I am glad to meet you comrade, I do not belong to any body of organised Socialists myself, but I am with you heart and soul. I remember Ernest Jones,[1] and have tramped miles to listen to him when I was but a boy, and now after many years of waiting, I thank God that those eyes of mine have been privileged to witness the formation of a party, which will follow in the footsteps of the Chartists, and with fuller knowledge will profit by their mistakes, and reap where they have sown."

"Thank you, comrade, I have no doubt we will succeed this time, and, old as you are, I would not be surprised if even you were in at the death of this accursed system."

As I spoke the old man's hand tightened in mine with a convulsive grasp and drawing me away from the crowd who had gathered around us, he whispered excitedly in my ear.

"Yes, yes, that is it, in at the death, that is what I want to be, and it is for that that I have toiled by day and night to master the secrets of science, and now, friend (his voice at this point grew almost into a shriek) I have a secret to impart to you, a secret which will send this movement of ours forward with a rush, and enable us at next election to sweep the country before us."

"Well, what is your secret," I asked, rather incredulously.

"You don't believe me. But you shall believe, you shall believe; ay, and tremble as the devils do in hell; excuse the allusion. But I cannot tell you here. Come to my house tomorrow—there is my card—and you will know all, all. He grinned almost sardonically in my face; then, as I drew back alarmed at his excited manner, his countenance changed, and, clasping both my hands between his own, he asked almost beseechingly.

"Won't you come? Excuse an old man's hastiness, comrade; promise

---

1   Ernest Charles Jones (1819-1869) Chartist, journalist, and acquaintance of Marx and Engels.

to come, won't you?"

I promised.

* * * * *

Twelve o'clock next day found me seated in a house in one of the lowest parts of the city, in an old arm-chair, divested of my coat and vest, while my limbs were securely fastened to the arms and legs of the pieces of furniture on which I sat. Opposite me, grinning in the most self-satisfied manner, sat my old friend of the evening before.

More out of curiosity than with any other feeling, I had searched out the house at the address I had found in the card he had given me. Welcoming me in the friendliest manner possible, he had no sooner seen me comfortably seated, than he placed in my hand a glass, apparently of lemonade, and bade me drink. As I complied he hastily latched the room door on the inside, and seizing a huge chest dragged it against it as if to barricade it against intrusion from the outside. Alarmed at such extraordinary behaviour, helping as it did to confirm me in a previously formed opinion that the old gentleman was not altogether responsible for his actions, I rose, intending to demand a reason for such conduct. But as I stepped forward for that purpose, my brain seemed to lose its balance, my legs reeled under me, I felt as incapable as a man in the last stages of intoxication, and could not raise a hand to defend myself when, lifting a heavy chair and swinging it round his head the scoundrel who had trapped me, brought it down with crushing force upon my head, stunning me with the blow.

And now having me well secured and perfectly helpless, he stood and gloated over me as I slowly regained consciousness and looked around the room in which I was imprisoned.

Well, my agitator friend, how are you."

"You treacherous scoundrel, what do you mean by such conduct as this?"

"Ha, ha, I've got you nicely friend, got you nicely. But don't be alarmed, your usefulness in the cause of socialism will not be prematurely cut short, your revolutionary career is not ended. Oh, no, its only beginning, only beginning. Ha, ha." And he laughed a quiet sardonic laugh, leaning forward until his face almost touched mine and his laughter grated on my ear as the rasping of a file grates upon the nerves, Realising my helplessness in the position in which I had been placed, I restrained my desire to exhaust my vocabulary of abusive epithets upon my captor, and sullenly watched his actions as pouring forth a torrent of words, now descending into a whisper and now rising into a veritable shriek, he unfolded to me the diabolical plan in pursuance of which he had lured me to my doom.

"Ah, ha, my friend, yesterday you said to the crowd in the market place that you ought to think yourself well repaid if you go down to the grave with the consciousness that you opened up a way to freedom for the toiling people of the world. Now, I will give you that opportunity, and will endow you with that consciousness, endow you with it in a manner you could never hope to achieve by mere sterile propaganda, such as you have been pursuing. What, not sterile, you say? Bah, why should you be so optimistic? Why shut your eyes to facts? You ought to know ere now that the British working-man is perfectly hopeless material from a revolutionary standpoint, Karl Marx notwithstanding. What! Marx never praised the British workmen. I know he did not, but he taught that the development of capitalism inevitably produces a race of propertyless workers, a proletariat who by their economic environment are converted into a revolutionary force, and thus capitalism produces its own grave-diggers.[2] Therefore the nation in which economic development is most advanced ought logically to possess the most socialistic working class. But England is the most commercially developed of all European countries, and its workers are yet the most reactionary, Question! You say question. Who would dare to question such A self-evident fact. Question! Did not Mr. Thomas Wilson of Hull, the Liberal shipowner, tell the Hull dockers that he would spend a quarter of a million of money (drawn from their sweat and blood) in breaking up their union and in bringing them to their knees, and didn't he starve them and their wives and children; and didn't they at last election return him with thousands of a majority over

---

2   "What the bourgeoisie, therefore, produces, above all, is its own grave diggers. Its fall and the victory of the proletariat are equally inevitable." Karl Marx and Friedrich Engels, *The Communist Manifesto* (Penguin: London, 1967; 1985), 94.

the socialist candidate. Question indeed. Were not the colliers of West Salford starved for sixteen weeks by Mr. Thos. Knowles until women and children were perishing of hunger, and didn't they return him at the head of the poll, and, taking the horses out of the carriage, drag him through the street. Question, Bah, talk of a revolution in Britain; you sneer at the ignorant Irish, but who could imagine an Irish tenant voting for a Lord Clanricarde, as your free-born Britisher does for his sweating employer."

"Well, but what has this to do with me."

"Ha, ha, you are anxious to learn, are you, then I will tell you. I want to be in at the death of the system. The number of enthusiastic workers in the movement are too few, I want to increase it, and you must help me. Listen, I am an unlicensed surgeon, a quack. I have a large practice among the poor; they have implicit confidence in my skill, and rightly. Silence, sir; do you see this lancet. I intend with it to open one of your veins and let the rich blood flow until I have secured a sufficient quantity for my purpose. Bleed you to death. Ah, no. I, sir, am a surgeon, I will not kill you, I will keep you here, I will feed you on the best; but I shall periodically draw from the richest blood in your veins. Ah, ha, you shall not die for the cause, you shall live for it, live for it, and on the morrow of the revolution you shall go free. Thou wilt thus advance socialism. Listen, the human body is made of numberless minute particles of which the mind is but a form, and of which the blood is the very essence. Incarminated in the minute globules of which the blood is composed science reveals the germs out of which, given a congenial environment, there may be recreated form with all the mental and physical powers and potentialities of the human being from which in the first instance it was withdrawn.[3] The secret of this germ, this protoplasm, which baffled science and philosophy so long, *I have at last discovered.*"

As he hissed the last sentence into my ears his whole face lit up with an almost demoniacal gleam of satisfaction, and I could not repress a

---

3   Incarminated may be a typo for incarnate as 'incarminated' is not recognised as a word by the Oxford English Dictionary. However, there is an example of its use in the sermons of Father Arthur Stanton (1839-1913), who was curate of St. Alban's Holburn from 1862 to 1913 and a well-known preacher. It is from a sermon he gave on 15 October 1911 and it too may be a typo for incarnate. "I might say that every page of the Bible is incarminated with the Blood of the Everlasting Covenant." See *Father Stanton's Last Sermons in S. Alban's Holborn* (London: Hodder & Stoughton, 1911), 296.

shudder of horror, as I reflected upon the hopelessness of my position in the hands of such a maniac. Taking a piece of cord he proceeded to fasten it firmly round my left arm just below the elbow, drawing it tight until I felt it cut into the flesh, and was compelled to clench my teeth to stifle the cry of pain that arose to my lips. Stepping back as if to survey his work, he caught sight of my face, and must have read the look of agony upon it, for as if to intensify my pangs he brought out a case of surgical instruments, and placing them within a foot of where I sat bound and helpless, began deliberately to turn them over and examine them, while dilating upon their value to the medical profession. Then suddenly resuming the thread of his discourse, he went on: "Yes, comrade, ha, ha, comrade, this secret I have at last discovered, and I now inform you that the discovery enables me to extract from common clay, the medical and hitherto unknown properties, which combined with a minute globule of human blood, produces the vital force of a human being. But I do not intend to experiment in the production of entirely new human beings as I might do without the necessity of invoking the aid of the passions of love or lust. I do not wish to create fresh armies of surplus labourers to enrich the dividend-hunting capitalist, or to become what Krapotkine[4] calls "more dung to manure the pasture lands of the rich expropriator."[5] No, I wish to destroy, not to help, the robber crew. Now, listen: this knowledge of mine enables me to create a human form, but that is not my wish, but, mark my words, taking the blood of a strong, self-willed man or woman, uniting it with the secret property extracted from the earth, and transfusing it with the blood and into the veins of a weaker willed person previously doctored into a state of congenial receptivity, this new protoplasm grows in vigour

---

4   Peter Kropotkin (1842-1921) Russian anarchist and proponent of anarchist communism. His surname was sometimes spelt as "Krapotkine." For example, see "Krapotkine Expelled from France," *Edinburgh Evening News*, 6 March 1896, 2.

5   "Do you want your husband, your lads to be ever at the mercy of the first comer who has inherited from his father a capital to exploit them with? Are you anxious that they should remain slaves for a master, food for powder, mere dung; wherewith to manure the pasture lands of rich expropriators?" Peter Kropotkin, 'An Appeal to the Young', *Justice*, 11 October 1884, 3. Connolly reused his version of Kropotkin's words in *The Reconquest of Ireland* (Dublin, 1915), 43: "The children were only children of the poor, and the poor—whether Protestant or Catholic—were only esteemed, perhaps only esteemed today, by the rich, as in Kropotkin's words, "mere dung to manure the pasture lands of the rich expropriator." See also "German and Irish Schools," *Irish Worker*, 5 December 1914, 1, for the original article republished as part of *The Reconquest of Ireland*.

and strength, spreads throughout the entire system, takes possession of the mind, the heart, the soul, the will, until finally some in the outward mash of form and feature, the subject becomes, in everything that goes to determine conduct or form character, a virtual copy, a mental or spiritual reproduction, of him or her whose blood they have absorbed. Now, my friend, observe the application of this startling fact. You are a young man. You, like most socialist propagandists, are a man of strong will and great force of character. You are enthusiastic in the cause of socialism, and have publicly declared you would be satisfied even in death if you had the consciousness of having opened up a way to freedom for the toiling people. Ah, ha, how I laughed when I heard that statement. Now, comrade, I propose to tap your blood, to slowly drain you of that priceless liquid, and then, by means of that chemical knowledge I have acquired, to use it to recreate the protoplasm of a human being, and then, by allying with my medicines, and administering it to my patients, to transfuse it to their blood, and then let it work its mission, which will mean that your Socialist spirit and determination incarnated in the blood I have withdrawn from your veins, will gradually dominate their consciousness and possess their being to the exclusion of all other thoughts, and thus thousands will be converted by your blood for one who would be converted by your speeches; and thus will the revolution come, for I will give my medicine free, free.

His voice rose into a shriek, his whole body seemed to dilate with the passion of his madness, the foam rising to his lips as he clutched a lancet from the case and hurled himself upon me.

Home and all that it means rose to my mind in that instant, the little children who would never see their father more, the wife who would wait in vain for her husband, the father who would mourn his son, the thousand and one ties that bound one to life, surged up before my agonised vision, and, in the frenzy of despair, as the lancet touched my naked arm I made one supreme effort and drawing my arms together tore asunder the chair to which I was bound, rose to my feet, and hurled my whole weight, bound and hampered as I was, upon the maniac, bearing him down with a terrific crash to the ground.

"Hello, hello, what's all the row about," shouted my landlord coming to the door of my bedroom in his nightdress, "what the devil is the matter with you."

"Where is he," I shouted, glaring wildly around me, as I gathered myself up from the floor on which I found myself with the bedclothes twisted round me like a rope, "where is the old villain."

"Oh, go to bed and be hanged to you, and take a comrade's advice, and in future eschew beefsteaks for supper."

PART III
LOST LETTERS

*****

CONNOLLY TO KIER HARDIE
1894[1]

[1894]
6 LOTHIAN STREET

D EAR HARDIE,
I enclose an open envelope with letter for Frank Smith ILP, whereth I give you permission to read and then forward to his address. You will see by the contents that we are asking him to stand as our candidate for the Central Edinburgh Parliamentary Division. You must really help us in this situation, we have tried everywhere. Hobson, Tattersall, Marsden,[2] Kennedy of Carlisle, Stirling Robertson of Montrose, Glasier of Glasgow [...] and have either received a definite no or were too late. Nairn is hinted at in my other letter to Smith. There is talk among the liberal wire-pullers of Mr. M'Ewan getting rewarded for funding the Liberal Party by being created a peer and the worst of the position is that it is said the new Liberal candidate would be our [...] labour candidate. John Wilson has developed into a full-blown Liberal-Labour man. You understand the damage. Our position will be simply intolerable and the seat will be completely lost <u>unless our man is in the field first</u>. If he is our position is sound and secure, and I question if Watson would consent to oppose us. But prompt action is absolutely necessary. I think a word or two from you would influence Mr Frank Smith a great deal, try it anyhow. In the meantime the news herein contained must be kept absolutely secret, out

---

1 "J. Connolly to Hardie (Edinburgh), 1894," ILP/4/1894/226, Francis Johnson Correspondence, London School of Economics Library and Archive, London.

2 Appears to have been Edward Marsden.

of newspapers etc as even a hint would precipitate the calamity we dread.

Yours fraternally,

JAMES CONNOLLY.

P.S. That foolish threat of an anti-Irish crusade uttered by Adam Anderson on Mid-Lanark, will do us an incalculable amount of harm. It is already being paraded as proof of our vile designs Could the —— not think such things without blurting them out.

*****

CONNOLLY TO KIER HARDIE
12 APRIL 1897[1]

IRISH SOCIALIST REPUBLICAN PARTY
67 MID. ABBEY STREET
DUBLIN
12 APRIL 1897

DEAR HARDIE,

In response to your letter I have sent app per assistant secretary a copy of our new pamphlet which I hope you will <u>review</u>, and a copy of the *Daily Independent* on Thursday, 6th, giving an account of one of our meetings.

You will gather from them much information as to how the land lies in Ireland, and also as to the position and policy of our party. You will see that we are <u>not</u> Home Rulers, but oppose the Home Rule parties as traitors to the cause of real nationalism as understood by the "rebel leaders" of Ireland in the past.

We consider that mere Home Rule would only strengthen the launch of reaction and flood Ireland with a corrupt gang of middle-class place-hunters. But in thus advocating full national independence as the only political change of any value we do not preach national hated, but only that we desire to stand towards the people of Great Britain in the same relation as we stand towards the people of France or America; neither more nor less; friendly to the people but independent of their gov-

---

1   "Connolly to Hardie (Dublin), 12 April 1897," ILP/4/1897/30, Francis Johnson Correspondence, London School of Economics Library and Archive, London.

ernment.

You of course could not very well take up such a position in speaking or writing about the Irish, it is only possible for the people of Ireland themselves to assume such a position, and it is the only line of policy upon which socialism can succeed in Ireland. You could scarcely credit the attention it has effected in the attitude of the people towards us.

Another point I would like to refer to is in your speculation on the probable attitude of the Home Rule members towards the Liberals, will they strike out an independent line? Now if you will allow me to say so, it is this position of mere friendly criticism which you and other English socialists adopt towards the Home Rule party which stultifies every effort to win the Irish in Britain to socialism. The Home Rule party are not a democratic party at all, do not even profess to be, and will always be an obstacle on the path to freedom until they are crushed and ousted from their place. When you talk of making terms with them, or expect democratic action from them, you are doing as much to hold back socialist action among the Irish democracy as Mr Sam Woods, John Burns, or H. Wilson are doing among the English workers. The positions are exactly analogous.

Another point which causes much confusion and loss to socialism is the mistaken reference to the "Irish vote" in English elections. Strictly speaking there is no such thing as the Irish vote. The majority of the Irish follow the lead of the National League and votes against a socialist. Straightaway goes up a howl from all our SDF and ILP platform against the "Irish vote." But a majority, an overwhelming majority of the Scotch and English follow the lead of the Liberal or Tory associations and also vote against the socialist, and I listen in vain for a single word of denunciation of the "Scotch vote" or the "English vote." Why? I am sure that at every election in which a socialist stands, a respectable majority of Irish men vote the socialist ticket, and in view of that fact it would be well if in future references to "Irish votes" were quietly dropped. There are in Ireland, as in England, a conservative class and a democratic class, wherever Irishmen go they carry that party division with them, and a solid Irish vote on any political subject has never yet been realised, even in the parliament days of Parnell.

As far as my personal experience, or rather my personal financial position in Dublin is concerned, well I think I have about reached the bottom rung of the ladder. I am poorer than I ever was before and am undergoing a gentle process of scientific slow starvation. An agitator's lot (in Ireland) is not a happy one, no lectures fees, no big bazaars, no enthusiastic election meetings; nothing but a constant grind, stump and grind, nothing left but "the joy of the onset."[2]

Yours fraternally,

JAMES CONNOLLY.

---

2   Possibly from *Song of the Red Republican* by Gerald Massey (1828-1907), poet, Chartist and socialist. "And O joy of the onset! sound trumpet, array us; / True hearts would leap up were all hell in our path. / Up, up from the Slave-land; who stirreth to stay us, / Shall fall, as of old, in the Red Sea of wrath." Connolly also uses the line in his letter to Hardie, 8 September 1897, attributing the line to Whitman but I have been unable to find any such line by him.

*****

CONNOLLY TO KIER HARDIE
8 SEPTEMBER 1897[1]

75 CHARLEMONT STREET

DUBLIN

8/9/97

DEAR HARDIE,

Your letter to hand with cheque for which thanks. It came just in the nick of time. I quite agree with your remarks about the labour liberals or liberal labours. The time for conciliating them has gone past, socialism has been long enough a factor in politics for them to have made up their minds on it, long ere this, and as literature on the subject is so accessible there is no reason to treat them as persons honestly ignorant of its meaning, or indeed to treat them in any other way than as malignant opponents. As your [...], well I think Jim was a trifle disappointed at [...] and perhaps is tired waiting [...] not [...] if a single—towards [...] not show the abiding rarity of a socialist. But it's ill judging. The Socialist Labour Party of America are issuing an American edition of our pamphlet *Erin's Hope* with an appendix by their Executive appealing to Irish American working men and an official appendix from our party doing likewise.

La Petite République the organ of the Parti Ouvrier of France, published an account of our suppressed meetings on the occasion of the Duke's visit and *Le Journal en Voyage*, a French illustrated paper is going

---

1   "Connolly to Hardie (Dublin), 8 September 1897," ILP/4/1897/60, Francis Johnson Correspondence, London School of Economics Library and Archive, London.

to give an illustrated account of our jubilee procession and a reproduction of the coffins we carried on that occasion. Would you give me the address of your Paris correspondent as I want to have a handy way (priority) of bringing reactionary utterances of the Home Rule press under the notice of the French socialist journals. Miss Maud Gonne, the editor of *L'Irlande Libre*, a Franco-Irish journal published in French, holds her paper to the extent of two columns open to me per an article on our aims and methods whenever I want it, but as she does not believe in the necessity of exposing the middle-class nationalists, and as I do, I must have some means for revealing to the French the deficiencies she would hide. I hope by so doing to induce them to realise the fact that until those people are kicked down and out, progress is impossible. She is at one with us in our objects, despises the Home Rulers quite as much as I do, but imagines she can use them and is instead used by them, not an uncommon occurrence.

Our progress is not as much in membership, as in influence among her and her colleague, the editor of the *Shan Van Vocht* in Belfast, Miss Milligan, and is getting our literature sold all over Ireland. Our meetings: at first decidedly cold and often hostile are now decidedly enthusiastic, and our audiences neither fail, and when you remember that it is always the same speakers you will realise that it cannot be mere curiosity which brings them. We are developing new speakers and officials (I am only a private member now) and only require to be allowed to go our own way and learn the value of fighting our own battle, to make socialism a power in Ireland. Of course we will make no *great* progress until we contest a parliamentary election. Personally, the capitalist boycott was too strong for me and I have sunk to the position of a peddler, and am struggling to earn a precarious livelihood in that avocation. I have often heard socialism discredited in England, as a bread and butter question, but here in Ireland it only means to bread without the butter. The long drawn out misery of such a life would be insupportable were it not for what Whitman calls the "joy of the onset."

Yours in the cause,

JAMES CONNOLLY.

PART IV
EARLY WRITINGS
NEVER REPUBLISHED

*****

SOCIALISM IN DUBLIN
[MANIFESTO OF THE IRISH SOCIALIST REPUBLICAN PARTY]
LABOUR LEADER
20 JUNE 1896, P.210

Irish Socialist Republic
to the Irish People

FELLOW COUNTRYMEN—We are today face to face with a new crisis in Irish political history. The reactionary Tory party—sworn supporters of every kind of royal, aristocratic, and capitalistic privilege—once more dominates the English Parliament; the Liberal party, long and blindly trusted by so many of our fellow-countrymen, has proven itself to be today as treacherous and corrupt as it has ever been in the past, when it succeeded in obtruding its slimy influence across the field of Irish politics, the Home Rule party, split up into a dozen intriguing sections, seek by senseless vilification of each other's character to hide their own worthlessness and incapacity; in the country the tenantry seek in vain for relief from the economic pressure born of landlord robbery, and in the towns the employing class strive by every means in their power to still further reduce the wages and deepen the misery of their unfortunate employees.

On all sides personal vanity, personal ambition, and overmastering greed are seen to be the controlling factors in public life, and truth, freedom, and justice, are forgotten, or remembered only to round off a period or give a finish to a peroration in the speech of some huckstering politician. Such is the state of Irish politics today.

Fellow workers, the struggle for Irish freedom has two aspects: it is national and it is social. Its national ideal can never be realised until Ireland stands forth before the world, a nation free and independent.

It is social and economic; because no matter what the form of government may be, as long as one class own as their private property the land and instruments of labour, from which all mankind derive their subsistence, that class will always have it in their power to plunder and enslave the remainder of their fellow-creatures. Its social ideal, therefore, requires the public ownership by the Irish people of the land and instruments of production, distribution, and exchange, to be held and controlled by a democratic state in the interests of the entire community.

But every Irish movement of the last 200 years has neglected one or the other of these equally necessary aspects of the national struggle. They have either been agrarian and social, and in the hunt after some temporary abatement of agricultural distress have been juggled into forgetfulness of the vital principles which lie at the base of the claim for National Independence, or else they have been national and under the guidance of middle class and aristocratic leaders, who either did not understand the economic basis of oppression, and so neglected the strongest weapon in their armoury, or, understanding it, were selfish enough to see in the national movement little else than a means whereby, if successful, they might intercept and divert into the pockets of the Irish middle class a greater share of that plunder of the Irish worker which at present flows across the channel. The failure of our so-called "leaders" to grasp the grave significance of this two-fold character of the "Irish Question" is the real explanation of that paralysis which at constantly recurring periods falls like a blight upon Irish politics. The party which would aspire to lead the Irish people from bondage to freedom must then recognise both aspects of the long continued struggle of the Irish nation.

Such a party is the newly formed Irish Socialist Republican party. In its resolve to win complete separation from all connection with the British Empire, and the establishment of an Irish Socialist Republic, it embodies to the full the true Irish ideal—an independent nation with a social democratic organisation of society—thus adapting to the altered environment of the nineteenth century the vital principle of common ownership of the means of life which inspired the Brehon Laws of our ancient forefathers.

In its programme of immediately practicable reforms will be found the only feasible proposals yet formulated, either for averting from Irish farming the ruin with which it is threatened by the competition of the mammoth farms and scientifically equipped agriculture of America and Australia, for lessening the tide of emigration, or for using the political power of the Irish people with potent effect in paving the way for the realisation of a revolutionary ideal.

We ask you then to join our ranks, to spread our ideas, to work for our success, which means your emancipation; to help us to blend the twin streams of national and industrial freedom into one irresistible torrent, sweeping all obstacles before it, and bearing grandly onward on its bosom the toiling millions of the Irish race, proudly enthusiastic in their desire to join the mighty ocean of lovers of humanity who in every clime under the sun are working and hoping for the time when oppression and privilege will be no more; when "every man will be a kaiser, every woman be a queen."[1]

Youth of Ireland! stand prepared.
Revolution's red abyss
Burns beneath us, all but bared;
And on high the fire-charged cloud
Blackens in the firmament,
And afar we list the loud
Sea voice of the unknown event.
Youth of Ireland! stand prepared
For all woes the meek have dreed.
For all risks the brave have dared
At far suffering so far deed.
Stand prepared![2]

-JAMES CLARENCE MANGAN

---

1   From "Progress of the Peoples" by Will Hubbard-Kernan (1845-1905). "As we higher march and higher on into this light serene, / Every man will be a kaiser, every woman will be a queen." Will Hubbard-Kernan, *The Flaming Meteor: Poetical Works of Will Hubbard-Kernan* (Chicago: Charles H. Kerr and Co., 1892), 187-188.

2   Taken from "The Peal of Another Trumpet" by James Clarence Mangan (1803-1849).

James Connolly, formerly of Edinburgh, moved the adoption of the above, which was seconded by Robert Dorman,[3] Dublin, and carried almost unanimously. Hitherto save for branches in Belfast, Waterford, and Dublin—in which latter city there is also a Fabian society—there has been no distinctively Irish Socialist organisation. This new movement, born on Irish soil and inaugurated by Irishmen, will appeal to the Irish people as nothing else has yet done, and the times we believe to be ripe for this development. Not only the land nationalisers, but the fighting men of the old Fenian movement, who are sick of the trivialities of the Home Rule movement in these the days of its decadence, will rally round this new standard and carry it to an ultimate triumph. The development of the movement will be watched with intense interest, not only by millions of Irishmen the wide world over, but by all lovers of freedom.

---

3   Robert Dorman (1859-1937). Long-time political activist in Dublin.

*****

INTRODUCTION TO
THE RIGHTS OF IRELAND AND THE
FAITH OF A FELON
SEPTEMBER 1896

T HE PRESENT PUBLICATION is the first of a series of pamphlets the
Irish Socialist Republican Party propose to issue on the political and
social position of the Irish people.

They will aim at familiarising the reading and thinking public with
that interpretation of the recorded facts of our national history which at
once explains and justifies the uprise of a Republican and Socialist Party in Irish political life. Hitherto Irish history has been written almost
exclusively from a middle-class standpoint with results that can only be
fully appreciated by those whose historical studies have rested upon a
thorough scientific basis, and who are therefore competent to place in
their proper relation to each other, the heterogeneous mass of facts and
fictions) which pass muster as history. The materialist conception of history—the truth that a rational explanation of the course taken by human
society must be sought in the influence which their material environment
has had upon the minds of the men and women with whom history has
to deal—furnishes this scientific basis. Applying it to the present, we find
that the government of every civilised country is simply a committee of
the rich who conduct the affairs of state in the interests of the upper class,
and that, in like manner, every political party is the party of a class and
seeks to acquire power in the interest of the class who officer its organization and furnish its finances. In other words, a political party is the
weapon with which a particular class in the community seeks to create
and maintain the conditions most favourable to its own class rule, to se-

cure for its own members the greatest share of the wealth which exists as the common product of society.

There are in Ireland today, apart from The Socialist Republican Party, two political parties. The Conservative Party—the party of the rent-receiving landlord, and the so-called Home Rule party—the political guardian of the profit-grinding capitalist. Between those two there exists an apparent antagonism, but a real identity of interests. The one, openly conservative, seeks to retain intact the institution of private property in land; the other, while professedly democratic and national, also opposes any solution of the land question which by rooting the peasantry on the soil would deprive the Irish middle-class of the services of those landless labourers, who thronging into the towns and competing for employment, drive down wages and so become the human stepping stones by which their wealthy compatriots pass to ease and fortune. The first party openly relies on the British connection for the maintenance of its prerogatives, the second keeps up a continual sham fight with the official representatives of that connection, but in the wildest flights of its ultra-patriotic orations, secretly relies on a timely manifestation of imperial power to provide a decent excuse for eating their words and counselling "prudence" when the time comes for revolutionary action.

In opposing both parties, as enemies to Labour, the Irish Socialist Republican Party stands today in much the same position as Fintan Lalor occupied in '48. Indeed a most striking parallel exists between his time and our own. In '48 there stood on the one side the landlords backed up by the government in demanding their rents, while the people were left to starve in the midst of plenty. On the other side, there stood, nominally in opposition to the government, the two sections of the Repeal Party. Of these two sections, one, the Repeal Association, was tame, constitutional, and time-serving, its only hope being to secure the good offices of middle-class English politicians, repealers and repealers only. The other section, the Confederation, intelligent, honest and sincere, according to their lights, but (with a few exceptions, such as John Mitchel) like the first, thoroughly conservative on the really fundamental question of property, firm believers in rent, interest and profit, outvying even the government in their insistence on the landlord's right to his rent, also repealers only, but, under a multitude of grandiloquent phrases hiding even from themselves the utter paltriness of their ideal. To-day we have in our midst the same story repeated. In the Home Rule camp again exist two opposing sections, the most advanced of whom are as hopelessly conservative as ever in their opposition to the claim of the labourer to the full produce of his toil. Under these circumstances, the Irish socialist Republican Party, as the only political party in Ireland which fully accepts Fintan Lalor's teaching, from his declaration of principles to his system of insurrection, hope that in issuing this pamphlet they will succeed in bringing home to the minds of their fellows, a realisation of the necessity which exists for the creation of a party which shall aim at giving effective political expression to the twin ideas of national and industrial freedom now so hopelessly divorced in the public life of Ireland.

Of the man himself it may not be amiss to inform our readers that he was descended from a family noted in Irish history for their rebellious tendencies, that is, for their restlessness under injustice. One of the seven septs of Leix (Queen's Co.) they were transplanted to Kerry in 1609 by Chichester under orders from James I. They had rebelled eighteen times against the plantations ordered by Queen Mary and Queen Elizabeth, and had been nearly exterminated in consequence, and the government hoped by thus removing them to remote and unfamiliar territory to curb their native impetuosity But at each successive rebellion they were always running back to their old tribelands, and it was probably in this way the ancestors of our author found their way to, and eventually settled at Tenakill. Fintan Lalor himself was born in 1809, but did not come into public life until 1847. After the suppression of the *United Irishman* newspaper and the sentence upon its editor, John Mitchel, of 14 years transportation, Lalor stepped into the breach as principal writer to the *Irish Felon*, edited by John Martin. The *Irish Felon* was also suppressed and Lalor arrested at Ballyhane, County Tipperary, where he was endeavouring to organise a revolt of the peasantry. He was removed to Newgate prison, Dublin, where he was confined, until, his health completely breaking down, he was released—to die. He died as he had lived, a revolutionist and a rebel against all forms of political and social injustice, and for nearly fifty years the middle-class "patriots" who write Ireland's history have honoured his memory by boycotting his writings and slurring over his name. May the labours of our Irish democracy inscribe on the pages of their country's history a more fitting tribute to his genius.

*****

IRISH REVOLUTIONS:
UTOPIAN AND SCIENTIFIC
NOVEMBER 1896[1]
WATCHWORD OF LABOUR
21 AUGUST 1920, PP. 2–3[2]

THE SUBJECT I have chosen for my paper tonight is "Revolution: Utopian and Scientific." Perhaps some members of our society may be of [the] opinion that the title itself savors just too strongly of the melodrama to be altogether appropriate for the purpose of such a gathering as ours. But such an opinion, if held at all, can only arise from a misconception of the meaning of the word revolution itself, and as the purpose of this paper is to remove that misconception and to endeavour to convey to my fellow members and the audience generally a clear and accurate grasp of what I personally and those who think with me understand by such terms. Perhaps the best title I could have chosen should be one which, like the present, will be certain to excite adverse criticism, and therefore to provoke thought. We have, then, at the outset, to clearly and definitely impress upon our minds what we mean by this term revolution, as only by doing so will it be possible to intelligently discuss the position of the revolutionary intent in Ireland, and to determine which are the Utopian, and which are the scientific methods of attaining to that ideal.

In the mind of the average man in the street and his instructors, the

---

1   Text of a lecture given to the Dublin Literary Society, 38 Upper O'Connell Street, on 10 November 1896. See "Dublin Literary Society," *Evening Telegraph* (Dublin), 10 November 1896, 2.

2   In a note on 28 August 1920 the *Watchword of Labour* said that the following was printed before the editors had an opportunity of correcting and editing the proofs. It is reproduced here as printed by *Watchword* on 21 August.

party journalists and the party politicians, revolution is inseparably connected with bombs and barricades, and destruction by force of arms of legally constituted authorities.

This, however, is obviously inaccurate and misleading, since a revolution may, and frequently does, take place without violent insurrection entering into the operations in matters where the use of force is absolutely inconceivable. A revolution may be taken as connoting such an organic change in any sphere of human thought or action as shall destroy an outworn and effete system or method, and replace them by a better system or method, founded entirely upon new principles and producing more satisfactory results. Such is a revolution, and the men and women who consciously place themselves on the side of the forces working to attain that end are revolutionists.

The introduction of chloroform or anaesthetics into the use of surgery, of steam to the service of industry, of the democratic ideal into politics, was in each case a revolution, and those who worked to effect such introduction were in the true sense on the side of the revolutionary forces. The non-use of force is entirely valueless as an indication of the revolutionary character of any movement. The French Revolution was a revolution not because it was accompanied by force, but because it inspired a new conception in politics, and gave public expression and power to a radical change already realised in the sphere of industry and commerce, that radical change consisting of the transfer of economic power or commercial importance from the hands of the landed aristocracy into the grasp of the manufacturing class. The Revolution was but the reflex of this economic change. This is the conception of revolution held by the men who are working for the establishment of an Irish Socialist Republic, and as it is identical with the views of the revolutionary party in Europe in general, we may fairly accept it as the basis of our further inquiry.

What, then, would this mean in Ireland, what would in this sense of the word be an Irish Revolution? We must consider it in its two aspects—political and economic. Politically, Ireland is a nation subject to and ruled in the interests of another nation. This fact is, however, hidden from some very innocent people by the circumstances that the people of Ireland enjoy the same political freedom as their fellow subjects in England or Scotland. But this apparent equality is neutralised by the fact that the inhabitants of the two countries are not one, but two and two entirely distinct peoples, with different racial, national and consequently individual characteristics and ideals. The consent of the majority being essential before any step can be taken to legislaturely express the will of the people, and the most deeply cherished ideal of the one nation being often most utterly abhorrent to the views of the other, the practical effect of the connection between them has also been that the interests of the one nation have been sacrificed to suit the convenience of the other; the larger country has often with the best intentions rode roughshod over the heart of the smaller.

In Ireland the will of England is paramount, to make the will of Ireland paramount would therefore be a revolution, since it would be a change for the better, and productive of more satisfactory results, and more in consonance with the spirit of human freedom. The conquest of complete autonomy of national independence, by every nation possessing an organic unity, a distinct national life of its own, is, we believe, as socialists, an absolutely essential step in the upward march of the human race. The scientific revolutionist then looks to the complete separation of Ireland from the authority of the British Crown as that organic change in the political world most in accord with the times, which he as a socialist is bound to labour for, as part of the world-wide crusade for the extirpation of injustice. Home Rule he regards as an ingenious, but rather belated, scheme to increase the effectiveness of the British Constitution by a devolution of its least important powers, for as he considers the British Empire itself as an organised system of commercial piracy and oppression, whose course is almost run, he cannot fail to regard the efforts of Home Rulers with the same mixture of amusement and contempt with which the skilful physician, equipped with all the knowledge of his art, views the efforts of the quack who strives to stem disease with the discredited remedies of a bygone generation.

Economically, the position of Ireland is worse than it is politically. The political subjection of Ireland destroys the national life of the people, and constantly tends to obliterate all those finest racial characteristics, which in a free nation might have acted as powerful factors on the side of human progress. But the economic subjection of Ireland does more than thwart the free development of the people, it destroys the people themselves. How far this exterminating process has gone can be best realised by a brief glance at the figures supplied by the middle class statistician, Mr. M. Mulhall.[3] Mr. Mulhall is well known as an optimist of the first water. With him the present system of society is the best that could be devised and uniformly productive of the most beneficial results, that the British Empire is an ideal incarnation of all the social and political blessings the most benign providence could possibly shower upon an ungrateful generation.

We may then fairly assume that his figures are not likely to exaggerate the evils arising from the landlord and capitalist system as we know them in Ireland, but rather to minimise them wherever possible. Here, then, are his figures of Irish progress during the fifty years from 1837 to 1887. Died of famine, 1,225,000; persons evicted, 3,668,000; emigrants, 4,186,000.[4]

The mere enumeration of these figures conveys but a faint idea of the suffering and misery they serve to chronicle. When we remember the pangs of anguish which must lacerate the bears of the man or woman who see their homes broken up, their household goods scattered, their children thrown houseless and homeless upon the mercy of the world, often beneath the rigours of winter, and then remember that more than three millions of our fellow-beings have been subject to this inhuman treatment at the hands of their fellow-countrymen, the Irish landlord class, that a million and a quarter human beings, women and children, made, we are told, by an Almighty Creator in his own divine image, have actually died of the most horrible deaths we can conceive of, the death by slow starvation; when we remember this we begin to grasp the central fact of the socialist position, that all questions of political freedom, of religious equality, of national glory take of necessity a minor and a very subordinate position beside the question of social justice, which in its last analysis means how best to secure to the labourer the fruits of his labour.

To speak of any form of Home Rule as a remedy for such evils is but

---

3   Michael George Mulhall (1836-1900), Irish author, statistician, economist and newspaper editor.

4   "The present reign has been the most disastrous since that of Elizabeth, as the following statistics show:—Died of famine 1,225,000; Persons evicted 3,668,000; Number of emigrants 4,186,000." Michael G. Mulhall. *Fifty Years of National Progress 1837-1887*. (London, 1887), 114.

to mock as with Dead Sea fruit[5] the victims of our unjust social system. All through the long continued reign of hunger which has marked modern Irish history, Ireland has continually exported more food than is sufficient to support a far larger population than she bears upon her surface. She exported this vast amount of foodstuffs while her sons and daughters were perishing of hunger, not because her Parliament sat at Westminster instead of College Green, but because the land of Ireland was held, not by the people for their own welfare but for a landlord class for the sake of plunder they might extract from the Irish people. If the Union had never been enacted the presence of the Irish legislature at College Green would not have sufficed to save the Irish people, unless they had been inspired with totally different and more democratic ideas than those which inspire our present representatives. Everyone of our political parties at present seem to hold the belief they do their duty when they attack any individual case of landlord tyranny, and are, therefore, free to support the system of private property which makes that tyranny possible.

As agriculture, the staple industry of Ireland, like every other industry, is conducted really in the interests of the privileged few as a matter of private gain, and not at all in order to serve the people, and as it is this false conception of property which lies at the root of Irish misery, so that change in the social system which shall abolish a society founded upon property, and replace it by a society founded upon justice, which shall abolish the landlord and the serf, the capitalist and the drudge, the prince and the pauper, the millionaire, and the outcast, which shall relegate to the limbo of exploded superstitions all the monarchical, aristocratic and financial castes which thrive so luxuriantly upon our Irish soil, which shall make the maintenance of all its own people the first concern of statesmanship the paramount public service and public duty, this change will be, in economics, the revolution we work for. This is Socialism. The scientific revolutionist is, then, a Republican in politics, because he wishes to win for his country her invaluable heritage—independence; he is a socialist because he wishes to base that independence upon the broadest possible foundations a free nation can rest upon—the recognition of equality among its citizens, the establishment of justice in its social

---

5   Something that appears to be beautiful or full of promise but is in reality nothing but illusion and disappointment. "Like Dead Sea fruits, that tempt the eye, / But turn to ashes on the lips!" Thomas Moore, *Lalla Rookh: an Oriental Romance* (London, 1817), 222.

relations, the perfection of democracy as its political ideal. But the utopian revolutionists, who include among their number nearly all the public men in Ireland, have other ideas on the question of Ireland's misery, and other so-called remedies.

We have already glanced at Home Rule, let us next consider some other ideas outside the actual region of politics. To begin with technical education. Perhaps on no question is there greater unanimity than on this. From every platform and in every public pronouncement of our leaders, lay and ecclesiastical, we are told of what technical education can do for the Irish people. We are informed that Germany has educated all her people in this manner, and as a consequence is assuming control of the markets of the world. Let us do likewise, educate our children on technical matters, and we will accomplish the same result as Germany.

This seems very plausible, but is nevertheless absurd.

Technical education benefits Germany commercially because she alone possesses it as a nation; the day on which the other civilised nations of the world possess technical education also, on that day it ceases to be of special benefit to Germany, or to any other country. In this respect it resembles elementary education. Fifty years ago a workman possessing an education as good as the average man in this room was a rarity, and today as a result educated workers are a [drug?] in the market, a clerk can be got for less than a hod carrier, and we have B.A.'s acting as bootblacks, and D.Sc.'s carrying sandwich boards. It will take at least a generation before we can realise the benefit of technical education, and when that generation has elapsed every other nation in Europe will be technically educated also, there will, in consequence, be no benefits to realise.

Certain other reformers pin their faith to land bills fixing what is known as fair rent. But a fair rent is as impossible economically as it is absurd historically. It is impossible economically because the competition of American farmers is continually depressing the price of agricultural products, and, as although the nominal rent may be stationary, the real rent varies with every fluctuation in agricultural prices, it constantly happens that the fluctuations of the market convert the fair rent of the land court into a terrible engine of oppression. It is absurd historically because the land of Ireland has only passed into the hands of the landlord class by virtue of Acts the most infamous recorded in history, and the rents claimed by its present owners from the occupiers of the soil in town and country are but the latter-day equivalent for the tribute exacted at the point of the sword.

Rent paid to a private individual is, of necessity, an unjust tax upon honest industry, and a fair rent is as absurd an expression as an honest burglary. Peasant proprietary also finds favour with a large number of people, but in view of the statement of the greatest agricultural authority in these islands that five-sixths of our Irish farms yielded no economic rent valuation, peasant proprietary may also be classed as utopian. Economic rent in the sense in which he employed the term meant the surplus produce of a farm, after provision had been made for the support of the people who tilled it. If five-sixths of the farms in Ireland yielded no such surplus, then the most peasant proprietary would do would be to provide the farmer with a hand-to-mouth existence in times of prosperity, and in times of agricultural depression to provide fresh victims for those financial leeches we call moneylenders. This has been the case in France; we have every reason to believe it would be so in Ireland also.

Some other fervent Nationalists are continually reminding us of the sudden development of industry which took place under Grattan's Parliament, and prophesying similar happy results for our country with the return of our native legislature, as they somewhat facetiously style that abortive product of political intrigue—Home Rule. But in reality the sudden bound of prosperity in the period in question was almost solely due to the fact of the introduction of mechanical power and the consequent cheapening of manufacturing goods. It was the era of the industrial revolution, when the domestic industries we had inherited from the middle ages were finally replaced by the factory system of modern times. The water frame invented by Arkwright in 1769, the spinning-jenny patented by Merrygrews in 1770, Crampton's mechanical mule, introduced in 1779, and the application in 1788 of the steam engine to blast furnaces, all combined to cheapen the cost of production and lower the selling price of every article in the various industries affected.[6] This immediately brought into the field fresh hosts of consumers and so gave an enormous fillip to trade in general, every section of the community benefiting from the increased prosperity of the manufacturing classes.

---

6   See "Socialist Economics," *Edinburgh Evening News*, 12 February 1894.

In the years between 1782 and 1803 the cotton trade more than trebled itself, and between 1783 and 1796 the linen trade nearly trebled itself, and in the eight years from 1788 to '96 the iron trade doubled in volume. The latter trade had at one time occupied an important position among Irish industries, but did not long outlive this sudden burst of prosperity. The invention of smelting by coal instead of by wood in 1750, and the application of steam to blasting furnaces, already spoken of, had placed the Irish manufacturers at an enormous disadvantage in competing with his English rival, but in the halcyon days between 1780 and 1800 this was not very acutely felt. When, however, trade once more assumed its normal aspect of keen competition, Ireland, without a native coal supply and entirely dependent on imported English coal, found it impossible to compete with her better situated rival, who, with abundant supplies of coal at their own door, found it very easy before the days of railways to undersell and ruin the unfortunate Irishmen. The same fate, and for the same reason, overtook the other important Irish industries. The period we have spoken of as marked politically by Grattan's Parliament was a period of commercial inflation due to the introduction of mechanical improvements into the staple industries of our country; as long as such machinery was worked by hand Ireland could maintain her place on the market, but with the introduction of steam to the service of industry, which began on a small scale in 1788, and the introduction of the power-loom, which first came into general use about 1813, the immense natural advantage of an indigenous coal supply finally settled the contest in favour of England and effected the ruin of Irish manufacturers.

A whole paper, much larger than this one, might be written upon this question alone, but I think I have said enough to prove my point—that the national prosperity of Ireland during this period was due to a concentration of circumstances, never likely to occur again, operating quite independently of any action on the part of the College Green collection of needy place-hunters and aristocratic nominees whom the arms of the Volunteers frightened for a few years into a simulation of public decency.

A native legislature might have hindered the subsequent decay as an alien parliament might have hastened it, but the process was one of the most significant signs. The *report of the Commission of the financial relations between Great Britain and Ireland* furnished the last rallying cry of the utopian reformers.[7] Ireland is overtaxed to the extent of £3,000,000 per annum, says the report.[8] "Here," cry the utopians, "is the cause of Irish discontent, here is the excuse for the Irish agitation, here is the cause of Irish misery." A most sapient conclusion, truly. The population is at present over four millions. For the purposes of easy calculations let us say three millions. Over-taxation to the extent of three millions on a population of three million people is equal to twenty shillings a head per annum, twenty shillings per head is less than sixpence per week, sixpence per week is less than a penny per day; so that we are asked to believe that over-taxation to the extent of less than a penny per head per day has made all the difference between Irish happiness and Irish misery, Irish loyalty, and Irish rebellion. Ireland is overtaxed, let us all admit, but attaching undue importance to that fact only serves the purpose of those who wish to draw a red herring across the track of real reform.

After this brief glance at the proposals of reform most in popular favour today, it behooves me now to indicate what I consider the scientific basis of the revolutionary party whose ideal I have before outlined.

I start with the important postulate that no British Parliament is ever likely to enact a series of reforms necessary to make that ideal of Irish freedom possible. Self-interest bars the way. For the same reason no British Parliament is ever likely to pass any measure of Home Rule as would enable the Irish people to obtain these desired conditions for themselves, British rule in Ireland, in other words, the power of the Imperial Government, is now, as in the past, the great barrier which lies across the path to Irish freedom. This we freely admit, in conjunction with all far-seeing and honest nationalists. Further, we are prepared to concede the point, if only in order to narrow the field for discussion, that Ireland is not able to bring into the field any insurrectionary force sufficiently strong to make headway against the government. This island is so small, and the railway and telegraph system so effective, that within a few hours of the receipt of the news at Dublin Castle a practically overwhelming force could be

---

7   *Final Report by Her Majesty's Commissioners Appointed to Inquire into the Financial Relations between Great Britain and Ireland* (1896).

8   "If the proportion of revenue to be raised from Ireland is to be regulated solely by a reference to a "taxable capacity" of the two countries the proportion of 1/20th appears to me to be fair, and on this assumption Ireland may be said to be overtaxed at the present time to the extent of nearly 2 ¾ millions annually." Report by Sir David Barbour in *Final Report*, 119-120.

concentrated upon any district in which rebellion on the old lines might be contemplated.

The political and military system of Great Britain is, indeed, one of the strongest in the world for ensuring rapidity of action in times of an emergency. I would ask you, however, to transfer your attention for a time from the military and political structure of the British Empire to the social and economic basis upon which that structure rests. It is absolutely essential for the purpose of obtaining a clear insight into the position of any movement that those who engage in it may know exactly the power and the weakness of the forces arrayed against them. The British Empire we find to be, in the last analysis, a capitalistic power whose interests are inextricably bound up with the present social system, rising and falling with the success or failure of the individualist experiment in civil government and social order.

The ruling idea of this individualist system, as expressed in the teachings of what is called the Manchester School of Political Economy[9], may be stated as the theory that wealth consists in the accumulation of commodities or articles which can be exchanged for current coin of the realm. Thus a nation which, like Ireland, Spain or Portugal, produces its own food and feeds its own people, is still considered a poor country if it possesses no manufacturers; while a nation which, like England, does possess manufacturers, is regarded as a rich, wealthy country, even although absolutely dependent for food upon other soils than her own, British statesmen adopting this theory, viz., the perfection and development of the capitalist system within their shores.

To such an extent has this been carried that agriculture has been entirely neglected, and the national dependence on manufactures so far increased that at present the population of Great Britain for nine whole months in the year is absolutely dependent for daily bread upon the agricultural produce of other countries—America, Australia, Russia or Ireland.

Now consider:

---

9   A political and economic school of thought led by Richard Cobden (1804-1865) and John Bright (1811-1889) that promoted free trade, free competition, and freedom of contract. Arose out of meetings of the Manchester Chamber of Commerce in 1820.

(1) agricultural produce to England, because the manufacturers of that country enable its people to pay a good price for the food thus imported;

(2) when they are no longer able to pay for it it will no longer be imported;

(3) if they had not their manufactures they would not be able to pay for it.

Therefore not only the power but the very life of England and its people depend under the present system on the maintenance of her industrial supremacy; but that supremacy is rapidly becoming a thing of the past.

This is the one universally recognised fact today—England, which at the close of the Napoleonic wars, was practically in undisputed control of the markets of the world, is steadily being driven from those markets by her foreign rivals, and can hardly hold her own, even in the home market. Belgium and Germany have successfully invaded the iron market, Russia now produces her own coal, India places her linen in competition with the product of the Ferringher, and China and Japan are quietly taking possession of the cotton trade.

There are a few figures which will help to convey to your minds the enormous growth of trade in Japan, and when you remember that in all the articles produced by Japan she is entering into direct opposition with Great Britain, you will realise what fate has in store for that country. According to an article in the *Indian Daily News*, and quoted from Japanese official reports, the production of textile fabrics in that country increased between 1885 and 1895 from the value of 511,900 dollars to 22,177,626 dollars, or, in other words, it multiplied itself not twice or thrice, but forty times. And in the production of cotton umbrellas multiplied itself four hundred and ten times. Vases and other cheap curios rose from two millions to over eleven millions. [10] This in the staple industries—cotton,

10   "Textiles rose from $511,900 to $22,177,626, matting from $935 to $3,461,369. In the ten years under contemplation the export of cotton umbrellas, those twelve-anna luxuries with which the maidan is dotted at every shower, was multiplied *four hundred and ten times*, and the total value of the 'Satsuma' and Kaga vases and other cheap curios, which the China Bazaar offers to smarten modest Calcutta house-keeping, went up from over two million dollars to over eleven million." "Japanese Competition," *Indian Daily News*, 3 September 1896, 10.

linen, and iron. British supremacy is doomed, while in the production of articles of household use and adornment the handwriting on the wall can already be seen in the words, "Made in Germany", written, printed, or stamped on the majority of such articles used in English, Scotch or Irish homes.

The words of the great English Free Trader, Cobden,[11] written many years ago, indicate with almost prophetical accuracy what the result will be. "When the time comes," he said, "that some other nation is able to produce cotton or linen goods cheaper than England can, then thither to that nation will the trade of the world fly though it were to the uttermost ends of the earth, and the cities and towns of Great Britain will be as deserted as are the streets of Tyre and Carthage today."[12] Well, this time has now arrived, and cheaper products of another nation are already in the market, the commercial glory of England is already on the wane, and before the present generation shall have run its course the industrial supremacy of Great Britain, and, perhaps, the British Empire itself will only be a historical tradition as anything human can be, that upon the knowledge and temper of that class will hinge the future of civilisation.

If there is in existence a socialist party strong, resolute, and alive to its opportunities and commanding public respect and confidence, I do not see what can prevent it seizing upon the reins of power and guiding the peoples from the treacherous deeps of individualism into the sheltering harbour of social democracy; but, on the other hand, if when the crisis comes, as come it will, perhaps like a bolt from the blue, the people are found still trusting in the illusory theories of capitalist economy, then I know of nothing short of a miracle which will suffice to save civilisation from destruction at the hands of those barbarians within our gates, the myriads of degraded labourers, whom the exigencies of commercialism has gathered together in our towns and cities, and who will not long starve in quiet or stay their hands from vengeance on the society which has lured them to their ruin.

For civilisation the choice will lie between a bold forward move into socialism, or a relapse back into the horrors of barbarism, when art and literature and science have been swept away, or have as little meaning to

---

11   Richard Cobden of the Manchester school of political economy.

12   I have not been able to find the source of this quote.

men as the glories of Maeven (the warrior queen of Ulster) have to the present-day tenants of our Dublin slums.[13] The scientific Irish revolutionist, then, derives his confidence in future victory from his knowledge that there are working in the very bosom of the commercial system from which his enemy derives his power, certain forces which in due time will lay in ruins the system which has called them into play, and which in the act of doing so will also prostrate that British Empire, the political reflex and most perfect embodiment of the lowest and meanest phase of human slavery that ever disgraced this old earth of ours. He lays no stress whatever on the national ill-will which the party organs of France or Germany or Russia may manifest against England. He knows too well that the anti-English shrieks of foreign newspapers today may be exchanged for the diplomatic kiss of peace tomorrow, and knowing this he resolves to rely only on the brave hearts and active brains of his own fellow-countrymen, convinced that a nation which cannot work out its own redemption is not fit for the responsibility of freedom.

At the street corner, in the lecture hall, through the press, wherever tongue or pen can convey a message he labours incessantly to inspire his fellows with his hopes and ideas, and the ballot-boxes will sum his victories or record his defeats as he presses unweariedly onward in his task of gathering the democracy beneath the revolutionary banner, so when the oppressors' power is in its last struggle with the economic forces which will sink its power beneath the historical horizon, a united nation may know its strength and seize the propitious moment to lift up amid the acclaim of democracy the world over the glorious sunburst of Irish Freedom.

---

13   "As things stand today capitalist civilization cannot continue; we must either move forward into socialism or fall back into barbarism," Karl Kautsky, *The Class Struggle (Erfurt Program)* (Chicago: Charles H. Kerr, 1910), 118. First published in German in 1892 and translated into English by Daniel de Leon in 1894 for *The People* (New York).

*****

IRELAND'S ADDRESS TO THE WORKING CLASS IRISH OF AMERICA[1]
THE PEOPLE (NEW YORK)
26 SEPTEMBER, 1897, P.1

To THE WORKING-CLASS IRISH OF AMERICA, GREETING:

The publication in the United States, under the imprint and by the authority of an American political party, of a pamphlet originally published in Ireland, and dealing with the social and political conditions of the latter country, marks, we venture to hope, the beginning of a new era in our international politics.

The history of the great American Republic, from the date on which the first general Congress of the United States addressed from Philadelphia their message to the people of Ireland asking the sympathy of that people, until the present day, has been a subject of the most intense interest and pride to Irishmen in general. This pride has, to a large extent, arisen from the fact that multitudes of Irishmen have contributed by their valor and genius to build up, and, when built, to safeguard the liberties of the Republic. Whereas our countrymen, in the service of the continental powers of Europe, sank to the position of hired mercenaries of foreign despots, as often suppressing liberty as fighting for it, in the United States our exiles of the working class have, on the whole, been, or meant to be the champions of freedom.

It is but fitting, therefore, that when the people of America are just

1   "Address from this party to working class Ireland in the States. Address prepared and read by comrade Connolly—it was unanimously adopted." Entry for 2 September 1897, *Minute book of the Irish Socialist Republican Party, Dublin, containing many entries by James Connolly, secretary, 29th May 1896 to 18th September 1898*, Ms. 16, 295, William O'Brien Collection, National Library of Ireland, Dublin.

beginning to realize that a more deadly foe to their liberties than any encountered by their fathers has established itself in their midst, and when the shadow of the impending and inevitable conflict between that foe and the champions of human freedom already gathers upon the horizon, the working class at home should desire to gain the ear of their compatriots in America in order to point out the absolute identity of the ideal sought after by the Socialist Labor Party of the United States with that hope which, vague and undefined, fired the imagination of Irish poets and martyrs in the past, and which, at last is clearly and definitely expressed, finds its place in the programme of the Irish Socialist Republican Party today. This identity once realized, the Irish working class in America will, it is to be hoped, awake to the fact that no stronger blow could be struck for the liberties of "the old land" than will be given on the day when a majority of the electorate of the United States vote for the installation of a socialist administration, pledged to uproot that last and meanest form of human slavery, the wage system of capitalism.

The international effect of such action will be best understood by Irishmen when it is remembered that, according to the report of a Judiciary Committee to the fifty-first Congress of the United States, no less than 21,000,000 acres of the soil of that country are at present in possession of titled aliens—members principally of the British and Irish aristocracy; and of the United States railroad and land bonds over 100,000,000 acres are likewise owned by the vulture investing classes of the same British Empire.[2]

How deeply those hereditary enemies of the Irish people, the English governing classes, are interested in the maintenance of the capitalist system in America is further daily illustrated by the "sympathetic" response of the London Stock Exchange to every rise and fall on Wall Street, by the unconcealed delight of the English capitalist press at every reverse of the working class movement in America (as in the case of McKinley) and by their persistent and successful attempts to inoculate the upper-class circles of American society with a desire to reproduce on American soil the political and social conditions peculiar to monarchical countries

---

2   The appendix to the US edition of *Erin's Hope* says: "...and of the United States railroad stocks and bonds and other American securities to the value of over $1,000,000,000 are likewise, according to the statements of well-informed financial writers, owned by the vulture investing classes of the same British Empire."

such as Great Britain.

The only measure which can effectually checkmate this conspiracy against the liberties of America, and at the same time lay broad and deep the foundations of Irish freedom, is socialism. The Socialist Labor Party carries its banner in America as the Irish Socialist Republican Party does in Ireland. Given the triumph of the one and the other is within sight of its goal.

Working class Irish of America, rally to the support of the only American political party which, recognizing that the interests of the oppressed are the same the world over, aids the revolutionary working class party of Ireland to spread a knowledge of its doctrines among the scattered children of the Clan-na-Gael.

*   *   *

AN APPEAL OF THE IRISH SOCIALIST REPUBLICAN PARTY TO THE WORKING CLASS IRISH OF AMERICA[3]
APPENDIX TO *ERIN'S HOPE*, US EDITION, DECEMBER 1897[4]

DUBLIN, SEPTEMBER 15, 1897

The publication in the United States, under the imprint and by the authority of an American political party, of a pamphlet originally published in Ireland, and dealing with the social and political conditions of the latter country, marks, we venture to hope, the beginning of a new era in our international politics.

The history of the great American Republic, from the date on which

_____

3   This article is a slightly revised/updated version of "Ireland's Address to the Working Class Irish of America," *The People* (New York), 26 September, 1897. Both are reproduced here for comparative purposes.

4   "The pamphlet *Erin's Hope*, with an appendix containing a call of the Irish Socialist Republican Party to the working class Irish of America and a call of the National Executive Committee SLP to our Irish fellow workers, is now ready, and orders can be filled at short notice. Price for single copies five cents. Discount to dealers and for larger quantities." *The People* (New York), 19 December 1897, 4.

the first general Congress of the United States addressed from Philadelphia their message to the people of Ireland asking the sympathy of that people, until the present day, has been a subject of the most intense interest and pride to Irishmen. This pride has, to a large extent, arisen from the fact that multitudes of Irishmen have contributed by their valor and genius to build up, and, when built, to safeguard the liberties of the Republic. Whereas our countrymen, in the service of the continental powers of Europe, sank to the position of hired mercenaries of foreign despots, as often suppressing liberty as fighting for it, in the United States our exiles of the working class have, on the whole, been, or meant to be the champions of freedom.

But the people of America are just beginning to realize that a more deadly foe to their liberties than any encountered by their fathers has established itself in their midst. The shadow of the impending and inevitable conflict between that foe and the champions of human freedom already gathers upon the horizon. It is but fitting, therefore, that the working class at home should desire to gain the ear of their compatriots in America in order to point out the absolute identity of the ideal sought after by the Socialist Labor Party of the United States with that hope which, vague and undefined, fired the imagination of Irish poets and martyrs in the past, and which at last is clearly and definitely expressed in the programme of the Irish Socialist Republican Party today. This identity once realized, the Irish working class in America will, it is to be hoped, awake to the fact that no stronger blow could be struck for the liberties of "the old land" than will be given on the day when a majority of the electorate of the United States vote for the installation of a Socialist administration, pledged to uproot that last and meanest form of human slavery, the wage system of capitalism.

The international effect of such action will be best understood by Irishmen when it is remembered that, according to the report of a Judiciary Committee to the Fifty-first Congress of the United States, no less than 21,000,000 acres of the soil of that country are at present in possession of titled aliens—members principally of the British and Irish aristocracy; while United States railroad stocks and bonds and other American securities to the value of over $1,000,000,000 are likewise, according to the statements of well-informed financial writers, owned by the vulture investing classes of the same British Empire.

How deeply those hereditary enemies of the Irish people, the English governing classes, are interested in the maintenance of the capitalist system in America is further daily illustrated by the "sympathetic" response of the London Stock Exchange to every rise and fall on Wall Street; by the unconcealed delight of the English press at every reverse of the working class movement in America; by their shrieks of joy upon the triumphs of undisguised reaction in American politics, and by their persistent and successful attempts to inoculate the upper-class circles of American society with a desire to reproduce on American soil the political and social conditions peculiar to monarchical countries such as Great Britain.

The only measure which can effectually checkmate this conspiracy against the liberties of America, and at the same time lay broad and deep the foundations of Irish freedom, is socialism. The Socialist Labor Party carries its banner in America as the Irish Socialist Republican Party does in Ireland. Given the triumph of the one and the other is within sight of its goal.

Working class Irish of America, rally to the support of the only American political party which, recognizing that the interests of the oppressed are the same the world over, aids the revolutionary working class party of Ireland to spread a knowledge of its doctrines among the scattered children of the Clan-na-Gael.

*****

INTRODUCTION TO '98 READINGS
DECEMBER 1897[1]

The series of '98 Readings which commence with this issue will, in no sense, aspire to present to the readers a philosophical or critical *resume* of the great revolutionary movement of the United Irishmen. Indeed, the Editor, so far from obtruding his own views upon the reader, will rather seek to suppress himself, and allow the men of '98 to present in their own language the principles and ideas which animated them; and to recapitulate the deeds which have made their name and memory so dear to every friend of Freedom. The reasons for taking such an unusual course are such as the thoughtful reader will, no doubt, appreciate. It is, perhaps, a misfortune that almost all popular histories of Ireland have been written by men who were themselves prominently identified with some particular phase of the public life of their country, and who were, therefore, insensibly constrained to write Irish history, from the peculiar standpoint of the particular party to which they themselves belonged. In consequence, when reading the history of our country, we are scarcely ever allowed to forget the personality of the writer, but are constantly recalled from studying the movements of the past, and plunged afresh in the controversies of today by our endeavour to appraise at their proper value, the meaning and significance of that interpretation of history revealed by the comments of our historians on the events they record. The politician turned historian can scarcely avoid making his statement of

---

1   The *Freeman's Journal* for 15 December 1897 (page 7) states: "the [Executive Council of the '98 Centenary Committee] desired to direct attention to the announcement that "'98 Readings" would be published at one penny each fortnightly, and would consist of articles from the *Press* newspaper, and might be ordered from the editor at 67 Middle Abbey Street.'" A copy of the pamphlet (LO P 69) in the National Library of Ireland has '1897' written on it in pencil.

history a long drawn-out justification of the course pursued by the political party of which he is a member, and so, whilst it may be, believing implicitly in his own impartiality, unconsciously colours his narrative to endorse his opinions. But it is the aim of this publication to present to the people of Ireland a complete picture of the men and ideas of one hundred years ago, and although the Editor might feel a longing to describe in his own language the period dealt with, he recognises that the same influences which prejudicially affect the efforts of other historians to give an impartial narrative of modern Irish history, operate no less powerfully upon himself. Therefore, the plan of reproducing all the best available literary material of the stirring period culminating in the "Great Rebellion," exactly as it issued from the hands of its authors, has been adopted as the one most likely to please all parties in the Ireland of today.

The Editor says in effect:—Here are the materials, here are the intellectual products and military achievements of the United Irish movement told by the actors on both sides in that great drama, now let every man construct therefrom his own theory of history. Every available source will be laid under contribution for that purpose. As there can be no pretence of originality in reprinting historical documents, if we utilise the works of other collectors, it is not in the spirit of plagiarism, but with an honest desire to popularise a knowledge of the result of their researches. Use will be made from the *Press* newspaper (the Dublin organ of the United Irishmen), songs and ballad sheets in use among the people, manifestos and addresses issued by the United Irishmen, and addresses from other reform organizations, official despatches and patriotic accounts of the battles of the Rebellion, speeches by leading Irishmen on the state of Ireland, reports of the Secret Committees of the House of Lords and Commons, and many other sources. As far as possible each reprint will be published in its due order in point of time. For instance, the various versions of the battles of the Rebellion will be issued on the centennial of the battle itself. It is to be hoped every patriotic Irishman will assist in bringing the work under the notice of his friends and fellow countrymen.

In conclusion, before finally leaving the explanatory stage of his work and assuming the more mechanical functions he has allotted himself, the Editor desires to point out that the mere fact that it is not yet possible to speak or write of '98 without arousing a host of stormy passions, hopes and fears, proves indubitably that the cause which produced such a host of apostles and martyrs in that fateful year is ***not yet a lost cause***; and is not regarded as such, either by friends or enemies.

*****

THE RIGHT TO LIFE AND THE RIGHTS OF PROPERTY[1]
(MAUD GONNE AND JAMES CONNOLLY)[2]
MAY 1898[3]

'The use of all things is to be common to all. It is an injustice to say this belongs to me, that to another. Hence the origin of contentions among men.'
—HIS HOLINESS POPE CLEMENT I

'God created all things that their enjoyment might be common to all, and that the earth might become the common possession of all. Only unjust usurpation has created the right of private property.'
—BISHOP AMBROSIUS

'Let them know that the earth from which they sprung, and of which they are formed, belongs to all men in common, and that therefore the fruits which the earth brings forth must belong without distinction to all.'
—HIS HOLINESS POPE GREGORY THE GREAT, 600 A.D.

'It is an age of social battlings for justice to all men, for the right of all men to live in frugal comfort, becoming rational creatures, to all of whom birth into the world gives title to a sufficiency of the things of the world.'
—ARCHBISHOP IRELAND AT BALTIMORE (see *Catholic Times*, November 3,

---

1   "The right to life and the rights of property," LO P 114 (45), National Library of Ireland, Dublin. The text was republished, with minor changes, in *Workers' Republic*, 17 September 1898, 7. The original version is reproduced here.

2   Although published under Maud Gonne's name, the leaflet was co-written with Connolly. "Connolly was perturbed about the famine. He had terrible reports from Kerry. The people must be roused to save themselves and not die as in 1847. That evening we drafted a leaflet. "The Rights of Life and the Rights of Property."' Maud Gonne, *The Autobiography of Maud Gonne: A Servant of the Queen* (Chicago: University of Chicago Press, 1995), 239. Gonne slightly misremembered the original title.

3   "Received... The Right of Life and the Rights of Property," *Labour Leader*, 7 May 1898, 154.

1893)

'In case of extreme need of food all goods become common property.'
—CARDINAL MANNING

'If rulers exact from their subjects... anything by use of force against justice, it is robbery like the doings of highwaymen. Hence (St) Augustine says, "Justice apart, what are kingdoms but organised brigandage?"'

—ST THOMAS AQUINAS (*Summa Theologica*)

F ELLOW COUNTRYMEN—at the present juncture, when the shadow of famine is already blighting the lives of so many amongst us, when famine itself in all its grim horror has already began to claim its victims; when the cry for food for the starving Irish people is once more arising to the heavens; we desire to offer a few words of calm advice to those amongst you in whose homes the pinch of starvation is actually present, in hopes that we may move you to action before it is too late; and in order to point out to you your duty, whether as fathers or sons, as husbands, or as Irishmen.

In the year 1847 our people died in thousands of starvation, although every ship leaving an Irish port was laden with food in abundance. The Irish people in that awful year might have seized that food, cattle, corn, and all manner of provisions before it reached the seaports, have prevented the famine, and saved their country from ruin—but did not do so, believing such action to be sinful, and dreading to peril their souls to save their bodies. But in this belief, we now know, they were entirely mistaken. The very highest authorities on the doctrine of the Church agree that no *human* law can stand between starving people and their *right to food*, including the right to take that food whenever they find it, openly or secretly, with or without the owner's permission. His Holiness Pope Leo XIII has lately recommended the writings of St. Thomas Aquinas as the very best statement of Catholic Doctrine on faith and morals.

Listen, then, to what St. Thomas teaches on the rights of property when opposed to the right of life. In *Summa Theologica* Question 66, article 2—he asks:

"Is it lawful to steal on the plea of necessity?"

And answers:

"The institution of human law cannot abrogate from natural law or divine law ... therefore the division and appropriation of goods that proceeds from human law cannot come in the way of man's needs being relieved out of such goods... Hence St Ambrose says 'It is the bread of the hungry that you hold back, the clothing of the naked that you keep in store, the ransom and deliverance of the unfortunate is contained in the money that you bury in the earth!... If, however, a need be so plain and pressing that clearly the urgent necessity has to be relieved from whatever comes to hand, as when danger is threatening a person and there is no other means of succouring him, *then the man may lawfully relieve his distress out of the property of another, taking it either openly or secretly.*"

"To use the property of another, taking it secretly in a case of extreme need, cannot, properly speaking, be characterised as theft, because what one takes for the support of life is much his by sheer necessity."

If this is a correct statement, and coming from such a source, we are sure you will not venture to call it in question. What is your duty to yourselves and those dependent on you? British law—always on the side of the rich against the poor—tells you to die of hunger rather than infringe the rights of property. But divine law tells you that your right to food is greater than any human law, that to die of hunger while there is food within reach is an act of suicide, and will be adjudged as such, and the common sense of humanity outside these islands stands ready to aid you, in purse of otherwise, once you show your determination to stand by your rights as men.

We ask you, then, fellow countrymen, by all you hold sacred, by your devotion to your wives and children, to your fathers and mothers and, last but not least, by your love for the poor motherland, whose hope is in you, to rouse yourselves in this awful crisis of your fate, and *be men*, and like men, take with the strong hand, if need be, that which rightfully belongs to you—the food without which the famine-stricken corpses of the poor children of the Irish race will once more bestrew the land—and show the world that you are resolved never again to let the sun shine upon the spectacle of Irish men and women dying as dogs would die—of hunger in sight of food.

*****

A WORD FOR MUNSTER
SHAN VAN VOCHT
7 FEBRUARY 1898, PP.30–31

IN A NOTE attending Dr. Sigerson's translation of a poem by Mícheál Óg Ó Longáin, as it is reprinted in a recent issue of the *Shan*, I notice an error, which, by some means, has escaped the vigilance of our usually alert and well informed editor. This is in reference to the supposed peaceful attitude of Munster during the year of rebellion, 1798. In one place it is stated that "While Ulster, Connaught, and Leinster were striving .... Munster took no part in the fray"; and in another we are treated to a recapitulation of how Munster retrieved her reputation in the next century.

This is all, to me, at least, a little incomprehensible. There is on record the account of one considerable battle fought in Munster between the King's troops and the United Irishmen, in which the rebels displayed an amount of gallantry and daring not excelled in any other province. At Ballynascarty, on the road between Clonakilty and Bandon, 220 men of the Westmeath Regiment of Militia, under the command of Lieutenant-Colonel Sir Hugh O'Reilly, and accompanied by two six-pounders, were attacked on the 19th of June by a body of 300 or 400 men, mostly armed with pikes. The troops were a trained, disciplined, and well-armed body, but so fierce was the attack and so well arranged the preparations of the insurgents that the Irish carried all before them for some time, and would undoubtedly have won the day but for the unexpected arrival on the scene of battle of another Royalist force, consisting of 100 men of the Caithness Legion, under a Major Innes. These coming up on the flank of the rebels opened fire upon them, and the two detachments of the King's forces thus uniting, the Republicans were forced to retire, as they were almost totally unprovided with firearms. This engagement took place on the 19th of June, two days before the battle of Vinegar Hill. Had it been a Republican victory it would probably have been the prelude to a general uprising throughout Cork county, as the battle of Oulart Hill (similar in many of its details) had been to the Wexford uprising. The fact that it occurred during the progress of the Wexford fight explains why the poet, Mícheál Óg Ó Longáin, could write regretfully of "Munster's Slumbers"; he being in Wexford knew nothing of the brave attempt in Cork county. But that which was pardonable in him is inexplicable on the part of people writing a century later. It might also be added in defence of Munster that, considering the difficulties which must have attended the transmission of news in those days, the fact that an attempt, and a gallant one, was made in three weeks from the time Wexford took the field speaks volumes for the spirit then animating the common people of that province.

*****

SOCYALIZM W IRLANDYI
ŚWIATŁA (LONDON)
APRIL 1898, PP. 30-34

REDAKTOR „Światła" zażądał ode mnie, bym napisał dla czytelników tego pisma krótki obraz położenia i sił naszego ruchu w Irlandyi. Rad jestem, o ile mi siły pozwolą, wypełnić to życzenie; ale czuję, że jest ono zbyt zaszczytnem dla partyi naszej, która jest tak jeszcze młodym rekrutem w międzynarodowej armii socyalistycznej, iż prawie nie może sobie rościć pretensyi do posiadania własnej historyi. Historya samej partyi naszej, tak dotąd krótka, może nie warta jest opowiadania. Ale zato szczególne położenie naszego kraju, jego stan ekonomiczny i polityczny muszą zainteresować towarzyszy naszych w Polsce, bo położenie Polski da się pod wielu względami porównać z naszem. To też postaram się dać krótki zarys dziejów Irlandyi i nauki, które my z nich wyciągnęliśmy.

Ludność Irlandyi liczą obecnie na cztery i pół miliona. Olbrzymia większość tej ludności zajęta jest pracą rolniczą. Przemysłu fabrycznego w kraju naszym właściwie niema, z wyjątkiem niektórych okolic północnej prowincyi Ulster i wschodniej prowincyi Leinster.

Irlandya jest pod rządem angielskim już od 700 lat, a w ciągu tego czasu kraj nasz był widownią prawie ciągłych wojen części irlandczyków przeciwko rządom najezdniczym. Aż do 1649 roku wojny te były prowadzone nie tylko przeciwko władzy politycznej Anglii, lecz i przeciwko porządkom społecznym, zaprowadzanym przez anglików. Może zdziwi polskich czytelników, że aż do 1649 r. irlandzkie porządki społeczne z wyjątkiem małego kawałka ziemi naokoło stolicy Irlandyi, Dublinu,— opierały się na gminnej, rodowej własności ziemskiej. Wódz irlandzki, chociaż uważany na dworach Francyi, Hiszpanii i Rzymu za równego panującym książętom Europy, zależał w istocie najzupełniej od woli swego ludu.

W tych częściach Irlandyi, gdzie w 500 lat po pierwszym tak zwanym podboju wielkorządcy angielscy mogli ukazać się nie inaczej, jak na czele potężnej armii, porządki społeczne, które panowały w Anglii (feudalizm), były nieznane. W takiem położeniu była większa część naszej wyspy. To też wojna z obcym najezdnikiem znaczyła tyle, co wojna z prywatną własnością ziemską. Ale gdy w 1649 r przemocą zniszczono irlandzki ustrój rodowy, znikł też społeczny charakter walk narodu irlandzkiego; nabrały one znaczenia wyłącznie politycznej walki o niepodległość. Było to w każdym razie nieuniknione. Gminna własność ziemska ustąpiłaby miejsca prywatnej własności landlordów (wielkich posiadaczy ziemskich), nawet gdyby Irlandya zachowała swą niepodległość. Stało się jednak inaczej zmiana ta nastąpiła nie przez działanie sił ekonomicznych wewnątrz kraju, lecz dzięki przemocy zewnętrznej siły zbrojnej. To też szerokie masy ludu irlandzkiego gorzko i słusznie były tem rozjątrzone. Do dziś jeszcze marzenia ludu irlandzkiego o wolności narodowej łączą się z tęsknotą do przywrócenia starożytnego sposobu władania ziemią, chociaż dziś powrót do starych porządków własności ziemskiej jest zupełnie niemożliwy.

Rozbicie ustroju rodowego naturalnie położyło kres znaczeniu wodza. Dzisiejsza irlandzka arystokracya—to potomkowie cudzoziemskich najezdców lub zdrajców kraju. Dzięki temu, kierunek wszystkimi ruchami patryotycznymi w Irlandyi dostał się do rąk wyłącznie klasy średniej—właściwej burżuazyi. Nasze ruchy patryotyczne stały się po większej części zależne od interesów burżuazyi. Czasami ci lub owi patryoci burżuazyjni, by wzbudzić zapał i zapewnić sobie poparcie wydziedziczonych mas ludu, wypowiadali w poezyi i w opowiadaniach narodowych poglądy, zbliżone do socyalizmu. Byly to poglądy na dzisiejszy ustrój społeczny podobne do zapatrywan pierwszych (utopijnych) socyalistów europejskich. Ale w okamgnienin znajdował się zaraz jakiś inny patryota burżuazyjny, który śpieszył uspokoić burżuazyę jakiemś powiedzeniem wręcz przeciwnem. Jeżeli poglądy społeczne jednego były napól-rewolucyjne, to drugi napewno wyrażał zdania zupełnie wsteczne. Jedno ładnie wyrównuje drugie, a w ten sposób chcianoby stworzyć tak zwany „ruch prawdziwie narodowy", to jest, ruch, w którym każda klasa społeczeństwa uznawałaby prawa wszystkich innych klas, w którym zarazem wszystkie klasy odkładałyby na stronę swe specyalne dążenia i połączyły się w walce narodowej przeciwko wspólnemu wrogowi—Anglii. Niema co mówić, że takie gadania oszukiwały tylko jedną klasę—klasę robotniczą. Jeżeli przestaniemy zajmować się klasowymi interesami, jeżeli przestaniemy rozpatrywać specyalne interesy różnych klas, to zyska na tem klasa posiadająca, klasa chcąca zachować swe lupy. Burżuazya może zatrzymać swe panowanie, swe zdobycze tylko wtedy, jeśli nie będziemy przyglądali się jej położeniu klasowemu, jeśli będziemy milczeli o interesach różnych klas. Jak człowiek, który doszedł do majątku przeniewierstwami i oszustwem, burżuazya niczego tak się nie obawia jak bezstronnego i ścisłego wglądania w pochodzenie jej posiadłości. To też pisma burżuazyjne i politycy burżuazyi bez ustanku starają się roznamiętniać aż do gorączki umysły klasy robotniczej w sprawach nie naruszających klasowych interesów burżuazyi. Wojna, religia, rasa, język, reformy polityczne, patriotyzm—wszystko to służy w rękach klas posiadających do odwracania uwagi robotników od burżuazyjnego ustroju społecznego, wszystko służy do oddalania przewrotu społecznego. Wszystkie te sprawy mogą kierować umysły w stronę jak najdalszą od spraw ekonomicznych, a w ten sposób opóźniać rozwój klasowej świadomości proletaryatu. Takiem jest zadanie polityki dzisiejszej Irlandzkiej Partyi Parlamentarnej, czyli Partyi Home-Rule (samorządu).

Burżuasya irlandzka oddawna uprawia taką taktykę i—przyznaćtrzeba—znalazła dla siebie w robotnikach-rodakach znakomity, podatny materyał. W ciągu ostatniego stulecia każde pokolenie w Irlandyi było świadkiem prób powstania przeciwko rządowi angielskiemu. Większość zwolenników każdego takiego spisku lub powstania pochodziła z niższych warstw ludności wiejskiej i miejskiej. A jednak pod wpływem garstki przywódców burżuazyjnych zgóry usuwano na bok wszystkie sprawy robotnicze i postanawiano, że powstańcy w razie zwycięstwa niemi zajmować się nie będą. Myślano, że takie postępowanie zapewni powstaniu pomoc wyższych klas i sprowadzi je pod sztandar rewolucyi.

Ale rezultat takiego postępowania prawie zawsze był jednakowy. Robotnicy co prawda dostarczali większość rekrutów do szeregów rewolucyjnych, większość ofiar więzienia i rusztowania; jednak cała masa robotnicza nie mogła, dzięki takiemu postępowaniu przywódców powstania, na tyle przejąć się ogniem rewolucyjnym, by poważnie zagrozić najazdowi trwającemu już 700 lat. Wszyscy robotnicy co prawda z serca chcieliby niepodległości narodowej, ale rozumieli, ile ofiar musi kosztować jej wywalczenie. Gdy zaś przywódcy powstania na dobitke wyraźnie im powtarzali, ze lud pracujący nie powinien spodziewać się nawet od zwycięskiego powstania żadnej zmiany w warunkach niewoli społecznej, to cóż dziwnego, że masa ludu robotniczego cofała się przed walką, a tylko jednostki najbardziej szlachetne i rycerskie szły do szeregów na bój nierówny i padały ofiarą zemsty wroga?

Wyższe klasy również pogardliwie głuche były na umizgi burżuazyjnych patryntów. Klasy wyższe cieszyły się własnością, ruchomą i nieruchomą. Pod opiekuńczą władzą Anglii czuły one swe posiadanie zabezpieczone, ale bynajmniej nie były pewne, jakie losy by je spotkały w razie zwycięstwa ruchu rewolucyjnego. To też wieley posiadacze ziemsey (landlordowie) stale byli wierni Anglii. Gdy poeci i marzyciele burżuazyjni roztkliwiali się nad „zgodą wszystkich stanów i wyznań", tymczasem arystokracya broniła swych prywatnych interesów przed drobnymi dzierżawcami tak nieubłaganie, że nieomal zupełnie wyludniła kraj. Doszło do tego, iż angielskie pismo burżuazyjne, londyński *Times*, oświadczył, że „imię landlorda irlandzkiego jest hańbą dla chrześcijaństwa!"

Drobna burżuazya w przeszłości dała sprawie narodowej wielu szczerych paryotów, pełnych poświęcenia. Ale wogóle niepewny to żywioł. Z jednej strony rada by ona zadowolnić swych upośledzonych rodaków i dla spokoju własnego sumienia krzyczy najgłośniej o swej niewyczerpalnej miłości dla sprawy swobody. Jednak cała klasa drobnej burżuazyi ciągle stara się skierować umysły społeczeństwa na drogę agitacyi legalnej za takiemi reformami, które by usunęły drażniące i zbyteczne wyskoki rządów angielskich urzędników, lecz nie naruszyły samych podstaw niewoli narodowej i ekonomicznej. W ten sposób w oczach nierozważnego tłumu mogą oni uchodzić za gorących patryotów. Zarazem zaś mogą korzystać ze wpływu swego, jako „przywódcy patryotyczni", na to, by potępiać wszelki poważny ruch rewolucyjny, który by od nich wymagał większych dowodów szczerości, niż hałaśliwe gardłowanie, lub większych ofiar z ich kieszeni.

W 1879 roku bardziej postępowi z chłopów, uprawiających rolę wydzierżawioną od landlordów, rozpoczęli ruch przeciwko wyzyskowi dziedziców. Był to czas dobrze wybrany, bo w rolnictwie panował wielki zastój, chętnie więc słuchano nowej ewangelii, która z początku była wygłazana z prawdziwie rewolucyjnym zapałem i silą. Ruch wzrastał wbrew oporowi duchowieństwa i burżuazyjnych polityków; wreszcie klasy te zaczęły się obawiać, że utracą swoje wpływy na lud, i dla zapobieżenia temu przyłączyły się do ruchu, stopniowo go osłabiając i studząc zapał. Wkrótce ruch rolny zupełnie stracił początkowe właściwości socyalistyczne. Po pewnym czasie wszystkie cele pierwotnych założycieli rachu spokojnie schowano do kieszeni, a wystawiono natomiast wyłącznie „Home Rule" (samorząd dla Irlandyi).

Od tego czau politycy burżuazyjni na dobre rozpanoszyli się w Irlandyi. Socyalizm aż do ostatnich czasów wywierał bardzo mały wpływ na umysły ludu irlandzkiego; znano go tylko z gazet angielskich, to też patrzano nań ze wstrętem jako na „angielski" wymysł. Robotnicze związki zawodowe są u nas coprawda rozpowszechnione, ale prowadzone są w ten sam sposób, co najbardziej zacofane ze związków angielskich. Działalność polityczna jest wyraźnie wykluczona z tych stowarzyszeń; to też członkowie ich łączą się dla walki z przedsiębiorcą w fabryce, a tymczasem we wszystkich kwestyach politycznych poza murami fabryki idą posłusznie za tym samym kapitalistą. Związki te dążą tylko do drobnych polepszeń losu, robotniczego, ale uważają cały ustrój dzisiejszy za wiecznie trwały, niezmordowanie więc zapewniają o swej dbałości o interesy kapitalisty i o chęci utrzymania „zgody między kapitałem a pracą."

Takie jest położenie Irlandyi, w której na początku 1896 roku Irlandzka Socyalistyczna Partya Republikanska rozpoczęła propagandę. Partyę tę założyło kilku robotników, którzy przyjęli zasady socyalizmu, ogłoszone przez Marksa i Engelsa. Rozpoczęto walkę słowem i pismen, które pomimo olbrzymich trudności już zdążyły głęboko wpłynąć na umysły ludu i zapewne w blizkiej przyszłości zupełnie zmienią polityczne położenia Irlandyi.

Treść nauki, z którą partya nasza zwróciła się do ludu irlandzkiego, jest następująca:

Wsystkie poprzednie ruchy patryotyczne w nowoczesnej historyi irlandakiej dążyły li tylko do zniesienia lub zmian rządu angielskiego w Irlandyi. Ale właśnie dzięki rządom angielskim w Irlandyi klasy, które zrabowały ziemię naszych przodków, zabezpieczyły sobie posiadanie nieprawnych łupów. Dziś zaś rząd angielski jest jedyną materyalną gwarancyą, zapewninjącą naszej burżuazyi jej panowanieklasowe klasowe i epokój w wysyskiwaniu pracy. Jedyną zatem klasą, zdolną do ruchu rewolucyjnego, jest klasa robotnicza. Ale klasa robotnicza, chcąc utrzymać swą energię rewolucyjną, musi pozbyć się wszelkich związków z partyami burżuazyjnemi. Może zaś to uczynić, jednie organizując się w klasową, partyę polityczną, w Socyalistyczną Partyę Republikańską. Działalność tej partyi prędko zapędai wszystkie żywioły zacofane do jednego obozu, do obozu zwolenników dzisiejszych porządków zarówno politycznych jak i społecznych. Socyalizm może byé urzeczywistniony tylko wtedy, gdy klasa robotnicza ujmie w swoje ręce ster rządu i przeprowadzi swą wolę zgodnie z prawami rozwoju ekonomicznego. To też pierwszym krokiem do zwycięstwa—jak to uznają wszyscy zwolennicy socyalizmu naukowego—jest zdobycie władzy rządowej—jeśli można—w drodze pokojowej, jeśli trzeba—siła.

Stąd wypływa potrzeba organizowania i kształcenia klasy robotniczej, by z zupełną świadomością swego powołania dziejowego mogła ona zająć w Irlandyi wszystkie stanowiska obieralne. Będzie to krokiem przedwstępnym do ujęcia w swe ręce samej władzy rządowej i zastąpienia rządów cudzoziemskich urzędników przez zorganizowane siły irlandzkiej demokracyi.

Przekonani jesteśmy, iż taka polityka jest w najzupełniejszej zgodzie ze wszystkiemi dążeniami ludu irlandzkiego, a zarazem opiera się na zasadach walki klasowej, na zasadach, których zastosowanie pozwoliło partyom socyalistycznym całego świata przezwyciężyć wszystkie przeszkody, obalić wszystkie zawady i dojść do stanowiska dzisiejszego, z którego blisko już widać cel naszego ruchu.

Wreszcie chciałbym w imieniu swych towarzyszy zapewnić braci polaków, że dążenie Irlandzkiej Socyalistycznej Partyi Republikańskiej do niepodległości narodowej Irlandyi bynajmniej nie wypływa z szowinizmu (źle zrozumianego patryotyzmu, nienawiści narodowej) lub wrogich uczuć względem angielskiej klasy robotniczej. Nie, do niepodległości Irlandyi dążymy dlatego, że jesteśmy przekonani, iż ruch robotniczy międzynarodowy musi zarazem organizować się narodowo i odpowiadać charakterowi i uczuciom narodowym.

ENGLISH TRANSLATION

The editor of *Light* has asked me to write its readers a brief account of the position and strength of our movement in Ireland. I am happy, if my strength allows me, to fulfil this wish; but I feel that it is too honourable for our party, which is still such a young recruit in the international socialist army that it can hardly claim to have a history of its own. The history of our party, which remains rather brief, is perhaps not worth telling. But the particular situation of our country, its economic and political state, must be of interest to our comrades in Poland, because Poland's situation can be compared with ours in many respects. I will therefore try to give a brief outline of Irish history and the lessons we have learned from it.

The population of Ireland now stands at four and a half million. The vast majority of this population is engaged in agricultural work. There is virtually no factory industry in the country, except in some areas of the northern province of Ulster and the eastern province of Leinster.

Ireland has been under English rule for 700 years, and during that time our country has been witness to almost constant wars by a section of Irish people against the invading governments. Until 1649, these wars were fought not only against England's rulers, but also against the social order established by the English. It may come as a surprise to Polish readers that until 1649 the Irish social orders with the exception of a small piece of land around the Irish capital, Dublin, were based on communal, ancestral land ownership. The Irish chieftain, although regarded at the courts of France, Spain and Rome as equal to the reigning princes of Europe, depended in fact most completely on the will of his people.

In those parts of Ireland where, 500 years after the first so-called conquest, the English grandees could appear no other way than at the head of a mighty army, the social order which prevailed in England (feudalism) was unknown. This was the position most of our island was in. It was also the case that war against a foreign invader meant as much as war against private landowners. But when the Irish ancestral system was destroyed by violence in 1649, the social character of the Irish people's struggle disappeared too; it took on the appearance of a purely political struggle for independence.

This was in any case inevitable. Communal land ownership would have given way to private ownership by landlords (large landowners) even if Ireland had retained its independence. What happened instead was that this change came about not through the action of economic forces within the country, but through the violence of external armed force. This is why the broad masses of the Irish people were bitterly and rightly angered by it. To this day, the Irish people's dreams of national freedom are still linked to a longing for the restoration of the ancient form of land ownership, although today a return to the old orders of land ownership is completely impossible.

The breakdown of the family system naturally put an end to the importance of the chief. The Irish aristocracy of today are the descendants of foreign invaders or traitors to the country. As a result, the direction of all patrilineal movements in Ireland fell into the hands of the middle class alone—the bourgeoisie proper. Our patrilineal movements have become, for the most part, dependent on the interests of the bourgeoisie. Sometimes this or that patrician of the bourgeoisie, in order to arouse the enthusiasm and secure the support of the disinherited masses of the people, would utter in poetry and in national stories views akin to Socialism. These were views on the present social system similar to those of the first (utopian) European socialists. But in the next minute there was another bourgeois patriot, who hastened to reassure the bourgeoisie with a saying to the contrary. If the social views of one were semi-revolutionary, the other certainly expressed completely retrograde opinions. The one nicely balances the other, and in this way one would like to create a so-called "truly national movement", that is, a movement in which each class of society would recognise the rights of all other classes, in which at the same time all classes would put aside their specific aspirations and unite in a national struggle against a common enemy, England. Needless to say, such talk deceived only one class—the working class. If we cease to concern ourselves with class interests, if we cease to consider the specific interests of different classes, it is the possessing class that gains, the class that wants to keep its magnifiers. The bourgeoisie can only retain its rule, its gains, if we do not look at its class position, if we keep silent about the interests of the different classes. Like a man who has arrived at his wealth by infiltration and deception, the bourgeoisie fears nothing so much as an impartial and close inquiry into the origin of its possessions. It is for this reason that the bourgeois magazines and the politicians of the bourgeoisie endeavour incessantly to embitter to the point of fever the minds of the working class on questions which do not violate the class interests of the bourgeoisie. War, religion, race, language, political reform, patriotism—all these serve in the hands of the possessing classes to divert the attention of the workers from the bourgeois social system, all serve to distance social upheaval. All these things can direct minds as far away from economic matters as possible, and thus retard the development of the class consciousness of the proletariat. Such is the task of the politics of to-day's Irish Parliamentary Party, or Home-Rule Party (self-government).

The Irish bourgeoisie has long practised such tactics and, it must be admitted, has found for itself excellent, fertile material in the workers-radicals. Over the last century, every generation in Ireland has witnessed attempts to rise up against the English government. The majority of supporters of any such conspiracy or uprising have come from the lower strata of the rural and urban population. Yet, under the influence of a handful of bourgeois leaders, all workers' issues were brushed aside and it was decided that the insurgents would not be concerned with them in the event of victory. It was thought that such a course of action would secure the help of the upper classes and bring the uprising under the banner of revolution.

But the result of such conduct was almost always the same. The workers admittedly supplied most of the recruits to the revolutionary ranks, most of the victims of imprisonment and scaffolding[1]; but the working mass as a whole could not, thanks to such conduct on the part of the leaders of the insurrection, become sufficiently filled with revolutionary zeal to seriously threaten an invasion that had already lasted 700 years. All the workers admittedly wished from the heart for national independence, but they understood how many sacrifices are needed to win it. And when the leaders of the insurrection made clear to them that the working people should not expect even from a victorious insurrection any change in the conditions of social slavery, what wonder that the mass of the working people retreated from the struggle, and that only the most noble and chivalrous individuals joined the ranks for an unequal battle and fell victim to the enemy's vengeance?

---

1   **Ed. Note:** This refers to the gallows, a common form of punishment under British occupation in Ireland at the time.

The upper classes were also contemptuously deaf to the musings of the bourgeois patricians. The upper classes enjoyed property, movable and immovable. Under the protective power of England they felt their possession secured, but were by no means sure what fate would befall them in the event of the victory of the revolutionary movement. This is also why many landholders (landlords) were constantly loyal to England. While the poets and dreamers of the bourgeoisie were fretting about the "concord of all states and creeds," the aristocracy was defending its private interests against small landlords so relentlessly that it almost completely depopulated the country. It came to this: the English bourgeois paper, the London *Times*, declared that "the name of the Irish landlord is a disgrace to Christianity!"

The petty bourgeoisie has in the past given the national cause many sincere patriots, full of dedication. But in general it is an uncertain element. On the one hand, it is eager to please its underprivileged countrymen and, for the peace of its own conscience, shouts most loudly about its inexhaustible love for the cause of freedom. But the whole class of the petty bourgeoisie is constantly trying to direct the minds of the public down the path of legal agitation for such reforms as would remove the irritating and superfluous excesses of the rule of English officials, but would not violate the very foundations of national and economic slavery. In this way, in the eyes of the unconcerned public, they can pass themselves off as ardent patricians. At the same time, they can use their influence as "patrician leaders" to condemn any serious revolutionary movement that would require more evidence of sincerity from them than noisy garbling, or greater sacrifices from their pockets.

In 1879, the more progressive of the peasants, farming the land leased from the landlords, began a movement against the exploitation of the tenants. It was a well-chosen time, for there was a great stagnation in agriculture, so they were eager to hear the new gospel, which at first was touted with truly revolutionary fervour and strength. The movement grew against the resistance of the clergy and the bourgeois politicians; finally these classes began to fear that they would lose their influence over the people, and to prevent this they joined the movement, gradually weakening it and dampening its fervour. Soon the agrarian movement completely lost its initial socialist qualities. After a while, all the aims of the original founders of the bill were quietly put aside, and only "Home

Rule" (self-government for Ireland) was put forward.

Since then, bourgeois politicians have spread to Ireland for good. Socialism has had very little influence on the minds of the Irish people until recent times; it was known only from English newspapers and was looked upon with loathing as an "English" invention. Workers' trade unions are widespread in our country, but they are run in the same way as the most backward of English unions. Political activity is explicitly excluded from these associations; their members join together to fight against the entrepreneur in the factory, while in all political matters outside the factory walls they obediently follow the same capitalist. These unions seek only minor improvements in the lot of the workers, but regard the whole present system as eternally sustainable, and tirelessly assert their concern for the interests of the capitalist and their desire to maintain "harmony between capital and labour."

Such is the position of Ireland, where the Irish Socialist Republican Party began its propaganda efforts in early 1896. This party was founded by a few workers who embraced the principles of Socialism as promulgated by Marx and Engels. It began a struggle by word and writ which, despite enormous difficulties, has already succeeded in profoundly influencing the minds of the people and will probably in the near future completely change the political position of Ireland.

The content of the doctrine with which our party addressed the Irish people is as follows:

All previous patrilineal movements in modern Irish history have sought only to abolish or alter English rule in Ireland. But it was precisely because of English rule in Ireland that the classes who plundered the land of our ancestors secured possession of their unlawful spoils. Today, the English government is the only material guarantor, secured for our bourgeoisie its class rule and an epoch of sucking our labour. The only class, therefore, capable of a revolutionary movement is the working class. But the working class, if it wants to maintain its revolutionary energy, must get rid of all links with the bourgeois parties. It can only do this by organising itself into a class political party, the Socialist Republican Party. The activity of this party will quickly drive all the backward elements into one camp, into the camp of supporters of the present political and social order. Socialism can only be realised when the working class takes the helm of government in its hands and carries out its will according to the laws of economic development. This is why the first step to victory—as all advocates of scientific socialism recognise—is to gain governmental power—by peaceful means if possible, by force if necessary.

Hence flows the need to organise and educate the working class so that it can take up all elective positions in Ireland with a full awareness of its historical vocation. This will be a preliminary step to the seizure of governmental power itself and the replacement of the rule of foreign officials by the organised forces of Irish democracy.

We are convinced that such a policy is in complete harmony with all the aspirations of the Irish people and at the same time is based on the principles of class struggle, principles the application of which has enabled the Socialist parties of the world to overcome all obstacles, to overthrow all defects and to arrive at the present position from which the goal of our movement can be seen.

Finally, on behalf of my comrades, I would like to assure my Polish brothers that the Irish Socialist Republican Party's drive for Irish national independence is by no means motivated by chauvinism (misunderstood patriotism, national hatred) or hostile feelings towards the English working class. No, we seek Irish independence because we are convinced that the international labour movement must both organise nationally and conform to national character and feeling.

PART V
EARLY WRITINGS PREVIOUSLY REPUBLISHED IN PART

*****

SCOTTISH NOTES[1]
JUSTICE
26 AUGUST 1893, P.3

O UR FRIEND PAISLEY,[2] Vice-President of the Glasgow Trades Council, in a letter to the Press on cooperation, points out "that it is a question of dividend-hunting from stem to stern." Nevertheless he is a member, and says he intends to remain one for the purpose of advocating the true principles of co-operation. I want to ask our friend a question. Are the dividends received by co-operators received at the expense of their underpaid (less than trade union rate) *employés?* If so is our friend anything less than a sweater? When calling upon public bodies to pay trade union rates of wages, if the above be true, will our friend please tell us if he is uttering anything else than so much cant?

The bottle workers are at present on strike in Portobello, Alloa, and Glasgow for a slight increase in their miserable wages. A few weeks ago they appointed a deputation from among their number to wait upon the Masters' Association and proffer their modest demands. As there are a considerable number of foreigners engaged in the works, they included a few of these "blarsted furriners" in the deputation.

But, behold ye, the patriotic soul of the Scottish bourgeoisie rose in wrath against such an innovation. What! Were they, the descendants of the men who had fought and bled to preserve the soil of Scotland from the unhallowed grasp of the foreign foe, going to stand idly by while a few ignorant, selfish, and unpatriotic slaves, *their* workmen, *their* hands,

---

1   This is signed simply "Connolly."

2   James Paisley, secretary of the Amalgamated Society of Railway Servants in Scotland.

whom they had condescended to employ out of pure charity, mark ye, enter, in cold blood, into an agreement with the foreigner to demand a greater share of the fruits of their labour from their native masters? Impious thought! It was all very well to employ a foreigner at starvation wages' and so cut down the wages of the native; it was right enough to sweat, starve, overwork, degrade, and brutalise the foreigner and the native in the one shop and at the same occupation—but to treat with the foreigner, to discuss hours of labour and wages with men whom you had employed to enable you to have complete control of both. Why, it was preposterous. Accordingly, the Masters' Association refused to hear the deputation, assigning as their sole reason the presence of foreigners among them.

*****

CONNOLLY TO KIERHARDIE
3 JULY 1894[1]

EDINBURGH
3/7/94
21 S. COLLEGE ST

D EAR HARDIE,
Your letter interested, tho' it did not surprise me. As an Irishman who has always taken a keen interest in the advanced movements in Ireland, I was well aware that neither the Parnellites nor the McCarthyites were friendly to the Labour movement. Both of them are essentially middle-class parties interested in the progress of Ireland from a middle-class point of view. Their advanced attitude upon the land question is simply an accident arising out of the exigencies of the political situation, and would be dropped tomorrow if they did not realise the necessity of linking the Home Rule agitation to some case more clearly allied to their daily wants than a mere embarkment of national sentiment of the people.

If you can show them it would be to their interest politically to support us, they will do so. Now, can this not be done? I think it can be done if you would allow me to suggest to you a plan which I think would, if carried out, prove a trump card. There is a nucleus of a strong Labour movement in Ireland, which only needs judicious handling to flutter the doves in the Home Rule dovecot. Now if you were to visit Dublin and address a good meeting there, putting it in strong and straight, without

---

1   "J. Connolly to Hardie (Edinburgh), 3 July 1894," ILP/4/1894/140, Francis Johnson Correspondence, London School of Economics Library and Archive, London. Republished in part in *Socialist Review*, vol 25, no. 137 (March 1925), 118-119.

reference to either the two Irish parties, but rebellious, anti-monarchical and outspoken on the fleecings of both landlord and capitalist and the hypocrisy of both political parties for a finale.

Now I think a letter from you to the secretary of the Fabian Society care of Mr Doyle, 6 Swift's Row, Lower Ormond Quay Dublin, or to Mr Benjamin Pelin, president of the Knights of the Plough, Narraghmore, Athy, Kildare, asking them to arrange for a meeting to be addressed by you in Dublin would bring this matter to a head.[2]

If such a meeting were well billed it would be an important one. Get a resolution passed expressing the sympathy of the Irish people with the Labour movement in Britain, and as Dublin is the very heart of Parnellism, you would force the hand of Redmond and his clique. If you would arrange for the meeting to be organised solely from the Dublin side and an invitation sent to Field to take the chair, he could scarcely refuse and the resolution would if rightly and judiciously used knock the bottom out of the Irish opposition to our movement. Hoping you will excuse me for these hints on what might be done, but earnestly pressing the matter for your consideration.

I am
yours faithfully,
JAMES CONNOLLY.

---

2   This sentence is missing from the version published in *Socialist Review* in 1925 and in *Between Comrades* in 2007. Hardie took Connolly up on his suggestion and he met Pelin in Dublin later in the year. See "Mr Kier Hardie's Visit to Dublin," *Evening Herald*, 5 November 1894, 1. For more on Pelin and the Knights of the Plough see Fintan Lane, "Benjamin Pelin, the Knights of the Plough and Social Radicalism, 1852-1934," in *Defying the Law of the Land: Agrarian Radicals in Irish History*, ed. Brian Casey (Dublin: The History Press Ireland, 2013), 176-200.

*****

PLAIN TALK[1]
LABOUR CHRONICLE
15 OCTOBER 1894

T HE INTELLIGENT and hard-headed elector and the shrewd and practical-minded voter have arrived in Edinburgh. Rumour has it that they have already been heard of in St Cuthbert's Ward, where Mr Thomas Blaikie stands as ILP candidate against Lord Provost Russell, and no doubt they will soon be discovered in many other wards of the city.

They are at present the most important persons in the British Empire, and will continue so to be until 8 o'clock on the evening of the polling for the municipal elections. After that date they will disappear from our midst, and the columns of the Liberal and Tory newspapers will know them no more. Their places will, however, be taken by our other old friends, these "undesirable products of our civilisation," the mob, the lower classes, the great unwashed, the residuum, and other such great names the organs of the classes are so fond of applying to the masses. And the masses seem to like it.

The Lord Provost and Town Council propose spending a sum of £30,000 in erecting a number of one and two-roomed houses in the recently cleared space between High Street and Cowgate. In St Giles Ward, where this piece of municipal philanthropy is to be perpetrated, there are already more one-roomed houses than in any ward of its size in the city. Is this cause and effect, or what? This problem of the housing of the poor has engaged the attention of every social reformer for the last two generations. Indeed, no thoughtful man or woman could view with unconcern

---

1   Connolly used the pseudonym "R.Ascal" for these articles.

the enormous evils arising from the congestion of population in our large cities. The slums, those plague-spots of our civilisation, will not remain hidden from our sight. The vice, the misery, the disease, the moral and physical degeneration of such a large portion of our people, as that driven by our landlord and capitalist system to herd together in these dens, cannot be neglected without grave peril to our social welfare.

The slum-dwellers are what society has made them, and every effort to lift them to the higher plane of a useful and honourable life will fail of its purpose until we recognise that fact.

What is wanted in the slums is more fresh air, more sunshine, more elbow-room, larger houses with more apartments and cheaper rents. Does the proposal to build a number of one or two roomed houses in the most crowded and unhealthy part of Edinburgh meet this want? I commend the following utterance of the most eminent medical authority in Scotland to the attention of our *enlightened* Town Council.

Dr Russell[2], medical officer of health to the City of Glasgow, says:— "It would be well if those who live in large houses, in the customary enjoyment of all their privacies, were to make an effort to think out in detail what it would mean if their whole life, personal as well as family, were suddenly to shrink within the limits of a house of one or two apartments; if their opportunities of private ablutions, of retirement in the event of sickness, of birth or of death, were to be deprived of all those conditions of space they have come to regard as essential. *It is almost too horrible* to express in naked uncompromising language the terrible jostling of birth and death and all the functions of life, which must be the daily routine of one of these small houses."[3]

---

2   James Burn Russell (1837-1905), Glasgow's first full-time medical officer of health, 1872-1898.

3   Taken from James B. Russell, "The House," in *Glasgow Health Lectures* (Christian Institute: Glasgow, 1881), 50-51. There is a slight difference in words (but not meaning) between Connolly's quote and the original: "Those who live in large houses, in the customary enjoyment of all their privacies, ought to make an effort to think out in detail how they would feel if their whole life, personal and family, were suddenly to shrink within the limits of one or two apartments; if their refined ideas of delicacy, their virtues of modesty and propriety, their opportunities of private ablutions, their retirement in times of sickness, in the events of birth and of death,—were suddenly deprived of the conditions of space, which they have come to regard as essential. It is almost too horrible to express in naked, uncompromising language the jostling of birth and death, and the functions of life which must be the

And yet our civic rulers in the plenitude of their wisdom, propose to spend a large sum of money in building more of this type of dwelling in the least suitable spot a long and exhaustive search could reveal.

A wiser plan would be to make a clean sweep of the whole inner line of closes and courts between Borthwick's Close and Blair Street, and erect instead, either an immense playground for the children, with wash-house and drying-green for the inhabitants in general, or else, another public garden, planted with such trees and shrubs as would grow there. But this idea is not likely to occur to our Lord Provost, whose private garden is much larger than the whole space in question. Will the intelligent electors, &c., please note the following facts:—were a heavy tax placed upon unlet property, the landlord or his agent would be more willing to let it in order to escape the tax, and thus cheap houses would be procurable elsewhere than in the slums. Were the Corporation to undertake the erection of workmen's dwellings and let them at a rent to cover the cost of building and upkeep, the working-class would soon find relief from the merciless greed of our house landlords.

And, generally, were an honest attempt made to recover from the ground landlords of Edinburgh the wealth they have stolen from the people in the shape of ground rents, the money necessary for such schemes as the above would soon be forthcoming. The taxation of ground values ought to be an article of faith with every voter who believes the City of Edinburgh ought to belong to the people of Edinburgh and not to the idle descendants of the pimps, the panderers, and the flunkeys who in past generations have trafficked their honour for our lands. But a middle-class Town Council will do none of these things.

On Tuesday, 2nd October, Councillor Forbes-Mackay[4] gave notice of a motion that waterproof coats and leggings be provided for our city employees. Councillor Forbes-Mackay retires in November, and is seeking re-election. Have these two facts any relation to each other? Oh, dear, no. No gentlemen would suggest that the motion is only made in order to catch a few working-class votes. Yet it is a strange coincidence that the

---

daily experience of those small houses."

4   Lieutenant Colonel A. Forbes MacKay, regular army officer with the Gordon Highlanders. He topped the poll in George Square Ward with 1,655 votes. His son was the physician Alister Forbes Mackay (1878-1914) who was part of the Nimrod expedition to the Antarctic, led by Ernest Shackleton.

motion can only come up again after an interval of two weeks at least, that it will then be remitted to a committee to report upon, that before such report is made the election will be over, and that all through the elections this proof of Mr Forbes-Mackay's good intentions will be of immense service to his canvassers. Kind-hearted, innocent, unsophisticated Councillor Forbes-Mackay![5]

A Mr Gardener[6], who aspires to represent St Giles in the liberal and nationalist interest, addressed a meeting of city employees on Wednesday, 3rd inst., in pursuance of his candidature. He told the assembled electors that he claimed their votes as a Catholic and as an Irishman. Yet, if my information be correct, this gentleman figured as one of Mr Goschen's committee, and appeared upon his platform when that gentleman contested and won the parliamentary representation of East Edinburgh against Mr Costelloe; and at that time Mr Goschen's committee were placarding the town with anti-Catholic manifestoes.

Later accounts confirm us that Mr Mitchell is going to seek re-election, and the *Evening News* hopes Mr Gardener will see his way to retire. The Liberals believe Edinburgh Irishmen should have a representative upon the Town Council; but not at their expense!

The *Edinburgh Catholic Herald* had a leading article the other day on what it described in its placards as "ILP insolence." Some foolish utterance of the Labour candidate for Newcastle, to the effect that Irishmen would get Home Rule when they knew how to behave themselves, was taken as the text for the article.

Yet, on Saturday, Sept. 8th, the *Evening News*, in an editorial, gave the following advice to the Liberal leaders: "In view of the distracted and demoralised state of the Irish parties, would it not be well—to strike Home Rule out of the Liberal programme?" That is to say, the Irish parties are divided, therefore the Irish parties are weak, therefore we need not be afraid of them, therefore, hang Home Rule. Again, on Tuesday, October 2nd, it declared, "Irishmen should be told plainly that the country will not

---

5   Connolly gatecrashed an election rally for Forbes Mackay even though they were running in separate wards. See "Mr. Connolly's Practical Socialism," *Edinburgh Evening News*, 2 November 1894.

6   James Gardiner, vice-president of the Gladstone branch of the Irish National League. He finished last in the election poll, receiving 54 votes. Connolly received 263. "Gardener" could be a typo, but it could also be a jibe by Connolly.

stand another Home Rule campaign."

Yet, on neither of these occasions, and they are only a few out of many which might be quoted to the same purpose, did the *Catholic Herald* even refer to such "Liberal insolence," or treachery.

Some of my readers may have detected a tendency to lapse into humour on the part of our contemporary the *News*, Here is a delightful specimen. On Saturday, Sept. 29th, in dealing with a manifesto issued by the Parnellites, it enquired of them—"Leaving out the contribution of the Dublin publicans and their *beer-stained pence*, what good round sum have they to show for Ireland's gratitude?"

"Beer-stained pence" *is* good in Edinburgh. Of course when such pence are used to buy famous pictures for our workers to gaze at when they tire of the penny almanacks hanging on the walls of their own ancestral mansions, or to erect additions to our University, that the children of the middle and upper classes may, at less cost to their parents, be fitted out and equipped for their task of quartering their useless lives upon our labour—then, you understand, beer-stained pence is not a bad thing.

Charity is proverbially cold. But not necessarily so. And, therefore, it seems to me that the arrangements in force at the Children's Hospital Dispensary in Lauriston Lane might be altered for the benefit of the poor women and children who are compelled to attend there. I am informed that all children brought to the waiting-room must have all their clothes unfastened, and in some cases removed, while awaiting their turn to enter the doctor's presence. The result often is a severe cold to the already ailing infants, and perhaps death. The children may, of course, be protected by shawls, &c., but the wives of the workers have not always such wraps for the purpose. It is, of course, necessary to avoid any undue waste of time on the part of the medical gentleman, but surely it is scarcely necessary to remind the authorities that the lives and health of our children are also worthy of preservation.

*****

PLAIN TALK
LABOUR CHRONICLE
5 NOVEMBER 1894

THE BATTLE of the wards is now in full swing. The din of the battle is in our ears, and the voices of the combatants cleave the air. We are no longer a quiet unenthusiastic people, steadily plodding about our business, but are instead a shouting, cheering, arguing, debating, reasoning, hair-splitting, canvassing, promising, gibing, jeering, heckling, truckling, dogmatising, expounding, worshipping, denouncing, good-humoured, "motley lot."[1]

* * *

Yes; that is the word, Mr M'Laren[2]—a motley lot. The working-class voters, poor, ignorant despised drudges that they are, toiling, moiling, sweating, grinding, labouring, delving, digging, driving, exhausted, worn-out, and degraded, in order that our glorious institutions in church and state may have their due meed of honour! The motley lot are, indeed, beneath the contempt of the well-fed politician.

---

1   This is in reference to a comment made by a candidate at the nomination meeting for St. Giles Ward at the Free Tron Hall, Chambers Street, 24 October 1894. Those in attendance: Andrew Mitchell (who eventually topped the poll), Duncan M'Laren, James Gardiner, and James Connolly. See "The Municipal Elections—St Giles' Ward," *Edinburgh Evening News*, 25 October 1894.

2   Duncan McLaren, ironmonger. Conservative and Unionist candidate for St. Giles ward.

* * *

But it was really too bad of the Edinburgh Socialists to pack the St Giles Ward meeting, and then to crow over the feat as if they had accomplished something wonderful.[3] Why, it was not even an original idea. The Liberals have done it often before—many a time. But the socialists are always taking credit for other people's ideas.

* * *

But how does it happen that a band of men who a week or two ago were described as a "few noisy fanatics," were able by means of a few, a very few, post cards to the least active of their members, to pack a hall holding over five hundred people? If they can do this with their enrolled members only, then the fight in St Giles is as good as won already, and, in the interest of the ratepayers, the non-socialist candidates ought to withdraw, and save the expense of a contest.

* * *

If they will not all do this, then at least the two gentlemen who cater for the working-class vote as liberal and independent candidates, might be reasonably expected to do so, and leave the ground clear for the real battle of the election, betwixt the representative of rankest Toryism and the representative of militant social democracy.

* * *

---

3   "The nomination meeting for St Giles' Ward was held in the Free Tron Church Hall, Chambers Street, Last night. For a considerable time before the hour of start the hall was filled, the audience including a large proportion of ladies. In the centre part a number of 'socialists' had evidently got together, and passed the time singing of the 'Red Flag of Liberty' and the 'Social Reformation.'" *Edinburgh Evening News*, 25 October 1894.

But our lawyer and capitalist friends will not do so. They will prefer to stay in the fight and help to obscure the issues at stake by a loud-mouthed profession of reforming zeal. The mean innuendos and slanderous insinuations put in circulation by their canvassers will help, *they think*, to weaken the hands of the social democrat, and aid in the defeat of the cause of progress.

* * *

While on this topic it might be as well to ask a question. "Why did the Tories not oppose Mr Mitchell before Mr Connolly appeared in the field?" and to put in the answer, "Because they knew that Mr Mitchell was as great a Tory as any one they could bring forward." And why did they oppose him when the socialist champion did appear? And again the answer, "In order to strengthen Mr Mitchell's hands by an appearance of Tory opposition. "Did someone say, "A Tory dodge!" Yes, friend, exactly.

* * *

Mr Gardner, who seems to be a gentleman of a humorous turn of mind, at a meeting in Scott, Croall, and Company's Bazaar, described the socialist candidate for St Giles as "a young man with no business ability, advocating ideas repugnant to all right-thinking men."[4] This is a terrible accusation, and one which cannot be hurled back at the accuser, with the customary retort, "You're another."

* * *

---

4   "Mr James Gardiner, the independent candidate for St Giles Ward, addressed a meeting last night of the electors in Messrs Scott, Croall & Son's Bazaar. Castle Terrace... [He said that] Mr Connolly, the socialist candidate, was a young man who, without any business experience, sought to enter the Council in order to ventilate extravagant ideas repugnant to all right-thinking citizens." "The Municipal Elections–St Giles Ward," *Edinburgh Evening News*, 27 October 1894, 2.

Mr Gardiner is not a young man. He would scorn the idea. He does not wish to spend his time in advocating ideas. *It* is not even known that he has any. But he *has* "business ability"—*of a kind*, and the workers are just beginning to realise the fact that such men are too good judges of their own business interests to be safe custodiers of the business or affairs of the Democracy. As long as the ethics of the commercial classes are founded on the higgling of the market, and as long as flesh and blood, men and women, are regarded as mere items of expenditure in a merchant's balance sheet, so long must the business instincts of the classes be regarded with suspicion and distrust, instead of as a passport to the confidence of the self-respecting masses.

* * *

In all elections, the personality of candidates is apt to be pushed too much to the front by their too enthusiastic supporters. It seems impossible to enter into the spirit of an election contest, without representing your man as a sort of second edition of the Angel Gabriel, come to rally the just and righteous to his standard. On the other hand, it seems just as imperative that you should, by ways that are dark and tricks that are vain, convey to the minds of the electors that your opponent could give points in iniquity to Charles Peace,[5] Chantrelle,[6] or Jessie King.[7]

* * *

Mark Twain tells a story of how, when he stood for some official position in the States, his opponents first charged him with every crime in the

---

5   Charles Peace (1832-1879). Notorious burglar and murderer.

6   Eugène Marie Chantrelle (1834-1878). French teacher who worked and lived in Edinburgh. Convicted of murdering his wife Elizabeth Chantrelle and hanged on 10 May 1878.

7   Jessie King (1861-1889) was a baby-farmer (the practice of accepting custody of an infant or child in exchange for payment) and found guilty of the murder of two children. She was executed on 11 March 1889. Doubts remain about her involvement in the murders.

calendar, and a few specially invented for the occasion, and then engaged a dozen of the dirtiest and most naked-looking children in New York to rush upon the platform, and, clasping him by the knees, to call him "Father, father!" We are not yet quite so bad in this country: but it is only the courage that is lacking. Our opponents prefer to trust to backstairs slandering and to pose in public as champions of political purity.

* * *

The *Evening News* (the official organ of the associated undertakers of the east of Scotland), declares it has always contended that the socialists should have fair play. Of course it has! It was in order to ensure the socialists a fair hearing that the *News* referred to their candidates as "men with unwashed faces and corduroy trousers."[8] This classical style, which the *News* always adopts during an election, is a far handier method of meeting an opponent than attempting to refute his arguments. But it may be employed once too often; and then the workers might begin to reflect whether it would not be a more manly thing to meet argument with argument, and reason with reason, then to meet arguments with mud.

* * *

But of course arguments require brains to furnish them; reasons require well-balanced minds to elaborate them; but mud can always be thrown

---

8   "At last night's meeting in St Giles' Ward Mr Connolly stated pretty plainly that the working classes could not be properly represented except by one of their own number. Against this doctrine we must raise a protest. While we admit that it may be advantageous to have a sprinkling of representatives from the working classes in Council or Parliament, it is absurd to suppose that a man must have an unwashed face and corduroy clothes in order to have common sense and humane feelings towards the labouring class. Many a man has given his life to working for the welfare of those who were socially his inferiors. Mr Connolly's doctrine is an insult to all such men, not least to Mr Mitchell, who has given his best services to the city with absolutely no return, apparently not even that of gratitude. It is to be hoped that the electors of St Giles at the proper time will stamp out the spurious doctrine of equality, which places on one level the ignorant and educated." *Edinburgh Evening News*, 25 October 1894, 2.

by journalists who sell themselves for that purpose. Therefore, the editor of the *Evening News* shows his wisdom [sic] in preferring to devote his energies to mud-throwing. *It is more in his line.*

* * *

I know several working men who will not be able to rest in their beds at night until the Town Council decides who is to be Lord Provost. It is a most momentous question, no doubt. And yet it seems to me that we will still be rack-rented and sweated, over-worked and under-paid, insulted and bullied, humiliated and despised, ground beneath the heel of land-lord and capitalist, foreman and manager, whether the honours go round or remain in the hands of the Liberal ring.

* * *

Personally, I would be in favour of electing Bailie M'Donald our next Lord Provost. He could not be a greater flunkey than Sir James Russell, and there is just a probability that he would succeed in bringing the whole institution into contempt by some egregious blunder which Russell would avoid.

* * *

And to get the people to laugh at a Lord Provost is a consummation de-voutly to be prayed for.[9]

* * *

The houses to be built in St Giles are to be palaces in comparison with

---

9   *Hamlet* Act III, Scene I, lines 65-66. '...'tis a consummation / Devoutly to be wished.'

the hovels in which the people in the same district dwell today. And yet when those people want a representative they are told to vote for some individual drawn from the class whose rents and profits are the cause of the low wages which drive the workers into these slums.

* * *

But the people are learning wisdom, and perhaps the lesson of this contest in St Giles will be laid to heart by those poor dumb drudges (with corduroy trousers), who in the past have so humbly followed whither the party politicians have led them.

* * *

Perhaps they will learn how foolish it is to denounce tyranny in Ireland and then to vote for tyrants and the instruments of tyrants at their own door. Perhaps they will begin to see that the landlord who grinds his peasants on a Connemara estate, and the landlord who rack-rents them in a Cowgate slum, are brethren in fact and deed. Perhaps they will realise that the Irish worker who starves in an Irish cabin, and the Scotch worker who is poisoned in an Edinburgh garret, are also brothers with one hope and one destiny. Perhaps they will observe how the same Liberal Government which supplies police to Irish landlords to aid them in the work of exterminating their Irish peasantry, also imports police into Scotland to aid Scotch mine owners in their work of starving the Scottish miners. Perhaps they will begin to understand that the Liberals and Tories are not two parties, but rather two sections of the one party—the party of property. Perhaps they will learn that the interests of both sections of the party of property lie in draining the last drop of sweat from the pores of the labouring people. Perhaps they will lay seriously to heart the words of the statesman poet[10]:

---

10   James Russell Lowell (1819-1891), American poet, diplomat, and abolitionist.

Labourin' man and labourin' woman,
They one glory and one shame,
Everything as done in human
Bears upon them all the same.[11]

* * *

And if they do, then socialism will risk the storm.

---

11   From *The Biglow Papers* (1848), an anti-war satire by Lowell. "Laborin' man an' laborin' woman / Hev one glory an' one shame, / Ev'y thin' thet 's done inhuman / Injers all on 'em the same." Published as a standalone poem entitled *A Yankee's Notion about Enlisting in the Mexican War*. See *The Liberator* (Boston), 3 July 1846, 108, for one of its earliest iterations.

*****

PLAIN TALK
LABOUR CHRONICLE
1 JANUARY 1895

WHAT IS A LIVING WAGE for a town-clerk? £2,000 per year is the sum agreed upon by the Democratic Town Council who, in November last, from every platform in the city were proclaiming their love of the people and the people's cause. And the free and independent voters who elected them, as they wend their way homeward on a Saturday evening, with their princely salaries of eighteen bob a week,[1] think—well, I wonder what they do think?

* * *

"It is madness to attempt to keep up wages in face of a falling market." So said the politicians during the late miners' strike.[2] But in spite of this sage verdict the Edinburgh lawyers have succeeded in raising the salary of the aforementioned official by a cool £500 per annum.

* * *

The natural law of supply and demand, it appears, does not apply to the

---

1   Eighteen bob (shillings) a week would amount to around £47 a year.

2   In reference to a common phrase used during the 1893 miners' strike to justify wage cuts, e.g. "[The Miners' Federation of Great Britain] have to justify their contention and maintain their position; to keep up wages in face of a falling market—a feat never yet accomplished." *South Wales Daily News*, 10 January 1893, 4.

professional classes, but only to the common people. Who would have thought that nature was so one-sided? It would serve a good purpose if some of our "friends" of the workingmen in the Town Council were to look more sharply after their permanent officials. They would, if they looked deep enough, be able to unearth a few scandals little suspected by the ratepayers.

* * *

Take the fair wages clause in our city contracts as an instance. How is it observed? The Cleaning Department are in the habit of hiring every week a large number of horses and men from city contractors to assist in the work of cleaning the streets. A few men only are required during the summer, but in the winter months the number averages fifteen or twenty per week.

* * *

No questions are asked about wages. The contractor receives so much per day for man and horse, and pays his employees as he himself thinks fit. The wages of the men employed range from 17s. to 22s. per week, *but all are paid for at the highest rate by the city.*

* * *

Moreover, although the ratepayers are thus compelled to pay a standard price for the services of those men, who are themselves paid at starvation prices, it frequently happens that some of those men, after performing their day's work with the Cleansing Department, are employed for other two or three hours in their master's service. Although their day's work is already paid for.

* * *

I see our old friend Bailie Steel has been defending the action of Inspector Mackay[3] in working the carters in the Cleansing Department more than nine hours per day. He said that when the resolution on that subject was passed by the Council it was understood that there would be some difficulty in observing the rule.

* * *

Now the fact is that Inspector MacKay made no effort whatever to observe the rule. He never spoke to the carters on the subject, he never altered in the least the method of working, he engaged no new hands to cope with the work in the shortened day at his disposal, he habitually works the employees ten to eleven hours per day, and pays nothing for overtime.

* * *

Yet in the resolution referred to it was distinctly stipulated that where overtime was found necessary payment should be made for it at the rate of 6d. per hour.

* * *

A large number of the workmen in question voted for the Liberal candidate in the municipal elections. They are now getting their reward.

* * *

---

3   Inspector George MacKay, Lighting and Cleaning Department, Edinburgh Council.

"Mr Grundy, Inspector of Mines, in a report to the Government, states that he is unable to discover any distressing circumstances connected with the employment of females and children in mines. They appeared to him to be healthy and happy, and without the wages earned by their work many families would be miserably in want compared with their present prosperity. Mr Grundy therefore considers that the inhibition of female labour would have bad effects of a far-reaching character."[4]

* * *

With a few alterations this might be taken as an almost verbatim reproduction of the late Mr Bright's speech against the Factory Acts in England.[5] But it is only the same spirit breathing through the report of the government officials in India. We have brought the blessings of Christian civilisation (as we understand it) to the benighted nations of India, and, as a result, their women and children are working in the mines, and their factory engines are going eighteen hours per day.

* * *

Rule Britannia.

* * *

---

4   "In Indian mines much of the labour is done by women and children. Mr. [James] Grundy, one of the government inspectors in India, says he is unable to discover any distressing circumstances connected with the employment of females and children in mines. They appeared to him to be hearty and happy, and, without the wages earned by their work, many families would be miserably in want, compared with their present prosperity." *Echo* (London), 18 December 1894, 1. Also, James Grundy. *Report of the Inspection of Mines in India, for the year ending the 30ᵗʰ June 1894*. (Calcutta, 1894).

5   John Bright (1811-1889), MP, mill-owner, free-trader, slum-landlord, and fierce opponent of trade unions and social reform. He also opposed the factory acts of the 1840s, which aimed to limit the working day for women and children in cotton mills to ten hours.

Lord Sandhurst will receive 12,000 rupees per annum in his new post as Governor of Bombay. We will now take up a collection in aid of the fund for providing bibles to the poor heathen.

* * *

The bookbinders in Messrs Nelson & Company's establishment are at present receiving a lesson in political economy. It appears the introduction of a newly-invented labour-saving machine has had the effect of throwing one-third of the employees in one particular branch upon the unemployed list.

* * *

It has saved their labour, and they have lost their wages, and their employers have increased their profits, and the identity of interests between the capitalist and the labourer is now a recognised fact.

* * *

And any socialist who would venture to insinuate that it would be better for the nation at large if the industry in question were carried on by the workers themselves, and such inventions used to shorten the hours of their labour instead of to starve a third of their number is well ignorant of the laws of political economy and an unsafe guide of public opinion.

* * *

But I wish some philanthropic society would offer a prize for the best essay on the following subject:—"The Relation between Labour-saving Machinery and Insecurity of Employment." Competitors to be limited to the ranks of bookbinders out of work.

* * *

If the bookbinders are the intelligent persons I take them to be, I fancy I would have what our Liberal and Tory friends would declare to be, some strange economic heresies.

*****

PLAIN TALK
LABOUR CHRONICLE
1 FEBRUARY 1895

THE *LABOUR CHRONICLE* is a local journal of democratic socialism. Consequently, it deals in the main with local matters. Consequently, I write plain talk about local wants. Consequently, in obedience to this immutable editorial law, which like the "natural" law of supply and demand, cannot be set aside, I shall carefully avoid all mention of the great Liberal meeting at Cardiff. It is not a local matter.

* * *

At this great meeting, the Prime Minister[1] attacked Mr Balfour for daring to hint that the Liberal government were not as conservative of all our glorious institutions as ever the Conservative party could hope to be. "Why," he said, "we do not even propose to touch the House of Lords, but only to readjust its relations with the House of Commons."[2] The leader of the great Liberal party seemed justly indignant at being taken for a reformer, with more regard for popular rights than for worn-out institutions. And rightly so. *N.B.*—If I were allowed to mention this mat-

---

1   Archibald Primrose, 5th Earl of Rosebery (1847-1929). Liberal Party politician and UK Prime Minister (March 1894–June 1895). The meeting was held in Cardiff on Friday 18 January 1895. See *Glasgow Herald*, 19 January 1895, 8, for a full report of his speech.

2   "What institution is it that we propose to destroy? Why, gentlemen, we have distinctly announced that we do not propose to adjust the House of Lords. We only propose to adjust the House of Commons." *Glasgow Herald*, 19 January 1895, 8.

ter at all, I could work into this paragraph some fine scathing irony and biting satire; but, alas I must refrain. It is not a local matter.

* * *

Speaking on the Disestablishment question[3] Lord Rosebery declared that—[enough. ED., *Lab. Ch.*]

* * *

Lord Rosebery is in favour of a Second Chamber. So is Mr M'Ewan, and the majority of official Liberals. They wish to establish here a breakwater, like the American Senate, as a check to popular enthusiasm.

* * *

As a preparation for the coming contest between the forces of social democracy and the forces of capitalistic slavery, no other measure would serve them so well. The American Senate will be remembered in history chiefly as the last stronghold of the slaveholders; as the legislative chamber whose pliability in the hands of the slaveholding aristocracy cost the American Republic 900,000 lives, and £140,000,000 expended in a civil war, which a little wise legislation might have averted.

* * *

It is only natural therefore, that our far-seeing aristocracy, Liberal and Tory alike, should long for an effective Second Chamber, where defects will be more carefully concealed from the public eye, and therefore be less likely to arouse the popular wrath. This, however, is not a local matter.

---

3   Disestablishment of the Church in Wales and Scotland.

* * *

At the great Liberal meeting at Cardiff, the audience closed the proceedings by singing "Auld Lang Syne." This world is a vale of tears and suffering. If I had been allowed to even mention this meeting, how I might have delighted the readers of this paper by conjuring up before their mind's eye the truly humorous spectacle of 10,000 Welshmen, in the throes of a desperate struggle with the intricacies of the Scottish dialect, trying to sing "Auld Lang Syne" and look cheerful. Such are the humiliations we have to undergo at the hands of the Liberal government.

* * *

Oh, for the heroism of Wallace, the genius of Bruce, or wild sweeping sword of M'Gonagall, to avenge this outrage on "oor guid Scotch tongue."

* * *

I commend the following extract to those of our readers who imagine that their class will be benefited by a change of government from Liberal to Tory or *vice versa*. The *Investor's Review* is a journal published for the express purpose of enabling the upper class to learn where they can most profitably and safely invest their money. It is, therefore, a journal published by rich men for rich men; and yet, here is what its editor says of the prospect of a revival of trade. I reproduce from *Justice*.

* * *

"Of a truth the old order changeth, yielding place to new, and what the new will be no mortal man can yet say, whether a higher brotherhood among the nations and races of mankind, or an armageddon of fiends around which the civilisation of which we boast will disappear as completely as those of ancient Rome, or still more ancient Egypt. What we can see is the dead calm which preludes and ushers in a change. And all Europe stands armed, its best energies devoted to a preparation for war, which means the letting loose of hell. Sanguine indeed must the mind be which can expect a 'revival of trade' on the old lines under such conditions."[4]

* * *

And yet when the Social Democrat speaks of the necessity for a complete social revolution, he is by some highly respectable people looked upon as a crank, instead of an earnest priest of humanity, who desires the peoples of the world to set their house in order before the coming storm.

* * *

At a recent meeting of the National League in Edinburgh, a Mr James Sorden is reported to have said, that there was coming forward a Liberal candidate who would make Mr M'Ewan shake in his shoes.[5] Mr Sorden, however, is not to be taken too seriously, or at his own valuation. He only fills the part of a political supernumerary, and his duty is simply to strut pompously across the stage of public life, and by his clumsy antics and loud-mouthed inanities excite the laughter of his audience, while the real artful dodgers of the League slink away like whipped curs, spurned by the party for whose sake they sold their leader, their principles, and their manhood.

---

4   "Socialist Analysis in the 'City,'" *Justice*, 19 January 1895, 6. There are minor differences between the quote used and the one reproduced in *Justice*. The original reads: "...boast *shall* disappear...," "...preparation for *wars*, which *shall be* the letting loose of hell," (my emphasis).

5   The John Dillon Branch of the Irish National League met on Sunday 13 January 1895 at the Moulders' Hall, Edinburgh. "Mr James Sorden said that no matter what splits might occur in the Irish party, they were strongly united on two questions—Home Rule and the Land. Regarding the rumour that Mr Cunningham-Grahame, in contesting the Central Division, would receive the support of the Nationalists, there was not a particle of truth in it. But there was a Liberal candidate coming forward who would make Mr M'Ewan shake in his shoes." *Edinburgh Evening News*, 14 January 1895, 3.

* * *

The *Glasgow Weekly Mail* is a Liberal newspaper. It is the property of Dr Cameron, M.P.[6] It has repeatedly accused the Labour Party of receiving aid from the Tories and of being traitors to the cause of Liberalism. No single item of evidence in support of these assertions has ever been adduced, and yet they have always formed the chief weapons in the armoury of our opponents in the League. Now, at last, we can give them a Roland for their Oliver.[7]

* * *

The *Mail* on Saturday, 19th January, made a most remarkable statement anent[8] the character and motives of the Irish leaders in Edinburgh. It declared "they were playing the part of traitors in the camp," "they were egged on and *backed up* by the Tory party."

* * *

Now here is a definite charge. Many people wondered how a few Irishmen could speak of bringing forward a candidate in Edinburgh. Where would they get the money? The *Mail* lets in a flood of light upon the subject, thoroughly exposing the sham patriotism of these so-called Nationalists. "Egged on" means, as we all know, encouraged to proceed; but *backed up*, what means that, please, in the political world? Subsidised, financed, supported by contributions of Tory gold—that is the plain meaning of the charge the *Glasgow Weekly Mail* brings against those immaculate apostles of Whig Nationalism, Messrs Donworth, M'Aweeny,

---

6   Charles Cameron (1841-1924). MP for Glasgow College constituency. Carmeron lost his seat in the1895 election to the Conservative candidate, Sir John Stirling-Maxwell.

7   Tit for tat, a blow for a blow. Roland and Oliver were legendary medieval knights who fought each other to a draw in single combat.

8   Scots English for about, concerning.

Brennan, Sorden, and Co.

* * *

The charge is a grave one, and the virtuous Edinburgh public should insist upon a complete and satisfactory refutation, or else hunt those hypocrites from public life.

* * *

Aha, that is a local matter, and I have handled it well.

* * *

Chief Constable Henderson has received an increase of £100 per annum in his salary. The carters in the employment of the Cleansing Department are still working overtime without additional payment. As the *Evening News* remarks, "the citizens of Edinburgh have shown their wisdom in electing to the Council men of sound business instincts." Oh, yes!

* * *

A contemporary informs us that when the House of Commons meets there will be an attempt made to induce the War Office to increase the stock of cartridges. There is at present an agitation on foot, outside the House of Commons, to increase the wages of dockyard labourers in the service of the Government. In a contest between an increase of cartridges and an increase of wages, I will lay my money on the cartridges every time.

* * *

The Duchess of Hamilton's shooting-box in Leicestershire, Glen Hall, has been broken into, and £100 worth of jewellery stolen.[9] This is shameful. If Bill Sykes[10] the burglar will not respect the pile of his aristocratic fellow-craftsmen, or the adornment of their ladies, our old belief in the existence of honour among thieves will be rudely shaken.

* * *

A London newspaper ventures to prophecy that the frock coat will disappear from wear during the ensuing year.[11] Mine has disappeared long ago. Oh, my prophetic soul, *my uncle!*[12]

* * *

Sir Michael Hicks Beach[13], speaking at Bristol, said he did not believe the whole argument against the House of Lords was worth sixpence. Quite right, Michael; but then the House of Lords itself is not worth threepence, so we are still three copper pennies to the good. See.

* * *

---

9   "The Duchess of Hamilton's Leicestershire hunting box, Glen Hall, has been broken into and £100 worth of jewellery stolen." *Edinburgh Evening News*, 23 January 1895, 4. "A daring robbery was perpetrated the other evening at Glenn house, near Leicester, the hunting box of the Duchess of Hamilton. It appears that the Duchess and the remainder of the house party were at dinner, when the burglars obtained a ladder, placed it against the house, and thereby obtained access to the bedroom of the Duchess. This they rifled of the whole of the jewellery within reach, including a gold watch, gold pins, studs, seals, and pencil cases. The value of the stolen property is estimated at £100." *Stalybridge Reporter*, 26 January 1895, 6.

10   Character in *Oliver Twist* by Charles Dickens. Spelt "Sikes" in the book.

11   "A London newspaper ventures to prophecy that the frock coat will disappear from wear during the current year." *Edinburgh Evening News*, 23 January 1895, 4.

12   *Hamlet*, Act 1 Scene 5, line 41. 'O my prophetic soul! Mine uncle?'

13   Michael Hicks Beach, 1st Earl St Alwyn (1837-1916), Conservative MP for Bristol West (1885-1906). He became Chancellor of the Exchequer for the second time following the 1895 general election.

***

NATIONALISM AND SOCIALISM[1]
SHAN VAN VOCHT
8 JANUARY 1897, PP.7–8

IN IRELAND at the present moment there are at work a variety of agencies seeking to preserve truly national sentiments in the hearts of the people. These agencies, whether Literary Societies, Irish Language Movements, or Commemoration Committees, are undoubtedly doing a work of lasting benefit to this country by helping to save from extinction the precious racial and national characteristics and language of our people. Nevertheless there is a danger that by a too strict adherence to their present methods of propaganda and consequent neglect of vital living issues, they may only succeed in stereotyping our historical studies into a worship of the past, or crystallising nationalism into a tradition, glorious and heroic indeed, but still only a tradition.

New traditions may, and frequently do, provide materials for a glorious martyrdom, but can never be strong enough to ride the storm of a successful revolution. If the national movement of our day is not merely to re-enact the old sad tragedies of our past history, it must show itself capable of rising to the exigencies of the moment, it must demonstrate to the people of Ireland and the world at large that Irish nationality is not merely a morbid idealising of the past, but is also capable of formulating a distinct and definite answer to the problems of the present, and a political and economic creed capable of adjustment to the wants of the future. This concrete political and social ideal, I believe, will be best supplied by a frank acceptance, on the part of all earnest Nationalists, of the Repub-

---

1   Extracts from this article were reprinted in *The People* (New York), 14 February 1897, 2.

lic² as the goal of our endeavours.

The Republic, that is to say, the progressive applications of the principles of true democracy to the national, industrial, and agricultural affairs of our country. Not a Republic, as is France, where a middle-class monarchy with an elective head parodies the constitutional abortions of England, and in open alliance with the Muscovite tyrants of Poland, brazenly proclaims their apostacy to the ideals of their revolutionary forefathers; not a Republic, as in the United States, where the power of the purse has established a new tyranny under the forms of freedom, where one hundred years after the feet of the last British red-coat had polluted the streets of Boston, British landlords and financiers impose upon the necks of American citizens a servitude compared with which the tax of pre-Revolution days was but as is a pin scratch to a bayonet wound. No!

The Republic I would wish our fellow countrymen to set before them as their ideal should be of such a character that the mere mention of its name would at all times serve as a beacon light to the victims of every form of oppression, holding forth promise of freedom and plenty as the reward of their efforts on its behalf. To the tenant farmer ground beneath landlordism on the one hand and American competition on the other as between the upper and the nether millstone, to the wageworker in the towns, suffering beneath the exactions of the slave-driving capitalist; to the agricultural labourer, toiling his life away for a wage that is not sufficient to keep body and soul together, in fact to every one of the toiling millions upon whose misery the outwardly splendid fabric of modern civilization is reared, the Irish Republic might be made a word to conjure with, a rallying point for the disaffected, a haven for the oppressed, a point of departure for the socialist, enthusiastic in the cause of human freedom. This linking together of our national aspirations with the hopes of the men and women who have raised the standard of revolt against that system of landlordism and capitalism, of which the British Empire is the most aggressive type and resolute defender, would not in any sense import an element of discord into the ranks of *earnest* Nationalists, but would instead serve to place us in touch with fresh reservoirs of moral and physical strength, sufficient to lift the cause of Ireland into a more important and commanding position than it has occupied since

---

2   The edition in *The People*, 14 February 1897, reads "...of the Socialist Republic as the goal of our endeavors."

the day of Benburb.[3]

It may be pleaded that the ideal of a Socialist Republic, implying as it does a complete political and economic revolution (vesting the entire ownership of land, railways, machinery, and instruments of labour generally in the hands of those who use them in town and country, to be controlled by their own associations, freely elected on a basis of perfect equality and universal suffrage, subordinate to and represented in the Democratic Congress of an independent Irish State),[4] would be sure to alienate all our middle class and aristocratic sympathisers, who would dread the loss of their privileges and property. What does this objection mean? That we must conciliate the privileged classes in Ireland. But you can only disarm their hostility by assuring them that in a free Ireland their "privileges" will not be interfered with—that is to say, you must guarantee that when Ireland is free of foreign domination the green coats of an Irish army will guard the fraudulent gains of capitalist and landlord from "the thin hands of the poor"[5] as effectually and as remorselessly as the scarlet-coated emissaries of England do today.

On no other basis will the classes unite with you? Do you expect the masses to fight for this ideal? Or when you talk of freeing "Ireland," do you only mean the chemical elements which compose the soil of Ireland? Or is it the Irish people you mean? If the latter, from what do you propose to free them? From the rule of England? But all systems of political administration or governmental machinery are but the reflex of the economic forms which underlie them. English rule in Ireland is but the outward symbol of the fact that English conquerors in the past forced upon this country a property system founded upon spoliation, fraud, and murder. That, as the present-day exercise of the "rights of property" so originated involves the continual practice of legalised spoliation and fraud, English rule is found to be the most suitable form of government

---

3   Battle of Benburb, 5 June 1646, at which the Irish confederate army defeated the Scottish Covenanter Army at Benburb, Co. Tyrone. 5 June was also Connolly's birthday.

4   William O'Brien and Desmond Ryan removed the line in parenthesis from *Socialism and Nationalism* (1948).

5   "They guard our masters' granaries from the thin hands of the poor." From "The Famine Year" by Jane Francesca Wilde ("Speranza") (1821-1896). Originally published in the *Nation*, 23 January 1847 under the title 'The Stricken Land'. Connolly republished it in the *Workers' Republic*, 24 November 1900.

by which that spoliation and fraud can be protected, and an English army the most pliant instrument with which to execute the judicial murder when the fears of the propertied classes demand it. The Socialist who would destroy, root and branch, the whole brutally materialistic system of civilisation, which, like the English language, we have unconsciously adopted as our own, is, I hold, a more deadly foe of English rule and tutelage than the superficial thinker who imagines it possible to reconcile Irish freedom with those insidious but disastrous forms of economic subjection, landlord tyranny, capitalist fraud, and unclean usury: baneful fruits of the Norman Conquest, the unholy trinity of which Strongbow and Dermot M'Morrough—Norman thief and Irish traitor—were the fitting precursors and apostles.

If you could remove the English army tomorrow and hoist the green flag over Dublin Castle, unless you set about the organisation of the Socialist Republic, your efforts would be in vain. England would still rule you; she would rule you through her capitalists, through her landlords, through her financiers, through her usurers, through the whole array of commercial and individualist institutions she has planted in this country and watered with the tears of our mothers and the blood of our martyrs. England would rule you to your ruin even while your lips offered hypocritical homage at the shrine of that freedom whose cause you had betrayed. Nationalism without Socialism; i.e. without a reorganisation of society on the basis of a broader and more developed form of that common property which underlay the social structure of Ancient Erin, is only national recreancy, since it would be tantamount to a public declaration that our oppressors had so far succeeded in inoculating us with their perverted conceptions of justice and morality, that we had finally accepted them as our own, and no longer needed an alien army to force them upon us.

As a Socialist I am prepared to do all one man can do to achieve for our sireland, her rightful heritage, independence; but if you ask me to abate one jot or tittle of the claims of pure justice, in order to win the sympathy of the privileged classes, then I must decline. Such action would neither be honourable nor feasible. Let us never forget that he never reaches Heaven who marches thither in the company of the devil. Let us openly proclaim our faith, the logic of events is with us.

*****

THAT DIAMOND JUBILEE -
IRISH SOCIALIST REPUBLICAN PARTY TO IRISHMEN
THE PEOPLE (NEW YORK)
30 MAY 1897, P.1

FELLOW WORKERS—The loyal subjects of Victoria. Queen of Great Britain and Ireland, Empress of India, etc., celebrate this year the longest reign on record. Already the air is laden with rumors of preparations for a wholesale manufacture of sham "popular rejoicings" at this glorious commemoration (?). Home Rule orators and Nationalist Lord Mayors, Whig politicians and Parnellite pressmen, have ere now lent their prestige and influence to the attempt to arouse public interest in the sickening details of this Feast of Flunkeyism. It is time then that some organized party in Ireland—other than those in whose mouths Patriotism means Compromise, and Freedom, High Dividends—should speak out bravely and honestly the sentiments awakened in the breast of every lover of freedom by this ghastly farce now being played out before our eyes. Hence the Irish Socialist Republican party—which, from its inception has never hesitated to proclaim its unswerving hostility to the British Crown, and to the political and social order of which in those islands that crown is but the symbol—takes this opportunity of hurling at the heads of all the courtly mummers who grovel at the shrine of royalty, the contempt and hatred of the Irish revolutionary democracy. We, at least, are not loyal men. We confess to have more respect and honor for the raggedist child of the poorest laborer in Ireland today, than for any, even the most virtuous, descendant of the long array of murderers, adulterers and madmen who have sat upon the throne of England. During this glorious reign, Ireland has seen 1,225,000 of her children die of famine; starved to death, whilst the produce of her soil and their labor was eaten up by a vulture aristocracy, enforcing their rents by the bayonets of a hired assassin army, in the pay of the "best of the English queens"; the eviction of 3,668,000; a multitude greater than the entire population of Switzerland; and the reluctant emigration of 4,186,000 of our kindred; a greater host than the entire people of Greece. At the present moment seventy-eight percent of our wage-earners receive less than £1 per week, our streets are thronged by starving crowds of the unemployed, cattle graze on our tenantless farms and around the ruins of our battered homesteads, our ports are crowded with departing emigrants, and our poorhouses are full of paupers. Such are the constituent elements out of which we are bade to construct a national festival of rejoicing!

Working Class of Ireland—We appeal to you not to allow your opinions to be misrepresented on this occasion. Join your voice with ours in protesting against the base assumption that we owe to this empire any other debt than that of hatred of all its plundering institutions. Let this year be indeed a memorable one, as marking the date when the Irish workers at last flung off that slavish dependence on the lead of "the gentry," which has paralyzed the arm of every soldier of freedom in the past. The Irish landlords, now as ever, the enemy's garrison, instinctively support every institution, which like monarchy, degrades the manhood of the people and weakens the moral fibre of the oppressed: the middle class, absorbed in the pursuit of gold, have pawned their souls for the prostitute glories of commercialism, and remain openly or secretly hostile to every movement which would imperil the sanctity of their dividends: the working class alone have nothing to hope for save in a revolutionary reconstruction of society: they, and they alone, are capable of that revolutionary initiative, which with all the political and economic development of the time to aid it, can carry us forward into the promised land of perfect freedom, the reward of the age-long travail of the people. To you, workers of Ireland, we address ourselves—AGITATE in the workshop, in the field, in the factory, until you arouse your brothers to hatred of the slavery of which we are all victims—EDUCATE, that the people may no longer be deluded by illusory hopes of prosperity under any system of society of which monarchs or noblemen, capitalists or landlords form an integral part: ORGANISE, that a solid, compact and intelligent force, conscious of your historic mission as a class, you may seize the reins of political power whenever possible, and by intelligent application of the working-class ballot clear the field of action for the revolutionary forces of the future.[1] Let the "canting, fed classes"[2] bow the knee as they may, be you true to your own manhood, and to the cause of freedom, whose hope is in you, and pressing unweariedly onward in pursuit of the high destiny to which the Socialist Republic invites you, let the words which the poet puts into the mouth of Mazeppa console you amid the orgies of the tyrants today.

> But time at last makes all things even
> And if we do but watch the hour
> There never yet was human power
> That could evade, if unforgiven,
> The patient HATE and vigil long
> Of those who treasure up a wrong.[3]

---

1   "Educate. We shall need all our intelligence. Agitate. We shall need all our enthusiasm. Organise. We shall need all our force." Social Democratic Federation, *Socialism Made Plain: the Social and Political Manifesto of the Democratic Federation* (1883), 8.

2   "Therefore take courage, all you that Jacobins be, and stand upon your rights, and do your appointed work with all your strength, let the canting fed classes rave and shriek as they will. Where you see a respectable, fair-spoken Lie sitting in high places, feeding itself fat on human sacrifices, down with it, strip it naked, and pitch it to the Devil wherever you see a greedy tyranny (constitutional or other) grinding the faces of the poor, join battle with it on the spot, conspire, confederate, and combine against it, resting never till the huge mischief come down, though the whole "structure of society come down along with it." John Mitchel, *Jail Journal* (New York, 1854), 110-111.

3   Based on lines from *Mazeppa* (1819) by Lord Byron (1788-1824). The original lines are: "For time at last sets all things even— / And if we do but watch the hour, / There never yet was human power / Which could evade, if unforgiven, / The patient search and vigil long / Of him who treasures up a wrong." Connolly rather pointedly changed "search" for "HATE" in the final line, with "HATE" in bold.

*****

FAMINE IN IRELAND
THE PEOPLE (NEW YORK)
29 MAY 1898, P.1

DUBLIN, Ireland. May 22—It is possible that even amid the excitement of the Cuban War and despite the all-absorbing labours of the SLP[1] of America in its prosecution of the far more important class war, there may have reached the United States some information sufficiently explicit to bring home to the minds of our comrades there the alarming fact that in Ireland at the present moment a large section of the population is suffering from a lack of food, amounting to actual famine.

But as such news is bound to be discounted in its importance by the fact that it only filters through to the people by the medium of a sensational press; and as it is almost certain to be accompanied by suggestions for remedies ridiculously inapplicable to the evil itself, I have ventured to set down here a few of the facts which came under my own observation, in a recent tour through the distressed districts, and also some of the reflections which as a Socialist were forced upon me by these facts.

The particular district through which I extended my investigations is that known as the County of Kerry. My tour comprised within its area the portion of the county extending from the town of Kenmare round the southwest coast to what is known as the town of Cahirciveen. This is the famine-stricken district of that county. It is composed almost entirely of mountains and bog land.

From the point of view of the picturesque nothing can be finer than this countryside, sea and mountain combining to charm the eye; but from the point of view of the people who have to extract a living from the culti-

---

1   Socialist Labor Party.

vation of the soil no place on earth would be more dismal or less encouraging. There is no such thing as a large farm in the neighbourhood, from five to twenty acres being as a rule the extent of holdings, and the dwellings of the people, exterior and interior, being of the rudest and most comfortless description. Almost all the population engage during the season in the fishing off the coast in their own boats, but as these vessels are only of the smallest description they can not venture far from land, and in consequence they have had, during the past year, the mortification of seeing the larger and better equipped boats of other nations come to their shores and reap the harvest of the sea before it reached them. At the same time the potato crop was attacked with the blight and the greater part of it destroyed, rendered quite unfit for food, and as the potato forms the staple diet of the entire people this second loss was indeed the crowning stroke to their misery. Round a great part of this district it is the custom for the shopkeepers to advance the necessaries of life to their customers during the winter and spring, and to receive repayment for same out of the proceeds of the fishing in the summer, but the practical failure of the fishing last year rendered the latter engagement impossible. The debts remain unpaid, the credit of the customers with the shopkeeper and of the shopkeeper with the wholesale merchant is now exhausted, bankruptcy is imminent, and starvation walks abroad through the land.

I have personally visited and verified numerous cases in which the whole family have not even had the luxury of potatoes since September 1897, but have been living for months upon *two* diets, and for weeks upon *one diet per day*, and that diet composed exclusively of Indian meal and water, without even milk to wash it down. I have conversed with schoolmasters who told of children fainting on the schoolroom floor for want of food. I have seen women, mothers of families, for the sake of half a dollar's worth of provisions walk seven miles to a relief committee, wait three or four hours and then have to walk the same distance back, have heard from the lips of eyewitnesses (whose credibility I can vouch for) of the produce of shellfish mixed with meal and boiled in water being eagerly devoured by one famishing family, and of the carcass of a diseased cow serving as food to another, have visited districts in which disease (to which this physical weakness brought on by hunger makes these people peculiarly subject) have seized nearly every house, until the place was justly described as 'one vast hospital,' in short, I have in one short tour of three weeks' duration seen an amount of misery so great as to justify the sufferers and all humane men in taking every means in their power to hurl into destruction the power whose administrators and 'statesmen' either could not or would not remedy the evil and prevent its occurrence.

But the leaders of the Irish people at present are themselves as little capable of formulating any real remedy for the evil that even were the forces of England annihilated tomorrow, and our Home Rule politicians installed in power, the economic conditions which have produced the present famine would be left untouched and at full liberty to work similar ruin in the future. Greater promptitude in coming to the relief of the sufferers we undoubtedly would have, more liberal application of public funds to the relief of distress might certainly be expected, but any statesmanlike effort to *prevent famine by removing the cause* would only come by the application to agriculture of those 'wild' Socialist theories for which our bourgeois patriots have, or profess, such an aversion. For these people I have spoken of are not suffering because of the existence in their midst of an 'alien' government, but because of the failure of that system of small farming and small industry on which they depended for their existence, to overcome the natural difficulties presented by their rugged coast and moist climate. Even landlordism, the curse of the Irish race in times past, and the clog and hindrance of all administrative bodies in the present, is only in a minor degree responsible for the present crisis. The root cause lies in the system of small farming and small industry. Isolated on his little plot of ground which in the best of times scarcely affords more than a bare subsistence, the Irish peasant reaps none of the benefits of the progress of civilisation, knows nothing of the wonderful results of the organisation of industry, his mental horizon is bounded by the weekly 'patriot' newspaper crammed with tales and legends of ancient Erin and her chivalry, and destitute of all scientific or economic enlightenment to help the Irish of today, and thus when the full hand of disease is stretched forth over the poor potato crop each peasant strives to avert the catastrophe by his own effort and thus falls an easy victim to the blight which an organised people could easily avert or render innocuous. In the present instance the two disasters which combined to produce the famine, were both directly due to the want of such co-operative effort as it would be the first duty of a Socialist republic to organise, and without such Socialist reorganisation the perpetual recurrence of these scenes of misery may be regarded as a certainty, no matter whether our government be Irish or English, alien or native.

The difference between the Irish and English capitalist politician in this matter may be briefly stated as follows: The Irish member of Parliament is invariably a political adventurer depending upon notoriety to demonstrate his usefulness to the party paymasters, therefore he must occasionally create a "scene" in the House of Commons, or make a "fiery" speech outside. Thus does he earn his salary and justify his existence to those who subscribe it. The English member of Parliament, on the other hand, is as a rule a wealthy capitalist who occupies his position in virtue of his having made certain donations to the party exchequer, of being donor-in-chief to local charities and chief financial mainstay of the local branch of his party organization. Therefore he is not expected to show signs of political activity, but only of a plethoric purse. *The Irish nationalist politician is the financial dependent of his party, the English political parties are the financial dependents of the capitalist politicians.* To use a homely simile, the difference between the English and Irish bourgeois politicians is simply the difference of attitude between the man who has caught a train and the man who is running to catch it. The English party politician comfortably ensconced in the train of fully dominant capitalism, only requires to *sit tight* and smile his scorn of the voting cattle whom he calls his fellow-countrymen, but the Irish party politician not yet able to realize an assured Income independent of political activity, has not caught the train, and in his rush for it avails himself of every means possible to win the favor of his fellow countrymen that they might be induced to help him into the same position as his English rival.

The mass of the Irish people being engaged in agriculture, the Irish "patriot" bourgeois seeks to win their favor by demanding legislative enactments in the interest of the farming community, Land Courts to give fair rents (?), compulsory purchase of landed estates in order to establish peasant proprietory, State help in constructing railways, State subsidies for lines of Irish steamships trading for Irish ports, government loans for harbor construction; in fact, be invokes the aid of the State in a manner calculated to put to blush even the most hardened Fabian, and seemingly totally inconsistent with that individualism on which capitalism is based. But when measures in behalf of the working class are mooted, when legislative interference between capital and labor is the subject of debate, then the identity of interests between the English and the Irish bourgeois is made at once apparent by the all but unanimous front both parties present against such "interference with the liberty of the subject."

In this respect, it will be observed. They are only repeating the tactics of the bourgeois parties of all countries. Grasping the power of the State, they have ever used it remorselessly in their fight against the pretensions of the landed aristocracy, regarding it then as their savior and a potent instrument of the world's welfare; but once freed from the danger of aristocratic domination and confronted by a demand that the State power should extent its beneficent operations over the entire community, and raise the wage-slave in his turn to freedom, then the State becomes to the bourgeois anathema, rarely fit to serve as a gigantic policeman for the protection of the private property and furtherance of the private interests of the possessing class.

The English capitalist parties (liberals or radicals) had always looked upon the Irish with contempt in the past, until the year 1885, when a lightning flash of class-consciousness suddenly illumining their understanding they recognized in the Irish Home Rulers the image of their own younger brothers, seeking to realise the same ends as themselves, by methods foreign to the English bourgeois of today perhaps, but nevertheless wonderfully similar to those his fathers had employed at a similar stage of their economic development. Out of the sudden recognition of this economic affinity arose, over the Irish Home Rule bill, the so-called Union of Hearts (of the Irish and English politicians), a pitiful travesty of that free union of free peoples which Socialism alone can bring to fruition. But this alliance from which Irishmen hoped so much was of necessity short-lived. The Englishman, at first cordial in his friendship to the Irish agitator who only wished to mould Ireland on the political and economic pattern of England, suddenly cooled off when he reflected that if the political freedom of Ireland would indeed hasten the economic development of that country; then English manufacturers would be the first to suffer by the entrance on the industrial battlefield of such a competitor. Better keep Ireland fettered, even at the cost of a standing military garrison, than to allow her freedom and see her develop into another rival in the race for the markets of the world.

The Right Hon. Joseph Chamberlain and most of the wealthier men of the Liberal party had reasoned so all along and therefore remained Liberal Unionists, opposed to Home Rule and Irish measures in general. After the first flush of their love for Ireland had cooled a little, and given time for the selfish passions to reassert their sway, such arguments and reasoning made such wonderful headway among "the leaders of public opinion" throughout England that the Home Rule proposal at the very next election received a crushing defeat from which it is questionable if It will ever recover.

As Ireland lacks nearly all the requisites for an industrial country, the fear that inspired this revulsion of public opinion was, I believe, entirely baseless, but the result itself is by no means regrettable. The Home Rule bill was in fact perhaps the greatest legislative abortion ever foisted upon a people in the name of self-government. The net result of all this play and counter-play of political and social forces during the last twenty years is the utter discomfiture of the middle class politicians, the falsification of all their prophecies, and the wreck of all their organisations. Added to this the various 'splits' in the Home Rule camp, by leading the politicians to attack one another, have revealed to the astonished eyes of the multitude the sorry character of the men whom they once idolised.

The effect of this situation upon the problem caused by the present famine may be briefly told. The English Liberal allies of the Home Rule party represent, as I have pointed out, a fully capitalist nation, or, more accurately speaking, a nation in which capitalism is generally dominant and no longer requires the aid of the State to maintain its internal prestige over reactionary forces. In such a country and to such a party, the State is a veritable Frankenstein, and to the dominant class a thing to be restricted and fettered in every way. But the Home Rule party represent an imperfectly developed country, in which *land* and not *capital* is dominant, and which, therefore, requires the aid of the State to free itself from the fetters of feudalism. The famine, the direct product of this imperfectly developed state of industry and agriculture, can only be effectually grappled with by the State, and thereupon the Home Ruler advocates State aid, but in so doing receives little if any aid from the English Liberal, who instinctively shrinks from any proposal which might tend to popularise the idea of State interference. Thus the Home Ruler, our Irish bourgeois politician, is landed in a hopeless dilemma. He knows he will be utterly ruined without the English Liberal alliance, nobody will believe in him, nobody will subscribe his salary, he will be dropped like a useless tool. And the English Liberals will not assist him in his demand for State aid, if he pushes it, they will relinquish him. But his constituents, the Irish agricultural population, who believe State aid to be their only hope, will repudiate him if he does not demand it. In such a hopeless quandary the Irish patriot parties, save the mark, flounder along without a definite policy, without a programme, without hope for the future, each separate party seeking to hide its confusion by emitting, like the cuttlefish, a shower of abuse upon its rivals, who retaliate in kind, until the waters of Irish politics stink in the nostrils of decent Irishmen.

Two recent plans prove this:

First—Thanks to the clashing of bourgeois interests, the famine pursues its way unchecked.

Second—The class-conscious Irish members grow in strength, in hope and in public confidence.

*****

L'IRLANDE ET LE SOCIALISME[1]
L'IRLANDE LIBRE
1 AUGUST 1898, PP.1-2

L A VIE PUBLIQUE de l'Irlande a été en général si bien identifiée avec la lutte pour l'émancipation politique que, naturellement, le côté économique de la situation n'a reçu de nos historiens et de nos publicistes qu'un très faible degré d'attention.

Le socialiste scientifique admet la vérité incorporée dans cette proposition de Marx que « la dépendance économique des ouvriers par rapport aux monopoliseurs est la base de la servitude *sous toutes ses formes,* et la cause de presque toute la misère sociale, de la criminalité moderne, de la dégradation mentale et de la dépendance politique. » Aussi cette fâcheuse exagération de la forme purement politique qu'à revêtue en Irlande la lutte pour la liberté, doit sembler à ce socialiste une inexplicable erreur de la part d'un peuple aussi fortement opprimé que le peuple irlandais. Mais l'erreur est véritablement plus dans l'apparence que dans la réalité.

Mais l'attitude réactionnaire de nos leaders politiques actuels, la grande masse du peuple irlandais se rend assez nettement compte que cette liberté politique qu'il poursuit avec tant d'ardeur, il devrait, s'il l'avait une fois conquise, la manier comme un arme de rédemption sociale, avant qu'il pût s'assurer son bien-être.

Malgré tout on doit se souvenir qu'en se dirigeant déterminément, comme ils le font, vers un but purement politique, les Irlandais se rattachent tout à fait aux grandes lignes de conduite posées par le socialisme

---

1   English translation published in *Workers' Repub*lic, 3 September 1898, 3, with the title "Socialism and Irish Nationalism."

moderne comme la condition indispensable et librement requise du succès.

Depuis l'abandon de l'insurrection malheureuse des anciens sócialistes, dont les espérances se concentraient exclusivement sur le triomphe éventuel d'une émeute et d'un combat de barricades, le socialisme moderne, recherchent la méthode, plus lente, mais plus sûre, du bulletin de vote, à dirigé l'attention de ses partisans vers la conquête pacifique des forces gouvernementales, dans l'intérêt de l'idéal révolutionnaire. L'avènement du socialisme ne peut se produire, nous le savons que quand le prolétariat révolutionnaire, en possession des forces organisées de la nation, (la puissance politique du Gouvernement) sera parvenu à créer une organisation sociale conforme à la marche naturelle du développement industriel. D'autre part, l'effort coopératif (non-politique) dans a même direction doit infailliblement échouer en face de l'opposition intéressée des classes privilégiées retranchées derrière les remparts de la loi et du monopole.

C'est pourquoi, même quand il est, au point de vue économique, très ouvertement conservateur, le rationaliste irlandais, tout en restant d'accord avec son faux raisonnement, est un agent actif de régénération sociale, en ce qu'il cherche à investir d'un plein pouvoir sur ses propres destinées un peuple gouverné actuellement par les intérêts d'une aristocratie féodale.

La section de l'armée socialiste à laquelle j'appartiens, le parti républicain socialiste irlandais, pas plus ici que là, ne cherche à cacher son hostilité à l'égard des partis purement bourgeois qui à présent dirigent la politique irlandaise.

Mais, en inscrivant sur nos drapeaux un idéal auquel, du bout des lèvres, ils rendent eux aussi hommage, nous n'avons pas conscience d'être dans une voie qui puisse abaisser le Drapeau du socialisme révolutionnaire.

Les partis socialistes de France font de l'opposition aux purs républicains, sans cesser d'aimer la République; de même, le parti républicain socialiste d'Irlande cherche l'indépendance de la nation, en refusant de se conformer aux méthodes ou d'employer les arguments du nationaliste chauvin.

Comme socialistes, nous ne sommes pas poussés à des haines de nations ou de races par le souvenir que l'ordre politique et social sous lequel nous vivons fut imposé à nos pères à la points de l'épée; que, pendant 700 ans, l'Irlande a résisté à cette injuste domination; que la famine, la peste et un mauvaise gouvernement ont fait de cette île occidentale presque un désert et dispersé nos compatriotes exilés sur la face du globe.

L'évocation de faits pareils à ceux que je viens de citer ne sert pas aujourd'hui à inspirer ou à diriger les énergies politiques de la classe travailleuse militante de l'Irlande, telle n'est point la base de notre désir d'affranchir l'Irlande du joug de l'empire britannique. Nous nous rappelons plutôt que, pendant tous ces siècles, la grande masse du peuple britannique n'avait pas d'existence politique quelconque; que l'Angleterre était, politiquement et socialement, terrorisée par une classe gouvernante peu nombreuse; que les atrocités qui ont été perpétrées contre l'Irlande sont seulement imputables à l'ambition peu serupuleuse de cette classe avide de s'enrichir des dépouilles d'hommes sans défense; que, jusqu'à la présente génération, il ne fut pas donné à la grande majorité du peuple anglais d'avoit voix délibérative dans le gouvernement de son *propré* pays; qu'il y a, par suite, malhonnêteté é manifeste à charger le peuple anglais d'une faute qui est celle de *notre* gouvernement; et qu'au pis aller, on peut tout au plus l'accuser de sa criminelle apathie a subir lui-même l'esclavage et à se faire un instrument de coërcition pour l'asservissement des autres. Accusation applicable au présent aussi bien qu'au passé.

Ainsi, nous refusant à baser notre activité politique sur les antipathies nationales héritées, et souhaitant plutôt la camaraderie des travailleurs anglais que les regardant avec haine, nous désirons, avec nos précurseurs, les Irlandais unis de 1798, que nos animosités soient ensevelies avec les os de nos ancêtres. Mais, en même temps, il n'y a pas de parti en Irlande qui accentue davantage, comme un principe vital de sa joi politique, le besoin de se séparer de l'Angleterre, et de se rendre absolument indépendant.

Aux yeux de l'irréfléchi ou de l'ignorant, il peut y avoir là une inconséquence; mais j'ai in persuasion que nos frères socialistes de France reconnaitront tout de suite la justesse du raisonnement sur lequel est basée une telle politique.

1. On nous dit: L'émancipation économique du travailleur exige la transformation des moyens de production en propriété commune de la

société. Traduit dans le langage courant et la pratique de la politique actuelle, cela peut s'entendre de la marche nécessaire pour que le socialisme s'établisse: c'est-à-dire du passage des moyens de production d'entre les mains des propriétaires particuliers à celles des corps publics fortement soumis à la volonté populaire.

2. Le socialisme cherche donc dans l'intérêt de la démocratie, à fortifier l'action populaire sur tous les corps publics.

3. Les corps représentatifs en Irlande dépendraient nécessairement plus de la volonté du peuple irlandais que maintenant qu'ils résident en Angleterre.

Une République Irlandaise s'imposerait donc comme la dépositaire naturelle du pouvoir populaire, comme l'arme de l'émancipation populaire, comme l'unique chose exigée pour mettre à la pleine lumière du jour tous les antagonismes de classes et les lignes de démarcation économique actuellement obscurcies par l'écume du patriotisme bourgeois. En cela, il n'y a point trace de chauvinisme. Nous désirons conserver avec le peuple anglais les mêmes relations politiques qu'avec le peuple de France, d'Allemagne ou de n'importe quel pays. L'amitié la plus étroite possible, mais aussi la plus stricte indépendance. Frères, mais non camarades de lit.

Ainsi, inspiré par un autre idéal, conduit par la raison, non par la tradition, suivant un chemin différent, le parti républicain socialiste d'Irlande arrive à la même conclusion que le plus irréconciliable nationaliste. Le pouvoir gouvernemental de l'Angleterre sur nous doit être détruit, le lien qui nous unit à elle doit être brisé.

Instruits par l'histoire que tout mouvement bourgeois aboutit à un compromis, que les révoltés bourgeois d'aujourd'hui deviennent les conservateurs de demain, les socialistes irlandais refusent de noyer ou de perdre leur personnalité dans une alliance avec ceux qui saisissent seulement une moitié du problème de la liberté. Ils cherchent seulement l'alliance et l'amitié de ces cœurs d'élite qui aimant la liberté à cause d'elle-même, n'ont pas peur de suivre sa bannière quand elle est levée par les mains du peuple travailleur, qui en a le plus besoin. Leurs amis, ce sont caux qui n'hésitent pas à le suivre, cet étendard de la liberté, pour consacrer leur vie à son service, quand ils devraient aller jusqu'à l'arbitrage terrible de l'épée.

ENGLISH TRANSLATION

SOCIALISM AND IRISH NATIONALISM
WORKERS' REPUBLIC
3 SEPTEMBER 1898, P.3

Reprinted from *L'Irlande Libre*. The organ of the Irish Colony in Paris, edited by Miss Maude Gonne.

The public life of Ireland has been generally so much identified with the struggle for political emancipation, that, naturally, the economic side of the situation has only received from our historians and public men a very small amount of attention.

Scientific Socialism is based upon the truth incorporated in this proposition of Marx, that, "the economic dependence of the workers on the monopolists of the means of production is the foundation of slavery *in all its forms*, the cause of nearly all social misery, modern crime, mental degradation and political dependence."[2] Thus this false exaggeration of purely political forms which has clothed in Ireland the struggle for liberty, must appear to the Socialist an inexplicable error on the part of a people so strongly crushed down as the Irish.

But the error is more in appearance than in reality.

The reactionary attitude of our political leaders notwithstanding, the great mass of the Irish people know full well that if they had once conquered that political liberty which they struggle for with so much ardour, it would have to be used as a means of *social* redemption before their well-being would be assured.

In spite of occasional exaggeration of its immediate results one must remember that by striving determinedly, as they have done, towards this definite political end, the Irish are working on the lines of conduct laid down by modern Socialism as the indispensable condition of success.

---

2   From *Address and Provisional Rules of the Working Men's International Association* (London, 1864). Original quote: "That the economical subjection of the man of labour to the monopolizer of the means of labour, that is the sources of life, lies at the bottom of servitude in all its forms, of all social misery, mental degradation, and political dependence." See *Bee-Hive Newspaper*, 12 November 1984, 1.

Since the abandonment of the unfortunate insurrectionism of the early Socialists whose hopes were exclusively concentrated on the eventual triumph of an uprising and barricade struggle, modern Socialism, relying on the slower but surer method of the ballot-box, has directed the attention of its partisans toward the peaceful conquest of the forces of government in the interests of the revolutionary ideal.

The advent of Socialism can only take place when the revolutionary proletariat, in possession of the organized forces of the nation (the political power of government) will be able to build up a social organization in conformity with the natural march of industrial development.

On the other hand, non-political cooperative effort must infallibly succumb in face of the opposition of the privileged classes, entrenched behind the ramparts of law and monopoly. This is why, even when he is from the economic point of view, intensely conservative, the Irish Nationalist, even with his false reasoning, is an active agent in social regeneration, in so far as he seeks to invest with full power over its own destinies a people actually governed in the interests of a feudal aristocracy.

The section of the Socialist army to which I belong, the Irish Socialist Republican Party, never seeks to hide its hostility to those purely bourgeois parties which at present direct Irish politics.

But, in inscribing on our banners an ideal to which they also give lip-homage, we have no intention of joining in a movement which could debase the banner of revolutionary Socialism.

The Socialist parties of France oppose the mere Republicans without ceasing to love the Republic. In the same way the Irish Socialist Republican Party seeks the independence of the nation, whilst refusing to conform to the methods or to employ the arguments of the chauvinist Nationalist.

As Socialists we are not imbued with national or racial hatred by the remembrance that the political and social order under which we live was imposed on our fathers at the point of the sword; that during 700 years Ireland has resisted this unjust foreign domination; that famine, pestilence and bad government have made of this western isle almost a desert and scattered our exiled fellow-countrymen over the whole face of the globe.

The enunciation of facts such as I have just stated is not able today to inspire or to direct the political energies of the militant working class of Ireland; such is not the foundation of our resolve to free Ireland from the yoke of the British Empire. We recognize rather that, during all these centuries, the great mass of the British people had no political existence whatever; that England was, politically and socially, terrorized by a numerically small governing class; that the atrocities which have been perpetrated against Ireland are only imputable to the unscrupulous ambition of this class, greedy to enrich itself at the expense of defenceless men; that up to the present generation the great majority of the English people were denied a deliberative voice in the government of their own country; that it is therefore, manifestly unjust to charge the English people with the past crimes of their Government; and that at the worst we can but charge them with a criminal apathy in submitting to slavery and allowing themselves to be made an instrument of coercion for the enslavement of others. An accusation as applicable to the present as to the past.

But whilst refusing to base our political action on hereditary national antipathy, and wishing rather comradeship with the English workers than to regard them with hatred, we desire with our precursors the United Irishmen of 1798, that our animosities be buried with the bones of our ancestors—there is not a party in Ireland which accentuates more as a vital principle of its political faith the need of separating Ireland from England and of making it absolutely independent. In the eyes of the ignorant and of the unreflecting this appears an inconsistency, but I am persuaded that our Socialist brothers in France will immediately recognize the justice of the reasoning upon which such a policy is based.

1. We are told "the economic emancipation of the worker requires the conversion of the means of production into the common property of society."[3] Translated into the current language and practice of actual politics this teaches that the necessary road to be travelled towards the establishment of Socialism requires the transference of

---

3   From the *Gotha Programme of the Social Democratic Party of Germany*, May 1875. "Die Befreiung der Arbeit erfordert die Verwandlung der Arbeitsmittel in Gemeingut der Gesellschaft und die genossenschaftliche Regelung der Gesamtarbeit mit gemeinnütziger Verwendung und gerechter Verteilung des Arbeitsertrages." (The liberation of labour demands the transformation of the means of production into the common property of society and the associative regulation of the collective labour with general employment and just distribution of the proceeds of labour.)

the means of production from the hands of private owners to those of public bodies, directly responsible to the entire community.

2. Socialism seeks then in the interest of the democracy to strengthen popular action on all public bodies.

3. Representative bodies in Ireland would express more directly the will of the Irish people than when those bodies reside in England.

An Irish Republic would then be the natural depository of popular power; the weapon of popular emancipation, the only power which would show in the full light of day all the class antagonisms and lines of economic demarcation now obscured by the mists of bourgeois patriotism.

In that there is not a trace of chauvinism. We desire to preserve with the English people the same political relations as with the people of France, of Germany, or of any other country; the greatest possible friendship but also the strictest independence. Brothers, but not bedfellows. Thus, inspired by another ideal, conducted by reason not by tradition, following a different road the Socialist Republican Party of Ireland arrive at the same conclusion as the most irreconcilable Nationalist. The governmental power of England over us must be destroyed; the bonds which unite us to her must be broken. Having learned from history that all bourgeois movements end in compromise, that the bourgeois revolutionists of today become the conservatives of tomorrow, the Irish Socialists refuse to deny or to lose their identity in an alliance with those who only understand half the problem of liberty. They seek only the alliance and the friendship of those hearts who, loving liberty for its own sake, are not afraid to follow its banner when it is uplifted by the hands of the working class who have the most need of it. Their friends are those who would not hesitate to follow that standard of liberty, to consecrate their lives in its service even should it lead them to the terrible arbitration of the sword.

*****

PATRIOTISM AND LABOUR
SHAN VAN VOCHT
2 AUGUST 1897, PP.138-9

WHAT IS PATRIOTISM? Love of country, someone answers. But what is meant by "love of country?" "The rich man," says a French writer, "loves his country because he conceives it owes him a duty, whereas the poor man loves his country as he believes he owes it a duty."[1] The recognition of the duty we owe our country is, I take it, the real mainspring of patriotic action; and our "country," properly understood, means not merely the particular spot on the earth's surface from which we derive our parentage, but also comprises all the men, women, and children of our race whose collective life constitutes our country's political existence. True patriotism seeks the welfare of each in the happiness of all, and is inconsistent with the selfish desire for worldly wealth, which can only be gained by the spoilation of less favoured fellow-mortals.

Viewed in the light of such a definition, what are the claims to patriotism possessed by the moneyed class of Ireland? The percentage of weekly wages of £1 per week and under received by the workers of the three kingdoms is stated by the Board of Trade report to be as follows:— England, 40; Scotland, 50; and Ireland, 78 per cent. In other words, three out of every four wage-earners in Ireland receive less than £1 per week. Who is to blame? What determines the rate of wages? The competition among workers for employment. There is always a large surplus of unemployed labour in Ireland, and owing to this fact the Irish employer is able to take advantage of the helplessness of his poorer fellow-countrymen and compel them to work for less than their fellows in England receive

---

1   I am unable to source the origin of this quote.

for the same class of work.

The employees of our municipal Corporations and other public bodies in Ireland are compelled by our middle class town councillors—their compatriots—to accept wages of from 4s. to 8s. per week less than English Corporations pay in similar branches of public services. Irish railway servants receive from 5s. to 10s. per week less than English railway servants in the same departments, although shareholders in Irish railways draw higher dividends than are paid on the most prosperous English lines. In all private employment in Ireland the same state of matters prevail. Let us be clear upon this point. There is no law upon the statute book, no power possessed by the Privy Council, no civil or military function under the control of Prime Minister, Lord Lieutenant, or Chief Secretary which can, does, or strives to compel the employing class in Ireland to take advantage of the crowded state of the labour market and use it to depress the wages of their workers to the present starvation level.

To the greed of our moneyed class, operating upon the social conditions created by landlordism and capitalism, and maintained upon foreign bayonets, such a result is alone attributable, and no amount of protestations should convince intelligent workers that the class which grinds them down to industrial slavery can at the same moment be leading them forward to national liberty. True patriotism seeks the welfare of each in the happiness of all, and is inconsistent with the selfish desire for worldly wealth which can only be gained by the spoilation of less favoured fellow-mortals. It is the mission of the working class to give to patriotism this higher, nobler, significance. This can only be done by our working class, as the only universal, all-embracing class, organising as a distinct political party, recognising in Labour the cornerstone of our economic edifice and the animating principle of our political action.

Hence the rise of the Irish Socialist Republican Party. We are resolved upon national independence as the indispensable ground-work of industrial emancipation, but we are equally resolved to have done with the leadership of a class whose social charter is derived from oppression. Our policy is the outcome of long reflection upon the history and peculiar circumstances of our country. In an independent country the election of a majority of socialist representatives to the Legislature means the conquest of political power by the revolutionary party, and consequently the mastery of the military and police forces of the State, which would then become the ally of revolution instead of its enemy.

In the work of social reconstruction which would then ensue, the State power—created by the propertied classes for their own class purposes—would serve the new social order as a weapon in its fight against such adherents of the privileged orders as strove to resist the gradual extinction of their rule.

Ireland not being an independent country, the election of a majority of Socialist Republicans would not, unfortunately, place the fruits of our toil so readily within our grasp. But it would have another, perhaps no less important, effect. It would mean that for the first time in Irish history a clear majority of the responsible electorate of the Irish nation—men capable of bearing arms—had registered at the ballot-boxes their desire for separation from the British Empire. Such a verdict, arrived at not in the tumultuous and too often fickle enthusiasm of monster meetings, but in the sober atmosphere and judicial calmness of the polling-booth, would ring like a trumpet-call in the ears alike of our rulers and of every enemy of the British Imperial system. That system would not long survive such a consummation. Its enemies would read in the verdict thus delivered at the ballot-box a passionate appeal for help against the oppressor, the *moral* insurrection of the Irish people, which a small expeditionary force and war material might convert into such a *military* insurrection as would exhaust the power of the empire at home and render its possessions an easy prey abroad. How long would such an appeal be disregarded?

Meanwhile, there is no temporary palliative of our misery, no material benefit which Parliament can confer, that could not be extorted by the fear of a revolutionary party seeking to create such a situation as I have described, sooner than by any action of even the most determined Home Rule or other constitutional party. Thus alike for present benefits and for future freedom the revolutionary policy is the best. A party aiming at a merely political Republic, and proceeding upon such lines, would always be menaced by the danger that some astute English Statesman might, by enacting a sham measure of Home Rule, disorganise the Republican forces by an appearance of concessions, until the critical moment had passed. But the Irish Socialist Republican Party, by calling attention to evils inherent in that social system of which the British Empire is but the highest political expression, founds its propaganda upon discontent with social inequities which will only pass away when the Empire is no more, and thus implants in all its followers an undying, ineradicable hatred of the enemy, which will remain undisturbed and unmollified by any conceivable system of political quackery whatever.

An Irish Socialist Republic ought therefore to be the rallying cry of all our countrymen who desire to see the union and triumph of patriotism and labour.

PART VI
EARLY WRITINGS PREVIOUSLY REPUBLISHED IN FULL

*****

WHAT IS WEALTH?[1]
DUNDEE WEEKLY NEWS
8 AUG 1891, P.3

SIR,—What is wealth? Wealth may be defined as everything necessary to the comfort and well-being of the human race. Money is not in itself wealth, although in society today it is a medium by which we may possess ourselves of wealth. Is wealth unfairly divided? Such a question can only be decided by appealing to cold, hard facts, and ignoring all mere theorisings or speculations. As labour is the source of all wealth, and the support of all life, it therefore follows that the only just claim to the possession of wealth lies with those who have laboured to produce it. Is wealth, then, divided in accordance with any such basis of distribution? Let us see. To take the annual distribution of wealth in this country we find that the annual produce of labour is estimated at £1,230,000,000 of which 200 millions are taken from the workers in the form of rent, 250 millions as interest, and 300 millions as profit, or a total of 800 millions, the produce of labour, to be divided among 10 millions of the population, while the remaining 459 millions is all that is left for the purpose of providing for the wants and necessities of the 23 million workers whose labour produced the entire amount.

Examining particular instances of this unequal distribution, we find that Queen Victoria received £385,000 per annum, and that the average wage of a Dundee female millworker is about 10s per week, or £26 per annum, if she works full time. £385,000 per annum is more than £1000 per day, and a woman working in the brickfields at Stourbridge, England, handling furnace brick 7 lbs in weight, receives 2s 2d for a day's work of

---

1   This letter was republished by the *Treason Felony* Blog, 4 June 2020.

10 ½ hours. We find that in the royal residence in Windsor no less than £1000 is spent annually on intoxicating liquors, and that the total cost of providing 29,986 dinners to the Edinburgh poor, who applied to the soup kitchen during the winter of 1889, was stated at £162 14s 8d, or 1s 2d per 12 rations—in other words, there is spent on strong drink in the Queen's household nearly six times the amount thought necessary for supplying 29,985[2] free meals to the starving poor of Edinburgh to keep them alive during the winter. According to the official report of the Committee of Management, £15 bought the entire butcher meat needed for those 29,000 odd dinners, and the royal baron of beef on the Queen's table at Christmas weighed over 200lbs. The Duke of Argyll has a rental of £50,843, and there are 2,425 paupers in Argyllshire. The Duke of Hamilton receives in royalties on coal £114,489, and a miner for hewing the coal gets less than 1s per ton. The average annual income of the railways of the United Kingdom is £70,000,000, of which £33,000,000 are set aside as dividends to idle shareholders, while only £17,000,000, or little more than half, go as wages to the workers. The average annual profit realised by the firm of J. & P. Coats, thread manufacturers, Paisley, has been officially stated at £457,719, and the wages of the girl workers in their employment is less than 12s per week. As the firm employ over 6,000 workers the company thus make a profit of 30s per week or £76 per annum off each of its "hands."

In the face of such facts as these, surely no rational person can doubt that wealth is unfairly divided. But why is it so? Because the rich, who are the owners of the means of production and distribution, the land, the mines, machinery and factories, railways, docks, and shipping, do not work, but are enabled to live in idleness and luxury. The poor, owning nothing but their labour power, are therefore compelled by the fear of hunger to hire themselves out to the owners of property to work their machinery and land, at whatever wage the competition among themselves for employment will allow them to receive. And until the workers recognise that the existence of private property is the means of production and distribution, the tools with which we labour, which at present enable a class to live in idleness on the labour of their fellow-creatures, is the source of all social inequality and injustice, and, therefore, must be swept away, and the instrument of labour be made common property,

---

2   This slight discrepancy in the figures is in the original.

to be held and wrought by the workers for the workers—in short, until socialism becomes the creed of the people, the prince and the pauper, the millionaire and the outcast, must always remain with us, a blot on our civilisation, an insult to our intelligence, a reproach to our humanity.

*****

WHAT DO SOCIALISTS WANT?[1]
DUNDEE WEEKLY NEWS
24 OCT 1891, P.10

SIR—The meaning of socialism is not in the least obscure, and it is only the misrepresentations of our enemies which make it so. Common property in the means of production and distribution—i.e., the land and instrument of labour—is socialism as accepted by all schools of socialistic thought. The industries of the country to be held and managed by the workers, and production and distribution of all goods to be arranged to supply the wants of all, instead of, as at present, to make a profit for a few—all classes of labour to be equally rewarded. The labour of the architect requires greater skill, but it is also less protracted and disagreeable, and performed amid pleasanter surroundings than the labour of the hod-carrier, and without the labour of the hod-carrier the most sublime conceptions of the architect would remain mere valueless drawings on paper. A colliery manager is absolutely useless without the labour of the colliers, and the labour of the collier is of little use to dwellers in cities without the coal-heavers, who bring the coal to our doors. All are equally necessary; therefore, all should be equally rewarded.

---

1   This letter was republished by the *Treason Felony* Blog, 4 June 2020.

*****

THE WORLD'S WEALTH[1]
DUNDEE WEEKLY NEWS
31 OCTOBER 1891, P.9

SIR—Labour is the source of all wealth. Capital itself is produced by labour, and is useless without labour, and capital in private hands is simply the stored up unpaid labour of the workers kept back by a capitalistic fraud. Wages are only a part of the fruits of labour, the remainder is retained by the capitalist in the name of profits, and is utilised by him to create fresh capital and enable him to live in clover off the labour of others. The two cases I have quoted are instances of this general rule, which remains unaltered whether the dividend is twenty or only four per cent. The fact that capitalists often fail does not alter the amount wrongfully taken from the workers. What one loses another gains. If capitalist A fails it is simply because B, C, D, E, and F, his rivals in business, have taken his trade from him, and will therefore secure greater profits, because of the ruin of their rival. The matter is of as little interest to the workers, as a class, as the similar question of how thieves divide their plunder can be supposed to be to the unfortunate victim from whom it was stolen.

---

1   This letter was republished by the *Treason Felony* Blog, 4 June 2020.

*****

SCOTTISH NOTES¹
JUSTICE
22 JULY 1893, P.3

THE SCOTTISH SOCIALIST FEDERATION (Edinburgh) sends a delegate to Zurich². On many of the questions to be submitted to the Congress, the delegate will have a free hand, but on one point, at least, the SSF has given an imperative, definite mandate. It reads, "That our delegate to the International Workers Congress vote against any proposal to allow Anarchists as such to take part in its deliberations."

We feel that at a time when the class-conscious workers of the world are dressing their ranks for the coming grapple with the forces of privilege it would be scarcely less than idiotic, were they to admit to their councils men whose whole philosophy of life is but an exaggerated form of that individualism we are in revolt against.

As the SSF finds that the limited number of its outdoor speakers are unable to meet all the calls upon it for propagandists, it has established a speaking class for members desiring to share in the good work of

---

1   This was Connolly's first report published in *Justice* as secretary of the SSF, a position he took over in July 1893 and signed "James Connolley" [sic]. His brother, John, had previously held the position. See Ransom, "James Connolly," 37. Ransom does not mention the report published on 24 June 1893 in *Justice*, but it was written while John was still secretary and is signed "J. Connolly"—the shared initial between the two brothers a source of confusion for later editors of Connolly's work.

2   The International Socialist Workers Congress met in Zurich, Switzerland, 6-13 August 1893. The SSF delegate seems to have been John Connolly. See "The Workers Congress at Zurich," *Evening Telegraph* (Dublin), 5 August 1893, 2. For a report of the Congress by an unnamed delegate from Edinburgh (who references his colleague from the SSF) see "The Socialist Congress—Edinburgh Delegate's View," *Edinburgh Evening News*, 15 August 1893, 2.

spreading the gospel. A most worthy ambition. "How beautiful upon the mountains are the feet of him that bringeth glad tidings etc."[3] I should be obliged for any suggestions as to the best manner in which such a class should be conducted.

---

3   Isaiah 52:7. "How beautiful upon the mountains are the feet of him that bringeth good tidings, that publisheth peace; that bringeth good tidings of good, that publisheth salvation; that saith unto Zion, Thy God reigneth!"

*****
SCOTTISH NOTES
JUSTICE
12 AUGUST 1893, P.3

THE POPULATION OF EDINBURGH is largely composed of snobs, flunkeys, mashers,[1] lawyers, students, middle-class pensioners and dividend hunters. Even the working class portion of the population seemed to have imbibed the snobbish, would-be-respectable spirit of their "betters," and look with aversion upon every movement running counter to conventional ideas. So socialism in Edinburgh had to fight a hard up-hill battle against tremendous odds. But it has won it, hands down, and is now becoming respectable. More, it is now recognised as an important factor in the public life of the community, a disturbing element which must be taken into account in all the calculation of the political caucuses.

Leith, on the other hand, is pre-eminently an industrial centre. The overwhelming majority of its population belong to the disinherited class, and having its due proportion of sweaters, slave-drivers, rackrenting slum landlords, shipping federation agents, and parasites of every description, might therefore have been reasonably expected to develop socialistic sentiments much more readily than the Modern Athens.[2] But the reverse is the case. Whatever be the reason, whether it be for lack of backbone, or for want of knowledge, or through sheer unadulterated cowardice, it is hard to say. Yet the fact remains that there are only a few socialists in Leith, in spite of all the educational work performed at our open-air

---

1   Archaic term for fashionable young men of the late Victorian era, especially ones fond of the company of women.

2   Term used to describe Edinburgh.

meetings on the Links[3] every Sunday during the summer months. An attempt was made a few years ago to continue our course of lectures during the winter for the benefit of our few sympathisers and all enquirers, but the venture failed for lack of support, moral and material. Leith was therefore given up to the political light and leading dispensed by the petty shopkeepers, small tradesmen, foremen and their flunkeys, who constitute the Leith Liberal Club[4]. But the S.S.F. has resolved to make another attempt to gain a footing for social democracy in that town, and accordingly, if the men and women there who sympathise with us in our efforts have the courage of their convictions, give the movement the support it deserves by signifying their adhesion to our principles, they can best do so by joining our ranks. The politics of Leith will in the future be something different from what they are at present, a battle ground for the contending factions of Liberal and Tory, fighting for the lion's share of the plunder of labour.

---

3   Public park in the docklands area of Leith.

4   Founded on 22 September 1886 at Duke Street Hall, Leith. Its objects were "to further the progress of liberal principles by means of lectures, debates, and such methods as may be deemed desirable, and to advance and defend the liberal cause in the burgh." See *Glasgow Herald*, 23 September 1886, 6.

*****

PLAIN TALK[1]
LABOUR CHRONICLE
1 DECEMBER 1894, PP.6-7

THE CZAR IS DEAD[2] and the elections are over. The new Czar has issued a manifesto, and Bailie M'Donald is now Lord Provost. The peace of Europe is still maintained, the Nihilists are plotting in silence, and Councillor Waterston[3] has been and gone and done it.

* * *

A Tory Lord Provost rules over Liberal Edinburgh, and Councillor Sir James Russell sits and sighs and wishes his name was Blaikie.

* * *

Edinburgh Town Council attended Divine Service in Hope Park U.P. Church on Sunday, 18th November, *in honour of the Lord Provost*, who is a member of that congregation. I wonder if they meant it.

---

1   This article was republished in Dudley Edwards and Ransom, *James Connolly*, where it was given the erroneous title "Party Politicians—Noble, Ignoble and Local."

2   Czar Alexander III died 1 November 1894.

3   J.H. Waterston (d. 1904). Councillor for Canongate ward and president of Edinburgh Total Abstinence Society.

* * *

The Liberals have threatened to oppose Mr Waterston because he voted for Provost M'Donald. Councillor Robertson declared at the Council meeting he was in favour of the honours going round, and would have voted against Sir James Russell had a really capable man been brought forward, but he would not vote for M'Donald.

* * *

And yet they all went to church in honour of Lord Provost M'Donald. Otherwise, I presume, they would not have gone at all.

* * *

This is the final outcome of the municipal elections: all the old gang are returned to office, and the municipal life of Edinburgh in the ensuing year will be marked by the same scrupulous regard to economy (in wages) and efficiency (in jobbery) to which we have been so well accustomed in the past.

* * *

The Social Democrats were defeated. On the authority of the celebrated representative of culture, Mr Francis M'Aweeney[4], we are told they received "a crushing blow," yet a more jubilant lot of men and women it would have been impossible to find on the day after the election.

* * *

---

4   President of the W.E. Gladstone branch of the Irish National League.

An opponent passing under the windows of their Committee Room an hour after the result of the poll was declared, on hearing the jubilant speeches and enthusiastic cheering of the Socialists, was constrained to remark to a companion, that the Social Democrats receive a defeat better than their enemies do a victory.

And he was right. Some defeats are better than victories. A defeat endured as the result of contest conducted in a fair and honourable manner is a thousand times more creditable to the defeated party than a victory gained by all the mean and unscrupulous arts of the wirepullers.

* * *

The Socialists did not send any carriages for their lady supporters; they did not have committee rooms outside the polling booth, and, waylaying unfortunate voters, rush them in, and then escort them between tall hats and frock coats, to record their votes in favour of the rights of property; they did not tell Irish Catholics that Mr Connolly was a Freethinker, who wanted to overthrow the Church, and then tell old Scotch women of both sexes that Mr Connolly was an Irish Papist who wanted to introduce the Scarlet Woman[5]; they did not seek the support of the Unionists by telling of the letter of recommendation from a leading Edinburgh Unionist; and seek the support of the Home Rulers by calling to their aid every quondam Home Ruler, or leader, who could be induced to sell his name, and voice, and birthright for the ill-smelling pottage of Liberal promises[6].

* * *

---

5   The Scarlet Woman of the Apocalypse, Revelation 17:1. "And there came one of the seven angels which had the seven vials, and talked with me, saying unto me, Come hither; I will shew unto thee the judgment of the great whore that sitteth upon many waters." The Scarlet Woman / Great Harlot / Whore of Babylon was interpreted by early Protestant reformers such as Martin Luther, John Calvin, and John Knox as referring to the Roman Catholic Church.

6   Taking the soup. A reference to apocryphal stories of Irish Catholics forced to convert to Protestantism during the Famine in order to receive food. Having just dismissed religious sectarianism in politics, Connolly then relies upon a sectarian smear to make a political point.

The Social Democrats were defeated. But last year the vote polled in George Square Ward for the I.L.P. candidate was only one-thirteenth of the total poll, whereas in St Giles, the vote for the avowed Social Democrat reached one-seventh of the total poll. A great advance, truly.

* * *

The official Liberal—backed by all the strength, reputation, and admirable electioneering organisation of the combined Liberal and Nationalist parties, and aided by the avowed support of the most influential Unionists in the ward, with a known man and a lawyer as their candidate, were yet only able to obtain a majority of four to one over a party the most revolutionary and the most recent in public life, with no electioneering organisation, and with a candidate known to earn his bread by following an occupation most necessary in our city life, but nevertheless universally despised by the public opinion of aristocratic Edinburgh.

* * *

It is to be hoped that next year the Ward will not be troubled with the presence of another bogus Unionist candidate.

* * *

Had there been no Unionist, and had the advanced working-class voters been left free to choose between the revolutionary Social-Democrat and the orthodox Liberal and defender of the rights of property, there is little doubt the result of the poll would not have brought much comfort to the enemies of Socialism.

* * *

But hundreds of men, who would otherwise have voted Socialist, cast their votes reluctantly for Mr Mitchell as the candidate most likely to ensure the defeat of the Tory.

* * *

They will now have twelve months in which to meditate on the difference between the Liberal Tweedledee and the Tory Tweedledum, and after having so meditated they are invited to record the result of their studies at the polling booth on the first Tuesday of November 1895, if not before.

* * *

There is great heartburning in certain Liberal circles in Edinburgh over a matter which does not affect the working-class voter. It is an invitation to an 'At Home,' to be held in the Waterloo Rooms, Glasgow [sic],[7] by Lady Helen Ferguson of Novar.[8]

* * *

All the gentlemen whose purses are in the habit of opening for the relief of distressed MPs and huckstering politicians in general, together with a few who have remained obdurate in spite of the pathetic appeals of

---

7   The event was held at the Waterloo Rooms, Edinburgh, 5 December 1894, and "attended by representative Liberals in the East of Scotland." See *Edinburgh Evening News*, 6 December 1894, 2.

8   Helen Munro Ferguson, Viscountess Novar (1863-1941). Her husband was Ronald Munro Ferguson (1860-1934), Liberal MP for Leith Burghs and member of the Liberal Imperialist faction within the Liberal Party which also supported working-class representation within the party.

Messrs Donworth[9] and Dillon,[10] are invited to this great social function.

* * *

Class the first will be thanked for their splendid devotion to the cause of Liberalism, and class the second will, it is hoped, be so overwhelmed with the magnificent display, and so enchanted by the bright smiles of the delegates from the Ladies' Liberal Association that they will open their hearts and their purses also, and all will be well.

* * *

By such means are replenished the Liberal coffers, and the Liberal working-man throws his cap in the air, and when he meets his Socialist comrade asks—"Where is the Tory gold?"[11]

* * *

And his Socialist comrade, who has been stinting himself of his glass of beer in order to pay the election expenses of *his* candidate usually scratches his head and wonders also—"Where is the Tory gold?"

* * *

Gold of any kind or colour is a very scarce commodity in a Socialist

---

9   Daniel Donworth of the John Dillon Branch of the Irish National League.

10   John Dillon (1851-1927), Home Rule MP for Dublin.

11   In 1885 a number of Social Democratic Federation (SDF) general election candidates were funded by elements within the Conservative Party with a view to splitting the Liberal vote. While not illegal, the "Tory Gold" scandal discredited the SDF and the party did not contest the 1886 election.

committee room. *N.B.*—those who do not believe this should come and join us and get a share of the plunder. Entry-money, sixpence; weekly subscription, one penny.—ADVT.[12]

* * *

Any orthodox Liberal or Tory politician will tell you that one cause of the great misery among the working-class is to be found in the alarming prevalence of early marriages.

* * *

Yet in face of this lamentable fact, we are informed that his Grace the Duke of Argyll, who is 71 years of age, is about to get married to his third wife.[13] As this step may lead to a still further increase in our pauper population, it is to be hoped wiser counsels will prevail and prevent the young couple taking the final disastrous step.

* * *

Ambrose Malvern [sic], aged 68, committed suicide by jumping from a hotel window.[14] This young man had married a widow the previous day. So I read in a contemporary. If some one will undertake to send this to his

---

12   Short for advertisement.

13   George Campbell (1823-1900), 8th Duke of Argyll (Scotland), 1st Duke of Argyll (UK). Married for the third time in 1895 to Ina Erskine McNeill (1874-1925).

14   Connolly appears to have gotten the surname mixed up with the location. "Ambrose Valentine (68), a retired officer of the Austrian Army, residing at Leamington, who was on a visit to Malvern on Friday, attempted to strangle himself in his bedroom and then jumped through the window, 30ft, from the ground. Death was instantaneous. Mr Valentine, who had been a widower for some years, was married on Thursday at Cheltenham to a widow a few years his junior. He had been in a depressed condition for some time." *Cardiff Times*, 24 November 1894, 3.

Grace the Duke of Argyll he might yet pause in his headlong career, and the nation be saved from an impending calamity.

* * *

Mr William M'Ewan, MP, gave £50,000 to assist in building a new wing to Edinburgh University. We gave thanks. Edinburgh Town Council, having a love for the beautiful, spent £70,000 in obtaining for the citizens a better view of M'Ewan's £50,000. Again we gave thanks. The first act of the newly-elected Town Council was to accept an estimate for the proposed widening of the North Bridge and refuse to insert in it a clause requiring the payment of the current rate of wages. The labouring people who voted for the return of the old gang to office are still giving thanks.

* * *

We are a great people.

* * *

I hear the Rev. Mr Jackson, at a meeting in the Albert Hall, on Sunday, 18ᵗʰ November, declared his Socialism was of the kind endorsed by the Trades Union Congress at their recent meeting in Norwich.[15] If this is

---

15   The title of the talk was "Ought Christians to be Socialists" and was held on Sunday 18 November at 3pm in the Albert Hall, Edinburgh. See "Public Notices," *Edinburgh Evening News*, 17 November 1894, 1. See also "Edinburgh," *Labour Leader*, 28 December 1895, 10, for Jackson chairing a meeting "having explained that he agreed to preside from friendliness to the general aims of socialism without committing himself to the SDF programme" and Connolly moving a resolution "That, believing social democracy to be the only rallying point for the forces of progress, this meeting pledges itself to support the programme and policy of the SDF." The same article carries a report of a lecture Jackson gave in the Albert Hall, Edinburgh on socialism and the family. "In the Albert Hall on Sunday last the Rev. Mr. Jackson lectured to a large audience on "Socialism and the Family." The lecture was a mixed and disappointing production, against which most of the Socialists present were

true the rev. gentleman is eligible for membership of the ILP or SSF, and I would advise him to enter into communication with one or other of these bodies, and take his proper place in the communion of the faithful.

* * *

But before admission he might, as a public character, be required to give some practical proofs of his sincerity. Not that we would expect him, as a follower of Him of Nazareth, to "sell all he has and give it to the poor,"[16] as one would-be follower was required to do. Oh, no, our latter-day Christianity is far too 'practical' to adopt such hare-brained theories of restitution as that implied in the aforementioned utterance of their Master.

* * *

But a certain colleague of Mr Jackson on the School Board has recently made an effort to deprive the women cleaners employed by that body of their wages, that is of their means of life, during sickness.[17] Will Mr Jackson preach a sermon on the subject, taking for his text the injunction, "Rob not the poor because he is poor."[18]

---

ready to protest had there been opportunity. The lecturer, after drifting about, and, while accepting the economic basis of socialism, finally assumed that because Bax and Morris had speculated on what the family relations might be under a realised and distant socialism, it must be held that Socialism attacks the family until some equal authority repudiates their speculations. Reasoning thus, what is a reader of the famous "Provincial Letters" to say when he finds that for some hundreds of years a leading party in the Church not only speculated on, but provided for the breach of all family relations?"

16   Matthew 19:21. "Jesus said unto him, If thou wilt be perfect, go and sell that thou hast, and give to the poor, and thou shalt have treasure in heaven: and come and follow me."

17   The move to limit sick pay paid to cleaners was initiated by Rev. Thomas Burns. See *Edinburgh Evening News*, 20 November 1894, 2.

18   Proverbs 22:22. "Rob not the poor, because he is poor: neither oppress the afflicted in the gate."

* * *

Or will he allow the Edinburgh Socialists the free use of his hall, or church, for the purpose of conducting a fortnight's mission to clergymen. Subject of mission: instruction in the use of the Divine command, "Love thy neighbour as thyself."[19]

* * *

Until our reverend friend is prepared to give such practical proofs of his Socialism will he please remember that "Faith without works is dead."[20]

* * *

The conduct of the Edinburgh School Board, coupled with the conduct of the Town Council in refusing to insert the fair wages clause in a most important contract, should help to clear the cobwebs from the eyes of the intelligent voters and enable them to appreciate the necessity for an infusion of new Socialistic blood into all our public bodies.

* * *

For some time to come the work of Socialists on all such bodies will not be so much to pass new laws as to infuse into their administration the spirit of the new life, to use all power to inaugurate the reign of justice, to convert our industrial system from a machine for making profit into an

19   Mark 12:31. "And the second is like, namely this, Thou shalt love thy neighbour as thyself. There is none other commandment greater than these."

20   James 2: 26. "For as the body without the spirit is dead, so faith without works is dead also."

instrument for sustaining life, to transform our politics from the government of men into the wise and well-ordered administration of things, to relegate to the limbo of exploded superstitions the old doctrine of freedom of contract between affluence and starvation, and thus, by constantly placing our doctrines and our efforts upon the same platform as the class interests of the workers, to create such a public feeling in our favour as shall enable us to bridge the gulf between the old order and the new, and lead the people from the dark Egypt of our industrial anarchy, into the Promised Land of industrial freedom.

* * *

The return of a Socialist candidate does not then mean the immediate realisation of even the programme of palliatives commonly set before the electors. Nay, such programmes are in themselves a mere secondary consideration, of little weight, indeed, apart from the spirit in which they will be interpreted.

* * *

The election of a Socialist to any public body at present, is only valuable in so far as it is the return of a disturber of the political peace.

* * *

Until Socialism attains such a foothold in this country as shall enable the Socialists to return a majority to the public bodies which rule the country, every fresh seat captured must simply be regarded as a fresh means of spoiling the little games of the Jabezian philanthropists[21], financial

---

21   Jabez Spencer Balfour (1843-1916), Liberal Party politician and fraudster. He ran the Liberator Building Society which collapsed in 1892 having defrauded thousands of people by diverting mortgage savings into speculative projects for his own personal gain. Balfour subsequently fled to Argentina but was extradited in

jobbers, and political thimbleriggers, who thrive on their reputations as Liberal and Tory politicians.

* * *

If only for the value of letting the light of public opinion in on the doings of officialdom, we should never relax our efforts until every representative body has its full quota of Socialist members.

* * *

While on this matter, it would be as well to keep in mind the fact, that under the Local Government (Scotland) Act, which comes into force in April of 1895, the Poor Law system of this country will be at last placed under democratic control.

* * *

The workers will then have an opportunity of humanising this iniquitous system, by placing upon every Parish Council a sufficient number of Social Democrats to counteract the despotic tendencies of our Liberal and Tory taskmasters.

* * *

The poor paupers, the war-worn veterans who have fallen in the battle of life, who are imprisoned in those bastilles of poorhouses, may now have the closing years of their lives lightened and brightened by the action of an intelligent Social Democracy.

1895 and sentenced to fourteen years' penal servitude.

* * *

To every upholder of the present system the poorhouse inmates are a mere burden on the rates, or an intolerable nuisance to honest folk, who are well done for if they are fed and sheltered at all. But to the Social Democrat they are unfortunate victims of an evil social system. They are our brothers and sisters, crushed beneath the wheels of a remorseless competition. They are the effect of which the landlord and capitalist are the cause.

* * *

We have so long been accustomed to receive without question the teachings of the master class, that it is no wonder the poorhouse dole and poor-relief should be regarded amongst us as degrading to the recipient instead of to society at large. But it is on society at large, and on its supporters and apologists, the real stigma should rest. Indeed, it would be well for the workers as a whole if they could come to look upon the poor-rates as their first means of relief instead of as their last resource.

* * *

Man, as a social animal, has a claim upon the society which gave him birth. This claim is his right to live as long as he is willing to perform his share of the labour necessary to his own maintenance and the maintenance of society at large. This claim involves, in the first place, the right of free access to the means of life; in the second place, the duty of contributing to the support of the weaker members of the community, i.e., children, the sick, infirm, and the aged.

* * *

Our Poor Law system is a grudging admission of the truth of this thesis, granted by the classes as an alternative to a troubled social upheaval. It has been surrounded since its inception with every form of insult and degradation their mean and petty minds could devise, until, today, the hideous uniform of the pauper is loathed more than the garb of the convict.

* * *

Thus, our masters have striven to debase this institution, whose existence in our midst they feel to be a standing reproach to the devil-take-the-hindmost theory, with which they wish to govern society.

* * *

To rescue our Poor Law from their hands, to relieve it from the false ideals with which its administration has been cursed, and to make its administrators in very truth guardians of the poor, this should be the aim of the workers. By so directing their efforts they may create, out of the framework of our Parish Councils, a public body, who, in solicitude for the public welfare and thoughtful provision for the weaker members of our human family, will find the same incentive to effort as the Liberal and Tory politicians find in the grosser pursuit of the glittering spoils of office.

* * *

But such a body can only arise out of that higher conception of human rights and duties which will flow from a wide and general acceptance of the principles of enlightened Social Democracy.

*****

CARMAUX SUNDAY
JUSTICE
9 NOVEMBER 1895, P.6

D EAR COMRADE, would you oblige by giving publicity, and if possible, your editorial endorsement, to the following suggestion. The capitalist journals of France and England are just at present engaged in endeavouring to foment feelings of hatred and distrust between the two peoples. As neither the French nor English workers can possibly benefit by any international conflict, it is our duty as socialists to do all in our power to counteract the effect of this poison so monstrously instilled by the reptile press. We must send to our French comrades some token of international amity which will bear upon its face such an unmistakable proof of our solidarity as will dissipate the clouds of suspicion and link the two people indissolubly together. How can this be done? The strike at Carmaux is at present riveting the attention of the civilised world.[1] The issues involved, the intervention of the French Government, the action of the Socialist deputies, the uncompromising attitude of the men in face of such odds, have all contributed to invest this struggle with an interest which secures for every actor in it a world-wide audience. Now, this is the time for British socialists to show the sincerity of their talk about international solidarity, and to show it in a manner the news of which will ring around the world. Let every branch of the SDF[2] and ILP[3] resolve to set apart one Sunday, say the 10th of November, as Carmaux Sunday, and

---

1   The Carmaux Glass Factory Strike of 1895. For more on this see Joan Wallach Scott, *The Glassworkers of Carmaux: French Craftsmen and Political Action in a Nineteenth-Century City* (Cambridge, Mass.: Harvard University Press, 1974).

2   Social Democratic Federation

3   Independent Labour Party

on that day throughout Great Britain let a public collection be taken at all our meetings by every branch (no matter how large or how small) on behalf of the Carmaux strikers, their wives, and little ones.[4] The editors of *Justice*, the *Clarion*, and *Labour Leader* may act as the custodians of the fund, which, I think, should be sent over in a bulk as a substantial proof of our comradeship. Such an act would be worth thousands of wordy resolutions affirming our belief in an abstract conception of universal brotherhood.

---

4   Such a collection was organised in Edinburgh on Sunday 27 October 1895. See *The Clarion*, 2 November 1895, 6.

*****

THE CORPORATION AND
THE FRANCHISE
EVENING TELEGRAPH (DUBLIN)
14 AUGUST 1896, P.3

SIR—Lord Salisbury,[1] on a memorable occasion, likened the Irish people to Hottentots[2] in their lack of legislative capabilities.[3] Between
the mind of the man who uttered this brutal phrase and the minds which
inspired the secret hostility of the Dublin Corporation to the franchise
clauses of their Water Bill there exists a strange family likeness. Both
dread the advent of the people, and in both cases, for the same reason,
lest they might be called upon to give an account of their stewardship to
the classes whose affairs they have so long mismanaged. Dublin holds an
unenviable position, in that it can claim to possess more slums at higher
rents, worse lighted streets and less public businesses under public control than any city of its size in the Three Kingdoms. Yet in face of this
truth, and with full knowledge of the fact that with the short time at the

---

1   Robert Gascoyne-Cecil, 3rd Marquess of Salisbury (1830-1903). Salisbury
was Prime Minister and leader of the Conservative Party at the time.

2   A word applied by Dutch settlers to the Khoekhoe people of southern
Africa. Now regarded as a racial slur.

3   This is in reference to a speech given by Lord Salisbury at the Annual
Conference of the National Union of Conservative Associations, St. James' Hall,
London, 15 May 1886. "In responding to a resolution of confidence unanimously
carried, his Lordship said the traditional policy of the Tory party was the maintenance of the Union... He denied that Ireland was a nation. Ireland was two nations
bitterly and antagonistically divided. They were asked to have confidence in the
Irish people, but confidence depended upon the people in whom they were going to
confide. Self-government, he held, only worked well when confided to people who
were of Teutonic race, and he did not believe in giving it [to] Hottentots, Hindoos,
Russians, or Irish." *Sunderland Daily Echo and Shipping Gazette*, 17 May 1886, 3.

disposal of the House of Commons, any important alterations in the bill by the Lords would mean the complete wrecking of the measure, their agents were, to judge by their speeches to the committee, more interested in tempting the Lords to reject the Franchise Clause, than in pressing forward the Bill itself. The result is just what the merest tyro in Parliamentary procedure knew it would be, the complete sacrifice of the entire Bill and the loss of the people's money. Some day the working classes of Dublin will have an opportunity of repaying in full the Salisburys, the Meades, and the M'Coys, our hereditary rulers, and their would-be imitators on Cork Hill.[4] May it come soon!

---

4   Location of City Hall, Dublin.

*****

IRELAND FOR THE IRISH[1]
LABOUR LEADER
10 OCTOBER 1896, P.356

"BEFORE THE TIME of the conquest, the Irish people knew nothing of absolute property in land. The land belonged to the entire sept; the chief was little more than managing member of the association. The feudal idea which came in with the conquest was associated with foreign dominion, and has never to this day been recognised by the moral sentiment of the people."[2]

In these few words of Mr. John Stuart Mill the impartial student may find the key for unravelling the whole tangled skein of Irish politics. Latter-day politicians, both on the English and Irish side, have done their utmost to familiarise the public mind with the belief that the Irish question arises solely out of the aspirations of the Irish people to have more complete control over the internal administration of the affairs of their country than it is possible for them to exercise while the seat of government is located at Westminster, and that therefore some form of local self-government, as, for instance, Mr. Gladstone's Home Rule, is all that is needed to settle this question, and lay for ever the troubled spirit

---

1   It was signed "James Connolly, Secretary Irish Socialist Republican League." The "Ireland for the Irish" articles were later republished as part of *Erin's Hope: the Ends and the Means* (1897).

2   John Stuart Mill, *England and Ireland* (London, 1868), 12. The original quote: "Before the conquest, the Irish people knew nothing of absolute property in land. The land virtually belonged to the entire sept; the chief was little more than the managing member of the association. The feudal idea, which views all rights as emanating from a head landlord, came in with the Conquest, was associated with foreign dominion, and has never to this day been recognised by the moral sentiments of the people."

of Irish discontent.

According to this luminous exposition of Irish history, we are to believe that the two nations have for seven hundred years been engaged in unceasing warfare, that the one country (Ireland) has during all that time been compelled to witness the merciless slaughter of her children by famine, pestilence, and the sword; that each succeeding generation has witnessed a renewal of the conflict and a renewal of the martyrdom, until the sensitive mind recoils from a perusal of Irish history as from the records of a shambles, and all for what, because previously Irishmen and Englishmen could not agree upon the form of political administration best suited for Ireland.

If this new reading of Irish history were true the intelligent foreigner might be forgiven for rating at a very low standard the intelligence of the two nations, which during seven hundred years had not evolved a satisfactory solution of such a simple question. At precisely the same low standard may safely be rated the political acumen of the English and Irish party leaders who are today complacently trotting out the discredited abortion of Home Rule as a sovereign remedy for Ireland's misery.

The Irish question has, in fact, a much deeper source than a mere difference of opinion on forms of government. Its real origin and inner meaning lay in the circumstance that the two opposing nations held fundamentally different ideas upon the vital question of property in land.

Recent scientific research by such eminent sociologists as Litourneau, Lewis Morgan, Sir Henry Maine, and others has amply demonstrated the fact that common ownership of land formed the basis of primitive society in almost every country.[3] But whereas in the majority of countries now called civilised such primitive communism had almost entirely disappeared before the dawn of history, and had at no time acquired a higher status than that conferred by the social sanction of unlettered and uneducated tribes, in Ireland the system formed part of the well-defined social organisation of a nation of scholars and students, recognised by Chief and Jurist, Brehon and Bard, as the inspiring principle of their collective life, and the basis of their national system of jurisprudence.

Such a striking fact will of course be interpreted in many ways, ac-

---

3   Charles Letourneau (1831-1902); Lewis H. Morgan (1818-1881); Sir Henry James Sumner Maine (1822-1888).

cording to the temperament and political or racial sympathies of the reader. The adherent of the present order of society will regard it as a proof of the Irish incapacity for assimilating progressive ideas, and will no doubt confidently assert that this incapacity is the real source of Ireland's misery, since it has unfitted her sons for the competitive scramble for existence, and so foredoomed them to the lot of hewers of wood and drawers of water.[4]

Those who believe in the strange theory that the progress of the human race has been in some strange manner pre-ordained to pass through the various stages of communism, chattel-slavery, feudalism, and wage-slavery as a preparation for the higher ordered society of the future, who teach that since society has walked along certain lines it might not under altered circumstances have reached the same high goal along totally different lines, will, of course, regard the Irish adherence to clan ownership at such a comparatively recent date as the seventeenth century as an evidence of retarded economical development, and therefore a real hindrance to progress.

But the sympathetic student of history, who believes in the possibility of a people by political intuition anticipating the lessons afterwards revealed to them in the sad school of experience, will be more inclined to join with the ardent Irish patriot in his lavish expressions of admiration for the sagacity of his Celtic forefathers who foreshadowed in the democratic organisation of the Irish clan the more perfect organisation of the democratic society of the future.

Whichever be the true interpretation of Irish history, one fact at least stands out clear and undeniable, viz., that the conflict between the rival systems of land ownership was the pivot round which centred all the struggles and rebellions of which that history has been so prolific. The real reason why the Irish regarded with such hostility their English rulers, and rose with such enthusiasm under their respective chiefs, was because they regarded this as the all-important question, and, in their eyes, English rule and Dublin parliaments were alike identified as the introducers and upholders of the system of feudalism and private ownership of land, as opposed to the Celtic system of clan or common ownership, which

---

4   Joshua 9:21. "And the princes said unto them, Let them live; but let them be hewers of wood and drawers of water unto all the congregation; as the princes had promised them."

they regarded, and, I think, rightly, as the pledge at once of their political and social liberty.

The English Government were also astute enough to perceive that the political or national subjection of Ireland was entirely valueless to the conquerors while the politically subjected nation remained in possession of economic freedom.

Consequently, we find that the first stipulation made to the Irish tribe upon its submission always was that the lands of the tribe should be regarded as the private property of the chief; that he should therefore accept them as a grant from the crown, from which he should in future hold them; that he should drop his Irish title, which proclaimed him the freely elected chief of a free community, and should instead accept an English title, such as duke or earl, and should in all things conform to English ideas of civilisation and social order.

All these stipulations were in the last degree repugnant to Irish ideas. The chief, as Mill has pertly observed, was but the managing member of the tribal association, although in the stress of constant warfare they usually limited their choice to the members of one or two families; yet the right of election was never abdicated by the tribesmen.

Whenever the restrictions of English gold overmastered the patriotism of an Irish chief, and succeeded in inducing his acceptance of the alien property system and the alien title (as in the case of Nat O'Neil and Nial Garu, O'Donnell, the Queen's O'Reilly, and the Queen's Maguire), they immediately elected another chief in his stead; and from that moment the unfortunate renegade became an outlaw from his own people, and could only appear in his native territory under an escort of English spears.

The Irish system was thus on a par with those conceptions of social rights and duties which we find the ruling classes today denouncing so fiercely as "socialistic." It was apparently inspired by the democratic principle that property was intended to serve the people, and not by the principle so universally acted upon today, viz., that the people have no other function in existing than to be the bondslaves of those who by force or by fraud have managed to possess themselves of property. They did not, indeed, regard all forms of productive property as rightfully belonging to the community; but when we remember that the land alone was at that time of importance, all other forms of property being insignificant by comparison, we see that they were as socialistic as the industrial development of their time would allow. The English civilisation against which they fought was, on the other hand, thoroughly individualistic; and, as it triumphed, we are reaping the fruits today in the industrial disputes, the agricultural depressions, the poorhouses, and other such glorious institutions in Church and State as we are permitted the luxury of enjoying in common with our fellow subjects in this "integral portion of the British Empire." The results of the change on the national type of Erin are well illustrated in the scornful words in which Aubrey De Vere apostrophises the "new race" of exploiters which then arose:

> The chiefs of the Gael were the people embodied;
> The chiefs were the blossoms, the people the root.
> Their conquerors, the Normans, high-souled and high-blooded,
> Grew Irish at last from the scalp to the foot.
> And ye, ye are hirelings and satraps, not nobles—
> Your slaves, they detest you; your masters, they scorn.
> The river lives on, but the sun-painted bubbles
> Pass quick, to the rapids insensibly borne.[5]

(SECOND ARTICLE NEXT WEEK.)

---

5   From "The New Race," by Aubrey Thomas De Vere (1814-1902).

*****

IRELAND FOR THE IRISH - II
LABOUR LEADER
17 OCTOBER 1896, P.364

THE BREAK-UP of the Kilkenny Combination in 1649 and the consequent dispersion of the Irish clans was the immediate cause of that confusion of thought and apparent lack of directness in aim which down to our day has characterised all modern Irish politics. Deprived of any form of political or social organisation which might serve as an effective basis for its practical realisation, the demand for the common ownership of the land naturally fell into abeyance until such time as the conquest of some form of political freedom should enable the dispossessed Irishry to substitute for the last tribal association the fuller and broader conception of an Irish nation as the natural repository and guardian of the people's heritage.

But when the fusing process of a common subjection had once more welded the heterogeneous elements of Irish society into one compact nationality it was found that in the intervening period a new class had arisen in the land—a class which, while professedly ultra-nationalistic in its political aims, had nevertheless so far compounded with the enemy as to accept the alien social system, with its accompanying manifestation, the legal dispossession and economic dependence of the vast mass of the Irish people as part of the natural order of society.

The Irish middle class, who then by virtue of their social position and education stepped to the front as Irish patriot leaders, owed their unique status in political life to two entirely distinct and apparently antagonistic causes. Their wealth they derived from the manner in which they had contrived to wedge themselves into a place in the commercial life of the

"Saxon enemy," assimilating his ideas and adopting his methods, until they often proved the most ruthless of the two races in pushing to its furthest limits their powers of exploitation. Their political influence they derived from their readiness at all times to do lip service to the cause of Irish nationality, which in their phraseology meant simply the transfer of the seat of government from London to Dublin and the consequent transfer to their own or their relatives' pockets of some portion of those legislative fees and lawyers' pickings then, as at present, expended among the Cockneys.

With such men at the helm it is no wonder that the patriot parties of Ireland have always ended their journeys upon the rock of disaster. Beginning by accepting a social system abhorrent to the best traditions of a Celtic people, they next abandoned as impossible the realisation of national independence. By the first act they set the seal of their approval upon a system founded upon the robbery of their countrymen, and by the second they bound up the destinies of their country with the fate of an Empire in the humiliation of whose piratical rules lies the Irish people's only chance of national and social redemption.

As compensation for this gross betrayal the middle-class politicians offer—Home Rule. To exactly analyse what Home Rule would confer on Ireland is a somewhat difficult task, since every person interprets the thing in their own way and according to their own peculiar bent. Perhaps the safest way, and at any rate the one least open to objection, will be to regard as Home Rule the Bill introduced by Mr. Gladstone.

As this scheme represents the utmost that the statesmanlike powers of Mr. Parnell, with a solid phalanx of eighty-six members behind him, could wrest from the fear or favour of English Liberalism, it is surely safe enough to assume that no other merely political body from Ireland is ever likely to improve upon this concession by any alliance with either of the great factions who watch over the interests of the English propertied classes. Home Rule proposed to establish in Ireland a domestic legislature, which would be carefully divested of all those powers and attributes which by the common consent of civilised peoples are regarded as properly belonging to the sphere and functions of government, which would have no power in controlling diplomacy, post-office, commerce, telegraphs, coinage, customs and excise, weights and measures, copyrights and patents, succession to the Crown, or army, navy, militia, or Volunteers.

The only conceivable result of such a state of affairs would have been to create in Ireland a host of placehunters and Government officials, who, secure in the enjoyment of a good income themselves, would have always acted as a barrier between the people and their oppressors. As a method whereby the English legislature might have been relieved of some of its duties at home, and thus left more free to pursue its policy of plunder and aggression abroad, it ought to have delighted the heart of the Jingo politician. That they were too dunderheaded to see their opportunity is a mercy for which far-seeing Irish democrats can never be sufficiently thankful.

But realising that, taken on its own merits, Home Rule is simply a mockery of Irish national aspirations, our middle-class leaders have industriously instilled into the public mind the belief that the advent of Home Rule would mean the immediate establishment of manufactures and the opening up of mines, etc., in every part of Ireland. This seems to them the highest possible ideal—an Irish society composed of employers making fortunes and workers grinding out their lives for a weekly wage. But, to say the least, the men who talk in this manner must either be woefully ignorant of the conditions of modern industry, or else, for some private reason of their own, must be engaged in deceiving those who believe in them. To establish industry successfully today in any country requires at least two things, neither of which Ireland possesses and one of which she never can possess.

The first is the possession of the wherewithal to purchase machinery and raw material for the equipment of her factories, and the second is customers to purchase the goods when they are manufactured. Well, we find that England, who has had the start in manufacturing over every other nation, who has been extending her commerce and perfecting her machinery for a hundred and fifty years at least, who has created a nation of highly skilled artisans, adept in every form of industrial achievement—England, the wealthiest country in the world, has brought her industries to such a degree of mechanical perfection that her customers cannot keep her going. She can supply goods of every description much quicker than the world is able to purchase and consume them, and as a direct consequence of this vast producing power she is compelled every few years to either wholly or partially stop her machinery and close her factories, to discharge her artisan subjects, and compel them to walk about in enforced idleness and semi-starvation until such time as the goods they had produced are purchased and consumed by their customers.

Bear this in mind, and remember also that Germany, France, Italy, Belgium, Austria, Russia, every state on the continent of Europe and America, India, China, and Japan are all entering into the struggle—that each of them are striving hard, not only to provide what they had formerly relied on England to provide, but also to beat England out of the markets of the world; remember that for all those countries the great difficulty is to find customers, that the oldest-established firm in the business—viz., the British Empire—finds that her customers cannot keep her mills and factories going; remember all this, and then tell me how your poor Ireland, exhausted and drained of her life-blood at every pore, with a population almost wholly agricultural and unused to mechanical pursuits—how is Ireland to establish new factories and where is she to find the customers to keep them going? She cannot create new markets. This world is only limited after all, and the nations of Europe are pushing their way into its remote corners so rapidly that in a few years at most the entire world will have been exhausted as a market for their wares.

Go to the factory towns, to the shipbuilding centres, to the coal mines, to the trade unions, or to the stock exchanges of England, the continent of Europe or America, and everywhere you will hear the same cry: "The supply of cotton and linen goods, of ironwork, of coal and of ships, of goods of every description is exceeding the demand; we must work short time, we must reduce the workers' wages, we must close our factories—there is not enough customers to keep our machinery going." In face of such facts the thoughtful Irish patriot will throw rant aside and freely recognise that it is impossible for Ireland to do what those other countries cannot do with their greater advantages, viz., to attain prosperity by establishing a manufacturing system in a world-market already glutted with every conceivable kind of commodity. It is well also to remember that even under the most favourable circumstances, even if by some miracle we were able to cover the green fields of Erin with huge, ugly factories, with chimneys belching forth volumes of poisonous smoke and coating the island with a sooty desolation—even then we would quickly find that under the constitution born of the capitalistic system our one hope of keeping our feet as a manufacturing nation would depend upon our ability to work longer and harder for a lower wage than the other nations of Europe in order that our middle class may have the opportunity of selling their goods at a lower price than their competitors. This is equivalent to saying that our chance of making Ireland a manufacturing country depends upon us becoming the lowest blacklegs in Europe.

Even then the efforts would be doomed to failure, for the advent of the yellow man into the competitive arena, the sudden development of the capitalistic system in China and Japan, has rendered for ever impossible the uprise of another industrial nation in Europe. "But," we are told by some of our leaders, "if we cannot compete with other countries in the world-market, we can at least produce for ourselves." Under no circumstances can we do so without bringing upon ourselves disasters as great as those we wish to escape from. With greater advantages and larger experience in the field than ourselves, the capitalists of other countries can easily undersell our goods, even in the home market, and if in order to give our manufacturers a chance we were to adopt Protection (impossible under Home Rule) the result would be to immediately increase the price of every kind of goods, while no one would benefit except the few capitalists for whose sake our Irish workers would be working harder and longer and paying higher prices than before.

Again, it is said we need not perhaps establish industry or try it, but we can at least establish peasant proprietary, and make every man the owner of his own farm, let every man live, if not under his own vine and fig tree, at least upon his own potato patch. In the first place I consider such an act to be, even if practicable, one of very questionable justice. To make the land of a country the property of a class is to my mind equally iniquitous whether that class number a few hundreds or a few hundred thousands. The land of a country belongs of right to the people of that country, and not to any particular class nor even to any single generation of the people in that country. The private ownership of land by the landlord class is an injustice to the whole community, but the creation of a peasant proprietary would only tend to stereotype and consecrate that injustice, since it would leave out of account the dispossessed millions of farmer tenants whom landlord rule had driven into the Irish towns or across the seas. It is manifestly impossible to reinstate the Irish people on the lands from which they have been driven, but that fact only lends additional point to the demand for the nationalisation of land in the hands of an Irish state. Setting that fact aside, however, have our advocates of peasant proprietary really considered the economic tendencies of the time and the development of the mechanical arts in the agricultural world. The world is progressive, and peasant proprietary, which a hundred years ago might have been a boon, would now be powerless to save from ruin the agriculture of Ireland. The days of small farmers, like small capitalists, are gone, and wherever they are found today they find it impossible to compete with the improved machinery and mammoth farms of America and Australia. How are our small farmers to compete with a state of matters like unto that revealed in the report of the American Social Science Association, even as far back as 1878?[1]

It tells how science and invention, after devoting so much time to industry, have turned their attention to agriculture, and as a result have effected almost a revolution in that branch of human activity. Ploughs which, driven by horses, plough more than five acres per day, or the extent of many an Irish farm, and steam ploughs which do much more; machines for sowing seeds, with which a boy and horse can do three times the work of a man, and do it much better; reaping machines, with which a man with one or two pairs of horses can do the work of at least sixty men with reaping hooks; reaping machines which not only cut the harvest but tie it as well are now so common in England and America as to fail to attract attention, and we hear on good authority of machines which cut, thrash, winnow, and sack it, without the intervention of any other human hands than those of the engineer who tended the machine. In cutting the corn a man or boy with a horse and machine can do the work of twenty men, cutting an acre an hour. All this, be it remembered, is possible only to the farmer who holds his thousands of acres. The first cost of any one of those machines would be enough to ruin the average small farmer in Ireland, and the result is that while he is painfully labouring on his farm his American competitor can bring in his harvest, send it thousands of miles by railroad, load it into ships, send it across the Atlantic, and eventually sell it practically at our own doors as cheap, and cheaper, than our home produce. The competition of New Zealand beef and frozen mutton has already inflicted incalculable harm upon the

---

1   William Godwin Moody, *Our Labor Difficulties, the Cause, and the Way Out; A Practical Solution of the Labour Problem* (Boston, 1878).

Irish cattle trade, and within the last few weeks I have received private information of a contract entered into with the Peninsular and Oriental Steamship Company to transport butter from the huge cattle ranches of Australia to any port in Great Britain or Ireland at a price that spells ruin to the dairy farms of these countries.[2] Where, then, is our hope of escape through peasant proprietary?

(THIRD ARTICLE NEXT WEEK.)

---

2 "Further supplies of Australian butter for the English market are to be expected from South Australia, the government of which colony have contracted with the Orient and the Peninsular and Oriental companies for the carriage of the article for two years at ¾ d [three farthings] a pound." *Cheltenham Chronicle*, 23 May 1896, 3.

*****

IRELAND FOR THE IRISH - III
LABOUR LEADER
24 OCTOBER 1896, P.372

E RE WE CAN forecast the future we must understand the present, and bring a just sense of proportion to our review of the history of the past. What, then, are the conditions which govern life in Ireland today, and of what are those conditions the outcome? According to the most eminent authorities who have ever dealt with the subject, the soil of Ireland is capable of sustaining a population many times larger than she has ever borne upon its surface, yet Ireland is in a state of chronic starvation. Every ship that leaves our ports is laden down with harvests for human consumption, while the people whose strong hands have reaped that harvest pine in wretchedness and want, or fly from the shores of this fertile island as from the arid sands of a desert. The landlord class, infatuated with that madness which always precedes destruction, press for their rents to the uttermost farthing wherever they can wheedle or coerce a too compliant legislature and executive to support them in their exactions.

The capitalist farmer, driven to the wall by the stress of competition, seeks in vain to maintain his foothold in life by an unceasing struggle with the lord of the soil on one hand and a ruthless oppression of the labourer on the other; the small farmer, bereft entirely of hope for the future, settles despairingly into a state of social wretchedness for which no savage land can furnish a parallel; the agricultural labourer, with his fellow in the towns, takes his strength, his brains, his physical and intellectual capabilities to the market, and offers them to his wealthier fellow-creatures, to be exploited in return for a starvation wage. On all sides anarchy and oppression reign supreme, until one could scarcely wonder if even the most orthodox amongst us were tempted to echo the saying of the Spanish Don Juan Dal Aguila[1] after the battle of Kinsale: "Surely Christ never died for this people!"[2]

These are the conditions under which life is endured in Ireland to-day. From what do such conditions spring? There are two things necessary for the maintenance of life in Ireland, as in every other country. They are land and labour. Possessed of these two essentials, the human race has at its command all the factors requisite for the wellbeing of the species. From the earth labour extracts alike its foods and the mineral wealth with which it contrives to construct and adorn its habitations and prepare its raiment. Therefore the possession of the soil is everywhere the first requisite of life. Granting this as a proposition too self-evident to need any elaborate demonstration, we at once arrive at the conclusion that since the soil is so necessary to our existence the first care of every well- regulated community ought to be to preserve the use of that soil and the right to freely share in its fruits to every member of the community, present or prospective, born or unborn. The moment when the land of a country passes from the care of the community as a public trust, and from being the common property of the entire people becomes the private property of individuals, marks the beginning of slavery for that people and of oppression for that country. With the land held as the property of individuals there are immediately created two antagonistic classes in society—one holding the land and demanding from the other a rent for permission to live upon it, and the other driven by the constant increase of their own numbers to offer larger and larger shares of the produce of their labour as tribute to the first class, who thus become masters of the lives of their fellow-beings. With the land held as the common property of the people an abundant harvest is eagerly welcomed as an addition to the wealth of the community, guaranteeing against want every one of its members. With the land held as private property the abundant harvest must be sold to satisfy the exactions of the holder of the soil, and as he jingles in his pockets the results of the sale of his tenants' produce the families who

---

1   Juan del Águila (1545-1602), served as general of the Spanish armies in the invasion of Ireland (1601-1602).

2   "Considering which humiliating picture, one might be tempted to repeat the bitter words of Don Juan D'Aguila—"Surely Christ never died for *this* people!"" John Mitchel, *The Last Conquest of Ireland (Perhaps)*. (Glasgow, 1861), 206.

reaped it may be perishing of want. As one crime begets another, so one economic blunder invariably brings in its train a series of blunders, each more fruitful in disaster than the first. When the production of food for public use was abandoned in favour of production of agricultural produce for private sale and private profit, it was almost inevitable that the production of every other necessary of life should be subjected to the same conditions. Thus we find that food, clothes, houses, and furniture are not produced in order that people may be fed, clad, sheltered, or made comfortable, but rather in order that the class who have obtained possession of the land, machinery, workshops, and stores necessary for the production of these essentials should be thereby enabled to make a comfortable living at the expense of their fellow-creatures. If the landlord and employing class in Ireland think they can make a rent or profit by allowing the Irish people to feed, clothe, or house themselves then they are allowed to do so under their direction—when, where, and how their masters please. If, on the contrary, they imagine it will pay them better to refuse that right (as they do in every eviction, strike, or lockout), then they do refuse that permission, and their countrymen go forth starving, their children die of want beneath their eyes, and their wives and mothers pine in wretchedness and misery in what their forefathers were wont to call the "Isle of the Blest."[3] By the operation of certain historic causes the workers have been deprived of everything by which they can maintain life, and are thus compelled to seek their livelihood by the sale of their capacity for work, their labour-power. The worker thus finds that the first and most essential condition which he must perform in order that he may possess his life is to sell a part of that life into the service of and for the profit of another. Whether he sells it by the hour, the day, the week, or the month is immaterial—sell it he must or else starve.

Now, the worker is a human being, with all the powers and capabilities of a human being within him, just as is a landlord, a capitalist, or any other ornament of society. But when he approaches the capitalist in order to complete that bargain, which means the sale of his life piecemeal in order that he may enjoy it as a whole, he finds that he must carefully divest himself of all claims to be considered as a human being, and offer himself

---

3   "Oh Brazil, the Isle of the Blest" by Gerald Griffin (1803-1840). "On the ocean that hollows the rocks where ye dwell / A shadowy land has appeared, as they tell; / Men thought it a region of sunshine and rest, / And they called it O'Brazil, the isle of the blest."

upon the market subject to the same law as governs the purchase or sale of any inanimate, soulless commodity, such as a pair of boots, a straw hat, or a frock coat. That is to say, the price he will receive for this piece-meal sale of himself will depend upon how many more are compelled by hunger to make the same horrible bargain. In like manner with the farmer seeking to rent a farm in the open market. Each competitor seeks to outbid the other, until the rent fixed is usually out of all proportion to the price which will in the future be obtained for the produce of the farm bidden for. The agriculturist finds that in years of universal plenty, when throughout the world the earth brings forth its fruits in teeming profusion, the law of supply and demand operates to lower the price of his farm produce, until it scarcely repays his labour in garnering it, and in times of scarcity, when a good price might be obtained, he has little to sell, his customers have not the wherewithal to buy, and the landlord or the money-lender are as relentless as ever in their exactions.

As a remedy for such an array of evils Home Rule stands revealed as a glaring absurdity. The Home Rule parties either ignore the question altogether or else devote their attention to vain attempts to patch up the system with schemes of reform which each day tends to discredit more and more, The tenant who seeks in the Land Court for a judicial valu-ation of his holding finds that in face of the steady fall in agricultural prices (assisted by preferential railway rates in favour of foreign produce) the fair rent of one year becomes the rackrent of another, and the tenant who avails himself of the purchase clauses of the Land Acts finds that he has only escaped from the personal tyranny of a landlord to have his veins sucked by the impersonal power of the money-lender. Confronted with such facts the earnest Irish worker turns in dismay and joins his voice to that of the uncompromising nationalist in seeking from the advocate of an Irish Socialist Republic the clue to the labyrinthine puzzle of modern economic conditions.

The problem is a grave and difficult one, alike from the general ig-norance of its controlling conditions and because of the multiplicity of vested interests which must be attacked and overthrown at every forward step towards its solution. The solution herein set forth is therefore not guaranteed to be ideally perfect in all its details, but only to furnish a rough draft of a scheme of reform by means of which the ground may be prepared for that revolutionary change in the structure of society which can alone establish an approximation to an ideally just social system. The agriculture of Ireland can no longer compete with the scientifically equipped farmers of America, therefore the only hope that now remains is to abandon competition altogether as a rule of life, to organise agriculture as a public service under the control of boards of management elected by the agricultural population, and responsible to them and to the nation at large, and with all the mechanical and scientific aids to agriculture the entire resources of the nation can place at their disposal. Let the produce of Irish soil go first to feed the Irish people, and after a sufficient store has been retained to ensure of that being accomplished, let the surplus be exchanged with other countries in return for those manufactured goods Ireland needs but does not herself produce. Thus we will at one stroke abolish the dread of foreign competition and render perfectly needless any attempt to create an industrial hell in Ireland under the specious pretext of "developing our resources." Apply to manufacture the same social principle, transform the capitalist from an irresponsible hunter after profit into a public servant, fulfilling a public function and under public control. Recognise the right of all to an equal opportunity to develop to their fullest capacity all the powers and capabilities inherent in them by guaranteeing to all our countrymen and women, the weak as well as the strong, the simple as well as the cunning, the honest equally with the unscrupulous, the fullest, freest, and most abundant human life intelligently organised society can confer upon any of its members.

"But," you will say, "this means a Socialist Republic; this is subversive of all the institutions upon which the British Empire is founded—this cannot be realised without national independence." Well, I trust no one will accuse me of a desire to fan into flame the dying embers of national hatred when I state as my deliberate and conscientious conviction that the Irish democracy ought to strive consistently after the separation of their country from the yoke that links her destinies with those of the British Crown. The interests of labour all the world over are identical, it is true, but it is also true that each country had better work out its own salvation on the lines most congenial to its own people. Now, the national and racial characteristics of the English and Irish people are different, their political history and traditions are antagonistic, the economical development of the one is not on a par with the other, and, finally, although they have been in the closest contact for 700 years yet the Celtic Irishman is today as much of an insoluble problem to even the most friendly of the English as on the day when the two countries were first joined in unholy wedlock. No Irish revolutionist worth his salt would refuse to lend a hand to the social democracy of England in the effort to uproot the social system of which the British Empire is the crown and apex, and in like manner no English social democrat fails to recognise clearly that the crash which would betoken the fall of the ruling classes in Ireland would sound the tocsin for the revolt of the disinherited in England.

But while awaiting the propitious moment there remains much to be done in the political field —work which can be pushed forward irrespective of Government opposition, work to which the Irish people can devote themselves, in open, public organisation while there is a rag of the constitution left. Pending the complete public organisation of agriculture let our representatives in Parliament press for the establishment in every rural district of depots for agricultural machinery of the newest and most improved pattern. Let such depots be established at the expense of the state and for the use of the agricultural population to whom the needful machinery for speedy and effective harvesting, etc., shall be supplied on hire at a charge carefully calculated to cover the cost of wear and tear of maintenance and construction alone. Take advantage of every political development to demand the nationalisation of Irish railways, and, when effected abolish at once the unfair charges by which the railway companies seek to injure home growers in favour of foreign importers. Our population are flying to the uttermost ends of the earth: seek to retain them at home by reducing the hours of labour wherever you have the power and by supporting every demand for legislative restriction. Your Irish railways employ thousands of men, whose working hours average twelve per day. Were they restricted to a forty-eight-hour week of labour employment would be provided for thousands of Irishmen who at present are driven exiles from their native land. Pledge every Irish representative to support an eight-hour bill for railways; if he refuses you will know that he considers profits as more sacred than patriotism, and would sacrifice his country on the altar of greed. Our Irish municipalities and other public bodies controlled by popular vote employ also many thousands of men. What are their hours of daily labour? On the average ten, and their wages just below starvation point. Insist upon the Irish corporations establishing the eight-hours day in all their works. They at least do not need to fear foreign competition. If you have no vote for the corporation you can at least help to hound off the political platform elsewhere every so-called patriot who refuses to perform this act of justice. Every Irish corporation which declines to institute an eight-hours working day at a decent wage for its employees has virtually entered into a conspiracy with the British Government to expatriate the Irish people, rather than pay an additional halfpenny in the pound on the rates. In all our cities the children of the labouring class are dying off before their time for lack of wholesome nourishing food. As our municipalities and public trusts provide water for the people free of direct payment and charge the cost upon the rates, let them also provide at our schools free breakfasts, dinners, and teas to the children in attendance there, and pay for it from the same source. No matter what may be the moral character of the parent, let us at least save the helpless children of our race from physical and mental degeneracy, and save our teachers from the impossible task of forcing education upon a child whose brain is enfeebled by the starvation of its body. As the next step in organisation let the corporations and public bodies everywhere throughout the country establish depots for the supply of bread and all the necessaries of life to the people at cost price and without the intervention of the middleman.

To save our struggling farmers from the merciless bleeding of our banking system and money-lenders in general, let our representatives in Parliament force forward the legislative abolition of our present banking houses and the suppression of all forms of interest mongering, and the establishment in their stead of state banking institutions, with popularly elected boards of directors, issuing loans at rates of interest as low as is consistent with economic soundness. When in addition to the foregoing we have abolished our hateful poorhouses, and by a tax upon all incomes over £500 per year provided comfortable pensions to the aged, the infirm, and widows and orphans we will have laid a substantial groundwork for a revolutionary movement, we will have amply demonstrated the sincerity of our patriotism, we will have stayed to some degree the tide of emigration (and kept at home the materials we will need when the time comes to strike), we will have welded the people of Ireland into one homogeneous whole, and fitted them to accomplish what they could never dream of attempting as a nation of masters and wage-slaves, landlords and tenants, we will have given even to those whom we must remove in

our onward march the assurance that if we crush their profit-making enterprises today yet when the sun dawns upon our freedom, if they have
served their fellow-creatures loyally in the hour of strife, they and their
children and their children's children will be guaranteed against want
and privation for all time by the safest guarantee man ever received, the
guarantee backed by all the gratitude, the loyal hearts, the brains and industry of the Irish people, under the Irish Socialist Republic.

*****

CAN IRISH REPUBLICANS BE POLITICIANS?
SHAN VAN VOCHT
6 NOVEMBER 1896, PP. 210–12

IN LAST MONTH'S issue of the *Shan Van Vocht*, the editor, in commenting upon the strictures passed by our contributor on the French
Revolution, asks for an expression of opinion on the relative merits of
[revolutionary uprisings and moral force agitations. As both the article in
question and the editorial] apparently take it for granted that the query
with which this communication is headed, must be answered in the negative, an assumption which I believe to be entirely erroneous, and the fundamental mistake in the calculation of our modern Irish revolutionists, I
would suggest that as the broader and more comprehensive question this
be instead the basis of the proposed controversy. [1] To make my position
more plain, I may say, I write as one who believes that the concession to
Ireland of such a limited form of local autonomy as that embodied in Mr.
Gladstone's Home Rule Bill would not in any sense be a step towards
independence, but would more likely create effectual barriers in the way
of its realization.

---

1   In the original, the words in the opening sentences are jumbled together.
It appears to have been a layout error on the part of the editor and/or printer. The
changes above are my own attempt to place some logic upon them. The original: "*In
last month's issue of the Shan Van Vocht, the editor, in commenting upon the strictures passed by our
contributor on the French Revolution, asks for an expression of opinion on the relative merits of As
both the article in question and the editorial revolutionary uprisings and moral force agitations, note
suggesting the discussion apparently take it for granted that the query with which this communication
is headed, must be answered in the negative, an assumption which I believe to be entirely erroneous, and
the fundamental mistake in the calculation of our modern Irish revolutionists, I would suggest that as
the broader and more comprehensive question this be instead the basis of the proposed controversy.*"

The question thus arises, are those who see in an Irish Republic the only political ideal worth striving for to eschew political action and seek in secret conspiracy alone to prepare for revolution? Up to the present every genuine Irish revolutionist has acted on this belief, that political action was impossible for republicans.

Now I assert the contrary. A revolution can only succeed in any country when it has the moral sanction of the people. It is so, even in an independent country; it is doubly so in a country subject like Ireland to the rule of another. Within this century no Irish revolutionist had obtained this sanction before he took the field. In 1848 the majority of the Irish people pinned their faith to the Repeal Association, which had disavowed even the right to resist oppression, and the Young Irelanders themselves had made no reasonable effort to prepare the popular mind for revolution, but had rather been precipitated into it against their will. Under such conditions failure was inevitable. Those who were willing to "rise" had no means of knowing how far their aspirations were shared by their fellow-countrymen elsewhere, and lacking confidence in themselves, with the recognised leaders of public opinion against them, the effort ended in disaster. The history of the Fenian movement was somewhat similar. The number of actually enrolled members formed but an insignificant minority of the population, the vast majority of our countrymen, though perhaps sympathising with the Fenian ideal, put their trust in politicians who preached tame submission under the name of "prudence" and "caution," and in the critical period of the movement flung the weight of their influence on the side of "law and order."

In both cases the recognised leaders of national thought were on the side of constituted authority and against every revolutionary effort. The facts are as undeniable as they are lamentable, and they speak in trumpet tones in favour of such a re-modelling of Irish and revolutionary tactics as shall prevent a recurrence of similar disasters in the future. This, I hold, can be best accomplished by a political party seeking to give public expression to the republican ideal. One point needs to be emphasised in this connection, viz., it is not republicanism, but the counsel of insurrectionary effort to realise republicanism, which gave to previous Irish movements their odour of illegality. A candidate for political honours (?) is as much at liberty to put the attainment of a republic on his programme as he is to pledge himself to Home Rule or any other scheme of

political reconstruction. Were a political party formed in Ireland to educate the people in sound national ideas by pledging every candidate to
openly repudiate the authority of the Crown and work for the realization
of republican principles, it would achieve a much needed transformation
in Irish politics.

Hitherto every Irish agitation has sought to make its programme as
broad and loosely defined as possible, in order to enrol under its banner
every section of Irish national opinion—loyal Home Rulers, Conservative Nationalists, Compromising Whigs, and Nationalist Democrats—
all alike were welcome. Such a basis is undoubtedly best for the purposes
of an "agitation," but it is worse than useless for the purposes of earnest
revolutionists seeking a definite end. But such a party as I speak of, with
an avowedly republican programme, would, in its very definiteness and
coherence, have immense advantages to recommend it to the consideration and support of practical-minded men. It would prevent the emas
culation of our young men by the vapourings of "constitutional" patriots;
it would effectually expose the sham Nationalists, and, let us hope, drive
them from political life; it would at every election in which it took part,
afford a plebiscite of the people for or against the republic; it would enlist
the sympathy of many earnest patriots whose open natures shrink from
secret conspiracy; it would ascertain with mathematical accuracy the
moment when the majority of the Irish people were ripe for revolution,
and *it could not be suppressed while representative government was left in
Ireland.* By adhering steadily to the policy of pledging every candidate
to its full programme, whether they stood for Parliament or local governing bodies, it would ensure that when a majority of the Irish people
had at the ballot-boxes declared in favour of the revolutionary party, every soldier of the cause would know that in the fight he was waging he
was not merely one of a numerically insignificant band of malcontents,
but a citizen soldier fighting under orders publicly expressed in face of all
the world by a majority of his fellow countrymen. This I hold to be an
eminently practical method of obtaining our end. It would exclude the
possibility of our national principles being betrayed in the moment of
danger, or compromised in the hour of success to suit the convenience
of interested party politicians. It would inspire confidence in the most
timid by its recognition of the fact that to counsel rebellion, without first
obtaining the moral sanction of the people, would be an act of criminal

folly which could only end in disaster. It would make Irish republicanism no longer the "politics of despair," but the science of revolution.

It may be urged against such a proposal that the first need of Irish politics is unity, and that such a party would only accentuate the division at present existing. This, however, could only be the case if our present representatives refuse to accept the pledge of loyalty to the free Irish Republic and to it alone. If they do so refuse, then they are unfit to be representatives of the Irish democracy and cannot be removed too soon. The objection in itself implies a suspicion of the genuine nature of the patriotism so loudly vaunted by our party politicians. Unity is a good thing, no doubt, but honesty is better, and if unity can only be attained by the suppression of truth and the toleration of falsehood, then it is not worth the price we are asked to pay for it. I would, in conclusion, earnestly recommend the readers of the *Shan Van Vocht* to study the suggestions contained in this paper, and if they approve of them, to act accordingly. Should this meet with a favourable reception, I may, if the opportunity occurs and the editor permits, give in a future issue my ideas on the programme of political and social reform, on which such a party might fight in Parliament and the country, while the public opinion of Ireland was ripening behind them, impending the arrival of the propitious moment for action.

*****

INTRODUCTION TO ERIN'S HOPE:
THE END AND THE MEANS
APRIL 1897[1]

THE FOLLOWING ARTICLE (1) was contributed in the first instance to the *Shan Van Vocht* of November, 1896, and is here reprinted, with the consent of the editor of that journal; first, in order to familiarize the reader with the conception of the function of the ballot-box as an adjunct to a revolutionary movement, and second, because the incorporation of this article in a pamphlet published under the authority of the Irish Socialist Republican Party, will serve to indicate the attitude of that party in Irish national politics. The remaining articles (2, 3, and 4), were written for the *Labour Leader* Glasgow, and though published anterior to the first, may be considered as an exposition of the political and social programme promised therein.

---

1   "The latest publication of the Irish Socialist Republican Party is entitled 'Erin's Hope, the Ends and the Means' by James Connolly. It indicates the attitude of the Irish Socialist Party towards Irish national politics, and is published at 67 Middle Abbey Street, Dublin, for 1d.'" *Reynolds's Newspaper*, 18 April 1897, 1.

*****

BRAVO IRELAND!
THE PEOPLE (NEW YORK)
18 JULY 1897, P.1

DUBLIN, IRELAND. July 2—If the reports of the festivities in connection with the Diamond Jubilee which reached America were at all like those which appeared in the English newspapers, our comrades of the SLP might be excused from asking: Where were the Irish Socialist Republicans during the anti-jubilee demonstrations in Dublin? To read the English press and the Irish weekly press one would imagine that the sudden outburst on the part of the Dublin workers was nothing more nor less than a 'Home Rule parade, arranged by the middle class politicians,' but those who either witnessed the anti-jubilee meetings and processions, or who had access to the Irish daily papers, are aware how little Home Rule or Home Rulers was in the minds of the multitude. The capitalist Home Rule press here pursues toward the Socialist Republican party a double-faced policy. In its weekly issues, intended for the consumption of rural districts and for abroad—all mention of the party is forbidden, and the boycott is strictly enforced, but in its daily issues, circulating in the cities, it is felt that the boycott would arouse the suspicions of the masses, who know of our activity, and consequently, a neutral attitude is observed, and meetings, etc., are briefly reported and general notices inserted. Consequently, the *Daily Independent* and *Evening Herald* (Panellite), *Freeman's Journal* and *Evening Telegraph* (Dillonite) reported our meetings during the jubilee, but the weekly editions of the same papers shamelessly attributed the entire outburst to the credit of their Home Rule sympathisers and ignored our existence.

But here are the facts. From the first suggestion of a diamond jubilee rejoicing down to the day itself, the middle class press in Ireland had exhibited the most shameless poltroonery and lack of moral courage. We would find one day in their columns a sneer at the jubilee and the next day four or five columns of space devoted to a glowing description of the preparations. We, on the other hand, from the first took up a strong attitude upon the matter, holding indignation meetings, exhibiting jubilee cartoons, and distributing 10,000 copies of the manifesto, lately reprinted in *The People*.[1]

For Monday, 21st June, the eve of jubilee day, we organised an anti-jubilee meeting, to be held in College Green, under the walls of the old Parliament House, and right in the midst of the illuminations, etc., prepared by the loyal flunkeys. One of our speakers on this occasion was the well-known editor of *L'Irelande Libre*, Miss Maud Gonne, the most popular woman in all Nationalist Ireland, lately described by the *Irish Republic* (New York), as 'Ireland's Joan of Arc.'

The announcement that this popular lady had chosen the socialist platform to speak from set all the political wirepullers by the ears, and in their chagrin every effort was made to prevent the success of the meeting. But in vain. The meeting was held. Comrade Connolly was in the chair, and a resolution, pledging those present to carry on the fight for a real Republican freedom was moved by Comrade Stewart, seconded by Mr. Shelly, of the Dublin Trades' Council, supported by Miss Gonne and carried with acclamation by an audience of five or six thousand. Then a procession was formed to escort our fair speaker through the street, with a black flag (symbolic of our jubilee feelings), at our head. The Trinity College students, bursting with loyalty for the empire which enables them to cultivate their brains at the expense of the toilers—sallied out, armed with cudgels, and attacked the procession, endeavouring to capture the flag. Then an 'iligant shindy'[2] took place; sticks rained down in all directions, broken heads were given and taken, and eventually the proletariat drove the bourgeoisie home in disorder, and marched in triumph to the Socialist club room, where Connolly addressed from the window a vast crowd, who closed a good night's work with three ringing cheers for the Socialist Republic.

1   See "That Diamond Jubilee—Irish Socialist Republican Party to Irishmen," *The People* (New York), 30 May 1897.

2   Elegant shindy, an Americanism to describe an Irish faction fight.

Next night, being jubilee night, the fashionable quarter of the city was illuminated to order, and immense crowds of the people filled the streets, singing rebel songs and waiting to see what the Socialist Republicans would do. Our preparations had been kept secret lest a police raid might spoil the fun, and, in consequence, when we did appear upon the streets it was as if we had risen from the earth. Our procession consisted of a wagonette and pair of horses, carrying a huge black banner, giving statistics of famine, eviction and emigration during the record reign, and winding up with the 'prayer,' From robber rule, O Lord, deliver us. Comrade Denis McDonnell, of the Lynn Massachusetts Section, SLP sat on the front beside the driver with a cudgel like a log of wood in his hand, and kept the enthusiasm of the people at boiling pitch along the entire route. Eight black flags, suitably inscribed by Miss Gonne, and a coffin with the 'British Empire' printed in white upon it, and carried on the shoulders of four stalwart members, formed the nucleus of our procession, which in less than half an hour from our appearance upon the main streets numbered nearly 20,000. Dublin has never witnessed such a scene before, such spontaneous enthusiasm, such fierce passionate earnestness, such willing recognition of a new leadership was a revelation to the old parties, who found themselves in a moment entirely forgotten.

After traversing the main streets, the procession was eventually broken up in Rutland Square by a baton charge of the police. A fierce fight between people and police occurred here, but of course discipline prevailed, and the people were routed. Over 200 cases were treated at the hospitals from broken heads and other wounds, and a number of men and boys received sentences of imprisonment for their participation in the 'riots,' and one old woman who got in the way of the baton charge has since succumbed to her injuries. The ordinary Home Rule capitalist parties took no part in the proceedings from first to last except by exhibiting a magic-lantern show from the windows of the National Club, outside of which the baton charge took place while our procession was passing. Since then their press has impudently striven to claim all credit for the demonstration by boycotting all reference to the Irish Socialist Republican Party, but too late. The people give honour where honour is due, and their feelings were amply testified to on Wednesday, 23rd June, evening, when a crowd of some 2,000 fresh from an encounter with the police marched spontaneously down Mid Abbey street, and, halting beneath the windows of the Socialist club room, cheered enthusiastically for the Socialist Republic.

I hope the editor of *The People* can find room for those few notes and so help in letting the Irish working class in the United States learn that Socialism has its message for Ireland, a message that is now awakening a grander and more confident hope in the breasts of many men and women wearied of the sordid intrigues and personal jealousies with which middle class leaders have disgraced our political life.

*****

BRITISH RULE IN INDIA
LIMERICK LEADER
12 JULY 1897, P.4

"The educated classes (of India) may find fault with their exclusion from full political rights... But it was by force that India was won. And it is by force India must be governed." —*London Times*, 1 February 1886.[1]

B RITISH RULE in India like British rule in Ireland is a political and social system, established and maintained by the conquerors in the interest of the conquered. So runs the legend. But there are not wanting men and women who, strangely enough, maintain that British rule, whether in India or Ireland, is one of the heaviest curses ever inflicted upon an unfortunate people, that its fruits are famine, oppression and pestilence, and that it has but one animating principle wherever found, viz., to extract the utmost possible tribute from the labour of its unfortunate subjects.

With that aspect of British rule peculiar to Ireland we are all in a position to be thoroughly acquainted, but there are, unfortunately, many reasons why a like acquaintance with the history and facts of British rule in India is impossible of attainment to the vast majority of our fellow-countrymen. Therefore, the writer, having had for some time exceptional opportunities for learning the real position of affairs in that country, feels he is doing a service to the cause of freedom and humanity

---

1   "The educated classes may find fault with their exclusion from full political rights. Political privileges they can obtain in the degree in which they prove themselves deserving of them. But it was by force, that India was won, and it is by force that India must be governed, in whatever hands the government of the country may be vested." *The Times* (London), 1 February 1886, 9.

in laying before the readers of the *Leader* a short sketch of the predisposing causes which have led up to the devastating famine which at present holds, and the incipient rebellion which threatens the Indian peninsula.

The first point to note is that the reader must in discussing Indian affairs at once rid himself of all the extravagant ideas about the "wealth of India" with which the reading public of these islands have been familiarised through the writings of ignorant English romancers, avaricious English adventurers, or unscrupulous English statesmen. India is in reality one of the poorest, if not the poorest, of all the countries in the world.

Her immense population live from generation to generation in a state of such chronic misery that deaths from actual hunger excites no comment whatever except when, as in the present famine, their numbers swell so that it is feared even the patient Hindoo may refuse to bear it longer.

Thus when we read that the tribute extracted from India by the Imperial Government in payment of home charges, pensions to retired officials, remittances, contributions to Imperial expenditure, etc., reaches an annual total of from 20 to 27 million pounds sterling, the sum, though large in itself, does not at first appear so exorbitant when levied on a population of over 200 million people. It is only when we are aware of the average daily income of the people upon whose labour this tax is levied that we begin to understand how it is that the 'inestimable benefits of British rule" (?) have been so potent a factor in working out the destruction of this people that the failure of a single harvest is enough to bring upon them all the horrors of famine.

The wages of the agricultural labourers of India—whence 70 per cent of the population derive their sole subsistence directly from the cultivation of the soil—are not such as to induce any very extravagant mode of living, or to fire the imagination of a glutton. In Behar, the northwest provinces, the greater portion of the Deecan and Oude, the average remuneration of the labourer is certainly not more than one anna, six pic, or 1 ½ d per day.

In some portions of East Bengal the wage sometimes rises to 3d. or 4d. per day—an almost princely remuneration. It should also be remembered that the entire native population is excluded from all share in the Government of their country, except in the most menial positions, and that on the other hand, the Indian Civil Service is entirely manned by Englishmen, whose salaries are the highest in the world for such services. Thus the poorest people under the sun are taxed to support the wealthiest (and most insolent) official class.

It might be interesting, in order to bring the contrast more vividly before the reader, to give a few instances of this disparity of means between official England in India and the unfortunate people upon whom it is quartered. The late Professor Fawcett, in an article upon a proposed loan to India, called attention to a few items, illustrating the extravagant expenditure of Anglo-Indians, when the cost of such extravagance can be saddled upon the Indian people. Two of these items, viz. £1,200 for outfit and passage of a member of the Governor-General's Council, and £2,450 for outfit and passage of the Bishops of Calcutta and Bombay, convey their own lesson so well that no words of mine could possibly add point to their eloquence.

£10,000,000 have been spent by the Imperial Government in erecting for their military garrison regimental quarters so luxuriously equipped that one Anglo-Indian writer, General Strachey, enthusiastically declared that "Our soldiers' barracks are now beyond comparison; the finest in the world," whilst Florence Nightingale, a thoroughly impartial witness, wrote—"We do not care for the people of India; the saddest sight in the East, nay, probably in the world, is the peasant of our Indian Empire." "We suppose," says a young Indian writer,[2] "it is inseparable from an alien rule that the living of an English soldier should be of primary importance." And again, "£10,000,000 wrung from the hard earnings of semistarved dwellers in mud hovels for the rearing of 'palatial' barracks. Surely we should pause before we congratulate ourselves upon this."[3]

We are constantly informed by all Anglo-Indian writers that the English in India have been mighty instruments in the hands of divine providence for winning the land from anarchy and oppression, bringing it within the era of civilization and order; and, finally, of introducing its people to all the inestimable benefits of modern civilization. We are,

---

2   Prafulla Chandra Ray (1861-1944)

3   Both quotes are from the essay, *India: Before and After the Mutiny*, which was written by Prafulla Chandra Ray in 1885 while a student at Edinburgh University. It was published anonymously in 1886 as *India in Revolt* by 'An Indian Student.'

of course, well enough acquainted on this side of the Channel with the ways of English officialdom to be able to discount, to a certain extent, the brightly-coloured reports of progress emanating from such sources, and they constitute the sole medium through which Indian news is allowed to filter through to the reading public of these islands.

But it would, nevertheless, be a mistake to suppose that the present writer denies that progress has been made in India under British rule. The only question is—in what degree is that progress due to British rule, and in what degree is it that progress which, under any circumstances, would have been made by an intellectual people with a continuity of literary and philosophic activity stretching back for 2,000 years and more? We are told that the English rulers of India were the first to abolish the hideous custom of suttee, by which the Hindoo widow was forced to sacrifice herself on the funeral pyre of her deceased husband. But an educated Hindoo, Ram Mohan Roy,[4] greatly venerated by his countrymen, had begun a crusade against the custom ten years before the edict was first formulated in 1829. It is more than probable that the exertions of this Indian patriot would eventually have been successful even without English intervention, which at the most, perhaps, hastened the desired consummation.

The vast irrigation works established throughout India are also often alluded to as specimens of the advance of civilisation in the East, largely resultant from the paternal efforts of the English Government on behalf of its Indian subjects. Here again the reader is apt to draw erroneous conclusions and picture to himself the Government of England laboriously instructing the ignorant Indian natives in the functions and uses, theory and practice of irrigation works. But the remorseless hand of history rudely shatters all belief in the fidelity to truth of any such picture.

So far from such irrigation works being the product of English enterprise or genius, they are, as a matter of fact, only feeble and halting imitations of the magnificent works and public enterprise of the former Mahommedan rulers whom the English have supplanted. Dr. Spry, writing in 1837, on "Modern India," declared—"It is in the territory of the independent native chiefs and princes that great and useful works are

---

4   Ram Mohan Roy (1772-1833) social reformer. The original *Limerick Leader* article misspelt the name as Ram Mahun Bay, but this was corrected by Connolly when he reprinted the article in *Workers' Republic*, 3 September 1898.

found and maintained. In our territories the canals, bridges, and reservoirs, wells, groves, etc., the works of our predecessors from revenues expressly appropriated to such undertakings are going fast to decay."[5]

It is noteworthy also that while the former rulers of India neither expected nor accepted any return for the money they voluntarily expended in their irrigation and other public works, the English Government could only be induced to embark on such enterprises by the hopes of reaping enormous profits therefrom—hopes which have never been realised. Lord Lawrence, in a letter to Lord Cranbourne, stated that the general opinion held that these works would yield an average profit of 20, 50, or even 100 per cent.

To the no small chagrin of the ruling classes of India, these high expectations were doomed to disappointment, the full measure of which is revealed in the words of Lord Salisbury, valuable as a, no doubt, unwilling tribute alike to British official incompetence, and to the superior engineering genius of their predecessors. "The irrigation works that have been carried out," he said, "if they had for their basis the former works of native rulers, have in many instances been a financial success. But... when we have begun the projects of irrigation for ourselves, we have not, I believe, in any instance the desired result of a clean balance sheet."[6] Will the reader please contrast this confession of bungling incompetence, added to a greed to pay dividends, with the conduct of Runjeet Singh, the "Lion of the Punjaub," whom the English have always vilified as a barbarian and a tyrant, but of whom Marshman tells us that "he always advanced money, free of interest, to his peasantry, for the purposes of irrigation."

That he was no exception to the rule, is amply borne out by the fol-

---

5   Henry Harpur Spry, *Modern India: With Illustrations of the Resources and Capabilities of Hindustan In Two Volumes: Volume II* (London, 1837), 11-12. Original quote: "The dedication of revenue, for the creation and support of a middle class in our Eastern dominions, has been, with few exceptions, utterly neglected. It is only in the territories of independent native chiefs and princes that great and useful works are formed or maintained. In our territories, the canals, bridges, reservoirs, wells, groves, temples, and caravansaries, the works of our predecessors, from revenues expressly appropriated for these undertakings, without any view to a direct return in profit, are going fast to decay, together with the feelings that originated them; and unless a new and more enlightened policy should be followed, of which the dawn may perhaps be distinguished, will soon leave to trace behind."

6   See House of Commons debates, East India Finance Motion For A Select Committee, 13 February 1877.

lowing significant statement in Arnold's "Dalhousie":—"The Musselman rulers were bold engineers in this respect; not only did they cover India with fine roads, shaded with trees in places which are now tiger-walks, but they remembered the Arabic proverb that 'water is the earth's wealth.' The irrigation works were so benevolently attended to, that the fees for wells and artificial reservoirs were always deducted from the produce of every village before the Government claim was paid." [7] In almost every detail of Indian administration the same tale remains to be told. India is regarded by its alien rulers as a huge human cattle farm solely in the interest of the dominant nation. Whatever is done for the development of its vast internal resources, is done not for the benefit of the Indian people, but primarily with a view to the dividends which the investing classes of England may draw from such development. The salt tax, a tax upon a first necessity of life, is ten times higher to-day than it was ever known to be under the Mussulman rulers of India. More than one humane English Governor has confessed his reluctance to increase this tax upon the helpless peasantry, yet it is today as high as 1,000 or 1,200 per cent.

As in Ireland during the famine years, the Government rated famine- stricken districts for the relief of their own poor, and so crushed into pauperism those who had managed to survive the loss of their potato crop; so in India, whenever the Government extends financial help to a famine-stricken population it seeks to recoup itself for the outlay by an increase in the salt tax. In other words it gives relief with one hand and with the other increases the taxes upon the food of a famishing people.

In the great famine of twenty years ago in Southern India when it was estimated that no less than six million people had perished of hunger, the salt tax was increased by forty-five per cent. The benevolent rulers of India have also, in order to secure this source of income to their exchequer, prohibited under severe penalties, all native manufacture of salt, and when the helpless people, unable to buy salt to season their food, endeavour to scrape a condiment from the deposits left by the receding ocean upon

---

7   Sir Edwin Arnold, *The Marquis of Dalhousie's Administration of British India: Volume the Second* (London, 1865), 279-80. "The Mussulman rulers were bold engineers in this respect; not only did they cover Hindostan with fine roads shaded with trees, in places which are now tiger-walks; but they remembered the Arabic proverb, that 'water is the earth's wealth.' Irrigation was so benevolently attended to, that the fees for wells and artificial reservoirs were always deducted from the produce of every village before the Government claim was paid, wherever it had a charge for it."

the rocks and pebbles of the seashore, they are prosecuted for defrauding the revenue. This devotion to the letter of the law in this respect stands out in marked contrast to their action in another, viz., in squandering in useless frontier expeditions the Famine Relief Fund, which, as its name indicates, was intended for emergencies like the present.

During the present century India has lost no less than sixteen million (16,000,000) people by starvation. All this time she has enjoyed the ameliorative influence of civilization on the British Imperial pattern, and in the full felicity borne of that enjoyment her children have died off like rotten sheep, while the apologists of the English governing classes have vied with each other in unctuous laudation of 'our civilizing mission' and our 'benign rule.' But at least, we may be told, India has profited intellectually by her subjection; is not education fostered by the Imperial Government? Yes, we spent on education in India one-fiftieth part of our net revenue there, whereas in England and Scotland alone we spent under the same heading about one twenty-fourth part of the revenue of the United Kingdom.

Again, as Irish Nationalists remember, that it was the wholesome fear engendered in the English governing classes by the Fenian conspiracy which led to the disestablishment of the Irish Church, so thoughtful Indians are not likely to forget that the year which saw the establishment of the universities of Bombay, Calcutta, and Madras, had also seen the smoke and fire of the Indian mutiny. England, in short, seen in India, a spot revealed by an All-wise Providence for the specific purpose of providing comfortable positions and fat salaries and pensions to the younger sons and poor relations of the English moneyed classes. Therefore, as any efforts to entrust the government of India to the children of the soil would necessarily displace those sinecurists from their snug berths and salaries, all suggestions pointing in that direction must be branded as rank heresy, if not political incendiarism.

In Java, under the rule of the Dutch, the natives share in the government of their country. In the words of Sir David Wedderbum, 'the Asiatic races are subordinated to their own recognised chiefs, and these are responsible to the Government for the maintenance of order.' Thus the most important official positions are open to the natives, who have never yet abused their trust. In the independent native States of India, before the Conquest, all posts, according to the Anglo-Indian writer, Marshman, were open to universal competition.

What, then, is the net result of British rule in India? 'The main evil of our rule,' said Sir T. Munro, Governor of Madras in 1819, 'is the degraded state in which we hold the native,' and as a corollary to this statement one of our contemporary writers, Sir James Caird, informs us from personal investigation that 'in the native States the people are more prosperous than under our rule, and they have not been driven into the evil hands of the sowcars (money lenders) as our ryots (peasants) have been.' At the present moment famine in all its horrors is once more devastating the country, and once more the native States are exempt from the calamity. The English Government officials for months denied the accuracy of the report which, despite their vigilance filtered through to Europe, and now when the awful truth can no longer be concealed, they, like Pilate of old, call heaven and earth to witness they are guiltless of the blood of this people. And once more they call upon the charitable to contribute to the relief of the destitute, whilst they prepare horse, foot, and artillery to insure that not one penny of the tribute, the exaction of which has created the destitution, shall be withheld from the British Exchequer, or devoted to the people they have ruined.

The people of India require justice, but justice is exactly what they must not expect. Justice is prosaic, dull and unsentimental, and cannot be advertised in Mansion House Funds, or prated about by royal and aristocratic dignities. Charity, however, though utterly useless for the purpose of staying the ravages of famine among a population of 36 millions perishing beneath it, yet fulfils the purpose of those who desire to hear their own trumpet blowing and see their names advertised side by side with the *elite* of society and in company with royalty. Above all it does not interfere with the ceaseless flow of Indian tribute into the coffers of their conquerors. Therefore, justice India must not expect, but Charity (D.V.) she will have. 'Look well at the background of this fine picture, and lo, the reeking shanks and yellow chapless skulls of Skibbereen and the ghosts of starved Hindoos in dusky millions.'[8]

---

8   Mitchel, *Jail Journal*, 106. "But look well at the background of this fine scene; and lo! the reeky shanks and yellow chapless skulls of Skibbereen!—and the ghosts of starved Hindoos in dusky millions." Mitchel took "reeky shanks and yellow chapless skulls" from *Romeo and Juliet*, Act IV, Scene I, line 83.

*****

OTHER PEOPLE'S OPINIONS
SHAN VAN VOCHT
4 OCTOBER 1897, P.188

"THE PEOPLE OF IRELAND," said Mr. Patrick McManus, in the September *Shan*[1] "are, with a few exceptions, republicans." So reasoned the men of '48; so reasoned the men of '67; and action based upon such reasoning brought their respective movements to an ignominious collapse amid the scorn and laughter of the enemy—and the world. Would it not be better for the reputation of our country to admit the fact that the earnest revolutionists of Ireland are, today, only a minority, than to be blatantly proclaiming that *all* Irishmen are Republicans, when all the world knows that the two Republican movements of this century were easily suppressed by a handful of constabulary? If friend McManus and those who think with him would take the scales from their eyes, and resolutely face facts, instead of crediting all our countrymen with their own generous enthusiasm, the result could not fail to be beneficial. Meanwhile, as a correction to his optimism, allow me to present here a few facts which seem to conflict with his sweeping statement.

Mr John Redmond, M.P., on Ireland's national demand:—"Separation from England was undesirable and impossible."
—Speech at Cambridge University, February 26th, 1895.

Irish Daily Independent on above speech:—"Mr. Redmond told his audience exactly what Ireland wanted."
—February 27th, 1895.

Mr Swift McNeill, M.P. for South Donegal, on the English Queen's reign:—"The Czar was now on a visit to ... our beloved Queen. Long may she continue to wear that crown upon which, for sixty years, her virtues have shed a transcendent lustre."
—Speech at Armenian Atrocities Meeting, Leinster Hall, September 25th, 1896.

---

1   *Shan Van Vocht.*

Mr. Alfred Webb on India:—"They (the Indians) know their duty to their Sovereign, and are loyal; they know their duty to themselves, and are resolved to be free. And free with them, as with us, in no sense implies a necessary desire for separation."
—*Weekly Freeman*, 17th July, 1897.

Daily Nation, on the solution of the Irish difficulties:—"The true and only solution of the difficulties which exist will be found when the Duke of York is sent here as permanent viceroy to read the *Speech from the Throne* at the opening of the first session of a re-constituted Irish Parliament."
—24th July, 1897.

Freeman's Journal on Monarchy:—"Irish people are willing to accept the Monarchy provided that national self-government is conceded."
—18th August, 1897.

Mr. Alderman Meade, a member of her Majesty's Privy Council, was recently elected unanimously to the executive of the new Parnellite organisation—the Irish Independent League.

All the different parties embraced in this list oppose and criticise each other on every pretext possible, yet neither from Press nor platform have we yet been treated to a denunciation of the above statements, full as they are of the foulest treason to the cause of freedom. Moreover, each of those factions pride themselves on their "discipline," and in holding each man accountable for his sayings, yet all these utterances have passed unchallenged. Friend McManus may say they are only exceptions, but they are the responsible leaders on Press and platform of political parties which at last election received the suffrages of 367,000 Irishmen; their constituents have in no case called upon them to withdraw their loyal expressions, therefore, I am justified in accepting those statements as an accurate reflex of Irish political opinion. If friend McManus were in Paris, as Wolfe Tone was one hundred years ago, endeavouring to convince the enemies of the British Crown that Ireland was ripe for a revolutionary movement, how would he feel if the Minister of War were to confront his absurd generalisations with the sober facts narrated above. How different it would be if those 367,000 men had declared for freedom. You may dismiss as chimerical the attempt to create a truly national party, if you persist in ignoring the politician; he will not be ignored. But if you adopt the ideas we advocate he may be suppressed—a much more desirable result. In conclusion, it is indeed a pity the whipped hounds can only whine in their master's hall, but it requires more moral courage to do even that than it does to sulk in our kennels, licking our sores in silence, while the curse who hold our jaws that the whip may be applied, pose before the world as the representatives of our principles.

*****

LA FAMINE
L'IRLANDE LIBRE
1 MAY 1898, P.2

*A Sneem, dans le comté de Kerry, la famine a été augmentée par des évictions, in-
humaines. Notre collaborateur M. Connolly a visité ce district pour pouvoir nous
envoyer un compte rendu très exact de la situation des infortunés paysans.*

JE ME SUIS rendu à Sneem pour faire une enquête sur la famine et sur
les évictions qui viennent d'y avoir lieu.

La solidarité des paysans et leur courage en portant secours aux
évincés leur ont attiré la sympathie publique.

La maison, ou plutôt la cabane de laquelle les dernières victimes de
la tyrannie du propriétaire ont été expulsées, consiste en une seule pièce
couverte par un toit de chaume endommagé qui laisse pénétrer la pluie.

Il y a soixante ans que cette chaumière fut construite par la famille
O'Sullivan, qui l'a habitée depuis, de père en fils, payant chaque année
un loyer pour ce triste privilège. Ce n'est pas pour ne pas avoir payé son
loyer que James O'Sullivan vient d'être expulsé. Tout pauvre qu'il était, il
ne devait rien à personne. Il a été expulsé parce qu'il a osé se payer le luxe
d'être charitable et miséricordieux.

Un de ses voisins, O'Neill, père de huit jeunes enfants, ayant été
réduit à la misère par une série de mauvaises récoltes, n'avait pas pu payer
son fermage et avait été chassé de sa maison. Deux fois des voisins re-
cueillirent la malheureuse famille et partagèrent leur modeste avoir avec
elle. Le propriétaire l'ayant appris, prévint aussitôt les fermiers que, s'ils
ne chassaient pas immédiatement O'Neill et ses enfants, ils seraient ex-
pulsés à leur tour. Alors les pauvres évincés furent obligés de s'en aller
grelottants de froid et de faim sous la pluie. O'Sullivan les voyant dans cet

état pitoyable les recueillit généreusement dans sa pauvre chaumière, bien qu'il connût la menace du propriétaire. Quelques jours après il recevait de celui-ci l'ordre de les chasser. Il refusa d'obéir, et pour ce refus le 3 mars dernier O'Sullivan fut expulsé grâce à la protection de la loi anglaise.

Mais O'Neill n'a pas partagé son sort. Les privations qu'il a subies et les nuits passées sous la pluie ont détruit sa santé, et le médecin a certifié qu'il était trop malade pour pouvoir être transporté sans danger.

Il a fallu cependant satisfaire aux formalités de la loi anglaise. Donc, l'huissier et les agents de police entrèrent dans la chaumière, éteignirent le feu, retirèrent une poignée de paille de la couchette du malade, en signe de prise de possession de la chaumière, puis ils s'éloignèrent laissant le malheureux attendre la mort comme une délivrances.

Quand j'ai visité la cabane, O'Neill gisait près du feu, couvert seulement de quelques haillons, avec ses enfants à peine vêtus groupés autour de lui. La faim était écrite sur leurs pauvres petits visages amaigris. Je n'ai jamais vu une scène plus douloureuse.

L'infortuné ne peut plus guérir, et le propriétaire n'attend que son dernier souffle pour pouvoir chasser sa famille de son dernier abri.

Il y a six ans que ce propriétaire, un Ecossais, a acheté ces terres pour la somme de 32.000 livres; le sol est très mauvais, composé pour la plupart de tourbières et de rochers, le revenu est évalué par le gouvernement a 1.862 livres, mais le propriétaire réussit à extorquer annuellement 3.000 livres de fermage des infortunés tenanciers qui sont au nombre de cinq cent trente et qui payent des loyers variant de 2 livres à 4 livres sterling.

Ce propriétaire exerce ses droits avec une extrême dureté; pas une pierre, pas un morceau de bois nu peuvent être pris sans paiement. On m'a cité un cas où il a fait payer deux sous à un paysan pour quelques branches de bois mort qu'il avait ramassées sur la route.

Ces deux dernières années, les récoltes ont été très mauvaises et la misère du peuple est terrible. J'ai visité un grand nombre des fermiers et causé avec eux; tous me disent la même chose. La nourriture manque, la famine existe en toute son horreur. Beaucoup de familles n'ont pour subsister qu'une poignée de farine de maïs par jour. Dans une chaumière j'ai vu une femme, Mme O'Connor, couchée sur son lit, attendre la mort sans audune nourriture ni médicament. Dans une autre chaumière un vieillard

Timothy Sullivan et sa femme subsistent avec un shilling par semaine !

Ce qu'il y a d'épouvantable surtout, c'est que la plupart des fermiers n'ont pas les semences nécessaires pour le printemps, et que la famine sera inévitable l'année prochaine.

ENGLISH TRANSLATION

At Sneem, County Kerry, inhumane evictions have increased starvation. Our contributor Mr. Connolly visited this district and gave us an accurate account of the situation of the unfortunate peasants.

I went to Sneem to investigate the famine and the evictions that have just taken place there.

The solidarity of the peasants and their courage in coming to the aid of the evicted people attracted public sympathy.

The house, or rather the cabin from which the latest victims of the landlords' tyranny have been evicted, consists of a single room covered by a damaged thatched roof which lets in the rain.

Sixty years ago this cottage was built by the O'Sullivan family, who have lived there ever since, from father to son, paying rent each year for this sad privilege. It wasn't for rent arrears that James O'Sullivan was evicted. Poor as he was, he owed nothing to anyone. He was made homeless simply for being charitable and merciful.

One of his neighbors, O'Neill, father of eight young children, had been reduced to poverty by a series of bad harvests. He was unable to pay his rent and was kicked out of his house. Twice his neighbors took in the unfortunate family and shared their modest belongings with them. Once the landlord heard of this he warned the neighbours that if they did not immediately expel O'Neill and his children, they too would be expelled. So the poor evictees were forced to leave, shivering with cold and hunger in the rain. Seeing them in this pitiful state, O'Sullivan generously took them into his poor cottage, even though he knew the landlord was threatening them. A few days later, he received an order from the owner to drive them out. He refused to obey and on 3 March O'Sullivan was evicted under the terms of English law.

O'Neill, though, didn't immediately share the same fate. The privations he had endured and the nights spent in the rain had destroyed his health, and the doctor certified that he was too ill to be transported safely.

However, English law must be obeyed. So, the bailiff and police officers entered the thatched cottage, extinguished the fire, removed a handful of straw from the sick man's bunk as a sign of taking possession of the cottage, and then walked away leaving the unfortunate man to await the delivery of death.

When I visited the cabin, O'Neill lay by the fire, covered only in a few rags, with his scantily clad children clustered around him. Hunger was written all over their poor, emaciated faces. I've never seen a more painful scene.

The unfortunate man will not recover from his illness, and the landlord is only waiting for him to draw his last breath so he can drive the family from their only shelter.

It's been six years since this landlord, a Scotsman, bought this land for the sum of £32,000. The soil is very poor, composed for the most part of peat bogs and rocks. The government estimates the income at £1,862, but the landlord extorts £3,000 a year in rent from the unfortunate tenants who number five hundred and thirty and who pay rents varying from £2 to £4.

This landowner exercises his rights with extreme harshness: not a stone, not a piece of bare wood can be taken without payment. I was told of one case where he made a peasant pay two pence for a few branches of dead wood he had picked up off the road.

Over the last two years, the harvests have been very poor and the people's misery has been terrible. I visited many of the farmers and talked to them; they all said the same thing. Food is in short supply, famine exists in all its horror. Many families subsist on a handful of cornmeal a day. In one thatched cottage I saw a woman, Mrs. O'Connor, lying on her bed, waiting to die without food or medicine. In another thatched cottage an elderly man, Timothy Sullivan, and his wife subsist on just one shilling a week.

The most appalling thing is that most peasants don't have the seeds they need for spring, and as a result famine next year is inevitable.

PART VII
PRIVATE LETTERS
PREVIOUSLY REPUBLISHED

*****

CONNOLLY TO LILLIE REYNOLDS
7 APRIL 1888/9[1]

APRIL 7TH
DUNDEE

L IL

For the first time in my life I feel extremely diffident about writing a letter. Usually I feel a sneaking sort of confidence in the possession of what I know to be a pretty firm grasp of the English language for one in my position. But for once I am at a loss, I wish to thank you for your kindness to me, and I am afraid lest by too great protestation of gratitude I might lead you to think that my gratitude is confined to the enclosure which accompanied the letter than the kindly sympathy of the writer. On the other hand I am afraid lest I might by too sparing a use of my thanks lead you to think I am ungrateful to you for your kindness. So in this dilemma I will leave you to judge for yourself my feelings towards you for your generous contributions to the 'Distressed Fund.'

So my love, your unfortunate Jim, is now in Dundee and very near to the 'girl he left behind him'[2] but the want of the immortal cash and the want of the necessary habiliments[3] presses me to remain as far from her

---

1   "Letter from James Connolly to Lillie Connolly," 7 April [no year], MS13,911/1, William O'Brien Collection, National Library of Ireland, Dublin. Although the letter lacks a year date, the address and contents are linked to the letter dated 17 April 188[8/9]

2   The popular song, "The Girl I left Behind Me" had many iterations, one of which was The Wandering [Migrant] Labourer, or An Spailpín Fánach. Connolly would later use the name "Spailpín" for his weekly column in the *Workers' Republic.*

3   Clothes; attire.

as if the Atlantic divided us. But cheer up, perhaps sometime or another, before you leave Perth if you stay in it any time, I may be available to see you again, God send it. I am glad to be able to tell you that I am working at present though and in another man's place, as he is off through illness. So perhaps things are coming round. I could get plenty work in England but you know England might be unhealthy for me, you understand. Excuse me for the scribbling as the house is full of people. It was only across the street from here a man murdered his wife and they are all discussing whether he is mad or not, pleasant, isn't it. Please write soon. It is always a pleasure to me to hear from you, and especially in my present condition, it is like a present voice encouraging me to greater exertion in the future. But I must stop, for I cannot compose my mind to write, owing to the hubbub of voices around me. I will watch for it expectantly, and believe me I will be glad to have the assurance of the sympathy of my own sweetheart.

Yours lovingly,

JAMES CONNOLLY
Address c/o Mrs Boyle, St Marys Street, Lochee Board, Dundee

*****

CONNOLLY TO LILLIE REYNOLDS
17 APRIL [1888/9][1]

St Mary's Street
Dundee
17 April 188[8/9][2]

I will meet you at Baggot Street Bridge and we will have a walk round Donnybrook. God's truth.

L ILLIE
There is something in your last letter I cannot understand, my weak
and feeble mind fails to grasp your meaning. You say you wrote to me on
the fifth and I have never wrote since to say whether I received your letter
or got work or aught else. Well I received your letter all right and also
the enclosure. I almost immediately after wrote to you, thanking you for
your letter and what it contained and informing you that I was working.[3]
Well, I am now puzzled by your saying that you cannot understand me
not writing before this. I was half expecting a compliment on my readiness in answering your letter, and instead of that I receive a rebuke. Alas

---

1   'Letter from James Connolly to Lillie Connolly," 17 April 188[8/9], MS
13,911/2, William O'Brien Collection, National Library of Ireland, Dublin.

2   In the original letter the final "8" in "1888" seems to have been changed
to "9." The letter was also originally dated "16ᵗʰ" but Connolly changed the "6" to
"7."

3   See Connolly to Lillie Reynolds, 7 April [no year].

this is a world of disappointment.[4] Man was made to mourn.[5] Well I will stop complaining and tell you about Dundee. This is the town, where the women rule the roost. According to the census there are supposed to be 11 (eleven) women to every two men in Dundee. And if you seen the street beside the mills at dinner hour or any [dull?] hours, just as the mills are coming out you would believe it, women, women hardly anything but women, women and girls of all shapes, descriptions, and sizes, short and small, long and tall, as beautiful as angels and as ugly as sin. And their talk, oh the Tower of Babel was nothing to it. You can hear at once all the twangs of every district in Scotland and the brogue of every county in Ireland. For there isn't a county in the Emerald Isle but what has sent its representatives here. I think Dundee has, as proportion to its population a stronger Irish population than any other town in Great Britain. The children here also work at six years of age going halftime to school and half to work. In the majority of families, both husband and wife work, the wife often earning more than the husband. Women can work when men can't get it here, and so the spectacle is often presented of the wife working while the husband sits idle at home. How would you like that, Lillie. It often made my teeth water when I looked at them, with envy (moryah[6]). I am not a bit surprised when I hear you saying you can't warm to the Perth people. If you knew what the newspapers call the lights and shadows of Scottish character as well as I do, you would like them less. Such affectedly pious God-fearing hypocritical skunks as the majority of them are not to be found on this side of the globe. Thank God. But when you do find a good old Scotsman or woman they are pure gold. I can hardly believe the socks you sent to me to be your first effort at knitting, they are absolutely the best I have ever seen. When my landlady saw them she said. 'Well Jim, the lass that sent you them didn't make a fool of you anyway.' And I echoed the sentiment, they didn't make a fool of me. God bless her is the prayer of her Devoted Sweetheart

---

4   "It is a world of disappointment—often to the hopes we most cherish, and hopes that do our nature the greatest honour." Charles Dickens, *Oliver Twist; or the Parish Boy's Progress* (Leipzig, 1843), 425.

5   Robert Burns. "Thro' weary life this lesson learn, / That man was made to mourn."

6   Moryah ("Mar dhea")—a sceptical Irish interjection used to cast doubt, dissent or derision. Approximate translation: "yeah right" or "as if."

JIM CONNOLLY.

Address c/o Mrs Boyle, St Marys Street, Lochee Board, Dundee.

I'll write soon & sudden.

*****

CONNOLLY TO LILLIE REYNOLDS UNDATED[1]

LILLIE
I was half amused and half vexed by the curt epistle I received on Friday. It seemed to me as if you had been studying the business epistles of some business house and applying them to me. However, when I come to think of it it is quite natural. It is a saddening indication of the condition to which I have fallen that, you who have been so usually effusive and affectionate, should be treating me to a letter like unto a summons for rent. I was rather amused to see that you treated my proposal to visit me in all seriousness. Do you think me 'daft' or what. ~~I wish to see you less.~~[2] I am getting vexed you see. I mean to say, I wish to tell you that I cannot bring myself to ask to meet you on Tuesday, or any other day for some time yet. I can not think but that my conduct is rather selfish in imposing on your good-nature as I have been doing and preparing to do. I think here is very dear. I [...] (confound these pens) if you can tolerate me any longer for a week or two, when I do see you next, it will be when I will not be quite so afraid of shaming you, as I have been. So Lillie, although I am very loath to be so long without seeing you and so near to you, still I am persuaded it is all for the best, better that it should be so. Don't think it is for any other reason. God knows I would like to see you and be with you every night in the week if possible and think myself happy if I was allowed to do so. But I cannot bring myself to inflict my presence, as I have been proposing to do, upon you. And while on this subject I may as well once more repeat what I said to you last time we met, that I hardly expected you would

---

1   "Letter from James Connolly to Lillie Connolly," undated, MS 13,911/3, William O'Brien Collection, National Library of Ireland, Dublin.

2   This line is crossed out in the original.

come to meet me. And the fact that you did come served to increase my love for the girl who could lower herself to be seen speaking to one who has descended so low in the social scale as myself. But cheer up, if with God's help I ever am able to make another [...] to better fortune I hope that I may be granted the pleasure and happiness of having my beloved Lillie by my side to share it with me and make it a blessing to be coveted. Although we cannot meet still I hope you will not forget to write quickly to yours lovingly,

JAMES CONNOLLY
c/o Mr Barret, 127 South Street, Perth

*****

CONNOLLY TO LILLIE REYNOLDS
UNDATED[1]

This is a love letter. This is a letter written by me, Jim, to the nicest girl between here and anywhere, to tell her that all her mistakes, her wilfulness, her troublesomeness, only make me love her the more, and make me more than ever determined to have the possession of [...] a delightful bundle of contradictions all to myself. You make things worse, indeed, the very idea is rank heresy, why if I was ever so miserable the thought of having such a sweet wife to come home to, a wife whom I love with all my heart and soul, the thought would make me brave in the face of any difficulty, cheerful in the face of any misfortune. You know me too well, Lillie, I think, to imagine I could be angry with you for long, if ever I felt inclined that way the thought of your sweet face and your lovable ways would make me ashamed of myself. Hoping I shall ever remain rich in the continuance of your love and that we shall soon see the accomplishment of that event which shall join our hands as [...] hearts have long been joined.

I remain, yours lovingly,

JIM.

P.S. NO, MY DEAR, you will not need to live with my mother. You shall

---

1   "Letter from James Connolly to Lillie Reynolds," undated, MS 13,911/4, William O'Brien Collection, National Library of Ireland, Dublin. The letter is slightly damaged which affects transcription. Although undated it is almost certainly from 1890 due to the discussion around wedding plans. Connolly and Lillie Reynolds married on 30 April 1890.

have a house of your own. My brother shall, I think be best man.
Write at once.

*****

CONNOLLY TO LILLIE REYNOLDS
6 APRIL 1890[1]

L IL
This is a letter full of reproach, abuse, and scolding, this is not a love letter. This is a letter written by me, James Connolly to my intended wife, Lillie Reynolds, on the style and after the manner of an old husband of nine or ten years standing. I have often [...] of your good nature, you will need it all before you are done reading this letter. Firstly, then I am angry with you, very angry indeed, because of your seeming or real carelessness of the interests of yourself and your humble servant, and because of your sublime ignorance of the most common and well known facts and thirdly for so easily forgetting what you have been told was necessary to remember. I am referring to the manner, the calm and unconcerned manner in which you inform me that you cannot leave London till the twelfth, after assuring me that you could always leave on the tenth of each month. By this change you have upset all my arrangements, and thrown me into a great deal of expense, and, more than all postponed our marriage for another week. You seem to imagine that to get married, all you have to do is to go to a clergyman and get the knot tied. But you are wrong in thinking so. The law of these countries require a great lot of formalities to go through which are necessary and without which a marriage is impossible. As I told you some time ago it is absolutely necessary that one or other of the parties must have resided in the parish in which the ceremony is to be performed, for 3 weeks *immediately* preceding the marriage. Now you see the effects of altering the date of your leaving London. It is impossible for me to reside in Perth for that time or anything like I would lose my work.

---

1   "Letter from James Connolly to Lillie Reynolds," 6 April 1890, MS 13,911/5, William O'Brien Collection, National Library of Ireland, Dublin.

So you must do it, it can't be helped and as I said before to you, you must undertake the duty or acquainting the registrar in order to get the necessary licence, without which the ceremony can't be performed. It's not me who is saying you must do this it is the law. I have to do it in my parish and the banns[2] are indeed already published here, and you must do it in Perth. There need be no trouble on your part. Get Mary Angus or some other person to go with you and let them introduce you to the registrar, merely saying 'this young lady wishes a form of notice of marriage', and he will ask your name and address and occupation which you will give him. (Perth address, of course). Then my name and address and occupation, (carter) which you will give him. Then you will get a paper which you will have to sign and get two householders to sign also. Your friend in Perth will get that done for you surely. Then return this paper to the registrar, and he will give you another, which you must get from home within fifteen days before the event. There is in reality not much trouble in this, but without it we cannot get married. Now for another distasteful job. You know before a catholic can marry a protestant he must obtain what is called a dispensation from the Archbishop. I have applied for this dispensation, and I am informed it can only be granted on condition you promise never to interfere with my observance of my religion (funny idea, isn't it,) and that any children born of the union should have to be baptised in the catholic church. Now, I know you won't like that especially as the priest will call on you to ask you. But, Lillie, if your brother attended chapel for nearly a year for the sake of his sweetheart, surely you will not grudge speaking for a quarter of an hour to a priest especially as the fulfilment of these promises rest with ourselves in the future, though I'd like you to keep them. Your brother you know, had to make the same promises, though perhaps, he did not let his family know. Believing you will oblige me in this instance I shall send your Perth address to the reverend gentleman, when he will either call on you or ask you to call on him.

Yours JIM

---

2   A notice read out on three successive Sundays in a parish church, announcing an intended marriage and giving the opportunity for objections.

*****

CONNOLLY TO LILLIE REYNOLDS
UNDATED[1]

Edinburgh Tuesday

L^{il}
I was very glad to receive your letter as it lifted quite a load off my heart. I was so afraid you had not gone to Perth. Your last letter was so very indignant with me. I am amused to see you are getting some of the anxiety which I have had this long time. But you need not be afraid. Mrs Angus is wrong. Six weeks was the old law but that has been altered in 1878. If you had done what I told you and gone to the registrar at once, you would have found out for yourself. Seven days is the time now, so please lose no time and go at once, and if all goes well I shall be with you next week and make you mine for ever. When giving your name to the registrar I gave it as Lillie.[2] By the way please write at once as soon as you get this letter and tell me your father and mother's names. Also your father's profession. I want it as soon as ever I can get it also your birthplace. When I gave your age I gave it as 22, was I right. How I am wearying to get beside you, and hear your nonsense once more. It is such a long time since we met, but I trust this time we will meet to part no more. Won't it be pleasant. By the way if we get married next week I shall be unable to go to Dundee as I promised, as my fellow-workmen in the job are preparing for a strike on the end of this month, for a reduction in the hours of

---

1   "Letter from James Connolly to Lillie Reynolds," undated, MS 13,911/6, William O'Brien Collection, National LIbrary of Ireland, Dublin. Although undated, the wedding plans place it in 1890.

2   The registrar spelt it as Lily.

labour. As my brother and I are ringleaders in the matter it is necessary we should be on the ground. If we were not we should be looked upon as blacklegs, which the Lord forbid. Mind don't lose a minutes time in writing, and you will greatly gratify.

Your loving JIM,
not JAMES as your last letter was directed.

*****

CONNOLLY TO KIER HARDIE
9 FEBRUARY 1894[1]

6 LOTHIAN STREET

D EAR COMRADE
I have been instructed by the Central Edinburgh Branch of the
Scottish Labour Party to inform you that owing to the extremely short
notice given them they find it impossible to send a delegate to the business meeting of the Party on Saturday 18th. They also desire me to protest,
in their name, against the manner in which the meeting as a whole has
been convened. While nearly two months' notice was given of a mere
conference of all sections of the working-class movement, binding on no
one, for a business meeting of the Party at which the whole policy and
programme of the Party is to be declared, we only receive four days' notice. And yet, according to one resolution on the agenda paper, one member of the Executive is to be chosen from Edinburgh. And we were never
invited officially to send in any motions or suggestions for the agenda of
the conference. Moreover, our meetings are held fortnightly, and for all
the convener of the business meeting may know, the invitation to attend
its deliberations will not be laid before the Edinburgh branches till next
week. For general meetings mean money, and we have none to squander.
When no Edinburgh delegates are present, who will choose the representative on the Executive.

Now that I have done grumbling, as per order, I have much pleasure

---

1   "J. Connolly to Hardie (Edinburgh), 9 February 1894," ILP/4/1894/20,
Francis Johnson Correspondence, London School of Economics Library and Archive, London. Republished in *Socialist Review* 25, no. 137 (March 1925), 120.

in wishing every success to the meeting, in spite of the gloom which our absence from the gathering must cast around you.

Fraternally yours,

JAMES CONNOLLY
Secretary
Central Edinburgh Branch
Scottish Labour Party

*****

CONNOLLY TO KIERHARDIE
28 MAY 1894[1]

NOTE NEW ADDRESS

21 S. COLLEGE ST
EDIN[BURGH]
28/5/94

D EAR KEIR HARDIE
Yours to hand. You may release Mr Beevers of any engagement you may have held him to in re Central Edinburgh. We have fixed nearer home, and are ready to begin as soon as we have succeeded in inducing the Trades Council and individual organised trades to embark along with us. I am to approach them at their first meeting, but can only hope to succeed by careful manoeuvring, which will most certainly fail if you persist in blurting out or allowing others to blurt out in the *Labour Leader* that the ILP in Central Edinburgh have selected a candidate and are expecting the workers to accept their choice without demur.[2] This would simply arouse every prejudice against us and deprive us of the opportunity of dilating on the cliqueism of the Liberal caucus. I want the ILP to act in con-

---

1   "J. Connolly to Hardie (Edinburgh), 28 May 1894," ILP/4/1894/106, Francis Johnson Correspondence, London School of Economics Library and Archive, London. Republished in *Socialist Review* 25, no. 137 (March 1925), 121.

2   "...and now I hear that Councillor Beever has been spending his Whit holidays in Edinburgh, where he is to be asked to contest the Central Division against brewer M'Ewan." *Labour Leader*, 19 May 1894, 2; "It seems that Councillor Beever, of Halifax, and William Small, of Blantyre, are the only men now in the running for the position of Labour candidate in Central Edinburgh." *Labour Leader*, 26 May 1894, 5.

junction with the Trades Council in promoting the return of a good Socialist and Independent Labour Candidate, who must be the free choice of a large number of the electors, who can be induced to sign a requisition asking him to stand <u>before we even announce him as our adopted candidate</u>. By such means we may hope to allay the prejudices of the electors, and draw many hundreds to our side who would be frightened away by any less cautious course. So whether you agree or not as to the wisdom of publicity we expect you will respect our wishes and observe a discreet silence until the time comes to speak. On what days in the week would it be possible for you to come to Edinburgh. By the way our choice of a candidate was in no way a reflection upon Beevers' abilities, but simply owing to the fact that a man nearer home was necessary in order to enable us to <u>cheaply</u> work up the constituency. We have secured such a man.

Yours fraternally,

JAMES CONNOLLY
Sec[retary]

*****

CONNOLLY TO KIER HARDIE
8 JUNE 1894[1]

EDINBURGH
8/6/94
21 S. COLLEGE ST

DEAR COMRADE HARDIE
I have written to Beevers. We have adopted as our candidate Mr William Small of Blantyre. He addressed one meeting in Edinburgh for the Central Branch the day after your <u>promised</u> visit.[2] He has since spoken in Leith for the Socialist Federation and speaks there to-night for the ILP. He has spoken for the Eastern last Saturday and on Sunday for the Socialists. At the latter meeting he had an audience variously estimated at 1,500 and 2,000 persons. It was the largest I have ever seen in the Meadows and he made a grand impression. The only discussion was after he had left the meeting and related to the remarks of other speakers. He speaks for the Southern Branch on next Wednesday (13th). I am taking him over the ground in this manner in order to work up the excitement and create a good impression all round. I wrote the Trades Council on their last meeting and they resolved by a three to one majority to co-op-

1   "J. Connolly to Hardie (Edinburgh), 8 June 1894," ILP/4/1894/118, Francis Johnson Correspondence, London School of Economics Library and Archive. Republished in *Socialist Review* 25, no. 137 (March 1925), 121-122.

2   "It was in support of this resolution that Mr. Kier Hardie was to have spoken, and there was an ominous silence as Connolly mounted the stool to apologise for his absence. He could only say that Mr. Hardie had promised to come and had been notified of the time and place of meeting but had not yet arrived. He promised that an apology from Mr. Hardie for the breach of faith would appear in the Labour Leader explaining the cause of his non-appearance." *Labour Leader*, 19 May 1894, 5.

erate with us and remitted it to their Parliamentary Committee to consider what steps they will take.[3] The Parnellite leaders in Edinburgh have privately promised their support and at their open meeting on Sunday will do it publicly and appoint a committee to help us. I intend as the climax to all these meetings to have a huge meeting in the Central on 25th June which will be advertised and will be billed, handbills for a week previously. We will then announce that Mr Small has consented to stand as a Labour candidate if a sufficient number of electors can be got to sign a requisition in his favour, to justify a fight being made. This requisition we can easily secure. Now I want to know if you can be with us on that date a Monday. Write soon and let us know. We are intending this time to make a supreme effort and from the very outset to act and talk as if we had got such promises of support that victory is certain. Do you think it would be possible or judicious to ask Mr Field MP for South Dublin to support Small at the next big meeting when the requisition will be presented. I know and this like the rest of my letter is confidential, that he has advised the Parnellites in Edinburgh to be friendly towards the Labour Party. Anxiously awaiting a reply.

From yours fraternally,

JAMES CONNOLLY
Secretary
Election Committee
Edinburgh

---

3   "...what steps they will take" is missing from *Socialist Review* (1925).

*****

CONNOLLY TO KIERHARDIE
19 JUNE 1894[1]

EDINBURGH
JUNE 19/94
21 S. COLLEGE ST

D EAR COMRADE HARDIE

I received your letter all right and was thankful for the information it contained. I am sorry Field can't make a good platform appearance it would have been a trump card. I asked you to see Redmond as soon as possible because the Parnellites here had resolved to ask his advice in order that their proposed manifesto in any form might have all the more force with their countrymen. If you had seen Redmond before he sent off his reply it might have helped to give a greater colour and force to his message. If you have not seen him I expect his letter will be pretty ambiguous and will throw the burden of choice of action upon the branch here. If he does, that will serve our purpose right enough. I resolved to take your advice and wait your coming in the autumn. Expense is a mighty factor in working out those problems. Will write and let you know result of meeting, of which I enclose a handbill.

Yours fraternally

JAMES CONNOLLY
Sec[retary]

---

1   "J. Connolly to Hardie (Edinburgh), 19 June 1894," ILP/4/1894/127, Francis Johnson Correspondence, London School of Economics Library and Archive, London. Republished in *Socialist Review* 25, no. 137 (March 1925), 123.

*****

CONNOLLY TO P. KAVANAGH
20 JUNE 1896[1]

75 CHARLEMONT STREET DUBLIN

DEAR COMRADE

I have been instructed to inform you that, in order to prevent unnecessary accumulation of arrears of weekly subscriptions, the financial secretary, Mr TJ. Lyng, will call upon all members once a week, from Sunday next, and collect said subscriptions which in all future communications will be termed dues. Club room, 67 Middle Abbey Street, open in future every night in the week.

Yours fraternally

JAMES CONNOLLY

---

1   "Postcard from James Connolly to P. Kavanagh regarding the collection of unpaid dues, 20 June 1896," MS 13,940/1/1, William O'Brien Collection, National Library of Ireland, Dublin.

*****

CONNOLLY TO T.J. O'BRIEN
1 JULY 1897[1]

67 MIDDLE ABBEY STREET DUBLIN

1 JULY 1897

DEAR O'BRIEN

Please remember that you have to write out certain minutes of our transactions, and as certain new members are expected tonight it is desirable to avoid any hitch in the proceedings. I will meet you at the rooms at 7 p.m.

Yours fraternally,

JAMES CONNOLLY

---

1   "Postcard from James Connolly to T. J. O'Brien [Assistant Secretary, Irish Socialist Republican Party] reminding O'Brien to prepare minutes before a meeting that evening, 1 July 1897," MS 13,940/1/2, William O'Brien Collection, National Library of Ireland, Dublin.

*****

CONNOLLY TO THOMAS J. LYNG
16 JULY 1898[1]

6 DRUMMOND STREET
EDINBURGH
16 JULY 1898

DEAR LYNG

I received your note all right and was glad to hear so good a report. I hope the boys will keep up to the scratch and not let the meetings drop off. They have now a good opportunity of showing the Dublin people that socialism does not depend upon any individual and I believe that when the people see that they will have more confidence than they otherwise would have in our party. I hope that Bradshaw and O'Brien will rally up and be men enough to do the part of men, and not be throwing it on the shoulders of others. I have been blowing my horn about you here at a great rate, and I hope you will not belie me by your inactivity. I have given out three subscription sheets for the paper, and I am confident each of them will bring in a few shillings at least. I have also been assured of a good many who will take the paper regularly and also get it into the newsagents.

I can now promise definitely that we will have a song from Leslie in the first issue.[2] I heard the first of it last night. I hope you are not forgetting about the trade unions. I am afraid you made a mistake when you resolved not to advertise this week, as a number of our readers will, I hope,

---

1   "Letter from James Connolly to Thomas J. Lyng, 16 July 1898," MS 13,912/4/3, William O'Brien Collection, National Library of Ireland, Dublin.

2   The song duly appeared, "Wolf Tone" by John Leslie, sung to the air of "The Farmer's Boy," *Workers' Republic*, 13 August 1898, 2.

be in Great Britain (and Ireland) and it is desirable to set them talking as soon as possible. What about advertising in *Justice* and the *Labour Leader*. If Graham is fixing his charge per column as moderately as you tell me I think you had better definitely decide on making paper as big as *Justice*. You could then decide on the number of columns each would take. Let Stewart make up his mind what space he will require for No.1 and act accordingly, only don't indulge too much in <u>long</u> articles. The article on the Tramway men is just the kind of thing wanted.[3] Same to Bradshaw, only as I am dealing with that Press banquet,[4] and incidentally with the politicians in the article on Wolfe Tone for which I hope T. J. O'Brien has copied out what I asked him, it would be desirable to avoid repetition. I would like Bradshaw to look up all the most reactionary sayings of the politicians and all the democratic sayings of the '48, '98 men, and prepare them for a two column setting forth side by side under a two column heading, saying Protests of Irish Patriotism (?). Ask Stewart to drop a note to Dr Watt and ask him to contribute some notes or an article on the subject of Socialism.

About coming back I will, I am sure, be able to get a good many people, of our own people that is, interested in the paper which [...] in the West of Scotland and it would be a pity to lose the opportunity. I may get some financial help likewise, and so I think it would be a mistake to be in too great a hurry home. But I can not say definitely as yet. It will all depend upon whether I get the requisite £.s.d. from the Greeks in the West for our paper. I don't mean the £50, but fresh subscriptions.[5] On our Sunday meetings here the collection was at Leith ten [shillings] three [pence], in the Meadows nineteen [shillings] five [pence] a record.

Yours fraternally,

James Connolly
P.S. I think I will have a fortnight idle owing to Summer holidays.

---

3   Yumen, "Dublin Tramways," *Workers' Republic*, 13 August 1898, 3-4. Yumen was a pseudonym used by E.W. Stewart.

4   Setanta, "Home Rule Journalists and Patriotism: An Object Lesson," *Workers' Republic*, 13 August 1898, 5. Setanta was a pseudonym used by Connolly.

5   Kier Hardie gave a loan of £50 towards the establishment of *Workers' Republic*. See "Receipt signed by James Connolly to James Keir Hardie for a loan given in order to establish 'The Workers' Republic', 20 September 1898," MS 49,491/1/330, William O'Brien Collection, National Library of Ireland, Dublin.

*****

CONNOLLY TO THOMAS J. LYNG
UNDATED¹

DEAR LYNG
The question you ask about the Editor's salary is too personal for me to attempt to answer. Please yourself. I would of course accept what you suggest, but follow your own mind on the matter. I am afraid that next fortnight I will be unemployed. You might call upon Mrs Connolly and let her know you have heard from me.

Yours

JIM

---

1   Letter from James Connolly [to Thomas J. Lyng] regarding the salary for the position of editor," undated, MS 13,912/4/1, William O'Brien Collection, National Library of Ireland, Dublin. A note on the NLI website reads: "A typescript copy of this letter, MS 13,912/4/2, carries 3 manuscript notes saying 'On tour in G.B', 'A spare copy' and '£1.00 per week.'" *Workers' Republic* was launched on 13 August 1898. The discussion in the letter on the level of wage for Connolly as editor would place its composition sometime in the late spring/early summer of that year. The letter has "1898" written on it but it is not in Connolly's hand and is in a different ink to the original.

PART VIII
SECONDARY REPORTS

*****

THE REPRESENTATION OF CENTRAL EDINBURGH[1]

SCOTSMAN

17 FEB 1891, P.6

A public meeting under the auspices of the Ward Labour Committee was held last night in the Labour Hall, South Bridge, Edinburgh, to consider the Parliamentary representation of the Central Division of Edinburgh... Mr. James Connolly, carter, moved the following resolution:—

> Resolved that this meeting record its most emphatic conviction that Mr William M'Ewan[2], the present member of parliament for the Central division of the City of Edinburgh, is no longer, if he ever was, a fit and proper person to represent the working classes of the Division in Parliament; that it recognises in his letter to the Chairman of the Central Liberal Association a conspicuous absence of any comprehension whatever of what was really involved in the late struggle between the railway companies and their employees[3]; that the recent railway strike has been productive of at least one unmixed good—viz, the shattering of the superstition that in our present industrial society, based upon monopoly on the one hand, and wage servitude on the other, there is, or ever can be, any true identity of interest between capital and labour; that recognising this fact, this meeting pledges itself to secure, if possible, the return to Parliament for the Central Division of Edinburgh of a la-

---

1   This report was rediscovered and reproduced online by the *Treason Felony* Blog, 4 June 2020.

2   William McEwan (1827-1913). Born in Aloa, Scotland. Opened the Fountain Brewery in Edinburgh in 1856. Liberal Party MP for Edinburgh Central, 1886-1900. Died in Mayfair, London, with a personal wealth of £1.5m.

3   The Scottish railway strike began on 21 December 1890 and involved three companies: The North British, the Caledonian, and the Glasgow and South Western Railways. The maximum number of men on strike was estimated at over 8,000 with around a hundred thousand persons out of work either directly or indirectly as a result. It ended on 29 January 1891. See James Mavor, "Scottish Railway Strike," *Economic Journal*, (March 1891), 204-219.

bour candidate at next general election; and that for the candidate it be made an indispensable condition of his candidature that he fully and freely recognises the antagonism of interest between the monopolisers of the means of production and distribution and the wage workers, or, in other words, that he expresses his belief in the existence of the class war.

The resolution, he proceeded, expressed the conviction of every honest man in the locality upon the matter...

*****

PROVINCIAL MEETINGS
FREEDOM (LONDON)
1 DECEMBER 1891, P.89

EDINBURGH—Nov. 11th, Scottish Socialist Federation. James Connelly [sic] opened the proceedings with a sketch of the events that led up to the Chicago tragedy. He concluded with a truly eloquent appeal to those present to put their heart and soul into the great work that lay to their hands, and by their efforts for the cause raise the grandest possible monument to those who had given up their lives for it. Comrades John Smith, Glasse, Gilray, Melliet, Campbell, Leslie, and Hamilton also spoke. "Annie Laurie," "The Carmagnole," Pierre Dupont's "Song of the Workers," and other revolutionary songs were sung. A Russian comrade rendered "the Marsellaise."

*****

EIGHT HOURS DEMONSTRATION AT EDINBURGH
EDINBURGH EVENING NEWS
8 MAY 1893, P.3

M R FRED HAMILTON, printer, moved the first resolution... Mr James Connolly[1] seconded. He said that wages were regulated by the men and women who were standing idle outside waiting for employment. Their hunger and misery were the factors the middle classes depended on when they offered such small remuneration. Their rulers had passed the unemployed by; they had not time for it; they were too busy to consider it, but he told them that they must settle the question; they must take up the eight hour day, with which was linked the other question of the unemployed. They must resolve to seize upon every centre of power in the country, from Parliament to Town Councils, and they must resolve to use them for their own interest, as their masters had used them for their interest.

---

1   "Mr James Connelly [sic], unskilled labourer, seconded the resolution, which was supported by Miss Conway, Independent Labour Party Executive." See "Eight Hours Demonstration in Edinburgh," *Glasgow Herald*, 8 May 1893, 7.

*****

EIGHT HOURS' DAY DEMONSTRATION – NO.3 PLATFORM
EDINBURGH EVENING NEWS
7 MAY 1894, P.3[1]

IT WAS ABOUT SIX O'CLOCK when speaking commenced at no.3 platform, which was under the charge of the Independent Labour Party and the Scottish Socialist Federation... The first resolution[2] was proposed by Mr J. Connelly [sic]. What, he asked, were all their strikes, lockouts, and such disputes, but the ebullition of their belief in the socialist movement—the evidence of their desires after freedom. They demanded not merely the right to vote, but the right to live—not the life of a human drudge, but the fullest and freest life that human society could put before its members. They denied the right of the capitalist to fleece them.

---

1   See also *Glasgow Herald*, 7 May 1894, 8. Same report is given.

2   "That in the opinion of this meeting of workers of Edinburgh and district, the time has come for the establishment of an eight hours working day, and that such relief from our industrial drudgery can be best secured by legislative enactment, compulsory in all cases, except where the organised workers of any trade or industry protest against it; and that, with the working class democracy of the world, we affirm our belief that the democratic administration of the industries by which they live is a necessary condition for the freedom of a people."

*****

THE KNIGHTS OF THE PLOUGH[1]
LEINSTER LEADER
25 AUGUST 1894, P.6

THE KNIGHTS OF THE PLOUGH held their monthly meeting in Narraghmore on Sunday 19th August 1894. Amongst those present were Messrs B Pelin in the chair, M Murphy, treasurer; D Nolan, P Byrne, J Bedoe, W Maher, N Murphy, Nicholas Maher. The following resolutions were proposed and passed unanimously.

> That we believe the best method whereby the House of Lords can be abolished is for the House of Commons to cease sending its ablest members into the said house. If the House of Commons ceased sending its best blood into this chamber it would quickly become a spectacle of stupidity to gods and men.

> That we approve of the suggestion of James Connolly, Edinburgh, Scotland, for the formation of a labour party, embracing the workers of the Three Kingdoms and adopting a common programme as we believe the cause of labour is the same in the three countries...

---

1   See Fintan Lane, "Benjamin Pelin," 190.

*****

A SOCIALIST MANIFESTO
EDINBURGH EVENING NEWS
29 JANUARY 1895, P.2

T HE SOCIALIST ELECTION COMMITTEE of the Central Division
 have sent out a manifesto to the electors, in which they justify the
position they took up in the general election of 1892, and review the
record of Mr M'Ewen and the Liberal party since that period. In conclusion they ask the electors to reserve their votes for a socialist candidate,
*"for the champion of a party pledged to uproot every form of political and
social bondage, to make the people in a democratic state the sole masters of
the land and instruments of labour by which they live, to organise and lead
the workers in their onward and upward pilgrimage from the dark Egypt of
our capitalistic anarchy to the Promised Land of Industrial Freedom."* [My
emphasis.]

*****

EDINBURGH SOCIALISTS AND THE CENTRAL DIVISION
THE SCOTSMAN
30 JANUARY 1895, P.6

T HE EDINBURGH SOCIALIST Election Committee have issued an address to the electors of the Central Division, in which the electors are asked to reserve their vote for a socialist candidate at the next election. The committee declare that the Liberals and Tories are not two parties, but only two sections of one party, and that their political antagonism has no deeper foundation than a difference of opinion as to the best way of keeping the poor contented in their misery, and excluded from their inheritance. The committee lay various charges at the door of the Liberal government, such as taking sides with the rich against the poor in the labour disputes at Hull, in Wales, and Yorkshire. The Liberal and Tory parties existed only to betray the working classes. The Socialist candidate would be the champion of a party pledged to "uproot every form of political and social bondage, to make the people in a democratic state the sole masters of the land and instruments of labour by which they live, to organise and lead the workers in their onward and upward pilgrimage from the dark Egypt of our capitalistic anarchy to the Promised Land of Industrial Freedom."[1]

---

1   Although unsigned, textual analysis identifies the manifesto as written by Connolly.

*****

EDINBURGH IRISHMEN AND THE POLITICAL PRISONERS
EDINBURGH EVENING NEWS
27 FEBRUARY 1895, P.2

A MEETING IN FAVOUR of the release of Irish political prisoners was held in the Masonic Hall, Melbourne Place, Edinburgh, last night— Mr H. M'Guinnes presiding. Mr Field, M.P., was to have addressed the meeting, but he was unable to get over from Belfast in time. The chairman referred to the disparity of the sentences upon the Irish political prisoners and those engaged in the anarchist movement in England. Mr Daniel Donworth moved:

> That this meeting declares its conviction that the Irish political prisoners should be released without further delay; declares that in view of the long term of imprisonment they have already endured, the doubtful nature of the evidence on which many of them were convicted, and the broken state of their health, there can be no real conciliation during the continued imprisonment of these men; and recommends the Irish electors of this city to vote only for those candidates who are prepared to vote for amnesty.

Mr James Connolly seconded, and Miss Maud Gonne, in supporting the resolution, said the Liberal government which was kept in power by the Irish votes, had failed to keep their promises to the Irish. The evicted tenants were as cold and homeless on the hillsides of Ireland as ever they were, and she had seen in Ireland evictions as cruel and as brutal as any she had seen under Mr Balfour. On questions being invited, Mr Fitzpatrick said that the member for the Central Division of Edinburgh had declared that he was opposed to amnesty, and asked whether any nationalist could conscientiously support such a man? Mr Patrick Connelly proposed that Miss Gonne should not answer that question. The member for the Central Division was not before them for election. The chairman said there was a probability that between this and the general election the member for Central Edinburgh might become sufficiently educated on the subject, or at any rate sufficiently sympathetic. The motion was unanimously adopted.

*****

SOCIAL PARADOXES
WORKINGTON STAR
1 NOVEMBER 1895, P.4

THIS WAS THE TITLE of a lecture on Sunday by Mr James Connolly, of Edinburgh, a smart socialist lecturer who has been here during the week for the Labour Party... Mr Connolly, in the course of an interesting address, said his intention was to examine the system under which we live in order to see whether it was worth supporting. As they proceeded they would find that the present system was in conflict with all the traditions that they were taught to believe in, and that nothing but the adoption of a collectivist system of society would prove to be a real remedy for existing evils. The capitalist and landlord classes had laid hold of every institution, from the school-room where their children were taught, to the House of Commons, where they manufactured the laws by which they were governed, and whatever charge might be brought against those classes there was one thing that could never be said about them, and that was, they could not be charged with neglecting their own interests, or refusing to support the system that kept them in comfort and luxury, and a large majority of the workers in misery and suffering.

From the Crown downwards they had a huge conspiracy to enable one class to live by exploiting another class. The workers had been taught to be thrifty till they forgot that the Chinese were thrifty and also very poor. The Turks were the most abstemious race they could find, and they were the most wretched and poverty stricken. But now the workers were beginning to see the cloven hoof; they were beginning to see that things were wrong, and the doctrine of collectivism was getting such a hold of them that it would never be rooted out by the lies of the other parties.

When their doctrine was beginning to spread their opponents tried their very best to show that it was absurd, but that had no effect except to help collectivism—out of their own mouths their opponents were condemned. That was the reason why they altered their mode of attack and adopted the old woman style of argument, such as telling them of the sacredness of freedom of contract and that sort of thing.

Freedom of contract was all right in theory. In theory no man could force an employer to engage him, and no employer could force a man to work for him. If that was so in practice they had no right to complain. If that were true, the capitalists were absolved from all blame.

But it was not true. It was true that no contract was legally binding where one man forced his views upon another. If a highwayman presented a pistol at a man's head and forced him to sign an agreement to pay him a certain sum, the agreement would not be legally binding. A gentleman was drowning in the Clyde; as he was going down for the third time a man rowed out to him in a boat, and told him that he would rescue him on one condition. He pointed out to the man that he was drowning, and that unless he (the man in the boat) rescued him he would perish, and then he said that if he would agree to give him everything he owned except what would just serve to keep him alive he would save him. But he was careful to tell him that he was not forcing him to do this; it was a perfectly free contract, and the man in the water could please himself whether he entered into it or not; but if he didn't he would drown. It might have been that the man in the water had made the boat, but he was entirely at the mercy of the man in the boat; he could either enter into this 'free contract' or drown.

It was exactly the same with the capitalist and the labourer today. The workers had made all the machinery, laid down all the railways, opened out the mines, and built the factories, but the capitalists had possession. The workers were not legally forced to work for the capitalists, but unless they entered into a 'free contract' to work for whatever the capitalist thought was sufficient to keep them alive, they might starve. That was what they called 'freedom of contract.' They were free to sell themselves into slavery or starve. The black slaves were never worse off than the white slaves of today. The black slave was never so happy as when his master couldn't find him; the white man was never so miserable as when he couldn't find a master.

As this season of the year they had harvest thanksgiving services all over the country. A Sunday was set apart on which to ask for an abundant harvest; afterwards another Sunday was set apart to offer up thanks for a good harvest, but they never heard of a Sunday being set apart to grumble about a bad one. A good harvest ought to mean happiness for the people, but under the present system that was not the case; a good harvest meant misery and poverty to a large number of people.

In 1835 they had an exceedingly good harvest. For nine months of the year they depended upon other countries for their food supplies; they only produced sufficient food to last them three months in the year. A large number of vessels were engaged in bringing imported food, and this provided work for sailors, dock labourers, ship-builders, ironworkers, miners, &c. In 1835, on account of the harvest being so abundant, it was not necessary to send for so much to other countries; this laid a lot of vessels idle and threw sailors and dock labourers out of employment. And as it was no use building more ships when so many were idle, shipbuilders were thrown out of work, and that, in turn, laid ironworkers, miners, &c, idle. So, because Great Britain was blessed with an abundant harvest, they had thousands of men thrown out of employment. Farmers could not get a good price for their produce, and because it was such a good harvest the landlords demanded a higher rent. Could anything be more absurd? His satanic majesty could not invent a worse system.

Take another illustration. The recent miners strike. They were told that their wages must come down because the supply of coal exceeded the demand for it. Coal was not harmful; it was a good thing. It did not contain cholera germs or fever microbes. All the industries depended upon it, and the men who risked their lives in the bowels of the earth winning coal ought to be highly honoured, and it ought to be impossible to get too much coal. If a son, by hard work, took an extra big wage home, his father would never think of taking him by the nape of the neck and trouncing him with a stick for working too hard. Or if the extra wage enabled him to fill the cupboard so that the door would not shut, the father would not tell the son that he would have to go without his breakfast every morning until the rest of the family ate sufficient to allow the cupboard door to shut. Yet the miners were asked to put up with lower wages because they got too much coal, and the very same applied to other industries.

They also heard a great deal about 'the horny handed sons of toil.' Labour was the source of all wealth, and to hear some people talk, one might think that the man with the horny hands would be looked up to and highly respected, and the other man who lived on the horny-handed toiler's labour would receive nothing but contumely.[1] But exactly the opposite was the case. Even working men themselves would not trust their fellow workers, and it was the men who did not work that they returned to their public bodies to represent them—the men who never had worked, and who, by the help of God and the ignorance of the people, would never work.

Then they were told that they were living under a Christian system of society, when the truth was, that if a man attempted to carry out the Christian ethics of the Bible he would starve to death in a month, unless he found himself in some lunatic asylum in the meantime. They were told to 'Love thy neighbour as thyself.' Suppose a man had built up a nice business, and was looking forward to the day when he would be able to retire; some man came in and told him that another man had set up in opposition to him in the same street; would he go down on his knees and pray for the success of the other fello? They might go to the same church and lend each other their hymn books, but how could they love their neighbour as theirself? Take the unemployed. Could a man looking for a job love his neighbour as himself? He knew that he had a wife and family depending upon him, and he knew that he could only get on by getting in front of his neighbour. If two men were after a job and only one man was wanted, could they love one another as they would love themselves or as they would love their families?

They were also taught, 'Thou shalt not kill'; yet they were spending millions of money in keeping up an army to cut the throats of their fellow creatures. When an army returned from some plundering expedition— perhaps from slaughtering a lot of poor half-naked uncivilized savages, they would go to some cathedral and offer up praises for their victory. If the British were going to war with Russia, the English ministers would pray to God to assist their army. The Russian priests would also pray for assistance, and between the two he thought God would have some diffi-

---

1   Harsh language or treatment arising from haughtiness and contempt.

culty in deciding what to do.

Let him not be misunderstood. He was not attacking Christianity; he was a Christian himself. What he was attacking was the sham Christianity practised. Under the present system of society real Christianity was impossible. They could only remedy these things by bringing about a collectivist system of society. So long as they tried to remedy the evils and upheld the present system they would always be beaten, because in the struggle for existence the nation that could work on the poorest food would be victorious, and the British would have to sink to the level of the Chinaman. They could only succeed by working longer hours for lower wages if they continued to uphold the present capitalistic system. The better way was to abolish the system altogether and set up a social democracy.

*****

DUBLIN TRADES' COUNCIL
LABOUR LEADER
12 SEPTEMBER 1896, P.325

AT THE LAST meeting a letter was read from Mr. James Connolly, the secretary of the Dublin branch of the "Irish Socialist Republican Party," enclosing a resolution adopted by that body with reference to Mr. Harrington, MP. The resolution declared that the attitude taken up by Mr. Harrington towards the Trades' Council proved his unfitness to act as the representative of an industrial constituency, and the Trades' Council were invited to appoint an election committee to co-operate with a similar committee from the Socialist Republic body in an effort to bring before the electors of the Harbour division a candidate more worthy to represent the interests of labour and champion the cause of national democracy. If the Trades' Council refused to act the opinion would gain ground that the council was a body of nonentities which any politician could afford to despise. It was decided to refer the letter to the executive.

*****

A BOOKISH CAUSERIE
LABOUR LEADER
3 OCTOBER 1896, P.344

THE[1] IRISH SOCIALIST REPUBLICAN PARTY has done well to make "the first socialist pamphlet, written, printed, and published in Ireland" a reprint of two articles from *The Irish Felon* of 1848 and written by James Finton Lalor. There is, as James Connolly in his introduction remarks, a striking parallel between Lalor's time and our own: "In Ireland in 1848 there stood on the one side the landlords backed up by the government in demanding their rents and on the other side the two sections of the repeal party—the one tame, constitutional, and time-serving, the other honest and sincere, but, like the first, thoroughly conservative on the really fundamental question of property." The articles themselves are marked by all the fire and vehemence which seem to be the birthright of Irish revolutionists, and I can conceive that the publication of this pamphlet and the series it begins will do more to reawaken Irish national feeling than reams of orthodox middle-class Home Rule. Home Rule is well, but home possession is better.

---

1   **Ed. Note:** preceding ellipsis removed for the purpose of typesetting.

*****

DUBLIN LITERARY SOCIETY
EVENING HERALD (DUBLIN)
11 NOVEMBER 1896, P.3

THE USUAL WEEKLY MEETING of the above was held last evening in Costigan's Hotel, Upper O'Connell Street, when Mr James Connolly read a paper on "Irish Revolution—Utopian and Scientific." ... Mr James Connolly, who, in the course of his paper, contended the present condition of society was rapidly passing away. The British Empire, the embodiment of capitalist government, was undergoing a remarkable change. England was losing her commercial supremacy—Germany was pushing her out, so was Japan, India, and China. And when these countries developed their powers of production, as they were only beginning to do, society in England would be brought face to face with a crisis when its choice would be between socialism and ruin. In these circumstances Ireland should look to her own future. She should not ambition to become an industrial hell like England. She should feed her own people first before feeding other peoples, and this could only properly and adequately be done in an absolutely free state, owning the land and the means of production and using them for the benefit of all. Mr H.P. Bell proposed a vote of thanks to the essayist... The meeting then adjourned.

*****

IRISH SOCIALIST REPUBLICANS
EVENING HERALD (DUBLIN)
7 DECEMBER 1896, P.3

THE USUAL WEEKLY LECTURE of the Irish Socialist Republican Party was delivered last night in the Foresters' Hall, 107 Talbot Street. The lecturer was Mr James Connolly, and the subject of his discourse was, "Why we are Revolutionists." He pointed out that the object of socialists is to improve the material condition of the working classes, and that to do this effectually it was necessary to take under national ownership and control all the means of producing and distributing the necessaries of life. The Irish people should be free, but they should have not only political but economic freedom. This, he said, is the revolution socialists are endeavouring to produce, and when the opportunity offered they would seize hold of the readiest and most effective means of producing it. An interesting discussion followed upon the subject of the lecture. These lectures are free to the public.

*****

SOCIALISM
REYNOLD'S NEWSPAPER
13 DECEMBER 1896, P.1

THE SECRETARY of the Irish Socialist Republican party, 67 Mid-Abbey Street, Dublin, sends to us a statement of their views, from which we gather that they favour the establishment of an Irish Socialist Republic, and the consequent conversion of the means of production, distribution, and exchange into the common property of society, to be controlled by a democratic state in the interests of the entire community. He informs us that our remarks with reference to one of the pamphlets of the Society some time ago secured them a number of members and subscribers from a place so far distant as Johannesburg in the Transvaal.

*****

IRISH SOCIALIST REPUBLICAN PARTY
EVENING HERALD (DUBLIN)
21 DECEMBER 1896, P.4

THE USUAL SUNDAY evening meeting of the Irish Socialist Republican Party was held last night in the Foresters' Hall, 107 Talbot Street. Mr Davison, who was the lecturer appointed, was unable to attend owing to illness in his family, and in his absence a lecture was delivered by Mr James Connolly upon "Socialism at Home and Abroad." During the course of his lecture Mr Connolly said that these islands, as far as democratic ideas are concerned, are the most backward and reactionary in the world. For in the parliament of these countries today there is no socialist party or representative, whereas in all the leading countries in Europe the socialist representatives form an important parliamentary party. Germany leads with forty-six socialist representatives. France comes next with about thirty-six, and in the other countries the numbers vary from six to thirty. In order to show the progress made by social democratic principles, the lecturer said that ten years ago two socialists contested a parliamentary division of Berlin. They received just sixty-nine votes. At the last election in the same constituency the socialist candidates polled 150,000 votes. An interesting discussion followed the conclusion of the lecture. These lectures are free, and public discussion is invited.

*****

SCENES ON THE STREETS OF DUBLIN
IRISH TIMES
22 JUNE 1897, P.6

A[1] GATHERING DESCRIBED as "a meeting of protest against the Jubilee celebration in Ireland," was held in Foster Place... The following resolution was moved by Mr. Connolly, seconded by Mr. Shelley, and passed:—

> That this meeting, recognising that the British Imperial system is hateful to the Irish People and impossible without the aid of an army of Irish mercenaries, prison cells and hangmen, regards the Diamond Jubilee celebrations in Ireland as the insolent triumph of the oppressors over the oppressed; and as the most fitting answer thereto this meeting hereby pledges itself to carry on the fight against that Empire until the republican faith of our fathers is finally realised.[2]

---

1   **Ed. Note**: preceding ellipsis removed for typesetting.

2   "The anti-Jubilee meeting was subsequently proceeded with. A black flag was borne by one of those present. It bore the following inscription:—'The Record Reign, '39-'97. Starved to death, 1,225,000. Evicted, 3,668,000. Forced to emigrate, 4,168,000.'" "Anti-Jubilee Demonstration in Dublin," *Freeman's Journal*, 22 June 1897, 6. The *Journal* said that the motion was raised by Mr Stewart and seconded by Patrick Shelley. However, the meeting was chaired by Connolly and it is almost certain that he was, at the very least, the author of the motion.

*****

IRISH SOCIALIST REPUBLICAN PARTY
IRISH INDEPENDENT
14 MARCH 1898, P.2

THE WEEKLY business meeting of the above party was held at 67 Middle Abbey street on Thursday evening. There was a full attendance of members, Mr Rafferty presided. After the transaction of routine business, some aspects of Local Government Bill were discussed, and, upon the motion of Mr J. Connolly, seconded by Mr E.T. Stewart, the following resolution was unanimously passed:—

> Whereas, an active interest in education and all matters pertaining thereto is an infallible sign of a people's fitness for freedom, and whereas no such interest can be expected whilst the educational institutions of a country are removed from public interest and management, and whereas national schools in Ireland are maintained by public funds, and ought, therefore, to be under public control, be it resolved that, whilst welcoming the Local Government (Ireland) Bill as an instalment of political freedom, this meeting regrets that, although extending democratic control over so many institutions, the framers of the Bill did not place the national schools of Ireland within the scope of its provisions; and, therefore, urges our Parliamentary representatives to press for the insertion of a clause in the Bill providing for the establishment in Ireland of a system of school boards—on a democratic franchise—as in England and in Scotland, to take over the entire management of the national school system in this country.

*****

THE COMMUNE OF PARIS
EVENING HERALD (DUBLIN)
15 MARCH 1898, P.1

A MEETING of the Irish Socialist Republican Party was held last evening at 87 Marlborough street, Mr T. Lyng presiding. The chairman, in his opening remarks, stated that that was the last indoor meeting of the session, and that all future meetings would be held in the open air. He then called upon Mr James Connolly to deliver his lecture on "The Commune of Paris." Mr Connolly accordingly proceeded to do so, and in the course of a lengthy address vividly described the harrowing scenes that preceded and succeeded that horrible epoch in the history of France, the Commune of Paris. The lecturer was frequently applauded throughout his address, and received the hearty applause of a very large audience when he concluded. Messrs E.W. Stewart, J. Toomey, G. King, J. M'Kenna, etc, having discussed the subject, and the lecturer having replied, the meeting dissolved with the singing of the French National Anthem, "The Marseillaise."

*****

GLEANINGS
CLARION
16 APRIL 1898, P.122

T HE GRIM SHADOW of famine is hovering over the poor peasantry in the county of Kerry in Ireland, and unless the problem of feeding and supporting them while the distress lasts is boldly faced, and a *comprehensive* scheme of succour formulated and put into practice at once, the terrible scenes which occurred in 1847 will be re-enacted. A correspondent writes[1] informing us that the people are even now starving, and the relief works only add to their misery. From 2s. 6d. to 5s. per week is the wages given for working at road making, and the unfortunates have to leave their small holdings just when they should be doing the spring work.

---

1   The correspondent was identified as Connolly in the same edition: "James Connelly [sic] (Dublin)—Many thanks for your letter and enclosure. We have used a portion of the latter in our "Gleanings" column. Regret we have not space for an article, but shall be glad to have a letter from you while you are in the distressed districts." "Notes to Clarionettes," *Clarion*, 16 April 1898, 126.

*****

THE VOLUNTEERS
EVENING HERALD (DUBLIN)
10 MAY 1898, P.2

A MEETING of the above[1] was held last Sunday evening at Foster place, under the presidency of Mr T. Lyng. There was a very large attendance of people taking an interest in the proceedings. The Chairman having explained what the meeting was for and what the organisation aimed at, Mr James Connolly proceeded to speak on the advertised subject. In the course of his address he referred to the Irish Volunteer movement, and in a very able manner showed up the halfway patriotism and indecision of the leaders of the movement. Continuing, he said that even Grattan shuddered at the idea of giving a farm labourer a vote. In support of his assertions Mr Connolly quoted Wolfe Tone's memorable criticism on Grattan and the Volunteers. The speaker concluded by saying that the most appropriate epitaph that could be written on the graves of the Volunteers was—"They could have made Ireland a nation and they left her a province" (CHEERS).

---

1   The Irish Socialist Republican Party.

*****

THE PRICE OF BREAD – THE IRISH
SOCIALIST REPUBLICAN PARTY
EARLY JUNE 1898[1]

T HE USUAL public meeting of above society was held last Sunday evening at Forster Place, Mr WJ Bradshaw presided. Although a heavy and disagreeable rain fell during the evening a large gathering was present... Mr Connolly also addressed the meeting on the subject, and in the course of his speech said that there was no use in expatiating on a grievance except one had a remedy to propose (HEAR, HEAR). The socialists, recognising this fact, never reverted to a grievance except they had a remedy. The remedy which he, in common with all other socialists, proposed in the present instance was for the Corporation to buy up and take control of all the bakers' shops and vend bread to the working people at cost price. Proceeding to another subject, the speaker informed his audience that it was the intention of the Irish Socialist Republican Party to start a paper soon which would champion in an uncompromising manner the grand and ever strengthening cause of labour (LOUD CHEERS). The chairman having made the usual formal announcements, the proceedings terminated.

---

1   Sourced from an undated newspaper cutting in ISRP minute book. "Evening Herald" is written in pen beside it, but the piece itself is undated. The cutting is after the official minute entry for 1 June 1898 which states: "It was decided to lecture on 'Price of Bread' next Sunday." This would place the date of the public meeting as 5 June 1898. "Minute Book of the Irish Socialist Republican Party 29th May 1896 to 18th September 1898," 1 June 1898, Ms 16,295, William O'Brien Collection, National Library of Ireland, Dublin.

APPENDICES
APPENDIX A
1894 LOCAL ELECTION CAMPAIGN

*****

THE MUNICIPAL ELECTIONS – ST GILES' WARD
EDINBURGH EVENING NEWS
23 OCTOBER 1894, P.2

ABOUT TWO HUNDRED persons assembled in the Free Tron Hall[1] last night to hear an address from Mr James Connolly, who enters the lists at socialist candidate for St Giles' Ward. Mr D. Dornan presided. Mr Connolly said that as social democrats they had no sympathy with the cant about non-political candidates. Mr Connolly then explained his views on the Fountainbridge improvement scheme, saying that the district would be improved, but the poorer tenants would be rack-rented out of their small shops and houses, and the propertied classes would get the benefit. He favoured the St Mary's Loch water supply scheme, and approved of the amalgamation of the Edinburgh parishes. Speaking of the housing of the poor, Mr Connolly denounced one-roomed houses, advocated the taxation of unlet property, and the acquisition of more open spaces. He was against the pensioning of highly paid employees, but some of the men, particularly firemen, should have a superannuation fund. Replying to a question, Mr Connolly said he was in favour of the people having control of the liquor traffic. On the motion of Messrs James Ewan and Walter Coutts, Mr Connolly was declared a fit and proper person to represent the ward in the Council.

---

1   122 High Street, Edinburgh.

*****

EDINBURGH MUNICIPAL ELECTIONS – A SOCIALIST CANDIDATE FORST GILES
EDINBURGH EVENING DISPATCH
23 OCTOBER 1894, P.4

ABOUT TWO HUNDRED persons met last night in the Free Tron Hall to hear Mr James Connolly, Socialist candidate for St Giles' Ward. Mr David Dornan presided. Mr Connolly stated that the Socialists had not been induced to enter the field out of any personal feeling towards the other candidates, but because they thought there were many matters of great importance not only to Edinburgh in general, but to St Giles' Ward in particular, which were being either entirely passed over or treated with insufficient knowledge. Social democrats had no sympathy with the cant about non-political candidates. Proceeding to deal with the Fountainbridge improvement scheme, he said the result would be to make the district more desirable, but then the poorer tenants would be rack-rented out of their small shops and houses, and the profit would go into the pockets of the propertied classes. As to a new water supply. he considered St Mary's Loch to have the weight of evidence in its favour. He approved of the amalgamation of the Edinburgh parishes. There should be no more one-roomed houses in St Giles' Ward; what they wanted were houses at smaller rents. Speaking next of pensions, he argued that high-salaried officials should have none, but that some of the city employees, particularly firemen, should have a superannuation fund. In reply to questions, he said that as a democrat he was in favour of the people having complete control of the liquor traffic; that he would, if returned, take steps for having Dr Littlejohn's statement about the death of infants from tainted milk being inquired into; and that he would do what he could to have the Castle Esplanade and certain gardens made more available for the public. At the close of the meeting. Mr Connolly was declared a fit and proper person to represent the ward.

*****

MR CONNOLLY'S CANDIDATURE
THE SCOTSMAN
25 OCTOBER 1894, P.7

Mr Connolly, Socialist candidate for St Giles' Ward, addressed a meeting of the men employed by the City Cleaning Department at King's Stables Road yesterday afternoon. There was a gathering of about one hundred and fifty. The candidate, who spoke from a lorry, apologised for starting without the usual formalities, as his chairman was not very good at speaking. It was perfectly well understood that his appearance there was somewhat of an innovation that would no doubt take a good many people by surprise, but he was not there of his own seeking. He had been repeatedly asked to come forward as a candidate in that constituency and had as repeatedly refused, until he saw the Liberal and the Tory parties working hand in hand in St Cuthbert's to secure the return of a Liberal, and in George Square working hand in hand to secure the return of a Tory, and until he realised that of all the men before the public in St Giles' Ward there was not one who seemed to be possessed of the faintest conception of the immense benefits to be conferred upon the working men by a wise and judicious use of the power possessed by the Town Council. (APPLAUSE.) The candidate proceeded to repeat his views on several local matters. The meeting closed without any vote of thanks or confidence.

*****

THE MUNICIPAL ELECTIONS – ST GILES' WARD
EDINBURGH EVENING NEWS
25 OCTOBER 1894, P.4

The nomination meeting for St Giles' Ward was held in the Free Tron Church Hall, Chambers Street, last night. For a considerable time before the hour of start the hall was filled, the audience including a large proportion of ladies. In the centre part a number of "socialists" had evidently got together, and passed the time singing of the "Red Flag of Liberty" and the "Social Reformation." When Bailie MacPherson took the chair the passages were blocked... Mr James Connolly got a loud cheer on stepping forward. He was there, he said, the nominee of an organisation largely recruited from the working classes—the motley lot which had been referred to. He was standing as a social democrat. (CHEERS AND HISSES.) There never was a proposal made which would sap the manliness of the city employees as the suggestion to give them pensions for meritorious services. It would be the greatest flunkeys that would get the pensions. (CHEERS.) He would oppose the erection of one-roomed houses. It was said that by comparison with the present houses the new ones would be palaces. That was an admission that the houses occupied by men at present were pig-styes. (CHEERS.) Among other reforms he would support would be the taxing of unlet property. Unlike other councillors, he himself, his wife, and children would benefit in every social reform that took place. If the working classes wanted properly represented, they should send one of their own class to the Council. Several questions were asked and answered... A vote of thanks to the chairman closed the proceedings.

*****

ST GILES' WARD
THE SCOTSMAN
27 OCTOBER 1894, P.11

L AST NIGHT Mr James Connolly, the Socialist candidate, addressed an open-air meeting in Chambers Street. He had an audience of about sixty. The members of the Town Council as it present constituted were, he stated, incapable of realising the wants and wishes of the working classes. In this connection, he alluded deprecatingly to the "dumping" of the smallpox hospital down in the Cowgate, and said that if there had been a socialist in the Council at the time Edinburgh would have been made to ring when the proposal was made. He considered that all ground in the city should be taxed. He was against the Fountainbridge improvement scheme, because the real people to benefit by the improvements, which would be carried out at the expense of the ratepayers, would be the landlords, whose property would increase in value and rents be raised accordingly. The meeting was also addressed by Mr S.G. Hobson, of Cardiff.

*****

ST GILES' WARD
EDINBURGH EVENING NEWS
27 OCTOBER 1894, P.2

M R JAMES CONNOLLY, the Socialist candidate for the ward, ad-dressed an open-air meeting in Chambers Street, last night. There were about sixty persons present. He said that members of the Town Council as at present constituted were incapable of realising the wants and wishes of the working classes. He considered that all ground in the city should be taxed. Mr S.G. Hobson of Cardiff also spoke.

*****

ST GILES' WARD CANDIDATES
EDINBURGH EVENING DISPATCH
27 OCTOBER 1894, P.4

LAST NIGHT Mr James Connolly, the socialist candidate, addressed an open-air meeting in Chambers Street. In the course of his remarks, he declared that he was against the Fountainbridge improvement scheme, because the real people to benefit by the improvements, which would be carried out at the expense of the ratepayers, would be the landlords.

*****

EDINBURGH MUNICIPAL ELECTIONS – MR CONNOLLY'S CANDIDATURE
EDINBURGH EVENING DISPATCH
29 OCTOBER 1894, P.3

M R CONNOLLY, mounted on a box, addressed an open-air meeting, attended by about one hundred people, in Parliament Square on Saturday. He was frequently interrupted by tipsy men while he repeated his views on several matters of local interest. When he was speaking of ground rents some of them shouted out "ravelled,"[1] and others as stoutly replied that he was not. Generally speaking, however, he had a patient hearing. At night he addressed a branch of the Independent Labour Party in the Moulders' Hall.

---

1   Tangled or confused.

*****

ST GILES' WARD
EDINBURGH EVENING NEWS
30 OCTOBER 1894, P.3

M R CONNOLLY addressed the city firemen at the fire station last
night, and spoke upon the pension scheme and other matters. He
received a hearty vote of thanks.

*****

THE SOCIALIST CANDIDATE FOR ST GILES' WARD
EDINBURGH EVENING NEWS
2 NOVEMBER 1894, P.2

THE SOCIALIST CANDIDATE for St Giles Ward, Mr Connolly, addressed an open-air meeting in Chambers Street last night—Mr Dornan in the chair. He said those who were responsible for Mr Mitchell's nomination betrayed the constituency last year by foisting upon it a notoriously unpopular employer; a step which was also attempted this year, but had to be abandoned in the face of popular feeling. Various questions were asked, and at the close a vote of confidence in Mr Connolly was unanimously passed. There were between three hundred and four hundred persons present.

*****

MR CONNOLLY'S PRACTICAL SOCIALISM
EDINBURGH EVENING NEWS
2 NOVEMBER 1894, P.3

THIS AFTERNOON Colonel Forbes Mackay, one of the candidates for George Square Ward, addressed a meeting of the workers in Messrs Miller & Richard's type foundry. The Colonel at the outset answered several questions put to him, and while doing so a note was handed him, stating that Mr Connolly wished to address the meeting. The Colonel stated that he had called the meeting, and asked the employer for leave to address the men, but he was willing to allow Mr Connolly five minutes. Mr Connolly then addressed the audience, observing that it did not lie with Mr Mackay to limit him to time, nor with the employer to say who the men were to hear, to which the Colonel replied, "Here is a grateful man." Mr Connolly monopolised nearly the whole of the time, and in concluding Colonel Mackay said he did not know what the electors of George Square had to do with St Giles. Mr Connolly replied that many of the electors although they worked in George Square voted in St Giles. The Colonel replied that he did not go a hunting in Mr Connolly's Ward, and he did not see what good Mr Connolly had to come and hunt in his. A vote of thanks to the Colonel closed the proceedings.

*****

ST GILES' WARD
THE SCOTSMAN
6 NOVEMBER 1894, P.3

MR JAMES CONNOLLY, socialist candidate, addressed a meeting of some four hundred to five hundred electors and others in the Free Tron Hall last night, a considerable proportion of the audience consisting of young men and lads. There were about a dozen ladies on the platform. Mr Dornan, who presided, called on a youth to give a socialist song by way of opening the proceedings. Mr Connolly spoke of this election battle as one of the most momentous, if not the most momentous, ever fought in Edinburgh, or in St Giles' Ward particularly, and he thought he might say without exaggeration that no other party in the city had as much reason to feel so light-hearted as they did as the result of their efforts up to the present. (APPLAUSE.) He repudiated the importance of the Lord Provostship as being the main question in the meantime, remarking that there was no topic on which he was so easy as to whether the honours should go round or not, because that matter sank into insignificance compared with the ordinary bread-and-butter problem that the working classes had to face. (APPLAUSE.) Between the other three candidates and himself he was quite willing that the electors should have their choice, and he hoped that today their vote would be given not merely for the working man, but for the Social Democrat as well. (APPLAUSE.) Replying to the attitude of those who represented the Irish party in the ward,[1] he quoted from the *Waterford News*:—"we see our fellow countryman,

---

1   This appears to be in response to the W.E. Gladstone (Edinburgh) branch of the Irish National League who said that Connolly was "serving the Unionist interest" by standing against the Lord Provost, James Alexander Russell. See *Edinburgh Evening News*, 29 Oct 1894, 2; *Edinburgh Evening Dispatch*, 29 Oct 1894, 3.

James Connolly—(APPLAUSE)—fighting a good fight for the St. Giles Ward in Edinburgh. We hope no Irishman will be found within the radius of the ward who will not accord to him ready sympathy and support, not so much on account of his nationality as on account of his sympathy with the aims and objects of the working classes."[2] (APPLAUSE.) The candidate was frequently interrupted in his remarks. At the close several questions were asked of and answered by Mr. Connolly, in whom a vote of confidence was passed unanimously, on the motion of Mr. Swan, seconded by Mr. Coutts.

---

2   This quote appears to have been made up by Connolly as a way to rebuff the Irish National League and its support for Lord Provost Russell—Connolly apparently picking an Irish newspaper which he knew would have little or no readership in Edinburgh.

*****

THE SOCIALIST IN ST. GILES
EDINBURGH EVENING DISPATCH
6 NOVEMBER 1894, P.2

M R JAMES CONNOLLY, socialist candidate for St Giles' Ward, addressed a meeting of some four hundred to five hundred electors and others in the Free Tron Hall last night. He repudiated the importance of the Lord Provostship as being the main question in the meantime, remarking that there was no topic on which he was so easy as to whether the honours should go round or not, because that matter sank into insignificance compared with the ordinary bread-and-butter problem that the working classes had to face. (APPLAUSE.) At the close of his address he was awarded a vote of confidence.

*****

ST GILES' WARD
EDINBURGH EVENING NEWS
6 NOVEMBER 1894, P.2

M R JAMES CONNOLLY, socialist candidate, addressed a large meeting—Mr Dornan presiding—in the Free Tron Hall last evening. Mr Connolly repudiated the assertion that the provostship was the most important issue of the elections—that matter sank into insignificance before the ordinary bread-and-butter problem which the working classes had to face. He hoped they would not vote for the working man alone, but for the social democrat as well. At the close of questions, a unanimous vote of confidence in Mr Connolly was passed.

*****

THE MUNICIPAL ELECTIONS
THE SCOTSMAN
7 NOVEMBER 1894, P.8

THERE BEING four candidates for St Giles' Ward, there was a great deal of stir in the vicinity of the Oddfellows' Hall, where the polling took place. The candidates and their immediate backers and supporters made a considerable company round the entrance, and the roadway was pretty crowded all day with carriages and sandwichmen. Mr Mitchell was announced on the posters as the tried representative of the people, and Mr Connolly as the man who would put down "swellocracy,"[1] while the other two candidates put forward their qualifications in other ways. Mr Connolly had his name writ large all over the pavement in the ward by some enthusiastic supporter who had started out early in the morning with a piece of chalk for the purpose; but Mr Gardiner, on the other hand, was quite unrepresented by placards or literature of any kind.

---

1   In the end, Connolly received 263 votes, coming third in a field of four. See *Edinburgh Evening News*, 7 Nov 1894, 2.

*****

A MUNICIPAL CANDIDATE AND HIS ELECTION
EDINBURGH EVENING NEWS
26 NOVEMBER 1894, P.3

A T A MEETING of the Cleaning and Lighting Committee of Edinburgh Town Council today, a matter connected with the recent municipal election came informally before the committee. It will be remembered that Mr James Connolly, the Socialist candidate for St Giles' Ward, sent a letter to his foreman when he agreed to stand as a candidate for municipal honours, stating in effect that he would be absent from work for some time, as he intended taking a more active part in the municipal contest, and expressing the hope that his place would be kept open. Since then Mr Connolly has never been at work, and one day last week he called on the inspector, Mr Mackay, asking to be reinstated. Nothing was done, and as the question was thought by Mr Mackay to raise some rather novel points, he submitted it "with-out prejudice" to the meeting today. After some discussion, a motion by Bailie Sloan was adopted, that as Mr Mackay had full power to deal with the men in the department under his charge, the case be left to him. The feeling among the majority of the committee was, we believe, in favour of Mr Connolly being taken back.

APPENDICES
APPENDIX B
1895 PARISH COUNCIL ELECTION

*****

EDINBURGH PARISH COUNCILS
THE SCOTSMAN
16 MARCH 1895, P.11

S⊤ GILES' WARD—Last night Mr James Connolly, social democratic candidate, addressed a meeting of about forty persons in South
Bridge school. The candidate devoted the whole of his address to the existing poor-law administration, and emphasised the necessity of sending
representatives from the working classes to the Parish Council if these
laws were to be reformed. He said he felt rather awkward asking for their
support to administer laws which he did not believe to be a necessary
part of their human society. In conclusion, he appealed to those present
to record their votes in favour of their own right as working men to have
control of all the boards that affected their own interests, and to begin
now and use that power and their influence to put their own representatives on all such boards as the Parish Council and Town Council, and
in returning them to see that they did their duty. He felt assured that if
they returned men of their own class they could expect a better and more
accurate appreciation of their wants and their interests than they could
from the classes who lived upon their labour. A resolution in favour of
Mr Connolly's candidature was unanimously carried.

*****

PARISH COUNCIL ELECTIONS
EDINBURGH EVENING NEWS
16 MARCH 1895, P.4

St Giles' Ward—Mr James Connolly, social democratic candidate, addressed a meeting last night in South Bridge school. About forty persons attended. Mr Connolly urged working men to return members of their class to all Boards that affected their interests, as they themselves had a better appreciation of their wants than those who lived upon their labour. Mr Connolly received a vote of confidence.

APPENDICES
APPENDIX C
LECTURE TOPICS AND
NEWSPAPER SNIPPETS

*****

Freedom (London), 1 April 1892, p.32.

"Edinburgh—March 17th, the Scottish Socialist Federation and friends held as usual a meeting in commemoration of the Commune of Paris. Leo Melliet, a member of the Commune, was in the chair. The speakers were Leslie, Melliet, Connelly, Bell, Gilray, Miss D. Forster, and Glasse."[1]

Leith Burghs Pilot, 13 May 1893, p.2.

"A great demonstration in favour of the principle of an eight-hours working day took place in Edinburgh last Saturday afternoon... At the third platform Mr John Leslie, labourer, acted as chairman, and with him were representatives of the Independent Labour Party, the Scottish Socialist Federation, and the Fabian Society... Mr. Fred Hamilton, printer, moved the first resolution. He said the greatest enemy the working-classes had to fight was not the employing class, but the vast army of unemployed, without whom the employing-class could not stand out for a single week against the workers. Mr James Connelly [sic], unskilled labourer, seconded the resolution, which was supported by Miss Conway, Independent Labour Party Executive."

Falkirk Herald, 19 May 1894, p.5.

"Socialism—On Sunday evening the first of a series of meetings in promotion of socialism was held on the Callendar Riggs. There was a fair gathering present, and an address on socialism in its religious aspect was delivered by Mr Connelly [sic], Edinburgh. At the close remarks were made also by several of those present."

Labour Leader, 19 May 1894, p.5.

"Edinburgh and District—The Central Division branch of the La-

---

1   Although the account mentions only Connolly's surname, the list of speakers is almost identical to those who spoke at an event to mark the Haymarket massacre the previous year, which included James. See "Provincial Meetings," *Freedom* (London), 1 December 1891.

bour Party held a meeting on the East Meadows, on Monday last, to hear addresses from J. Kier Hardie, MP, and councillor Beever of Halifax... After Mr Beever had spoken, another resolution was moved by Mr. Swan and seconded by Mr. Grady. It was in support of this resolution that Mr. Kier Hardie was to have spoken, and there was an ominous silence as Connolly mounted the stool to apologise for his absence. He could only say that Mr. Hardie had promised to come and had been notified of the time and place of meeting but had not yet arrived. He promised that an apology from Mr. Hardie for the breach of faith would appear in the *Labour Leader* explaining the cause of his non-appearance."

CLARION, 23 JUNE 1894, P.6.
"EDINBURGH—...A largely-attended meeting of members of local branches [of the Independent Labour party] was held in the Moulders' Hall last Saturday evening to consider the final selection of a candidate for the Central Division. A. Dickinson presided, and James Connolly submitted an account of what the Central Branch had done in the matter up to date of summoning the meeting. The action of the Central Branch received the endorsement of the whole party on the motion of Edward Watt (South Division) seconded by John McKenzie (Eastern Division)... A good beginning is of the upmost importance. Clarionettes should not need to be told twice. Jas. Connolly is election secretary.

JUSTICE, 21 JULY 1894, P.5.
"A CONFERENCE of Scottish socialists was held in Dundee on Saturday July 14. Delegates were present from Edinburgh, Dundee, Falkirk, Glasgow, and Aberdeen... Comrade Connolly (Edinburgh) moved as an amendment that "the secretaries of the various organisations send their notes direct to *Justice*, and that the editor be asked to devote one column weekly to notes on the Scottish movement." The amendment was carried by a small majority."

LABOUR LEADER, 4 AUGUST 1894, P.8.
"JAMES CONNELLY [sic] (of Edinburgh) will lecture on Cathedral Square, on Sunday, August 5, under the auspices of St. Rollox branch SLP, at 2:30 and 6:30. 2:30—Socialism and the Living Wage; 6:30—The Capitalist a Thug."

CLARION, 25 AUGUST 1894, P.6.

"THE 'SOCIALIST RAMBLYNGE CLUB' visited Loanhead on Saturday last, and Connolly explained the beauty of socialism as compared with coal strikes. Loanhead is a mining centre."

JUSTICE, 15 SEPTEMBER 1894, P.5.

"LAST SATURDAY comrade Nightingale, of Glasgow, paid his first visit to Edinburgh district, and addressed the miners at Loanhead. Comrade Connolly also spoke, and a debate was arranged with the leader of the Irish faction there for next Saturday."

CLARION, 22 SEPTEMBER 1894, P.6.

"WHILE THE TRADE COUNCILLORS, assisted by IL Peers, were collecting for the miners last Saturday, a spirited debate was being conducted before a large audience of miners at Loanhead between James Connolly, of the Socialist Federation, and Bernard Donoghue, a leading Irish nationalist. A fact of much significance was that the nationalist champion conceded the wisdom and justice of the socialist demands, and the debate turned on 'Independent Political Action' v 'Liberal Labour Alliances.'

"The debate was fought out with coolness, skill, and great good humour between the two champions, and the audience took sides vigorously. Result: fifteen names were enrolled in the Federation, and a branch will probably be formed."

FALKIRK HERALD, 15 DECEMBER 1894, P.1.

"FALKIRK FOR SOCIALISM. Liberal Club, Falkirk. Sunday, 16th Dec— James Connolly, late socialist candidate for St. Giles Ward, Edinburgh, will lecture in above Hall. Subject—"Liberal Caucuses and Socialist Candidates." Questions and Discussion. Chair to be taken at 7. Collection."

JUSTICE, 22 JUNE 1895, P.5 (197)

"EDINBURGH... For daring to stand as a socialist candidate for the Town Council, and latterly for the Parish Council, our comrade James Connolly has found it impossible to obtain employment in this, his native town, and there can be no mistake that if Connolly is compelled to leave this district his loss will be a severe blow to the socialist movement here. Socialist are not in the habit of praising each other, and very often fail to give honour where honour is due; but in bearing testimony to the invaluable services to the cause rendered by our comrade, all who know him will agree with me in saying that his loss will have a very serious effect on the movement here. A fluent speaker, with a good strong voice, Connolly seems to have been specially created for outdoor propaganda, and these two qualifications, together with a thorough knowledge of his subject and untiring zeal and perseverance, has made our comrade what he is—a martyr, whose martyrdom could have been saved if certain men had been honourable enough to fulfil an obligation entered into, or at least give some reason for non-fulfilment. Connolly has more than sufficient time on his hands, and if any branch of the SDF or ILP is wishful to have an efficient and capable lecturer and organiser, letters addressed to James Connolly 65, Nicolson Street, Edinburgh,[2] will always find one.

JUSTICE, 29 JUNE 1895, P7 (207)

"SDF CLUB, Burnley. Dear Comrade, in your last week's issue, mention was made in the Edinburgh notes of the good work for socialism done by James Connolly of the Scottish Socialist Federation, and also of the inevitable reward, so it seems, for such work. I can also speak of the high esteem in which Connolly is held by his comrades. He wrote me that a couple of months retirement from Edinburgh will not do him any harm, and perhaps not the cause, as his absence may compel others to come forward and take a more active part in the work. I am going to arrange a lecturing tour for him if possible, and any branch desiring a speaker and out-door worker cannot do better than avail themselves of Connolly's services, and I am sure the advantage will be mutual. For terms, etc., apply to me as above. Yours fraternally, Dan Irving."

LABOUR LEADER, 29 JUNE 1895, P.5.

"JAMES CONNOLLY, Scottish Socialist Federation and ILP, is open to book dates for lectures. For terms etc., apply Dan Irving, SDF Club, St. James Hall, Burnley."

CLARION, 29 JUNE 1895, P.4.

"JAMES CONNOLLY, Scottish Socialist Federation and ILP is open to book dates for lectures. For terms, etc., apply Des Irving, SDF Club, Burnley."

---

2   Meeting room address of the SSF.

Justice, 29 June 1895, P.7.

"DEAR COMRADE, in your last week's issue, mention was made in the Edinburgh notes of the good work for socialism done by James Connolly, of the Scottish Socialist Federation, and also of the inevitable reward, so it seems, for such work. I can also speak of the high estimation in which Connolly is held by his comrades. He wrote me that a couple of months retirement from Edinburgh will not do him any harm, and perhaps not the cause, as his absence may compel others to come forward and take a more active part in the work. I am going to arrange a lecturing tour from him if possible, and any branch desiring a speaker and out-door worker cannot do better than avail themselves of Connolly's services, and I am sure the advantage will be mutual. For terms etc, apply to me as above. Yours fraternally, Dan Irving."

JUSTICE, 27 JULY 1895, P.4.

"ON SUNDAY, JULY 21, comrade Connolly addressed a good crowd.[3] He also addressed two meetings in Bury. At night a large audience in all the rain listened attentively to what he had to say. Good discussion afterwards, and as our comrade is stopping all the week we expect to do some good."

BOLTON EVENING NEWS, 6 AUGUST 1895, P.3.

"LECTURE ON SOCIALISM—Under the auspices of the Horwich Branch of the ILP, a lecture was given on the Market Ground on Monday evening, before a moderate audience, by Mr J Connolly of Scotland, on 'Social Paradoxes.'[4] Mr Connolly received an attentive hearing, and at the close invited questions, and quite a number were put pertinent to socialism, the proceedings at one period being very lively. Replying to a query, the lecturer denied the Independent Labour Party had tried to smash up the Liberal party, and said his party tried to return socialist candidates, and if the Liberals were smashed in the procedure that had nothing to do with the socialists."

---

3   This may refer to a meeting in Summerseat. The previous paragraph said the local activists had a meeting space 'offered us by a farmer in one of his fields' in the town.

4   Connolly gave a similarly-entitled lecture in Workington, Cumbria, on Sunday 27 October 1895. See "Social Paradoxes," *Workington Star*, 1 November 1895.

CLARION, 10 AUGUST 1895, P.252.
"WALKDEN AND DISTRICT ILP—Sunday, August 11th. Comrade Connolly, of Edinburgh, will lecture near Little Hulton Station and the Monument. Times of lectures will be advertised locally."

CLARION, 17 AUGUST 1895, P.260.
"SALFORD (WEST) ILP—Lectures by James Connolly, of Edinburgh. Sunday August 18th, at 11am, opposite Broad Street Baths, Pendleton. Subject, 'Progress and Social Discontent.' Afternoon, at 2.30pm, on Charlestown Fair Ground. Subject, 'The Abolition of the Working Class.' Evening, at 7, opposite Seedly Post Office. Subject, 'Individual Misfortune of Social Wrongs—which?' Wednesday, August 21st, at 8pm, near Woodbine Inn, West Liverpool Street. Subject, 'Political Reform or Social Revolution?' Thursday, August 22nd, at 8pm, in the ILP Club, Brindle Heath Road. Subject, 'The Social Question in Ireland.' Discussion invited."

CLARION, 24 AUGUST 1895, P.268.
"STOCKPORT (CENTRAL) ILP—Sunday, Aug. 25, James Connolly, of Edinburgh, will speak on open space, Chestergate Bridge, at 2.30pm; Armoury Ground, at 6.30pm. Monday, August 26th, on open space, Chestergate Bridge, at 7.15pm."

LABOUR LEADER, 24 AUGUST 1895, P.8.
"STOCKPORT CENTRAL ILP—Sunday, August 25. Comrade James Connolly, of Edinburgh, will speak at Spare Ground, Chestergate Bridge, at 2:30; Armoury Ground at 6:30. Monday August 26th, at 7:15, Chestergate Bridge. Will all ILPers show up at these meetings."

CLARION, 31 AUGUST 1895, P.276.
"WIGAN SDF, MINERS' HALL, MILLGATE—Sunday, September 1st, to Saturday, September 7th, Jas. Connolly, of Edinburgh. Sunday, 11am and 3pm, Big Lamp; 7pm, Miners' Hall. Monday and Tuesday, at 7pm, Big Lamp. Wednesday, at 7 pm, Miners' Hall. Thursday, at 7 pm, Lambourhead Green. Friday, at 7 pm, King William, Platt Bridge. On Saturday, September 7, a tea and social, at five o'clock, in the Miners' Hall. Tickets: Tea and social, 1s; social only, 4d."

Clarion, 7 September 1895, p.284.
"Liverpool SDF. Speaker Jas. Connolly of Edinburgh. Sunday, Sept. 8th, 11am and 3pm, Monument; 8 pm, Islington Square. Monday, 8pm, Crown Street. Tuesday. 8pm, Smith Street. Wednesday, 8pm, St. Domingo Pit. Thursday, 8pm, Edge Hill Church. Friday, 8pm, Islington Square. Saturday, 3pm, Monument."

Clarion, 21 September 1895, p.300.
"Alltrincham ILP—Tuesday, Sept. 24th, at 7.30, at the Big Lamp. Speaker, Connolly of Edinburgh ILP. Subject, 'Social Paradoxes.'"

Labour Leader, 21 September 1895, p.9.
"Sheffield—Next week we have here to lecture for us J. Bruce Glasier and Katherine St. John Conway, BA, also Fred Brocklehurst, and J. Connelly [sic]."

Leigh Chronicle and Weekly District Advertiser, 27 September 1895, p.5.
"Leigh Social Democratic Federation—The local branch of the above had the services of Mr J Connolly, of Edinburgh, at their usual Sunday lectures in the market-place, Leigh. Mr Connolly lectured on Sunday morning on 'Progress and discontent,' and in the evening on 'Social paradoxes,' to fairly large and attentive audiences; also on Monday evening, when the subject treated was 'The rich man a thief.' The branch hope to continue these meetings as long as the weather permits, as the attendances point to the fact that more people are becoming interested in the question of socialism."

Clarion, 19 October 1895, p.332.
"Salford Labour Church, Prince of Wales Assembly Rooms, Blucher Street, Liverpool Street, behind the Prince of Wales Theatre. Service on Sunday next, at 7pm. Speaker, Mr. J. Connolly, of Edinburgh. Subject, 'Socialism and Christianity.'"

Clarion, 19 October 1895, p.334.
"Coventry... James Connolly has been lecturing here for the SDF all the week. I had the pleasure of listening to an excellent address by him—subject 'Political Economy'—at the SDF branch."

LABOUR LEADER, 19 OCTOBER 1895, P.9.
"NOTTINGHAM—Socialism, and plenty of it, was meted out to the free and independent electors of nottingham on Sunday last and during the week, Miss Enid Stacy and J. Connolly, of Edinburgh, being the principal exponents of the doctrines enunciated by the ILP... Comrade Connolly addressed two meetings on Sunday, morning and evening, and has been occupied during the week in speaking to outdoor meetings."

NORTH BRITISH DAILY MAIL, 21 DECEMBER 1895, P.3.
"EDINBURGH SOCIALISM—What was described as a great socialist demonstration took place last night in the Music Hall, Edinburgh. The attendance, however, hardly justified such a description, the hall not being half-filled. The object of the gathering was to hear an address by Mr. H.M. Hyndman on 'Social Democracy, the only rallying point for the forces of progress.' ...At the conclusion of the address, Mr. Hyndman answered numerous questions, after which Mr. James Connelly [sic] moved a resolution pledging the meeting to support the programme and policy of the Social Democratic Federation. Mons. Leo Milliet seconded the resolution, which was unanimously adopted."

JUSTICE, 28 DECEMBER 1895, P.413.
"FOR THE FIRST TIME in its history the Edinburgh Trades Council was officially represented at a socialist meeting, the president and secretary of that body being on the platform... On the platform was quite a bevy of ladies, while comrades Melliet and James Connolly made a capital show, as well as good speeches... Discussion being disallowed owing to the lateness of the hour, comrade Connolly moved a resolution to the effect that, as socialism was the only rallying-point for the forces of progress, it was the duty of every man and woman to further the cause by all means at their disposal. This was seconded by comrade Melliet, and carried by acclamation."

LABOUR LEADER, 28 DECEMBER 1895, P.10.
"THE DEMONSTRATION of our SDF comrades in the Music hall on Friday the 20th inst, in spite of unfavourable weather, was a splendid affair... it was moved by comrade Connelly [sic], and seconded by comrade Leo Melliet, and carried by acclamation, 'That, believing Social Democracy to be the only rallying point for the forces of progress, this meeting pledg-

es itself to support the programme and policy of the SDF.'"

L̲ABOUR L̲EADER, 18 J̲ANUARY 1896, P.7.

"O̲N S̲UNDAY last the Rev. Mr Jackson again lectured in the Albert Hall to a large audience on 'Socialism and Marriage.' The Lecturer, while accepting the economic aims of socialism, continued as before[5] to give an undue place to the speculations of some socialistic writers as to what the marriage relation might be under realised socialism. At the close comrade Connolly, amid loud applause, took exception to the lecturer's method of treating socialism, and pointed out that it could only apply if he was prepared to saddle Christianity with the opinions and conduct of professing Christians."

L̲ABOUR L̲EADER, 15 F̲EBRUARY 1896, P.7.

"O̲N S̲UNDAY last a very large audience—the largest this season—turned out to hear Edith Lanchester lecture in the Operetta Hall, under the auspices of the SDF, on 'Socialism and the Family.' Comrade Connolly occupied the chair, and explained that socialism had no connection with speculations on family life and was nowise responsible for the opinions of individual socialists on the subject."

L̲ABOUR L̲EADER, 9 M̲AY 1896, P.7.

"A̲RBROATH held its first Mayday celebrations on Saturday afternoon, under the auspices of the Trade Council and the local group of the ILP... J. Connolly delivered a masterly address in support of a legal eight-hours day."

J̲USTICE, 30 M̲AY 1896, P.5.

"E̲DINBURGH—Since last I sent notes from Auld Reekie we have held a

---

5   "In the Albert Hall on Sunday last [22 December 1895] the Rev. Mr. Jackson lectured to a large audience on "Socialism and the Family" The lecture was a mixed and disappointing production, against which most of the Socialists present were ready to protest had there been opportunity. The lecturer, after drifting about, and, while accepting the economic basis of socialism, finally assumed that because Bax and Morris had speculated on what the family relations might be under a realised and distant socialism, it must be held that Socialism attacks the family until some equal authority repudiates their speculations. Reasoning thus, what is a reader of the famous "Provincial Letters" to say when he finds that for some hundreds of years a leading party in the Church not only speculated on, but provided for the breach of all family relations?" "Edinburgh," *Labour Leader*, 28 December 1895, 10

most successful May Day demonstration.[6] The meeting was held in the Meadows in the evening, comrades Connolly, Doyle, Brunton, and Scott addressing a large crowd; comrade Allan acting as chairman.

Comrade James Connolly has left Edinburgh for Dublin. A special meeting of the branch was held to present him with a testimonial in token of the respect and esteem in which he was held, and as a recognition of the splendid services he has rendered to the cause of socialism in this city. Connolly is one of the best propagandist speakers in the movement, and was indefatigable in preaching the principles of Socialism. His loss to us will be severely felt, but he may be trusted to continue the good work in the place to which he has gone."

IRISH TIMES, 1 SEPTEMBER 1896, P.6.
"THE FORTNIGHTLY MEETING of the Trades Council was held last evening in the Trades Hall, Capel Street... Mr Simmons read a letter from Mr James Connolly, secretary of the Irish Socialist Republican Party, asking that steps should be taken to oust Mr Harrington as member of parliament for the Harbour Division. Mr Kearns asked who the Irish Socialist Republican Party were? (LAUGHTER.) The President said he did not know. (LAUGHTER.) Mr Dunne moved that the letter be referred to the Executive Committee for consideration."

IRISH INDEPENDENT, 18 NOVEMBER 1896, P.7.
"THE INTER-CLUB billiard tournament promoted by the Workingmen's Club, Wellington Quay, bids fair to be a great success. A meeting of the delegates of the various clubs entered was held last evening at 10 Wellington Quay—Mr James Connolly presiding... The Chairman stated that at least a dozen clubs would take part, and it was decided to hold a draw on Monday evening, December 14, at 10 Wellington Quay, at nine o'clock. Routine business having been transacted, the meeting adjourned till that date."[7]

---

6   "About one hundred idlers met in the East Meadows, Edinburgh, yesterday [Friday 1 May] and labelled their meeting a Mayday celebration," *Greenock Telegraph and Clyde Shipping Gazette*, 02 May 1896, 3.

7   "...and last, but by no means least, the premier club, and, as far as this project is concerned, the initiatory one, the Workingmen's Club, Wellington Quay, in whose fine premises the meeting before alluded to was held, under the presidency of one of the most active and energetic members of the present House Committee, Mr. James Connolly." *Evening Herald* (Dublin), 7 November 1986, 7.

EVENING HERALD (DUBLIN), 5 DECEMBER 1896, P.7.
"IRISH SOCIALIST REPUBLIC; Labour Lectures, 107 Talbot street; James Connolly lectures on 'Why we are Revolutionists'; Sunday 8pm prompt; questions and discussion invited; admission free."

EVENING HERALD, 9 JUNE 1897, P.2.
"IRISH SOCIALIST REPUBLICAN PARTY. The usual open-air meeting of the above party will be hold tonight (Wednesday), 8 o'clock, at Foster Place, College Green. Subject, 'Socialism and Thriving.' Intelligent opposition invited."

DUBLIN DAILY NATION, 12 OCTOBER 1897, P.6.
"THE USUAL WEEKLY MEETING of the ['98 Centenary] Executive Committee was held on Saturday evening in the Council Chamber, City Hall, Dublin—Mr JM Johnson, CTC, Dundalk, in the chair... Mr [James] Connolly drew attention to the statement published by 'United Ireland' under the signature of Mr F Hugh O'Donnell, in which it was stated 'that Wolf Tone came to France cowering before the guillotine and worshipping a naked prostitute on the altar of Notre Dame.' Mr Connolly reminded the executive that Wolf Tone did not reach France until 1795, and the 'Enthronement of the Goddess of Reason,' the incident referred to, had occurred in 1793, two years previously. He thought such statements were not only inaccurate, but also tended to weaken the feeling in favour of the '98 movement."

DUBLIN DAILY NATION, 16 NOVEMBER 1897, P.6.
"ON SUNDAY night the first public meeting of the Irish Socialist Republican Party since they became affiliated with the Central Executive[8] was held at no 87 Marlborough Street. Mr D O'Brien presided and there were over one hundred members present. The proceedings were characterised by the greatest enthusiasm. Mr James Connolly delivered a lecture, which was well received, on 'The Men of '98: their Principles and their Aims.'"

IRISH INDEPENDENT, 4 MARCH 1898, P.7.
"IRISH SOCIALIST REPUBLICAN PARTY. A well-attended meeting of above organisation was held last Sunday evening in the rooms, 87 Marlboro' Street, under the presidency of Mr EW Stewart. After the chairman

---

8   The '98 Centenary Committee.

had made some brief statements as to the objects and ends of the association, Mr James Connolly proceeded to deliver a lecture on 'The Socialist Republican's Position in Ireland.' The lecturer dealt very ably with his subject, and at the conclusion of his address received the warm applause of an appreciative audience."

IRISH INDEPENDENT, 12 MARCH 1898, P.1.
"'VIVE LA COMMUNE!' Lecture by James Connolly on 'Commune of Paris,' tomorrow (Sunday), 7:30pm, at 87 Marlborough Street, under auspices of Irish Socialist Republican Party."

WEEKLY FREEMAN'S JOURNAL, 19 MARCH 1898, P.3.
"A CONVENTION of the General Executive of the '98 Centenary Committee was held in the Municipal Chamber, City Hall, Dublin, on Saturday. Mr. John O'Leary Presided... Mr. James Connolly (Rank and File Branch) moved the following amendment: 'That as this convention does not recognise the right of the British Parliament or Government, we cannot see that membership of that Parliament gives any right to membership in commemoration of the men of '98.'"

EVENING HERALD, 17 MAY 1898, P.2.
"THE USUAL weekly meeting of above party was held last Sunday evening at Foster Place, Mr. Lyng occupying the chair. There was a very large crowd of people present throughout the whole of the proceedings who accorded each speaker a patient and intelligent hearing. The chairman opened the proceedings by calling the attention of the meeting to the pamphlets dealing with the socialistic propaganda. The pamphlets he referred to were, 'Erin's Hope, the End and the Means,' by James Connolly; 'the rights of Ireland and the Faith of a Felon,' by the '48 hero, J Fintan Lalor; 'Socialism and the Worker,' by Sorge; ''98 Readings,' 'Looking Backwards,' by E Bellamy; 'Wages and Labour,' by Karl Marx, and 'Capital and Labour,' by the same author, &c. The chairman then addressed the meeting at some length, and concluded amidst applause.

Mr. EW Stewart, addressing the audience on the advertised subject, proceeded to point out the economic, social, and national causes that generated the revolt in Italy. He showed in a very comprehensive manner how the toilers of Italy, driven to despair by the ultra-tyranny of the capitalist or plundering classes of that country, found that the only way they could effectively assert their right to be maintained by the State when they laboured, was by a manly appeal to physical force.

Mr. James Connolly endorsed all that the previous speaker had said. Mr. WJ Bradshaw also addressed the meeting."

CLARION, 9 JULY 1898, P.223.
"SCOTTISH WESTERN FEDERATION... It was decided to engage James Connolly, of the Irish Socialist Republican Party, for two weeks."

EDINBURGH EVENING NEWS, 9 JULY 1898, P.1.
"LEITH BRANCH SDF—Meeting, Leith Links, Sunday first, at 2:30[pm]. Speaker—Jas. Connolly, Dublin, organiser of Irish Socialist Republican Party. Subject—'The Socialist Movement in Ireland.'"

EDINBURGH EVENING NEWS, 11 JULY 1898, P.1.
"SDF MEETING TONIGHT. Jeffrey St., 8pm. James Connolly—Trade Unionism and Democracy. Tuesday Night—Manderston St., Leith."

EDINBURGH EVENING NEWS, 12 JULY 1898, P.1.
"SDF MEETING TONIGHT, Manderston Street, Leith. James Connolly, 'Our Social Paradoxes.' Wednesday Night, M'Ewan Hall, 8pm."

EDINBURGH EVENING NEWS, 13 JULY 1898, P.1.
"SDF MEETING TONIGHT, M'Ewan Hall 8pm. James Connolly. Progress and Discontent. Thursday night, foot of Canongate."

EDINBURGH EVENING NEWS, 14 JULY 1898, P.1.
"SDF MEETING, foot Canongate, 8pm., Jas. Connolly, 'Individual and Society.' Friday, Nicolson Square."

JUSTICE, 23 JULY 1898, P.6.
"EDINBURGH—After having carried on the summer propaganda so far with our local speakers, we are having this week a visit from our old friend [and] comrade, James Connolly, Dublin, secretary of the Irish Socialist Republican Party, who is over for a short tour in Scotland. He opened with two splendid meetings on Sunday, the 10th, at Leith Links and the Meadows, where stirring addresses were given to large crowds."

CLARION, 30 JULY 1998, P.246.
"GLASGOW. Bridgeton ILP, 5 Graham Street—James Connolly of the Irish Socialist Republican League, will lecture on Bain Square, Calton, 2:30pm, on Sunday July 31; also Bridgeton Cross, 7pm."

BARRHEAD NEWS, 5 AUGUST 1898, P.2
"UNDER THE AUSPICES of the Barrhead Labour Party a lecture will be delivered by James Connolly (Secretary Irish Socialist Party[9]) at the Cross on Saturday first, at 7pm. Subject—'Socialism and Irish Nationality.'"

BARRHEAD NEWS, 12 AUGUST 1898, P.3.
"UNDER THE AUSPICES of the Labour Party, a lecture was delivered in the open air at the Cross last Saturday, by Mr James Connolly of Dublin. The subject was announced as "Socialism and Irish Nationality," but as the lecturer said he did not see any Irishmen about, it was changed to a more general one. There was a fair attendance."

LABOUR LEADER, 13 AUGUST 1898, P.7.
"COMRADE JAMES CONNELLY [sic], of the Irish Socialist Republican Party, delivered the last of a series of very interesting lectures on the Paisley Racecourse last Sunday. After hearing him on Irish topics, that distressful country's sons especially cannot fail to be impressed that socialism is not such a hideous crime as some party hacks would have them believe [...] Under the auspices of the Clydebank branch, and in connection with the Scottish Western Federation, James Connelly [sic], of the Irish Socialist Republican Party, has addressed two large meetings in Clydebank during his visit. Plenty of Irish wit, and somebody sorry they spoke."

---

9   The word "Republican" is missing in the original report.

APPENDICES
APPENDIX D
LETTER UNCHECKED
AGAINST THE ORIGINAL

Introduction

The National Library of Ireland holds six letters written by Connolly to Lillie Reynolds. Donal Nevin in *Between Comrades* reproduces all six plus one other dated 17 November 1889. However, I was unable to locate the original in time for the publication of this collection. It is reproduced below and while it is undoubtedly authentic, I did not include it in the Letters section given Nevin's record on errors and omissions with regard to Connolly's writings and work. It is reproduced here for reference.

*****

CONNOLLY TO LILLIE REYNOLDS 17 NOVEMBER 1889[1]

22 West Port
Edinburgh
17 November 1889

Lillie

I AM GLAD to see that you are beginning to be a little more pleasantly talkative in your letters. In the past your letters were mainly confined to a few short words, inquiries after my health, and at one time of appointments for a meeting. But your last letter is a really nicely discursive chatty and lively letter, and I like it. I have told you so often that your letters are always welcomed that I need not repeat, but in truth I was desirous of encouraging you in your letter writing that I am always reminding you that I want you to write whether you will be able to say anything remarkable or not. And let me tell you, Lillie, in all seriousness that your letters in reality form a really welcome change to the miserable monotony of my present existence. Lillie I am in truth dissatisfied

---

1   Nevin, *Between Comrades*, 80-81.

and surely troubled in my mind I have been trying hard to recruit myself principally since I came here but the incubus which I have mentioned to you before prevents me most effectually. I have had intentions of, when recruited a little endeavouring to settle down and trying to realise that ideal of home which I have formed in my mind. With your help Lillie, I had hoped to find happiness. In other words I had intended to ask you if you could find courage to risk your life and welfare along with such a scapegrace[2] as myself.

As far as love could carry me, I would do anything possible to secure such a prize as yourself and to guard it against harm, but, Lillie, much as I would love to have you in the near future as, let me say it reverently my wife, the consideration of my present poverty and the barrenness of the general outlook deter me. I am in a quandary, I am trusting but in spite of all my trust, I am often haunted by the fear that the much coveted prize may grow wearied of such an uninteresting body or person as my humble self. I want advice, give it to me, Lillie. For the attainment of my desire I would wait and work a lifetime and think myself happy if I was able to, at least succeed. But I do not want to wait and I am of opinion that another interested in the matter may object still more forcibly.

Of late our old happy walks and talks together are crowding on my memory, and making me long for something akin to that time, for the happiness of once more having my sweetheart by my side and being cheered and enlivened by her bright and happy ways. You see, mavourneen[3] you have conquered me and reduced me to slavery. What will you do with your prisoner. I will look forward with anxiety to your letter and be sure and fill your letters, continue the good beginning which you have made and let me know all about yourself and everything you are interested in, except the Protestant Girls Society of Ireland tell me about your present ways of amusing yourself and your delightful walks, and tell me that you miss me and so fill with gladness the soul of your loving sweetheart.

Write soon.

JIM

---

2   A mischievous or wayward person, especially a young person or child; a rascal.

3   My darling. From Irish, mo mhuirnín.

APPENDICES
APPENDIX E
WRITINGS OF
JOHN CONNOLLY,
BROTHER OF JAMES

*****

A SOCIALISTIC LABOUR PARTY IN EDINBURGH
EDINBURGH EVENING NEWS
8 NOVEMBER 1892, P.2

IN THE TRADES HALL, High Street, Edinburgh, last night, a meeting of those favourable to the formation of a branch in Edinburgh of the Scottish Independent Labour Party, was held. Mr Connelly [sic], secretary of the Scottish Socialist Federation, presiding.[1] The miserable social state in which the working classes were living today had been brought about, said the chairman, with the connivance, and largely with the help of political parties. No matter how advanced one of the political parties might be in their opinions, the men who really controlled the action and determined the policy of these parties were the monied men; and the only hope of escape from the present system of spoliation and degradation of the working classes was the discomfiture of the political parties, who upheld the social system which had such fruits.

---

1   Three months later, John Connolly wrote to *Justice* in February 1893 as secretary of the SSF, which lends weight to the assumption that he was the speaker at this meeting.

*****

SCOTTISH SOCIALIST FEDERATION[1]
JUSTICE
18 FEBRUARY 1893, P.4

THE QUARTERLY REPORT of the above society for the quarter ending December 31st, 1892, is full of interest to all those who have
watched the progress of the movement in Scotland, and who are aware
of the difficulties which the propagandist has to contend with in that
country, the "land o' the unco guid," sedate, douce, and, above all things,
respectable, caring nothing for religion in his own heart, but unyielding
in his demand for a rigid adherence to the outward show and semblance
of religion in others. The cautious Scot has ever looked askance upon the
new social gospel expounded for his acceptance by such unconventional,
unrespectable, irreverent Sabbath-breaking demagogues as were and are
the few enthusiasts who have dared to range themselves beneath the banner of Socialism. Had the doctrines of the Socialists been ushered into
this country beneath the aegis of the church's sanction; had its praises
been thundered forth from all our pulpits; had its criticism of the iniqui-
ties of our modern capitalist system been made the theme of the manifold
long-winded discourses inflicted upon the patient worshippers in all our
city churches Sunday after Sunday; had its message of hope to the worker,
its promise of a social redemption from the oppression, the misery, the
malevolence, the hatred, the ill-will, the antisocial strife and jealousy running rampant in our class society; had these excited in our churches one
tittle of the attention so freely given to the visit of a royal figurehead, or
the idolatry of stained- glass windows; socialism would have swept across
Scotland like a whirlwind, and would have been accepted almost without question by the majority of the so-called hard-headed working men

---

1   John Connolly signed the article "J.C."

who to-day affect to look upon it with such supreme contempt. But the churches, fortunately or unfortunately, chose to act otherwise, and the work of propaganda fell upon those, to whom it, after all, perhaps most properly belongs, the working-class Socialists themselves. Well, they have not shirked their task, in good and in ill report they have borne aloft the banner of the cause; and one item in the report above-mentioned, viz., £2 16s. 3d. for entry money and dues, proves that the seed so persistently sown in the past is at last beginning to bear fruit, and is moreover valuable as evidence of the good which can be accomplished by even a few enthusiasts linking themselves together in the name of a great cause. Literature sold during the quarter amounted to £3 11s. 4d., or nearly 6s. per week; while collections totalled up to £7 18s 6d thus showing that the sympathy at present extended to the movement takes a more tangible shape than mere words. While on the expenditure side the sum of £2 18s. for advertising shows that the local comrades neglect no means of bringing their cause before the public. Add to this, the changed attitude of the capitalist newspapers towards the movement, from contemptuous toleration or fulsome patronage to bitter, undisguised hatred and determined opposition, as well as the fact that the numbers attending our Socialist meetings are constantly increasing, and we can read from all these signs a promise of hope which nothing can dim, an assurance of triumph of which nothing can deprive us. Thus, though the enemies of progress may vent upon our heads all the malice, the meanness, and the calumny at the command of the supporters of a slowly-dying tyranny, serene and unruffled amidst the storm, we can await the dawning of the new industrial era with a confidence, a trust, and a joy that passeth all non-socialist understanding.

*****

SCOTTISH NOTES[1]
JUSTICE
24 JUNE 1893, P.3

IF LARGE AND ATTENTIVE audiences, brisk sale of literature, and generous collections are any criterion of the position our movement occupies in the public mind, then the Scottish Socialist Federation (Edinburgh) has every reason for just a little pride in the evidences, of the spread of socialist doctrines afforded by their meetings. It is no longer necessary for our speakers to mount the stool and bellow themselves hoarse in the effort to attract a crowd. The meadows of Edinburgh are a favourite resort of all sorts and conditions of men and women desiring to convert their erring fellow-mortals. Theological hair-splitting. Home Rule raving, Orange fulminating, atheistic sneering, all alike hold the field in our absence; but when, away in a select spot, far from the madding crowd, the Red Flag is uplifted to the breeze, then from all quarters come rushing the politicians, the bigots, the saints and the sinners, leaving their teachers with but the skeleton of an audience, and often no audience at all. Yea, it is well, for ours is the true gospel of social salvation.

And, plentiful as blackberries in summer, there glitter among our crowds the shining, resplendent tall hats of the superior persons, upon whose faces there can often be seen a most curiously blended look of mystification and anger, as their ears drink in the strange, new, wonderful doctrine expounded from the stool. But the only opposition ever offered

---

1   The article was signed "J. Connolly." John Connolly was secretary of the Scottish Socialist Federation until July 1893. See "Scottish Notes," *Justice*, 22 July 1893. It should be noted, however, that the sharp humour and bite of the article is very similar in style and tone to that of James. However, the available evidence, such as it is, points to John and not James as the signed author.

is that from the man who "sympathises with Socialists, don't you know? But they are so impracticable." The other Sunday, Miss Enid Stacey, addressed two meetings on behalf of the SS[F], at both meetings speaking the most uncompromising socialism, and completely enlisting the sympathies of her hearers, who greeted her at the close with three ringing cheers, somewhat of a phenomenon in Sabbatarian Edinburgh. Comrade Alexander had also offered to speak in Edinburgh on Saturday and Sunday, and his offer being accepted by both the Labour Party and the SSF, had been advertised accordingly throughout the week. But, alas! without acquainting the secretary of his intentions, our gay and festive lecturer waltzes off to Glasgow, breaking his promise as lightly as if it were an election pledge and he a politician out of office. Perhaps it amused him; but what about the comrade who had to explain his absence to a crowd of some two or three thousand people who had gathered together, partly in the expectation of hearing him?

*****

ALEC DICKINSON[1]
JUSTICE
14 DECEMBER 1895, P.5

O UR EDINBURGH COMRADES have this week to deplore the loss of a staunch comrade and faithful worker in the cause of socialism. Alec Dickinson, member of the South Edinburgh Branch of the ILP, Fabian representative on the Edinburgh School Board and at one time secretary of the local Fabian Society, though never enrolled in the ranks of the SDF, was yet a comrade whose breadth of sympathy and genuine enthusiasm in the fight against oppression overleapt all barriers, and had ever a hand and voice ready to assist every party engaged in the holy war against monopoly. With the health and constitution of an invalid, he, for the sake of socialism, undertook and accomplished the work of a giant. The memory of his life and work should remain with us an inspiration and an encouragement to those who weary not in well-doing, and as a mute reproach to those laggards in the cause whose lukewarm support of the principles they profess, materially contributed to increase his burdens. A funeral procession of at least two thousand mourners accompanied his remains to their last resting place, at which our comrade Dr. Glasse, officiating as clergyman of the church to which he had belonged, and our comrade Leo Melliet on behalf of his fellow socialists, paid the last tribute of respect in words none the less pathetic, because of the visible emotion of the speakers.

At the SDF meeting in the Operetta House a resolution, expressing sympathy with the relatives of our comrade, was passed in silence. It is not given to every one to elicit such expressions of respect, but in the case of

---

1   The article was signed "J.C", which was used by John Connolly. See "Socialist Scottish Federation," *Justice*, 18 February 1893.

our late comrade, they were felt to be but a fitting tribute to the worth of one who was both a soldier and a martyr.

APPENDICES
APPENDIX F
APOCRYPHA

*****

SCOTTISH SOCIALIST FEDERATION – EDINBURGH
COMMONWEAL
1 NOVEMBER 1890, P.351

GOOD MEETINGS were held on Sunday both here and at Leith. In the afternoon Mackenzie, Hamilton, and Connolly spoke in the Meadows, but cold and rain, or providence, drove the audience off. [1]

---

1 Could be either John or James Connolly. Bernard Ransom believed it referred to John.

*****

THE PROPAGANDA - NORTHERN NOTES
FREEDOM (LONDON)
1 JULY 1891, P.54

IN EDINBURGH the Scottish Socialist Federation, which consists of all schools of socialists and communists has lost two of its best speakers, T. H. Bell (Anarchist-Communist) and Hamilton (SD[1]). We have still the pleasure of hearing Davidson and Smith (AC) and Pearson (SD) and our new speakers are (Cyril Bell (AC) and Conolly [sic] (Socialist))[2]. There have been several conversions from opportunism to revolutionary anarchism, and our outdoor meetings have been strengthened by visits of Campbell (London SDF) and Glasier (Glasgow SL[3]). Our meetings have been held in Links and Meadows, one in Chambers Street and one on Grassmarket. We have given up Labour Hall and taken a new clubroom at 333 High Street.

---

1   Social Democrat.

2   More than likely this refers to James as the speaker is referred to as new, but I cannot be certain.

3   Socialist League.

*****

MR J. KIER HARDIE MP ON THE LABOUR QUESTION
THE SCOTSMAN
24 OCTOBER 1892, P.8

Mr J. Keir Hardie, M.P., lectured in the Free Tron Hall, Edinburgh, on Saturday night, under the auspices of the Edinburgh Fabian Society and the Scottish Socialist Federation. The hall, which holds about four hundred people, was nearly filled. Mr Connolly, vice-president of the Scottish Socialist Federation, presided[1], and he was accompanied on the platform by Messrs T. Blaikie, A. Purdie, A. M'Lean, J. Mackenzie, and R. Blackburn, members of the Edinburgh Trades Council, and others. The Chairman, in opening the proceedings, said they had forced upon them the fact that there could be no freedom for the working classes in any scheme of party policy. The widest political freedom was still compatible with the most grinding social tyranny.

---

1   Given that John Connolly was more than likely secretary of the SFF, it appears that James Connolly held one of the Vice-President roles, but in the absence of the minute book of the SFF I cannot be certain. It could very well be that the opposite was true, and James was secretary and John vice-president.

*****

SOCIALISM AND THE NON-CHURCH-GOING CONTROVERSY
EDINBURGH EVENING NEWS
21 NOVEMBER 1892, P.2

L AST NIGHT, at the usual meeting of the Scottish Socialist Federation in the Trades Hall, Edinburgh, Mr J. Connolly[1] dealt with the Rev. Mr Jackson's address of the previous Sunday on "Working Men and the Church." He submitted that the charge against the Church made by the non-churchgoers had been evaded. He endorsed the statement made at Mr Jackson's meeting that, so far from the Church representing the spirit of Christ, and being the true friend of social reform, it had enveloped in a cloud of sophistry and verbiage the most momentous of Christian truths, and had given a high place within its walls to usurers, sweaters, rackrenters, and slum-owners, who were the scourges of humanity. If the poor, persecuted, early Christian Church could overthrow chattel slavery, why did its rich, influential successor stand powerless before the problems of the present day. Mr Jackson referred to the work of Wilberforce; but when Wilberforce made England ring with denunciations of chattel-slavery, the unimpeachable evidence of Blue Books showed an unparalleled record of barbarous cruelty perpetrated in England itself on helpless wage-slaves under unrestricted competition. What people did was of more importance than what they said, and twenty-nine religious newspapers were published in 'rat shops.' The lecture was followed by a discussion.

---

1   I am unable to establish whether this is John or James. The meeting was advertised in *Edinburgh Evening News*, 19 November 1982, 1. It said: "J. Connolly will reply to Rev. Mr Jackson."

APPENDICES
APPENDIX G
CONNOLLY, GREAVES, & THE ARMY TALE

*****

CONNOLLY, GREAVES, &
THE ARMY TALE
CONOR McCABE

I T WAS SUFFICIENTLY WELL-KNOWN that Connolly was born in Scotland for a number of newspapers to report this fact in the wake of the 1916 Rising. Those that did usually said that he was born in Glasgow.[1] The most remarkable account was the one that appeared in the *Newcastle Daily Journal* on 2 May 1916.[2] Aside from a couple of minor errors on

---

1   Some examples: "[Connolly] was born in Scotland of Irish parents." "The Rebel Leader's Style," *Aberdeen Press and Journal.* 2 May 1916, 4; "Connolly was born in Scotland of Irish parents, and spent some time in America." "James Connolly," *Waterford Star,* 6 May 1916, 5; "Connolly, the founder of the Socialist Party in Ireland, is a man who, though of Irish parentage, was born and brought up in Glasgow." "Notes of the Week," *Alfreton Journal,* 5 May 1916, 1 (see also "A Warning to England," *Kerry Evening Post,* 6 May 1916, 3; "A Lesson from Ireland," *Wicklow News-Letter and County Advertiser,* 13 May 1916, 4, for same quote); "Born in Scotland of Irish parents, [Connolly] became an advanced socialist of the self-educated type, travelled to America, where he absorbed the new ideas of labour agitation, drifted back to this country, and eventually became Larkin's right-hand man in Dublin and his chief organiser." 'James Connolly," *Nottingham and Midland Catholic News,* 6 May 1916, 5; "Socialistic ideas were first spread in Ireland by two men, who, though of Irish parentage, were born and brought up in large industrial centres in Great Britain—James Connolly from Glasgow, and James Larkin, from Liverpool." "Seeds of Socialism," *Blackpool Gazette and Herald.* 9 May 1916, 7.

2   "James Connolly, who was previously reported shot, and is now said to have surrendered with the other rebel leaders, was born in Edinburgh, on the 6th June, 1866, in Campbell's Close, in the Cowgate, the house where he was born being no longer in existence. His parents were Irish, and his father worked as a carter in the service of Edinburgh Corporation for 42 years, when he received a pension. James learned the tile laying trade, and later entered the Corporation service as a carter, and became prominent in Labour disputes. As a boy he showed a great deal of intelligence, and was marked among his companions for the ready way in which he grasped things. On Sundays and holidays he would go for long rambles into the country,

dates, it was surprisingly accurate. It gave his correct place of birth (Cowgate, Edinburgh); that his parents were Irish; that his father worked as a carter; that he went to school and afterwards learned the tile-laying trade (something that Connolly himself once mentioned in a letter);[3] that he ended up as a carter; that he married an Irish woman who was working in Perth; that one of his children died in a fire while he was in America; and that he opened a boot repair shop. It also correctly stated that his brother John was in the army. What is also notable is that it made no mention of Connolly ever having been in the army—indeed, it is never mentioned until Desmond Greaves published his biography in 1961.

The tale of Connolly's army career, as told in *Life and Times*, is well known. He signed up to King's Liverpool in 1882 and was stationed in Cork where he stood guard the night of the execution of Myles Joyce. His battalion then moved to the Curragh in 1884. The following year it was sent to Dublin and by 1886 he was stationed in Beggars Bush. He met

---

and so great was his power over the other boys of his own age that they would do anything he asked them. He received his education first at the Catholic School in Lothian Street, and later at the school in Market Street. He married a Dublin girl who was in service in Perth, and he had six children, five of whom are still alive. The other child was burned to death through her clothes catching fire. Connolly was at that time in America, and his wife was preparing to follow him. On leaving his employment with the Corporation he started a small boot repairing business in Buccleuch Street, and later he received an invitation from the Socialist party in Ireland to take up organising work there, and some time afterwards he went to America as a Socialist lecturer. He remained in America for 10 years, and returning to Dublin he again took up socialist work there, publishing his book, *Labour in Irish History*, and writing a great many pamphlets. He also acted as Irish correspondent of *The Forward*. While in Edinburgh he stood as a Socialist candidate for the representation of St. Giles Ward in Edinburgh Town Council at the November election of 1894. He was one of the first Socialists to stand in an Edinburgh municipal contest, and came out third on the ward poll. On his election posters Connolly was announced as "the man who would put down 'swellocracy.'" He also stood for the Parish Council, and was defeated. Connolly was in Edinburgh and Leith in October, 1913, in support of the Dublin strikers. He was the principal speaker at a demonstration, organised by the Edinburgh Trades Council and other Labour organisations, at the bandstand in the Meadows. On that occasion he was described as "Larkin's lieutenant." Connolly's brother John, who has just been discharged from the National Reserve, resides with his family at 57 Calton Road, Edinburgh. He has served twenty years in the Army, and two of his sons have been killed at the front, while one is a prisoner of war in Germany." "General' Connolly," *Newcastle Daily Journal.* 2 May 1916, 5.

3   "Connolly to Matheson, 9 March 1903," MS 13,906/2/11, William O'Brien Collection, National Library of Ireland, Dublin.

Lillie, his future wife, around this time at a tram stop at Merrion Square and in February 1889, with only a few months left to serve, he decided to go AWOL and return to Scotland as his father had fallen ill. He initially moved to Dundee to 'lie low' until he found civilian clothes and in 1890 he returned to Edinburgh to marry Lillie.[4] Almost every biography of Connolly since 1961 has reproduced this tale. The problem is that there is no evidence to support it.

Greaves' *Life and Times* has all the appearance of meticulous research but is severely lacking in pathways for third-party verification—namely sources, citations, and references. This meant that later historians had to take Greaves at his word, which for the most part they did. He had a certain amount of credibility, having uncovered Connolly's birth certificate in 1951, establishing once and for all that Connolly was born in Edinburgh in 1868.[5] However, in terms of the army story all that Greaves would say was that he got it from two sources: an old associate and friend of Connolly named 'Jack Mullery of Liverpool' and 'from the statements of contemporaries in Edinburgh...'[6] No other details were given and Jack Mullery was a mystery as there was no known associate of Connolly with that name. That changed in 2019 when the journals of Desmond Greaves were made available online.

Jack Mullery was John Mulray. He was born at 24 Devon Street, Liverpool, on 8 February 1879. His father, Michael Mulray, was Irish and a tailor by trade. The family moved to Dublin soon afterwards and were living at 7 Great Longford St when his brother, Richard, was born.[7] His mother, Catherine Mulray, died of tuberculosis ("phthisis") on 3 June

---

4   Greaves, *Life and Times*, 19-29. The one major variation on this tale is that told by Samuel Levenson who argued in his 1973 biography that Connolly signed up to the Royal Scots. However, later biographers have essentially followed Greaves over Levenson.

5   C. Desmond Greaves, "Connolly in Scotland: Some New Facts," *Irish Democrat*, March 1951, 4-5.

6   Greaves. *Life and Times*, 9; 24.

7   As of 17 December 2023 the surname is transcribed as "Mulroy" on the Irish Genealogy website, but the name on the original document is "Mulray." See entry 180– https://civilrecords.irishgenealogy.ie/churchrecords/images/birth_returns/births_1880/02853/2045474.pdf. There is a photograph of 7 Great Longford Street available on the RTÉ archive website. It was taken around 1952/53. https://stillslibrary.rte.ie/indexplus/image/3009/063.html

1894.[8] By this time, they were living at 47 Marlborough Street. They were still living at this address in 1901 when John, his three brothers, his sister, and widowed father, occupied one room in the tenement building.[9] He was now a qualified tailor.

It was as an apprentice tailor, four years previously, that Mulray first met Connolly. He worked at 67 Middle Abbey Street, below the offices of the ISRP, where he 'used to see Connolly coming in and out.'[10] They got chatting and eventually this led to Mulray joining the party. His membership was approved on 30 December 1897.[11] By 1903, however, relations seemed to have soured somewhat and Mulray was among the ISRP members who voted to accept Connolly's resignation from the party, leading to Connolly's emigration to the United States later that year. 'My career has been unique in many things' he wrote in a letter to William O'Brien in August 1903. 'Men have been driven out of Ireland by the British Government, and by the landlords, but I am the first driven forth by the "Socialists?"'[12]

Not long afterwards, Mulray also emigrated to America and met Connolly by accident one day in New York.[13] They were not on speaking terms beforehand but it is clear from the few surviving letters between them that they soon became friends once again—in one Connolly signed it as 'your affectionate comrade', the only record we currently have of him

---

8   See entry 329–https://civilrecords.irishgenealogy.ie/churchrecords/images/deaths_returns/deaths_1894/05968/4696283.pdf

9   House 47.7 Marlborough Street. https://www.census.nationalarchives.ie/pages/1901/Dublin/Mountjoy/Marlborough_Street/1327892/

10   "10 June 1956," Desmond Greaves Journal, Vol.12, 1956-7, accessed 5 May 2024, https://desmondgreavesarchive.com/journal/desmond-greaves-journal-vol-12-1956-7/. Greaves refers to Mulray as Mulray throughout his journal. He changed the name to Mullery when he finally published *The Life and Times of James Connolly* in 1961.

11   "New members: J. Mulray. 47 Marlboro' St." "Minute book of the Irish Socialist Republican Party, Dublin, containing many entries by James Connolly, secretary, 29th May 1896 to 18th September 1898," 30 December 1897, Ms. 16,295, William O'Brien Collection, National Library of Ireland, Dublin. Mulray is also mentioned in the ISRP minutes for 6 November 1898 as a member and living at 47 Marlborough Street.

12   Connolly to O'Brien, MS 13,908/1/89.

13   "10 June 1957," Desmond Greaves Journal, Vol.12, 1956-7.

using that phrase.[14] In 1907 Mulray was one of the founding members, along with Connolly, of the Irish Socialist Association.[15] He left for Ireland not long afterwards. He seems to have dropped out of socialist politics around 1912, although he was active up until that time. He was married in Liverpool in 1925 (under the name John Mullery), his wife died in 1936,[16] and it is in that city in 1957 that Greaves tracked him down to 32 Exmouth St, Everton.

He got the address from Ina Connolly-Heron.[17] Her sister, Nora, had received a congratulatory telegram from Mulray when she was made a senator in May 1957, on the nomination of the Taoiseach, Éamon de Valera.[18] Greaves first visited Mulray on 10 June 1957 and he appeared to him to be 'very well preserved, somewhat deaf, but in full possession of his faculties...'[19] At first they talked about his stint in America before Mulray brought up the story of how Connolly first met Lillie:

> He was in uniform at the time... He ran for a tram for Kingstown or Black-rock at the corner of Merrion Square. The conductor did not stop, so he and an attractive young girl missed it together. That started the relationship, since they fell talking. There was never a cross word between them, but sometimes they would jokingly say, "That tram!" The conductor had not seen them, he supposed. In those days the trams would stop anywhere they were hailed.[20]

The story as recounted by Mulray differs from the final version, published without reference or attribution, in *Life and Times*:

> It was in Dublin that Connolly met his future wife, Lillie Reynolds, during

---

14   "10 June 1957," Desmond Greaves Journal, Vol.12, 1956-7; "Connolly to Mulray, 19 June 1905," MS 13,909/11, William O'Brien Collection, National Library of Ireland, Dublin. In the same letter Connolly wrote "... it is to Ireland that all my thoughts turn when dreaming of the future. I suppose I will never see it again, except in dreams."

15   "Dr Brahn's Attack," *Daily People* (New York), 30 May 1907.

16   "Deaths," *Liverpool Daily Post*, 29 February 1936, 1. The notice read: "Mullery—February 27, in hospital, Eileen, dearly-beloved wife of John Mullery, 32, Exmouth Street, Everton. Interment at Ford Cemetery on Monday next, at 4pm." They had previously lived at 8, Shallcross Street, Everton. See "John Rafferty," *Liverpool Daily Post*, 21 July 1933, 1.

17   "31 May 1957," Desmond Greaves Journal, Vol 12, 1956-7.

18   "Senate Now Complete," *Cork Examiner*, 16 May 1957, 7.

19   "10 June 1957," Desmond Greaves Journal, Vol.12, 1956-7.

20   "10 June 1957," Desmond Greaves Journal, Vol.12, 1956-7.

an evening trip to Dún Laoghaire, then Kingstown. Connolly strolled from Beggars Bush to near Merrion Square for the tram. The trams used to then to stop wherever they were hailed. On this occasion both he and a young woman of his own age, fair, small and refined in an unassuming way, were left behind by an impatient driver and entered into conversation. Their friendship ripened quickly and by the end of 1888 they had decided upon marriage.

Greaves embellished the story with details that were not in the original. Mulray's speculation that the tram driver did not see them instead becomes a statement of fact—'left behind by an impatient driver'—as if Connolly or Lillie had said it and not Mulray. The tram's destination may have been Kingstown or Blackrock, but Greaves had no time for such ambiguity and so it became Kingstown with Connolly intent on an evening trip. Furthermore, Greaves had Connolly strolling from Beggars Bush to Merrion Square in order to catch a tram to Kingstown—even though Mulray made no mention of Beggars Bush. Finally, Greaves had Connolly walk towards Merrion Square to catch a tram to go to Kingstown, which is in the opposite direction, even though he could have caught it at any point along the route. This falsification, seemingly small, is nonetheless significant. Greaves had Connolly coming from Beggars Bush because the King's Liverpool regiment was stationed there in the mid-1880s. Greaves invented this detail in order to link Connolly to the regiment.

Mulray was also the sole source for the story of Connolly stationed in Cork in 1882. Greaves wrote the following in his journal on 10 June 1957, quoting Mulray:

> He was at Spike Island—that affair about Myles Joyce. They were on trial, didn't understand English and were all hanged. Connolly told me—'I was on guard that night.' My God! I was sorry for them." I was a little confused about Spike Island as the matter rang a bell, yet seemed not quite right. "Which Spike Island do you mean?" I hazarded. "Oh! There's only one. Don't you know—near Queenstown." So I was to gather Connolly was stationed at Cobh.

Myles Joyce was executed in Galway on 15 December 1882. He was one of ten men found guilty of the murder of five people in Maamtrasna on the Galway/Mayo border in August of that year. Joyce spoke only Irish, his barrister did not understand any Irish, and the court proceedings were all in English. He was widely perceived to have been innocent.[21]

---

21   For more on this see Margaret Kelleher, *The Maamtrasna Murders: Language,*

Although unsure of its veracity, Greaves nonetheless wanted to use the Spike Island story and so he simply altered the parts he did not like in order to make the Mulray's memories 'fit' the King's Liverpool hypothesis. The tale as told by Greaves is thus:

> Very few details of Connolly's army life are known. He told Mullery of spending the night on guard, at Haulbowline in Cork Harbour, when Myles Joyce was executed for his part in the Maamtrasna massacre. There is no doubt that Joyce was innocent, and had he been able to speak or understand English he might have been acquitted. Connolly spent the whole night thinking about the impending execution, all his sympathy going out to the men convicted of "agrarian crime."[22]

Greaves changed Spike Island to Haulbowline and added the poetics of Connolly brooding on men convicted of agrarian crime. According to Mulray, Connolly said he felt sorry for them; it was Greaves who added the 'agrarian' dimension. Quite remarkably, Greaves then explained why he changed Mulray's story:

> Mullery said "Spike Island" but the King's Liverpool Regiment had no men there on the day the records were made up: possibly there may have been a small detachment sent to Spike Island to relieve the Oxfords, but more likely the two stations, which are in very close proximity, were confused.[23]

Quite apart from the ethical and professional issues around changing witness testimony to suit a hypothesis, Greaves now faced a problem with Mulray's memories in that, by Greaves' own admission, they were faulty. Which parts were to be believed and which parts discounted? In the absence of any firm supporting evidence for Mulray's memories regarding Connolly's army career and courtship of Lillie, Greaves' criteria was whether they proved his King's Liverpool theory or not—and when they did not *he changed Mulray's memories*.

Soon after their meeting Mulray wrote to Greaves to say he was sorry that he had not told him more about Connolly and asked him to get in touch. In the meantime Mulray was admitted to hospital. Greaves visited him at the Royal Infirmary in Liverpool around 10 July 1957. They only spoke for a few minutes and there is no record at present available

---

Life and Death in Nineteenth-Century Ireland (Dublin: UCD Press, 2018). Joyce was granted a posthumous pardon by President Michael D Higgins in 2018.

22   Greaves, *Life and Times*, 26.

23   Greaves, *Life and Times*, 26.

of Greaves meeting with him again. Mulray died on 13 July 1958. His son, John, wrote to William O'Brien in December of that year. 'Apparently you have not heard of the death of my father, Jack Mullery' he said. 'He had an operation on his arm but he never recovered his strength after leaving hospital.' O'Brien had kept in touch with Mulray over the years—in 1951 Mulray told O'Brien that 'Connolly never mentioned to me where he was born.'[24] The letter from the son is the earliest reference in the O'Brien archive to John Mulray as Jack Mullery.

The second major source for Greaves' army story was 'the statements of contemporaries in Edinburgh.' On 13 November 1956 Greaves wrote to William O'Brien to ask for his assistance for details regarding Connolly's army career.[25] 'Peadar O'Donnell with whom I had lunch a few days ago' wrote Greaves, 'told me that you also knew that he was in the Militia and stationed in Dublin, a fact I learned from old schoolfellows of his in Edinburgh some years ago... Some of my informants in Edinburgh told me he enlisted under a false name. One man thought it was Reid but was not sure.'[26]

Greaves wrote about meeting the 'old schoolfellows' in his journal entry for 13 September 1956. It took place six years previously in 1950 when he was researching Connolly's connections with Edinburgh. He met a man named Conlon, 'an old man of about 75 in a top-floor tenement, who had liked his drop and had an air of mischief about him.'[27] Conlon was a 'special friend' of Connolly's brother, John. Greaves wrote:

Conlon stopped speaking to me and turned to Geddes. "He was born in the Coogate," he said. "That's what you call the Cowgate," said Geddes. Then Con-

24   "Notes by William O'Brien of statements by Mark Deering and John Mulray regarding the birthplace of James Connolly, Nov-Dec 1951," MS 13,942/1/14, William O'Brien Collection, National Library of Ireland, Dublin.

25   "C. Desmond Greaves to William O'Brien, 13 November 1956," Ms 13,961/3/72, William O'Brien Collection, National Library of Ireland, Dublin.

26   O'Brien never replied to Greaves. He wrote a letter on 31 January 1957 to a person named "Jack" where he referred to Greaves as the "editor of the 'Irish Democrat,' a disguised communist paper run by the Connolly Association to trap the Irish elements in Great Britain. He is writing a book on Connolly and appealed to me for assistance twice but I have ignored him." "William O'Brien to 'Jack,' 31 January 1957," Ms 13,942/1/17, William O'Brien Collection, National Library of Ireland, Dublin.

27   "13 September 1956," Desmond Greaves Journal, Vol.12, 1956-7.

lon said even more mischievously, "Did you hear he was in the army?" He explained that John Connolly joined under the name of John Reid, but could not remember what name James took. The regiment was the King's Liverpool. "But you can check the birth at the Registry Office," he declared. "This is quite different from the accepted story," I demurred. "Ay, indeed. There was some fellow over writing a book about Connolly. But we didn't like the look of him so we told him nothing."[28]

There is no mention of this encounter in the online edition of his journal for 1950, so we have to rely on his memory of the event six years later. It appears though that it was only one person who told him about Connolly in the army, while in his letter to O'Brien it is plural. Greaves also referred to the event in *Life and Times*, writing about 'old associates... deliberately misleading visitors from Dublin out of concern to protect Connolly's reputation.'[29] Conlon said nothing of the sort. It happened once and they simply didn't like the look of the man.

It was this encounter that appears to have led Greaves down the path of Connolly and the King's Liverpool regiment, one that he stubbornly stuck to over the years. While no army record for Connolly has been found, his brother's record does exist and is available online.[30] He enlisted under the name James Reid (not John as stated by Conlon who would have been around two years of age when his 'close' friend signed up) and served sixteen years with the Border Regiment. He reenlisted in December 1914, this time with the Royal Scots, and was discharged due to ill-health on 1 February 1916. He died on 22 June 1916, around seven weeks after his brother's execution.[31]

---

28   It was this encounter that led Greaves to pay for a registry search, leading to the discovery of Connolly's birth certificate. See "13 September 1956," Desmond Greaves Journal, Vol.12, 1956-7.

29   Greaves, *Life and Times*, 24.

30   The record is available on findmypast.co.uk. (subscription required) under James Reid, service number 20308. Rather confusingly, it consists of two separate files for two different men named James Reid. John Connolly is the second one, with the address 7 Fountain Place and married to Elizabeth Atchieson in 1891. Search result here: https://www.findmypast.ie/search/results?datasetname=british+army+service+records&sid=103&firstname=james&firstname_variants=true&lastname=reid&servicenumber=20308.

31   Commonwealth War Graves. Corporal John Connolly, service number 20308.   https://www.cwgc.org/find-records/find-war-dead/casualty-details/416281/john-connolly/ accessed 6 May 2024.

In August 1957, Greaves wrote to the War Office in the hope of finding Connolly's army record. They wrote back to tell him that his enquiry had been sent on to the Public Records Office and that they thought they had the information he was looking for, "in the 'musters' of the King's Liverpool regiment."[32] 'I am looking for a name appearing as a recruit in July 1882, and a disaster (or casualty) in February 1889, who was also in Cork Harbour in November 1882' wrote Greaves in his journal. 'It may be discoverable.' At this point the journal stops for three years. We do not know the precise wording that came back from the Public Records Office, but we do know the search drew a blank. Greaves was now left with a heaving bag of hearsay for his King's Liverpool thesis. He had spent years searching for proof that Connolly served in the British army to no avail and yet seemed determined to publish the story as incontrovertible fact. In the end his argument came down to mathematics:

> Connolly spent seven years in America. If he was right in saying that he spent twenty years among the exiles in Britain, then he must have spent twenty-one years in Ireland. These are known to have included 1896-1903, and 1911-16. It has been shown that the missing seven years cannot be placed between 1870 and 1880, so they must fall between 1882 and 1889. If Connolly was in Ireland then, as he must have been on his own statement, what was he doing? There is no alternative to set against the fact that the first battalion of the King's Liverpool Regiment was in Ireland from precisely July 1882 to February 1889. Those who reject this must tell us what else he was doing.[33]

Let us park the logic at play here and focus instead on Connolly's statement that he 'spent twenty years among the exiles in Britain.' Greaves implies that it dates from 1916 and involves calculations for Connolly's years in the US and subsequent return to Ireland. Yet the line, as Greaves was aware, was from his 1902 US lecture tour—Greaves even referenced it as such later on in *Life and Times*.[34] It first appeared in *Workers Republic* in August 1902 in the article 'Our American Mission.' It was reprinted in *Daily People* (New York) on 24 August 1902. The publicity for the speaking tour said that Connolly was born in Monaghan in 1869.[35] Con-

---

32   "17 August 1957," Desmond Greaves Journal, Vol.13, 1957, 1960-61, accessed 6 May 2024, https://desmondgreavesarchive.com/journal/desmond-greaves-journal-vol-13-1957-1960-61/.

33   Greaves, *Life and Times*, 25.

34   Greaves, *Life and Times*, 148.

35   Mark Deering, "The Irish Agitator," *Weekly People* (New York), 26 July

nolly privately criticised that statement as inaccurate,[36] yet declined to say when and where he was born.[37] He never contradicted such statements in public, allowing assertions of Ireland as his place of birth to pass without any comment or clarification. To complicate matters further, he listed himself as born in Monaghan in both the 1901 and 1911 Censuses.[38] He was not only content for the assumption he was born in Ireland to continue, he actively pushed it in official documents. When Connolly used the words 'twenty years' in 1902 he was making a point about his skills as an activist, not leaving little easter eggs for future biographers to decode.

It is wild, to say the least, that after years of research and digging, this was the best that Greaves could come up with regarding Connolly's supposed stint in the army—a back-of-the-envelope calculation based on a mis-sourced line in a single article in order to support a veritable feast

1902, 3. The article said he 'was born in 1869, near Clowes [sic] in the county of Monoghan [sic], Ireland.'

36   "The fiend who wrote that preposterous biography, and created a new birthplace and a new year of birth for me, will I hope suffer in this life all the tortures of the damned. 'May life's unblessed cup for him / be filled with miseries to the brim.' The yahoo!" "Connolly to Unknown Recipient. 7 August 1902," MS 13,912/1/23, William O'Brien Collection, National Library of Ireland, Dublin. The quote is from Thomas Moore. *Lalla Rookh.* (London, 1817), 222: "May Life's unblessed cup for him / Be drugged with treacheries to the brim."

37   William O'Brien met Mark Deering on 1 December 1951 and asked him about the piece in the *Weekly People.* "Deering replied that he did not write the note but he allowed his name to be put to it. Connolly told him that he was not born in County Monaghan, but did not say where he was born. Deering added that he understood that Connolly had spent some time in County Armagh." "Notes by William O'Brien," MS 13,942/1/14. It appears from the minutes of the ISRP that although the broad biographical sketch itself was written by Connolly, it was agreed to by the party "on the understanding that particulars as to Connolly's birthplace, age, etc and his special characteristics be added to same." "Minute Book No. 4 of the Irish Socialist Republican Party," 8 July 1902, MS 16,266, William O'Brien Collection, National Library of Ireland, Dublin. Connolly was not present at the meeting. He was in Salford (Trafford Road) that evening, speaking on socialism and imperialism. See "James Connolly," *Clarion,* 4 July 1902, 4.

38   See household return form for 54.3 Pimlico, 1901 census, and household return form for 70 Lotts Road, South, 1911 census. https://www.census.nationalarchives.ie/search/. It is worth noting that in the 1891 census he is listed as born in Edinburgh. See census 1891 return for "James Conaly" [sic] 75 St. Mary Street, parish of Old Church. St. Giles, Edinburgh. ref: 685/3 93/ 2. Scotlandspeople.gov.uk [paid subscription] https://www.scotlandspeople.gov.uk/image-viewer/census/census-17315362_4579_685_3_93_?search_token=306465037663be0e284d65.

of conjecture and speculation. What is unforgivable, though, is the sheer invention that followed. There is no evidence Connolly served in the King's Liverpool; no evidence he was stationed in Haulbowline; no evidence he was stationed in the Curragh; no evidence he was stationed in Beggars Bush; no evidence he deserted; no evidence he went on the run to Dundee; no evidence he did so to help his sick father; and no evidence that he chose Dundee to change into civilian clothes. All of these details are today accepted as fact, and all of them were invented by Greaves.

Connolly once wrote that he knew a thing or two about the army, 'having slept in the same room as a militiaman.'[39] He was, of course, referring to his brother John, with whom he was quite close. Almost every army story told of Connolly can equally be explained by Connolly talking about his brother rather than himself. At the same time it is important to say that future investigation may yet yield results, but at the moment there is *no evidence* that Connolly served in the army. One of the the short stories rediscovered as part of the research for this collection has as its protagonist a private in the army, which will add to the speculation but, unfortunately, will not help us escape from it. We have only the hearsay memories of men in their seventies, interviewed in the 1950s, as they tried to disentangle decades of bar-stool stories from the actual contemporary truth. No supporting contemporary documentary evidence exists for those memories. We do not know if the elderly men got Connolly mixed up with his brother John; nor do we know if the hit-pieces written in 1913 in the anti-ITGWU newspaper, *The Toiler*—which said that Connolly served in the 'Monaghan Militia' before deserting to Scotland—got fused with their memories over the years, adorning the clothes of truth through sheer repetition.[40]

---

39 "Home Thrusts," *Workers' Republic*, 26 November 1899, 1.

40 The editor of *The Toiler* was Patrick J. McIntyre (sometimes referred to as MacIntyre), journalist and trade unionist affiliated with the Workers' Union, an English-based trade union with a small presence in Ireland. It became known as a 'scab' union. McIntyre was virulently anti-Larkin, anti-ITGWU, and anti-Connolly. He was taken prisoner during the 1916 Rising, although he played no part in it, and was executed without trial on 26 April 1916 along with Francis Sheehy-Skeffington and Thomas Dickson. The murders caused an outrage and the officer in charge, Captain J.C. Bowen-Colthurst from Cork, was later court-martialled and found guilty but insane. However, he was released after three years and moved to Canada where he died in 1965. For 'scab' reference see Charles McCarthy. *Trade Unions in Ireland 1894-1960*. Dublin: Institute of Public Administration, 1977, 15; James Curry. 'The Irish

The issue of Greaves and his King's Liverpool conjecture, however, is much wider than the question of whether or not Connolly was a private in the army. The story is used to 'explain' the missing portion of our knowledge of Connolly's life—namely from the 1881 census when he was recorded as an apprentice baker,[41] to his letters to Lillie in 1889 which he wrote when he was in Dundee. We can infer from at least one of those letters that he was in Dublin for a portion of this time.[42] We also know that he worked as a tile-layer, but for how long—and when—we don't know, nor has there been any great rush to find out. The army story put paid to any curiosity regarding Connolly's early life and activities; it pushed back the age he left school from twelve to the age of ten or eleven according to Greaves[43] and the age of nine according to Nevin[44]—and, having ruled out any real formal schooling, it magically explained Connolly's education and formidable writing skills. The reason for this backwards leap was to account for the jobs he held—the years 1882 to 1889 having been ruled out of contention by Greaves and his King's Liverpool conjecture. It should be noted that primary school attendance was mandatory (if not always entirely enforced) for all children in Scotland between the ages of five and thirteen under the Education (Scotland) Act 1872, and although this would not preclude children from work, Connolly's age was given as thirteen in the 1881 census, even though he was twelve on 3 April, the night it was taken.

And yet, as this collection shows, there are riches to be uncovered regarding Connolly if one is of a mind to dig for them. One such example is a previously unknown body of work that includes four fictional writings (including the long-lost sketch, *An Agitator's Wife*), an election manifes-

---

Transport and General Workers' Union and the labour press in Ireland, 1909-1920.' Dissertation. University of Galway, 2017, 104

41   Household return for King's Stables, 2, St Cuthberts, St Georges, Midlothian, Scotland. 1881 Census. Findmypast.co.uk. https://www.findmypast.co.uk/transcript?id=GBC%2F1881%2F0028913803.

42   'I will meet you at Baggot Street Bridge and we will have a walk round Donnybrook. God's truth.' "Connolly to Lillie Reynolds, 17 April 1889," MS 13,911/2, William O'Brien Collection, National Library of Ireland, Dublin.

43   Greaves, *Life and Times*, 18.

44   Nevin. *A Full Life*, 5. There is absolutely no evidence that Connolly left school at age nine. It is astounding that such baseless conjecture was allowed into print.

to, and a letter that were all published in the year before the formation of the ISRP and presented here in this collection for the very first time under Connolly's name.

BIBLIOGRAPHY
MANUSCRIPTS, NEWSPAPERS, & PUBLISHED MATERIALS, ETC.

*****

MANUSCRIPTS, NEWSPAPERS, &
PUBLISHED MATERIALS, ETC.

MANUSCRIPTS

C. Desmond Greaves Journals, Desmond Greaves Archive (online).

Francis Johnson Correspondence, London School of Economics Library and Archive.

William O'Brien Collection, National Library of Ireland.

Witness Statements, Bureau of Military History (online).

NEWSPAPERS

Aberdeen Press and Journal

Alfreton Journal

Barrhead News

Bee-Hive Newspaper

Blackpool Gazette and Herald

Bolton Evening News

Cardiff Times

Cheltenham Chronicle

Clarion

Commonweal

Cork Daily Herald

Daily People (New York)

Dublin Daily Nation

Dundee Advertiser

Dundee Weekly News

Economic Journal

Edinburgh Evening Dispatch

Edinburgh Evening News

Edinburgh Evening Post

Evening Herald (Dublin)

Evening Telegraph (Dublin)

Falkirk Herald

Freedom (London)

Freeman's Journal

Glasgow Herald

Greenock Telegraph and Clyde Shipping Gazette

Indian Daily News

Irish Democrat

Irish Independent

Irish Press

Irish Times

Irish Worker

Irish World (New York)

Justice

Labour Chronicle

Labour Leader

Leith Burghs Pilot

Leigh Chronicle and Weekly District Advertiser

Liberator (Boston)

Limerick Leader

Liverpool Daily Post

L'Irlande Libre

Newcastle Daily Journal

North British Daily Mail

Nottingham and Midland Catholic News

People (New York)

Reynold's Newspaper

Scotsman

Shan Van Vocht

South Wales Daily News

Stalybridge Reporter

Sunderland Daily Echo and Shipping Gazette

Światła (London)

The Times (London)

Toiler

Watchword of Labour

Waterford Star

Weekly Freeman's Journal

Weekly People (New York)

Wicklow News-Letter and County Advertiser

Workers' Dreadnought

Workers' Republic (1898-1903)

Workington Star

Published Material

Amel, Mahdi. *Arab Marxism and National Liberation: Selected Writings of Mahdi Amel*. Edited by Hicham Safieddine. Translated by Angela Giordani. Chicago: Haymarket Books, 2020.

Arnold, Sir Edwin. *The Marquis of Dalhousie's Administration of British India: Volume the Second*. London: Saunders, Otley & Co., 1865.

Barton, Brian. *The Secret Court Martial Records of the Easter Rising*. Cheltenham: The History Press, 2010.

Byron, Lord. *Poetical Works*. London: Oxford University Press, 1973.

Callow, John. *James Connolly and the Re-Conquest of Ireland*. London: Evans Mitchell Books, 2013.

Collins, Lorcan. *James Connolly*. Dublin: O'Brien Press, 2012.

Communist Party of Ireland, ed. *James Connolly Collected Works Vol I*. Dublin: New Books, 1987.

———, ed. *James Connolly Collected Works Vol II*. Dublin: New Books, 1988.

Connolly, James, ed. *The Rights of Ireland and the Faith of a Felon, by James Fintan Lalor*. Dublin: Irish Socialist Republican Party, 1896.

———, ed. *'98 Readings* Dublin, 1897

———. *Erin's Hope: The End and the Means*. Dublin: Irish Socialist Republican Party, 1897.

———. *Home Thrusts, by Spailpin*. Dublin: Irish Socialist Republican Party, 1901.

———. *The New Evangel*. Dublin: Irish Socialist Republican Party, 1901.

———. *Socialism and Nationalism*. Dublin: Irish Socialist Republican Party, 1901.

———, ed. *Songs of Freedom by Irish Authors*. New York: J.E.C. Donnelly, 1907.

———. *Socialism Made Easy*. Chicago: Charles H. Kerr & Company, 1909.

———. *The Axe to the Root: Industrial Unionism and Working Class Political Action*. Melbourne: Socialist Party of Victoria, 1910.

———. *Labour, Nationality and Religion*. 1910.

———. *Labour in Irish History*. Dublin: Maunsel & Co., 1910.

―――. *The Re-Conquest of Ireland*. Dublin: Liberty Hall, 1915.

Connolly, Frank. 'The Agitator's Wife.' *Liberty*, February 2024, 15.

Connolly, Nora. *The Unbroken Tradition*. New York: Boni and Liveright, 1918.

―――. *James Connolly: Portrait of a Rebel Father*. Dublin: Talbot Press, 1935. Reprint, Dublin: Four Masters Press, 1975.

―――. "Nora Connolly O'Brien." In *Survivors*, edited by Uinseann Mac Eoin, 183-215. Dublin: Argenta Publications, 1980.

Cork Workers' Club, ed. *The James Connolly Songbook*. Cork: Cork workers' Club, 1972.

―――, ed. *The Connolly-Walker Controversy on Socialist Unity in Ireland*. Cork: Cork Workers' Club, 1974.

―――, ed. *Ireland Upon the dissecting Table: James Connolly on Ulster & Partition*. Cork: Cork Workers' Club, 1975.

―――, ed. *The Connolly-DeLeon Controversy on Wages, Marriage & the Church*. Cork: Cork Workers' Club, 1976.

Cronin, Fintan. 'Notes on Sources.' *Saothar* 7 (1981): 112-113.

Cronin, Sean. *Young Connolly*. Dublin: Repsol Books, 1978.

Irish Communist Organisation, ed. *Connolly: Yellow Unions in Ireland and other Articles*. London: Connolly Books, 1968.

―――, ed. *Connolly: Press Poisoners in Ireland and other Articles*. London: Connolly Books, 1968.

―――, ed. *Connolly: Socialism and the Orange Worker*. London: Connolly Books, 1969.

―――, ed. *The Connolly-Walker Controversy*. London: Connolly Books, 1969.

Davies, Dr. Noëlle. *Connolly of Ireland: Patriot and Socialist*. Liverpool: Brython Press, 1946.

Deasy, Joseph. *The Teachings of James Connolly*. Dublin: New Books, 1966.

De Vere, Aubrey. *Poems of Aubrey De Vere*. Dublin: The Educational

Company, 1900.

Devine, Francis. *Organising History: A Centenary of SIPTU*. Dublin: Gill & Macmillan, 2007.

Dick, Maria-Daniella, Kirsty Lusk and Willy Maley. "'The Agitator's Wife" (1894): the story behind James Connolly's lost play?' *Irish Studies Review* 27, no.1 (2019): 1-21.

Dillon, Paul. 'James Connolly and the Kerry Famine of 1898.' *Saothar* 25 (2000): 9-42.

Dobbins, Gregory. "Whenever Green is Red: James Connolly and Postcolonial Theory." *Nepantla: Views from the South* 1, no.3 (2000): 605-48.

Dooley, Pat. *Under the Banner of Connolly*. London: Irish Freedom, 1945.

Edwards, Owen Dudley and Bernard Ransom, eds. *James Connolly: Selected Political Writings*. London: Jonathan Cape, 1973.

Edwards, Ruth Dudley. *James Connolly*. Dublin: Gill & Macmillan, 1981.

Ellis, P. Beresford, ed. *James Connolly: Selected Writings*. London: Penguin Books, 1973.

Fox, R.M. *James Connolly: The Forerunner*. Tralee: The Kerryman, 1946.

Galvin, Patrick. *Song for a Raggy Boy*. Dublin: Raven Arts Press, 1991.

Glazier, J. Bruce. "James Connolly: In Memoriam." *Labour Leader*, 17 May 1917, 7.

Greaves, C. Desmond. "Connolly in Scotland: Some New Facts." *Irish Democrat*, March 1951, 4-5.

———. *The Life and Times of James Connolly*. London: Lawrence & Wishart 1961.

Griffin, Gerald. *The Poetical and Dramatic Works of Gerald Griffin*. Dublin: James Duffy, 1857.

Gonne, Maud. *The Autobiography of Maud Gonne: A Servant of the Queen*. Chicago: University of Chicago Press, 1995.

Grundy, James. *Report of the Inspection of Mines in India, for the year ending the 30ᵗʰ June 1894*. Calcutta, 1894.

Harkin, Shaun. *The James Connolly Reader*. Chicago: Haymarket Books, 2018.

Heron, James Connolly. *The Words of James Connolly*. Cork: Mercier Press, 1986.

Hubbard-Kernan, Will. *The Flaming Meteor: Poetical Works of Will Hubbard-Kernan*. Chicago: Charles H. Kerr and Co., 1892.

Hyland, J.L. *James Connolly*. Dublin: Historical Association of Ireland, 1997.

ITGWU. *The Attempt to Smash the Irish Transport and General Workers' Union*. Dublin: ITGWU, 1924.

ITGWU. *Some Pages From Union History*. Dublin: ITGWU, 1924.

Jones, Sir William. *Poetical Works of Sir William Jones*. London: Cadell & Davies, 1807.

Kelleher, Margaret. *The Maamtrasna Murders: Language, Life and Death in Nineteenth-Century Ireland*. Dublin: UCD Press, 2018.

Kautsky, Karl. *The Class Struggle (Erfurt Program)*. Chicago: Charles H. Keer, 1910.

Lane, Fintan. "Benjamin Pelin, the Knights of the Plough and Social Radicalism, 1852-1934." In *Defying the Law of the Land: Agrarian Radicals in Irish History*, edited by Brian Casey, 176-200. Dublin: The History Press Ireland, 2013.

Leo XIII, Pope. *Rerum Novarum—Encyclical Letter of Pope Leo XIII on the Conditions of Labor*. 1891.

Leslie, John. *The Irish Question 1894*. Cork: Cork Workers' Club, 1974.

Levenson, Samuel. *James Connolly: A Biography*. London: Martin Brian & O'Keeffe, 1973.

Little, George A. 'About Malahide.' *Dublin Historical Record* 10, no.1 (Mar-May 1948): 1-16.

Lowell, James Russell. *The Biglow Papers*. 3ʳᵈ ed. London: Trübner and Co., 1861.

Lynch, David. *Radical Politics in Modern Ireland: The Irish Socialist Republican Party 1896-1904.* Dublin: Irish Academic Press, 2005.

MacAonghusa, Proinsias and Liam Ó Régáin, eds. *The Best of Connolly.* Cork: Mercier Press, 1967.

Mallock, William Hurrell. *Labour and the Popular Welfare.* London: Adam & Charles Black, 1893.

Mariátegui, José Carlos. *Selected Works.* Translated by Christian Noakes. Madison: Iskra Books, 2021.

Marx, Karl and Friedrich Engels. *The Communist Manifesto.* Penguin: London, 1967.

Marx, Karl and Frederick Engels. *Ireland and the Irish Question.* Moscow: Progress Publishers, 1971.

Massey, Gerald. *Poems by Gerald Massey.* Boston: Ticknor & Fields, 1907.

Mayor, James. "Scottish Railway Strike." *Economic Journal* (March 1891): 204-219

McCarthy, Charles. *Trade Unions in Ireland 1894-1960.* Dublin: Institute of Public Administration, 1977.

McCarthy, Conor, ed. *The Revolutionary and Anti-Imperialist Writings of James Connolly 1893-1916.* Edinburgh: Edinburgh University Press, 2016.

McKenna SJ, Lambert. *The Social Teachings of James Connolly.* Dublin: Catholic Truth Society, 1920. Reprint, Dublin: Veritas Publications, 1991.

McNulty, Liam. *James Connolly: Socialist, Nationalist & Internationalist.* Dagenham: Merlin Press, 2022.

Mill, John Stuart. *England and Ireland.* London: Longmans, Green, Reader and Dyer, 1868.

Mills, Leif. *Men of Ice: The Lives of Alistair Forbes MacKay (1878-1914) and Cecil Henry Meares (1877-1937).* Whitby: Caedmon of Whitby, 2008.

Mitchel, John. *Jail Journal, or Five Years in British Prisons.* New York:

The Citizen, 1854

Mitchel, John. *The Last Conquest of Ireland (Perhaps)*. Glasgow: Cameron & Ferguson, 1861.

Moody, William Godwin. *Our Labor Difficulties, the Cause, and the Way Out; A Practical Solution of the Labour Problem*. Boston: A. Williams & Co., 1878.

Moore, Thomas. *Lalla Rookh: an Oriental Romance*. London: Longman, Hurst, Rees, Orme, and Brown, 1817.

Moran, James, ed. *Four Irish Rebel Plays*. Dublin. Irish Academic Press, 2007.

Morgan, Austen. *James Connolly: A Political Biography*. Manchester: Manchester University Press, 1988.

Morris, Catherine & Spurgeon Thompson. "Postcolonial Connolly." *Interventions* 10, no.1 (2008): 1-6.

Mulhall, Michael G. *Fifty Years of National Progress 1837-1887*. London: G. Routledge, 1887.

Musgrove, PJ, ed. *A Socialist and War 1914-1916 by James Connolly*. London: Lawrence & Wishart, 1941.

Nevin, Donal. *James Connolly: A Full Life*. Dublin: Gill & Macmillan, 2005

———, ed. *Between Comrades: James Connolly Letters and Correspondence 1889-1916*. Dublin: Gill & Macmillan, 2007.

———. 'Between Comrades.' *Saothar* 34 (2009): 135-138.

———, ed. *James Connolly Political Writings 1893-1916*. Dublin: SIPTU, 2011.

———, ed. *Writings of James Connolly: Collected Works*. Dublin: SIPTU, 2011.

Nic Foirbeis, Rút. *A History of Irish Republicanism in Dundee c.1840 to 1985*. Perth: Tippermuir Books, 2024.

O'Brien, William. *Forth the Banners Go: Reminiscences of William O'Brien as told to Edward MacLysaght*. Dublin: Three Candles, 1969.

Ó Cathasaigh, Aindrias, ed. *The Lost Writings: James Connolly*. London: Pluto Press, 1997.

———. 'Donal Nevin (ed), Between Comrades'. Saothar 32 (2007): 110.

———. 'Where, oh Where, is our James Connolly?' 12 September 2017, https://theirishrevolution.wordpress.com/2017/09/12/where-oh-where-is-our-james-connolly/.

O'Connor, Gerald. *James Connolly: A Study of his work and Worth*. Dublin: Curtis, 1917.

O'Connor Lysaght, Donal, ed. *Socialism Made Easy: James Connolly*. Dublin: Plough book Service, 1968.

———, ed. *Old Wine in New Bottles: Some Lessons of the Dublin Lockout*. Dublin: Self Published, 2013.

O'Riordan, Michael, ed. *Revolutionary Warfare by James Connolly*. Dublin: New Books, 1968.

Puirséil, Niamh. *The Irish Labour Party 1922-73*. Dublin: UCD Press, 2007.

Ransom, Bernard Campbell. "James Connolly and the Scottish Left 1890-1916." PhD diss., University of Edinburgh, 1975.

Ray, Prafulla Chandra. *India: Before and After the Mutiny*. India: Ministry of Information and Broadcasting, 2012.

Reeve, Reeve and Ann Barton Reeve. *James Connolly and the United States*. New Jersey: Humanities Press, 1978.

Rodney, Walter. *Decolonial Marxism: Essays from the Pan-African Revolution*. London: Verso, 2022.

Russell, James B. 'The House,' in *The Glasgow Health Lectures: Delivered for the "Coombe" Trust, Under the Supervision of the Glasgow United Young Men's Christian Association, During October, November, and December 1881*. Glasgow: J. Menzies & Co., 1881, 47-66.

Ryan, Desmond. *James Connolly: His Life, Work & Writings*. Dublin: Talbot Press, 1924.

———, ed. *Socialism and Nationalism: A Selection from the Writings of*

James Connolly. Dublin: At the Sign of the Three Candles, 1948.

———, ed. *Labour and Easter Week: A Selection from the Writings of James Connolly.* Dublin: At the Sign of the Three Candles, 1949.

———, ed. *The Workers' Republic: A Selection from the Writings of James Connolly.* Dublin: At the Sign of the Three Candles, 1951.

Saor Éire Press, ed. *Workshop Talks by James Connolly.* Cork: Saor Éire Press, n.d.

Scott, Joan Wallach. *The Glassworkers of Carmaux: French Craftsmen and Political Action in a Nineteenth-Century City.* Cambridge, Mass.: Harvard University Press, 1974.

Social Democratic Federation. *Socialism Made Plain: the Social and Political Manifesto of the Democratic Federation.* London: Social Democratic Federation, 1883.

Socialist Review, ed. "Letters of James Connolly." *Socialist Review* 25, no.137 (March 1925): 117-23.

Sozialistische Arbeiterpartei Deutschlands. *Das Gothaer Programm.* 1875.

Spry, Henry Harpur. *Modern India: With Illustrations of the Resources and Capabilities of Hindustan In Two Volumes: Volume II.* London: Whittaker & Co., 1837.

Thompson, Spurgeon. "Indigenous Theory: James Connolly and the Theatre of Decolonization." *Interventions* 10, no.1 (2008): 7-25.

Wilde, Lady. *Poems by Speranza.* Glasgow: Cameron & Ferguson, 1871.

Working Men's International Association. *Address and Provisional Rules of the Working Men's International Association.* London: Working Men's International Association, 1864.

Young, Robert J.C. *Postcolonialism: An Historical Introduction.* Oxford: Blackwell Publishing, 2001.

INDEX NOMINUM

INDEX

Milton Keynes UK
Ingram Content Group UK Ltd.
UKHW030653101124
450921UK00003B/60

9 798330 435319